Tracing and Documenting Nazi Victims Past and Present

Arolsen Research Series

Edited by the Arolsen Archives –
International Center on Nazi Persecution

Volume 1

Tracing and Documenting Nazi Victims Past and Present

—

Edited by
Henning Borggräfe, Christian Höschler
and Isabel Panek

DE GRUYTER
OLDENBOURG

On behalf of the Arolsen Archives.

The Arolsen Archives are funded by the German Federal Government Commissioner for Culture and the Media (BKM).

ISBN 978-3-11-066160-6
eBook (PDF) ISBN 978-3-11-066537-6
eBook (EPUB) ISBN 978-3-11-066165-1
ISSN 2699-7312

This work is licensed under the Creative Commons Attribution-NonCommercial NoDerivatives 4.0 License. For details go to http://creativecommons.org/licens-es/by-nc-nd/4.0/.

Library of Congress Control Number: 2020932561

Bibliographic Information published by the Deutsche Nationalbibliothek
The Deutsche Nationalbibliothek lists this publication in the Deutsche Nationalbibliografie; detailed bibliographic data are available on the Internet at http://dnb.dnb.de.

© 2020 by the Arolsen Archives, Henning Borggräfe, Christian Höschler, and Isabel Panek, published by Walter de Gruyter GmbH, Berlin/Boston
Cover image: Jan-Eric Stephan
Printing and binding: CPI books GmbH, Leck

www.degruyter.com

Preface

Tracing and documenting the victims of National Socialist persecution is a topic that has received little attention from historical research so far. In order to take stock of existing knowledge and provide impetus for historical research on this issue, the *Arolsen Archives* (formerly known as the *International Tracing Service*) organized an international conference on *Tracing and Documenting Victims of Nazi Persecution: History of the International Tracing Service (ITS) in Context*. Held on October 8 and 9 2018 in Bad Arolsen, Germany, this event also marked the seventieth anniversary of search bureaus from various European states meeting with the recently established *International Tracing Service* (ITS) in Arolsen, Germany, in the autumn of 1948.

More than 120 participants from around the world, including representatives from leading organisations and researchers from various disciplines, looked back over more than seven decades of tracing missing persons and documenting Nazi persecution. The consequences of Nazi persecution were and are manifold and they are still felt today. The loss of relatives, the search for a new home, physical or mental injuries, existential problems, social support and recognition, but also continued exclusion and discrimination have shaped the experiences and memories of those who were once persecuted, not to mention the effects on their relatives and on society as a whole. Tracing bureaus, archives and other agencies have played an important role in this field, and this is the subject of the articles that are collected in this volume.

The publication of these articles also reflects the transformation process undergone by what was then the ITS over the past decade. After years of international pressure, the former ITS, now the *Arolsen Archives*, was opened to the public in late 2007. This event triggered an ongoing radical transformation process, which has seen the institution make its documents accessible: to survivors and their relatives, to educators and researchers, as well as to the general public. The *Arolsen Archives* have adopted the goal of making their UNESCO-protected holdings easily accessible to a broad audience, of supporting research and education, and of increasing public awareness of the history of the victims of National Socialism.

It is my hope that this publication will inspire researchers, educators, and engaged citizens from all walks of life to explore the vast collections of the *Arolsen Archives* and that it will reveal their potential to augment knowledge about National Socialist persecution with regard to its victims, its consequences and the culture of remembrance. As soon there will be no witnesses and survivors of Nazi persecution left to tell us about their experiences, it is essential to make the documents speak in their stead, so that, paraphrasing Elie Wiesel, the documents become witnesses as well.

I would like to thank the authors of this volume very sincerely for their contributions and express my deep gratitude to the editors, Henning Borggräfe, Christian Höschler, and Isabel Panek, for the tremendous work they have done.

Floriane Azoulay,
Director of the *Arolsen Archives*

Table of Contents

Henning Borggräfe, Christian Höschler, Isabel Panek
Tracing and *Documenting* Nazi Victims Past and Present – Introduction —— 1

Dan Stone
On the Uses and Disadvantages of the *Arolsen Archives* for History —— 13

From Early Tracing Activities to Information for Descendants

Christian Höschler, Isabel Panek
The (Early) Search for Missing Nazi Victims
  Historical Precedents, Organizational Frameworks, and Methods —— 37

Linda G. Levi
Family Searching and Tracing Services of JDC in the Second World War Era —— 59

Christine Schmidt
Those Left Behind
  Early Search Efforts in Wartime and Post-War Britain —— 95

Maren Hachmeister
Tracing Services in Poland and Czechoslovakia after 1945
  Between Humanitarian Principles and Socialist Ideology —— 117

René Bienert
Survivors Helping Survivors
  Simon Wiesenthal and the Early Search for Nazi Criminals in Linz —— 131

Silke von der Emde
Caring for the Dead and the Living
  DPs and the Arolsen Archives of Feelings —— 155

Zvi Bernhardt
***Yad Vashem* and Holocaust Victim's Search for Family** —— 173

Diane Afoumado
ITS Research at the *United States Holocaust Memorial Museum* for Descendants of Holocaust Victims and Survivors —— 183

Ramona Bräu, Kerstin Hofmann and Anna Meier-Osiński
The New Tasks and Challenges for Tracing —— 201

Collections and Activities of Archives Dealing with Nazi Victims

Henning Borggräfe, Isabel Panek
***Collections Archives* Dealing with Nazi Victims**
    The Example of the Arolsen Archives —— 221

Rebecca Boehling
From Tracing and Fate Clarification to Research Center
    The Role of International Players and Transnationalism in Shaping the Identity of the ITS —— 245

Kerstin Hofmann
"It is our job to find out who did what."
    The *Central Office* in Ludwigsburg and Cooperation with the ITS —— 261

Tobias Herrmann
The *Federal Archives* and its Role in German Politics of Remembrance —— 279

Carola Lau
***Institutes of National Remembrance* and their Role in Dealing with National Socialism**
    An Examination of the Issues, Debates and Public Perceptions —— 291

Puck Huitsing and Edwin Klijn
Linking and Enriching Archival Collections in the Digital Age
    The *Dutch War Collections* Network —— 315

Contributors —— 339

Henning Borggräfe, Christian Höschler, Isabel Panek
Tracing and *Documenting* Nazi Victims Past and Present – Introduction

On March 11, 1948, a letter sent from a hospital in Aylesbury, England, reached the recently established *International Tracing Service* (ITS) in the small town of Arolsen in Northern Hesse. It had been sent by Maria Puszkariowa, who was looking for her husband, Marian Ćwierz, whom she had lost contact with in the last months of the war: "Until 1944 he was in Schevenhütte, Schill Str. 17, near Aachen. [...]. In January 1945 he was deported from the Herne prison near Dortmund to the Buchenwald concentration camp. Since then I have had no word from him."[1] This was just one of thousands of similar letters that arrived month after month in Arolsen and many other tracing offices, even three years after the end of the war. Maria Puszkariowa had sent an identical letter to the *International Committee of the Red Cross* in Geneva, which forwarded it to Arolsen, where it was registered two weeks later. Hundreds of thousands of people were still looking for friends and relatives who had been deported by the Germans to extermination camps, imprisoned in concentration camps and other detention facilities, or sent to the Reich for forced labor. But nearly three years after the liberation, how could the ITS find information about the fate of Marian Ćwierz in order to answer this letter? How were all of the missing persons supposed to be found – considering that millions of people had been murdered and could not come forward themselves, and that the confrontation between East and West had divided Germany and Europe, meaning it was often impossible to search for clues at the sites of persecution?

Personal documents were an important component in the effort to answer these questions – documents the Germans had produced for the purposes of persecution, but also documents the Allies had used to register and care for liberated prisoners. From the late 1940s onward, more than 30 million such documents were gathered in Arolsen. This resulted in the creation of one of the world's largest collections of documents on the victims of Nazi persecution, which is now being preserved, described and made publicly accessible by the

---

[1] The letter from Maria Puskariowa was addressed to the *Central Tracing Bureau*, the predecessor to the ITS, and bears the incoming mail stamp of the CTB, 11.3.1948, 6.3.3.2/90584689/ITS Digital Archive, Arolsen Archives.

 OpenAccess. © 2020 Henning Borggräfe, Christian Höschler, Isabel Panek, published by De Gruyter.
 This work is licensed under the Creative Commons Attribution-NonCommercial-NoDerivatives 4.0 License. https://doi.org/10.1515/9783110665376-002

*Arolsen Archives.*² The holdings include extensive documents from the Buchenwald concentration camp, which were secured by the US Army when the camp was liberated and were later made available for tracing purposes. According to these documents, Marian Ćwierz had been arrested in July 1944 in Meschede before being deported from the Herne police prison to Buchenwald as a political prisoner on January 6, 1945, by order of the Dortmund Gestapo. When he was registered in the camp, all of his personal belongings and a suitcase of clothing were taken from him. These personal effects, as they are known, were dispersed by the SS shortly afterwards, meaning that the property of the Polish forced laborer was distributed to the German population. Just three days after Marian Ćwierz arrived in Buchenwald, the SS transported him to the *Ohrdruf S III* subcamp, where the prisoners were forced to dig tunnels. He survived the murderous conditions in this camp for only a few weeks. As in tens of thousands of other cases, the ITS had to send his wife the sad news in May 1948 that, according to the concentration camp documents, her husband had died on March 22, 1945.³

The correspondence pertaining to the search for Marian Ćwierz can now be found in *Tracing/Documentation file (T/D file)* number 34. This was one of the first of a total of over three million case files that the ITS created starting in 1948 and that continue to be created by the *Arolsen Archives*. To this day, the *Arolsen Archives* receive around 15,000 inquiries annually relating to more than 20,000 people.⁴ When an inquiry is first received about a person, a *T/D file* is opened (though today these files are only digital). All further correspondence about the case, as well as any subsequent inquiries received about the person from other relatives or authorities, are also placed in this file.⁵ If they were stacked on top of one another, the huge volume of *T/D files* would reach a height of 6,476 meters, towering almost as high as Mont Blanc, the highest mountain in the Alps – and providing the title of this book. The terms *tracing* and *documenting* also delineate the subject matter addressed by these articles.

---

2 In May 2019, the name of the ITS was changed to the *Arolsen Archives – International Center on Nazi Persecution*. Regarding the history of the *Arolsen Archives*, see Henning Borggräfe, Christian Höschler and Isabel Panek (eds.): *A Paper Monument: The History of the Arolsen Archives, Exhibition Catalogue*, Bad Arolsen: Arolsen Archives, 2019.
3 ITS to Maria Puskariowa, 19.5.1948, 6.3.3.2/90584692/ITS Digital Archive, Arolsen Archives. See also Buchenwald Prisoner Documents on Marian Ćwierz, 1.1.5.3/5707125/ITS Digital Archive, Arolsen Archives; KZ Buchenwald, verstorbene Häftlinge in Außenkommando S III, 5.4.1945, 1.1.5.1/5347901/ITS Digital Archive, Arolsen Archives.
4 See https://arolsen-archives.org/en/living-history/annual-report-2018/. Last accessed: 8.8.2019.
5 Most of these files are found in sub-collection 6.3.3.2 Repository of *T/D* cases; other case files are in the other sub-collections of Group 6.3.3 ITS Case Files as of 1947.

In its original sense, *tracing* meant an active search for missing persons. The direct predecessor to this activity was the search for prisoners of war and missing civilians during the First World War by the *International Committee of the Red Cross* in Geneva.[6] The methods used for this included local investigations, correspondence with other tracing offices and authorities (such as resident registration offices or registry offices), compiling lists of names with findings (such as where individuals had been held or had died), and transferring this information to card files. In view of the scale of persecution in the Second World War, which left millions dead, *tracing* after 1945 quickly came to mean the evaluation of documents seized from Nazi authorities, as well as those that had been gathered by the Allies for the care of Displaced Persons (DPs), in the hopes that they might contain clues about missing individuals. The *clarification of fates* became another important term in this context.

In the late 1940s and early 1950s, these collected documents began to attract the attention of other entities, namely, German compensation authorities and the immigration authorities of many different countries which wanted to use historical sources to review claims and entry applications. Survivors, family members and their legal representatives also contacted the ITS to request documents proving that they had been persecuted or showing where they were after the war. In light of this, the ITS changed the name of its correspondence files in 1954 from *T files* (for *tracing*) to the above-mentioned *T/D files*, because the documents initially used for *tracing* were increasingly also being used for *documenting* the victims of Nazi persecution.[7]

Tracing and *documenting* thus overlapped when it came to evaluating the archival documents for information about individuals – and these activities continue to overlap at the *Arolsen Archives* today. Many *T/D files* testify to this dual use in that they contain both early correspondence pertaining to *tracing* and the *clarification of fates* and later correspondence pertaining to compensation or immigration proceedings. Finally – reflecting an even later transformation of the *tracing* process – the *T/D files* often include inquiries from the children or grandchildren of victims of the Nazis who want to learn more about their family history.

Documenting has yet another meaning in this context. It refers to the evaluation of historical documents, but in a broader sense it stands for the decades-long efforts of the ITS and many similar institutions to purposefully collect and organize these documents. It additionally represents the resulting creation of

---

6 See the chapter by Christian Höschler and Isabel Panek in this volume.
7 The cover of the file for Marian Ćwierz also bears the label "*T file*."

new collections of source materials, which are themselves historically valuable for researching victims of Nazi persecution. The collection of *T/D files* is a very good example of this. *Documenting* applies not only to the institutions that were established as tracing services, however, but also to those concerned primarily with the compensation of victims or prosecution of perpetrators, and to institutions founded for the purposes of remembrance and commemoration. They all documented victims of Nazi persecution using a variety of methods, and they created their own archives to do so.

The search for missing persons and documentary proof of persecution has occupied millions of victims and their relatives since 1945. Added to this are numerous institutions that were either established specifically for *tracing* and *documenting* or that pursued one or both of these activities as key tasks. We therefore consider *tracing* and *documenting* to be an important aspect of the *second history*[8] of National Socialism, meaning it is one of the fields that has attempted to reckon with the crimes of the Nazis since 1945. But this field has been given scant attention by scholars to date, and its importance to the victims of Nazi persecution and their families has not been sufficiently appreciated – unlike the compensation of Nazi victims, prosecution of Nazi perpetrators and development of public memory, which are comparatively well-researched fields.[9]

Tracing and *documenting* were largely overlooked by researchers for a long time compared to these three other fields, probably in part because the millions of individual *tracing* and *documenting* activities mostly took place out of the public eye – unlike criminal prosecution and commemoration – and were often conducted directly between the tracing and documentation offices on the one hand and the survivors and their relatives on the other. This also meant they were rare-

---

[8] Peter Reichel, Harald Schmid and Peter Steinbach (eds.): *Der Nationalsozialismus: Die zweite Geschichte: Überwindung, Deutung, Erinnerung*, Munich: Beck, 2009.

[9] Regarding the compensation of victims of Nazi persecution, see most recently Constantin Goschler (ed.): *Compensation in Practice: The Foundation "Remembrance, Responsibility and Future" and the Legacy of Forced Labour during the Third Reich*, New York/Oxford: Berghahn, 2017; on criminal prosecution, see Enrico Heitzer, Günter Morsch et al. (eds.): *Im Schatten von Nürnberg: Transnationale Ahndung von NS-Verbrechen*, Berlin: Metropol, 2019; Kerstin Hofmann: *"Ein Versuch nur – immerhin ein Versuch": Die Zentrale Stelle in Ludwigsburg unter der Leitung von Erwin Schüle und Adalbert Rückerl (1958–1984)*, Berlin: Metropol, 2018; regarding public memory, see Johannes Rhein, Julia Schumacher and Lea Wohl von Haselberg (eds.): *Schlechtes Gedächtnis? Kontrafaktische Darstellungen des Nationalsozialismus in alten und neuen Medien*, Berlin: Neofelis, 2019, and the conference proceedings from *Geteiltes Gedächtnis? Erinnerung an die NS-Zwangsarbeit im Europa des 21. Jahrhunderts*, 9.3.2016–11.3.2016, Hamburg, in: H-Soz-Kult, 14.9.2016. Available at: https://www.hsozkult.de/conferencereport/id/tagungsberichte-6697. Last accessed: 9.8.2019.

ly a topic of public discussion, as compensation was. At the same time, however, the institutions involved in *tracing* and *documenting* have always had many points of contact with these three widely researched fields of *second history*, a fact addressed by a number of the essays in this volume.

This book is based largely on an international conference held in October 2018 in Bad Arolsen with the title *Tracing and Documenting Victims of Nazi Persecution: History of the International Tracing Service (ITS) in Context*.[10] The conference was linked to ongoing research for the first permanent exhibition on the history of the *Arolsen Archives* that opened in June 2019. One aim of the conference was to discuss new research findings on the institution's history in a broader context. The goal was also to look at the full history of *tracing* and *documenting* – in terms of the many institutions that were active in this field particularly in the early post-war period, and with an eye to important turning points or processes of change and the reasons for them in the seven decades since the end of the Second World War.

In May 2017, after the documents of the German *Kirchlicher Suchdienst* (*Church Tracing Service*) were handed over to the *German Federal Archives*, a conference was held in Bayreuth dealing with tracing services and archival work. The *Church Tracing Service* had been responsible primarily for German expellees and refugees after 1945.[11] Then, in December 2018, *Yad Vashem* organized a conference entitled *Searching for Each Other: Survivors' Attempts in the Post-War Period to Locate Missing Relatives and Friends*, which focused specifically on the search for victims and survivors of the Holocaust.[12] These conferences not only indicate growing interest in the topic, they also show that *tracing* and *documenting* were not limited to Nazi victims after 1945. The *International Committee of the Red Cross* in Geneva, like many national tracing offices (which were often attached to local Red Cross societies), was concerned with everyone missing after the war. In occupied Germany, however, strictly separated structures were established for tracing foreigners from UN countries and victims of Nazi persecution

---

10 Conference proceedings from *Tracing and Documenting Victims of Nazi Persecution: History of the International Tracing Service (ITS) in Context*, 8.10.2018 – 9.10.2018, Bad Arolsen, in: H-Soz-Kult, 29.1.2019, www.hsozkult.de/conferencereport/id/tagungsberichte-8071. Last accessed: 9.8.2019.
11 Conference proceedings available at: https://www.bundesarchiv.de/DE/Content/Artikel/Ueber-uns/Aus-unserer-Arbeit/Textsammlung-Konferenz-Bayreuth-2017/2017-11-30_suchdienste-und-archivarbeit_laa.html?chapterId=36974. Last accessed: 9.8.2019.
12 "Searching for Each Other: Survivors Attempts in the Post-War Period to Locate Missing Relatives and Friends". Available at: https://www.yadvashem.org/sites/default/files/newsletters/files/Workshop%20Program%20Zborowski.pdf. Last accessed: 9.8.2019.

on the one hand, and German expellees, war victims and missing Wehrmacht soldiers on the other.

Although it would seem worthwhile to adopt an overarching perspective here, particularly in terms of documenting the history of tracing methods and the public discussion of the search for missing persons in the twentieth century,[13] scholars to date have continued to follow this separation established by the Allies. Additionally, in the interest of anchoring the topic of *tracing* and *documenting* more firmly in the *second history* of National Socialism, it makes sense to initially focus solely on the *tracing* and *documenting* of Nazi victims.

A moderate amount of research has been conducted to date. It is dominated by individual studies on the organizational history of various tracing and documentation offices. These were initially published mainly by the tracing institutions themselves, usually to mark memorial days or institutional anniversaries. They provide overviews of the tasks and goals of the tracing and documentation offices and are aimed primarily at the employees of similar institutions and interested members of the general public. Considering the context in which they were produced, many of them must be considered source materials rather than scholarly accounts.[14] It is only more recently that the topic of *tracing* and *documenting* has attracted the attention of historians. But the emphasis here is still very much on the early history of the search for missing victims of the Nazis in the immediate post-war period. The tracing of displaced children has also become a focal point in recent years – a trend reflected in other thematically related areas of research.[15]

When it comes to the topic of *documenting,* by contrast, a large number of studies have been produced. These are not positioned in a dedicated field of re-

---

[13] For research in this area with a broader perspective extending even beyond the Second World War, see Jenny Edkins: *Missing: Persons and Politics*, Ithaca: Cornell University Press, 2016.

[14] Deutsche Dienststelle (WASt) (ed.): *Narben bleiben: Die Arbeit der Suchdienste 60 Jahre nach dem Zweiten Weltkrieg*, Kassel: Volksbund deutscher Kriegsgräberfürhsorge, 2007; International Tracing Service (ITS) (ed.): *60 Years of History and Benefit of the Personal Documentary Material about the Former Civilian Persecutees of the National Socialist Regime Preserved in Bad Arolsen*, Bad Arolsen: International Tracing Service, 2003.

[15] Verena Buser: "Child Survivors and Displaced Children in the Aftermath Studies: An Overview", in Henning Borggräfe, Akim Jah, Steffen Jost and Nina Ritz (eds.): *Freilegungen: Rebuilding Lives – Child Survivors and DP Children in the Aftermath of the Holocaust and Forced Labor*, Göttingen: Wallstein, 2016, 27–39; Julia Reus: "'Everywhere where human beings are, we can find our children'": On the Organization of the ITS Child Search Branch Files", ibid., 41–49. See also Lynne Taylor: *In the Children's Best Interests: Unaccompanied Children in American-Occupied Germany, 1945–1952*, Toronto: University of Toronto Press, 2017.

search, however, but instead must be considered contributions to Holocaust *aftermath studies*[16] or research into the politics of history. For this reason, such works revolve less around the practical documentation activities of the respective institutions and more around the depiction and analysis of debates relating to the politics of the past.[17]

Greater attention has been paid to the history of the ITS in recent years, however. In 2011, Arolsen historian Bernd Joachim Zimmer published a detailed account of the organization's early administrative history.[18] A dissertation by historian Jennifer Rodgers looked at the creation and development of the ITS in the context of the conflict between East and West and showed how different international players used the archive for their own political gains during the Cold War. And on a scholarly meta-level, Dan Stone has investigated the potential and challenges of the ITS collection for producing a social history of the Holocaust and Nazi persecution.[19] When the *Research and Education department* of the ITS was established after the archive reopened to the public in 2007, research began to be conducted into the thematic areas covered by the collections in what are now the *Arolsen Archives*, including the death marches, life trajectories of Displaced Persons, early testimonies of victims of Nazi persecution, and the persecution and compensation of *forgotten victims*.[20] And the new permanent ex-

---

[16] Eleonora Bergmann: "Early accounts of survivors: The records of the Central Jewish Historical Commission at the Jewish Historical Institute in Warsaw", in René Bienert, Rebecca Boehling and Susanne Urban (eds.): *Freilegungen: Überlebende – Erinnerungen – Transformationen*, Göttingen: Wallstein, 2013, 138–151; Boaz Cohen: "The difficulties of creating a Holocaust archive: Yad Vashem and Israel Kastner 1947–1948", in *Jewish Culture and History*, 15/3, 2014, 173–187; Laura Jockusch: *Collect and Record! Jewish Holocaust Documentation in Early Postwar Europe*, Oxford: OUP, 2012.

[17] Matthias Haß: *Gestaltetes Gedenken: Yad Vashem, das U.S. Holocaust Memorial Museum und die Stiftung Topographie des Terrors*, Frankfurt/New York: Campus, 2002; Carola Lau: *Erinnerungsverwaltung, Vergangenheitspolitik und Erinnerungskultur nach 1989: Institute für nationales Gedenken im östlichen Europa im Vergleich*, Göttingen: V&R unipress, 2017; Edward Tabor Linenthal: *Preserving Memory: The Struggle to Create America's Holocaust Museum*, New York: Viking, 1995.

[18] Bernd Joachim Zimmer: *Der Internationale Tracing Service Arolsen: Von der Vermisstensuche zur Haftbescheinigung: Die Organisationsgeschichte eines "Ungewollten Kindes" während der Besatzungszeit*, Bad Arolsen: Waldeckischer Geschichtsverein, 2011.

[19] Jennifer Rodgers: *From the 'Archive of Horrors' to the 'Shop Window of Democracy': The International Tracing Service and the Transatlantic Politics of the Past*, PhD Diss., University of Pennsylvania, 2014; Dan Stone: "The Memory of the Archive: The International Tracing Service and the Construction of the Past as History", in *Dapim: Studies on the Holocaust*, 31/2, 2017, 69–88.

[20] Jean-Luc Blondel, Susanne Urban and Sebastian Schönemann (eds.): *Freilegungen: Auf den Spuren der Todesmärsche*, Göttingen: Wallstein, 2012; Henning Borggräfe, Hanne Leßau and Har-

hibition that opened in June 2019, entitled *A Monument of Paper: The History of the Arolsen Archives*, takes a critical and reflective look at the varied history of the institution.[21]

In a broader and more general sense, *tracing* and *documenting* are important aspects of *transitional justice*, or the establishment of justice in the transition from unjust systems to new forms of social and political coexistence. *Tracing* and *documenting* remain necessary tasks in the wake of wars and dictatorships in the twenty-first century as well. For example, an extensive body of specialized social-scientific and legal literature has been produced to deal specifically with the topic of *enforced disappearance*, which has been used a method of terror in conflicts since the second half of the twentieth century.[22] While this literature is very distinct from historical studies of the repercussions of World War II, taking it into consideration could open up interesting perspectives in terms of methodology and content for future research into the *tracing* and *documenting* of Nazi victims.

The goal of the book at hand is initially much more modest. It aims to bring together important aspects of the existing research on *tracing* and *documenting* in order to stimulate further research in this still underexposed area of study. The opening article grapples with a question that is closely tied to the subject of the book, but that also cuts across it: How can the paper legacy of seven decades of *tracing* and *documenting* be put to use today for research as well as educational and memorial work? The benefits and disadvantages of the ITS archive are the subject of the chapter by Dan Stone, based on a keynote presentation, which illuminates core elements of the collections of the *Arolsen Archives* from an epistemological perspective and demonstrates how the collections can be used for a social history of the Holocaust and Nazi persecution. Many of the essays under the heading *From Early Tracing Activities to Information for Descendants* look at the historical development of the *clarification of fates* and how the need for in-

---

ald Schmid (eds.): *Fundstücke: Die Wahrnehmung der NS-Verbrechen und ihrer Opfer im Wandel*, Göttingen: Wallstein, 2015; Akim Jah and Gerd Kühling (eds.): *Fundstücke: Die Deportation der Juden aus Deutschland und ihre verdrängte Geschichte nach 1945*, Göttingen: Wallstein, 2016. For a comprehensive list of a number of publications by the *Arolsen Archives*, see https://arolsen-archives.org/en/publications-downloads/. Last accessed: 9.8.2019.

21 Henning Borggräfe, Christian Höschler and Isabel Panek: *A Paper Monument*; an online tour of the exhibition is available at: www.arolsen-archives.org/exhibition. Last accessed: 28.8.2019.

22 See, for example, Gabriel Gatti: *Surviving Forced Disappearance in Argentina and Uruguay*, New York: Palgrave Macmillan, 2014; Council of Europe, Commissioner for Human Rights (ed.): *Missing Persons and Victims of Enforced Disappearance in Europe*, 2016. Available online at: https://www.refworld.org/docid/572233704.html. Last accessed: 28.8.2019.

formation and the practice of providing it have changed from the immediate post-war period to the present day.

The editors Christian Höschler and Isabel Panek provide an introductory overview of the early search for missing victims of the Nazis, particularly taking into account the activities of survivors, the early history of the ITS and the methods and tools that were used for *tracing* and *clarifying fates*, which have not yet been specifically studied by scholars. The search for Jewish victims of Nazi persecution is the subject of the chapter by Linda G. Levi, which looks at the activities of the *American Jewish Joint Distribution Committee* as well as the particular challenges of searching for survivors of the Holocaust and the associated issue of reuniting families. Christine Schmidt's article on the situation in Great Britain is a national case study that not only discusses *tracing* and the *clarification of fates* primarily in the context of Jewish migration, but also shows how the activities of the *British Red Cross Society* laid important foundations for the subsequent centralized *tracing* and *documentation* of Nazi persecution in Europe. The chapter by Maren Hachmeister, by contrast, turns the spotlight to Eastern Europe and explores the activities of the national *Red Cross Societies* of Poland and Czechoslovakia. It highlights the specifics of the search for Nazi victims in these two states while also revealing the global dimension of their work through their cooperation with international actors such as the ITS. With his chapter on the work of Simon Wiesenthal, René Bienert contributes a case study that uses Austria as an example of the engagement of survivors of Nazi persecution after 1945. One central finding is that the search for missing persons was sometimes carried out in the context of other activities – in this case, as part of the search for Nazi perpetrators. Silke von der Emde takes a literary studies approach to examining the role of Displaced Persons in the early years of the ITS. As survivors of Nazi persecution, they were not only the subject of many of the documents preserved in the archive, they were also involved in shaping the growing collection in Arolsen as an *archive of feeling* and making empathy an important component of tracing activities. Other chapters in this volume show how the focal points of *tracing* gradually changed and which additional tasks arose over the course of seven decades. Zvi Bernhardt, for example, describes how the *Yad Vashem* memorial played an insignificant role in the search for Holocaust victims for nearly three decades before developing into a key actor in the 1980s, one which continues to carry out this task in Israel today. Diane Afoumado offers an overview of the current information practices of the *United States Holocaust Memorial Museum* (USHMM), with a focus on the critically important use of the digital collections of the *Arolsen Archives* and the special aspects of providing information about Holocaust victims to second- and third-generation relatives. Finally, Ramona Bräu, Kerstin Hofmann and Anna Meier-Osiński document the many different layers of today's *tracing* at the *Arolsen Archives* in terms of the changing needs for information, the professionalization of the organization's visitor services and the *#StolenMemory* campaign, the aim of which is to return the personal effects stored in the *Arolsen Archives* to the relatives of the former concentration camp prisoners to whom they belonged.

The title of the second part of this book is *Collections and Activities of Archives Dealing with Nazi Victims*. The chapters in this section focus not on *tracing* and the *clarification of fates*, but rather on the farther-reaching activities and spheres of action of institutions with collections on the topic of Nazi persecution – including the acquisition of relevant documents, the establishment and preservation of collections, and the aspects of politics and memory culture that are tied up with the work of such institutions. Using the example of the *Arolsen Archives*, the introductory essay by the editors Henning Borggräfe and Isabel Panek identifies the characteristics of what are known as *collections archives* and explains not only the creation and structure of the ITS archives, but also their (in)accessibility for historical research and public memory over the course of decades. Rebecca Boehling considers the influence of international actors in her analysis of the transformation of the ITS from a pure tracing service to a place of documentation, research and remembrance of Nazi persecution, and shows how this transformation significantly affected the importance to memory culture of the documents now preserved in the *Arolsen Archives*. In his chapter about the *German Federal Archives* as an actor in German politics of memory, Tobias Herrmann describes various activities at the institution that contribute to the reckoning with Germany's Nazi past. He makes a distinction between legally defined responsibilities and activities that result from the self-conception of the *German Federal Archives* as a part of present-day memory culture. Carola Lau compares the creation, reception and impact of state documentation and research institutions in Poland, Slovakia and the Czech Republic. Her article focuses on the significance of the Nazi period for the work of what are known as *Institutes of National Remembrance* at the intersection between memory management, memory culture and the politics of the past in each country. The last chapter in this book is by Puck Huitsing and Edwin Klijn, who use the example of the *Dutch War Collections* project to examine current developments in the digitization of historical collections and public access to them. The authors see great potential in the systematic archival description and linking of digital holdings to enable new possibilities and approaches to discoverability and evaluation.

Although this volume once again pays special attention to the history of what was the ITS and is now the *Arolsen Archives*, our explicit goal is to consider the full spectrum and development of the field – not least in order to better understand what was unique about the history of the ITS or exemplary for other institutions and their respective fields of activity (even if only in certain periods of time). It would be interesting for future studies to look beyond the perspective of individual organizations and attempt an overarching history of the process of *tracing* and *documenting* Nazi victims. One important aspect of this, which is unfortunately entirely missing from this volume and all previous studies, would be an analysis that goes beyond the depiction of individual cases to recount the history of *tracing* and *documenting from below*, from the perspective of the people affected – first of the survivors and relatives of the missing themselves, then of the subsequent generations. The extensive *T/D files* of the ITS and similar collections of files from other organizations offer ample empirical material for this.

Our thanks go to everyone who contributed to the conference and to this volume, as well as to Sarah Hudson, Jessica Spengler and Anne-Marie Wilms for translating selected articles, and to Anna Metta and Margit Vogt for their editorial support. We would like to thank *De Gruyter Oldenbourg*, in particular Martin Rethmeier and Jana Fritsche, for the trust placed in us with the establishment of a new *Arolsen Research Series*; the book at hand is the first volume in this series. In addition to the printed book, a free and fully accessible version of the text is available online at https://doi.org/10.1515/9783110665376-002 in the interest of the open access philosophy of the *Arolsen Archives*. Finally, special thanks are due to our colleagues at the *Arolsen Archives* who, in various ways, supported the production of this book and the organization of the conference that preceded it.

Dan Stone
On the Uses and Disadvantages of the *Arolsen Archives* for History[1]

Abstract: The ITS digital collections are hugely revealing but also difficult to use and overwhelming in their size. Beginning by considering the disadvantages of ITS for historical research, I attend to the need for a critical approach that seeks to avoid the trap of positivism. Doing so puts the historian in a position to consider the uses of ITS. With a focus on the topics of sub-camps, death marches and liberation, this chapter shows that ITS can be used, with care, for the purposes of uncovering untold narratives and of discovering information about little-known sites and experiences of the Holocaust about which one finds out little by relying only or primarily on documents created by the perpetrators. The ITS collections, in other words, allow one to follow the trajectories of individuals and to situate them into bigger patterns of Nazi criminality. This social history of the Holocaust, or Nazism from the perspective of its victims, is one of ITS's main advantages and it provides an important counterpart to a perpetrator-centric narrative. The latter is no less necessary for understanding the pattern of Nazi crimes, but for a rounded history (or an *integrated history*), one which is attuned to the effects of the crimes on the victims as well as to the mechanics of the crimes, ITS is indispensable.

Introduction

> "The good historian is like the giant of the fairy tale. He knows that wherever he catches the scent of human flesh, there his quarry lies."
> Marc Bloch[2]

In the first few years after the Allies created it, the body that would come to be known as the *International Tracing Service* (ITS) underwent several institutional

---

[1] In 2019, the *International Tracing Service* (ITS) was renamed *Arolsen Archives*. The following article, however, uses the term ITS to refer to both the historical organization and its collections.
[2] Marc Bloch: *The Historian's Craft*, Manchester: Manchester University Press, 1967, 26. My thanks to Christine Schmidt for her comments on an earlier draft of this work. Research for

OpenAccess. © 2020 Dan Stone, published by De Gruyter. This work is licensed under the Creative Commons Attribution-NonCommercial-NoDerivatives 4.0 License.
https://doi.org/10.1515/9783110665376-003

makeovers and was rehoused on more than one occasion. This process of remaking in the light of changing circumstances was equally true for the *Child Search Branch*, which until 1950 was a separate body, based in a different location from the *Central Tracing Bureau* (CTB) or the ITS. Under rapidly changing conditions, and desperately trying to cope with the unexpectedly huge workload, both the adult and child tracing units were overwhelmed with tracing requests and, in the first few years of their existence, searching work in the field. That other distractions were unwelcome is clear from the irritated flurry of activity set in motion by an order from the *United Nations Relief and Rehabilitation Administration* (UNRRA) as that body was coming to the end of its administration of the CTB, stating that copies of all records were to be sent to UNRRA headquarters in Geneva by the end of September 1947.[3] In the *Child Search Branch*, the following question was raised: "Should we be doing something about Archives? Miss Heise did mention something about it with regard to our new filing system just before she left. However, we are not touching on the filing system until we get to Ludwigsburg." Child tracing officer Eileen Davidson's response was: "Please hold for time being. Miss Heise said your Dept. was setting up the filing system for our section!"[4] Among the many pressing things the child search teams had to deal with in 1947, creating a well-organised archive was not high on their list of priorities.

In light of these exchanges, which give us a glimpse of the tracing units' office culture, perhaps we – by which I mean scholars and researchers who use the ITS archive, primarily in digital form, today – should not be surprised to find that the 30 million documents that are now at our disposal are not easily navigated. If one thinks about ITS in terms of *archive biography*, one quickly understands that ITS did not emerge fully formed in 1948. Rather, its tasks, and the documents with which it worked to fulfil them, were constantly changing. ITS added documents to its collections at different stages throughout its history, although the bulk of them were acquired in the first ten years after the war. Furthermore,

---

this chapter was funded by a *Leverhulme Trust Major Research Fellowship*, grant number MRF-2015–052.

3 Paul B. Edwards, Zone Director, UNRRA U.S. Zone Headquarters, Heidelberg, Staff Memo No. 173, Subject: Records Disposition – Collection and Preservation of Documents, 9.5.1947, 6.1.2/82486049/ITS Digital Archive, Wiener Library; L. Doughty, Chief – Program Analysis, Inter-Office Memo, 10.5.1947, Subject: Collection of Documents, 6.1.2/82486054–82486056/ITS Digital Archive, Wiener Library.

4 R.P. [Ruby P.] to E.D. [Eileen Davidson]; E.D. to Miss [Sheila] Collins, PCIRO, US Zone Headquarters, APO 633, US Army, Inter-Office Memo, 14. and 15.7.1947, 6.1.2/82486052/ITS Digital Archive, Wiener Library.

the documents in ITS were there to be used by the staff for tracing work; that is to say, ITS was primarily interested in them insofar as names of individuals could be extracted from them (to be *carded*, in ITS jargon) so as to show the stations of a person's trajectory during the years of Nazi persecution. ITS is both like and unlike other archives. It is like them to the extent that one needs to understand the process whereby the archive came into being in order to make use of it – documents were acquired through active searches in German locations such as factories and hospitals; through donations from individuals who had preserved or come into possession of Nazi documents at the end of the war; through exchanges with other institutions, including legal depositions and newly-created museums; through Allied occupation authorities' orders to German civil servants; and through chance discovery. It is also like other archives insofar as there is – as the above facts imply – always a politics of the archive: the history of ITS, including the uses to which the West German government put it during the Cold War and its secrecy for the last two decades of the Cold War, under the administration of the *International Committee of the Red Cross* (ICRC), suggest that this is no mere empty vessel, just waiting for historians to reveal its holdings. These have always already been shaped, controlled and interpreted. But it is unlike other archives by virtue of the fact that ITS was not established as an archive, but as an institution with a different remit: tracing the missing. It is also unlike most other archives to the extent that it is no longer growing, or is growing now only slowly, as the current waves of tracing inquiries are handled and archived. Unlike most other archives – although this is perhaps less true today when bodies such as the *National Archives* in London seek to attract a wider user base – ITS is very conscious of the fact that, as an institution, it has commemorative and educational functions as much as narrowly archival ones.[5]

Perhaps we should celebrate these facts. Although it takes time and effort to use the ITS database, the fact that the material was collected for the purposes of tracing and not for historical research has advantages as well as disadvantages.

I will start with the latter, since the disadvantages are obvious to anyone who has used the archive. Not only is it hard to navigate, the rewards of persevering may sometimes appear limited. Tens of thousands of pages of lists of names, or blank pages, of Hollerith punch card results, or of inter-office memoranda of the trivial sort cited above are just some of the delights greeting the as-

---

[5] For more on these issues, see Dan Stone: "The Memory of the Archive: The International Tracing Service and the Construction of the Past as History", in *Dapim: Studies on the Holocaust*, 31/2, 2017, 69–88.

siduous researcher. Then there are thousands of pages documents copied from other archives, whether the *Zentrale Stelle* in Ludwigsburg, documents from the *International Military Tribunal* at Nuremberg, or the *Auschwitz-Birkenau State Museum*. It is useful to have so many of them in one place but it is not always easy to work out in advance of one's research what is original to ITS and what is not. Some of the ITS's institutional documents may be found in the *National Archives* in London, in the archives of the *International Refugee Organization* (IRO) in Paris, or in the *United Nations* (UN) *Archives* in Geneva and New York. Many documents are to be found in the *United States Holocaust Memorial Museum* (Washington, DC) or in *Yad Vashem* (Jerusalem), as well as in local archives across Germany, other European countries, or Israel.

More pressing than these – let us call them preliminary – issues is the question of what to do with the material that one does find. Before the ITS was opened to researchers (and the general public) just over a decade ago, scholars of the Holocaust were already well provided for in respect of archival material, especially since the end of the Cold War made archives in the formerly communist countries of Eastern Europe increasingly accessible – if not everywhere and at all times. Thus the problem is a more fundamental, theoretical one: how much material does a historian need? The question demands a return to Nietzsche's second essay in the *Untimely Meditations:* "on the uses and disadvantages of history for life."[6]

In that essay of 1874, Nietzsche famously distinguished between three kinds of history: monumental, antiquarian, and critical. The first refers to the great moments in the life of an individual, which should be highlighted for the benefit of future generations. Quite apart from Nietzsche's warning that to subscribe to such a monumental history means to forget large sections of the past, leaving only "embellished islands", one might wonder whether, after the events whose description one can find in ITS documents, the notion of a monumental history even has any validity or purchase any more. Further, since Nietzsche warned that monumental history can leave an age unable to distinguish between "a monumentalized past and a mythical fiction" and that it "inspires the courageous to foolhardiness and the inspired to fanaticism", one could justifiably ask

---

[6] "Vom Nutzen und Nachteil der Historie für das Leben". Notoriously difficult to translate, the essay has also recently been published as "On the Utility and Liability of History for Life", in Richard T. Gray (ed.): *The Complete Works of Friedrich Nietzsche, Vol. 2: Unfashionable Observations*, Stanford: Stanford University Press, 1995.

whether monumental history is one of the main causes of the evils of the twentieth century.⁷

For scholars who use ITS, Nietzsche's second type of history is more perilous. The antiquarian historian, Nietzsche tells us, "likes to persist in the familiar and the revered of old". The problem for the ITS researcher is unlikely to be quite the same: probably few of us delight in the past we find in ITS and want to preserve it because we admire the way of life contained therein – except, perhaps, insofar as the dedication of the tracers provides evidence of a desire to undo or at least to mitigate some of the negative effects of Nazism. Rather, the problem lies in being unable to negotiate a critical path through the piles of documents. Nietzsche's next warning, however, speaks much more directly to our concern: "The possession of ancestral goods", he writes, "changes its meaning in such a soul [i.e. in the antiquarian historian]: *they* rather possess *it*." Here Nietzsche sounds like Marx when the latter writes that the owner of an entailed estate is in fact owned by the property and feels the weight of its heritage as an obligation.⁸ Likewise, the antiquarian historian is unable to throw off the weight of the past and to select from it only what truly matters. "The trivial, circumscribed, decaying and obsolete", Nietzsche goes on, "acquire their own dignity and inviolability through the fact that the preserving and revering soul of the antiquarian man has emigrated into them and there made its home."⁹ Antiquarianism simply collects everything and does not know how to choose: it mummifies the past and thus the present too in "a blind rage for collecting, a restless raking together of everything that has ever existed."¹⁰

---

7 Friedrich Nietzsche: "On the Uses and Disadvantages of History for Life", in R.J. Hollingdale (ed.): *Untimely Meditations*, Cambridge: Cambridge University Press, 1991, 70 – 71. On historicism as part of the intellectual background to the Holocaust, see Dan Stone: *Constructing the Holocaust: A Study in Historiography*, London: Vallentine Mitchell, 2003.
8 Marx writes: "That which is permanent is entailed wealth, landed property. This is the preserving moment in the relation – the substance. The master of the entailed estate, the owner, is really a mere accident. Landed property anthropomorphises itself in the various generations. Landed property always inherits, as it were, the first born of the house as an attribute linked to it. Every first born in the line of land owners is the inheritance, the property, of the inalienable landed property, which is the predestined substance of his will and activity. The subject is the thing and the predicate is the man. The will becomes the property of the property." Karl Marx: *Critique of Hegel's Philosophy of Right*, ed. by Joseph O'Malley, Cambridge: Cambridge University Press, 1977 (1843), 106.
9 Nietzsche, "On the Uses and Disadvantages", 73.
10 Ibid., 75.

It is easy to see how research in ITS leads one to become "encased in the stench of must and mould".[11] Must one read every last document in sub-unit 6.1.2 in order to understand the workings of the *Child Search Branch?* Do we really need to know the contents of every memo sent between ITS director Maurice Thudichum and his staff or the minutes of every PCIRO sub-committee? How many thousands of cemetery maps does one need to examine before one understands the aims of the "graves recheck" programme? Beyond the problem of collecting for the sake of collecting, which is truly a form of antiquarianism, one then runs into the methodological problem that accompanies collecting without analysis: positivism. The aim of collecting all of this material, irrespective of whether it serves any analytical purpose or not, becomes to reconstruct, in extreme detail, "what happened" – again, without any regard for whether or not anyone needs to know.

It is out of a disdain for collecting and for the positivism that follows from it that Nietzsche says mankind also requires, besides the monumental and antiquarian modes of regarding the past, a third, *critical* mode of history. In Nietzsche's scheme, this is a process whereby the past is condemned, as if to say that what had gone before deserves to perish. As Nietzsche says, this is a potentially dangerous process:

> [M]en and ages which serve life by judging and destroying a past are always dangerous and endangered men and ages. For since we are the outcome of earlier generations, we are also the outcome of their aberrations, passions and errors, and indeed of their crimes; it is not possible to free oneself wholly from this chain.[12]

But the attempt to combat this heritage is a worthwhile one, Nietzsche seems to suggest, even though it is hard to know where the limits to rejection of the past should lie.[13] In the case of the Nazi crimes so amply documented in ITS, this critical approach to the past, in which we agree that the past deserved to perish, is surely the justification for the many hours spent in the archive. Negotiating a path between antiquarianism and critical historiography, between identifying material that contributes to an analytically or conceptually rigorous approach to history and tarrying with material of any sort, is the challenge that the researcher in ITS has to tackle. For historians of ITS, critical historiography

---

11 Ibid.
12 Ibid., 76.
13 Nietzsche uses the term *denial* rather than *rejection* but in the context of Holocaust history that has the potential to sow confusion. Nietzsche does not mean that we should deny that events have happened but that we should deny that they should have happened.

means subjecting documents to source critique, understanding the history of the archive, approaching the documents with research questions and in the spirit of dialogue with other historians in order to produce not the past as it was but an interpretation of the past. In reality there is no practical difference between the past and history, for history cannot recreate the past or judge its interpretations against the past; it can only produce substitutes for the past that adhere to rigorous disciplinary rules about relying on the traces of the past we call documents.

This negotiation is perhaps no different from what historians always do in archives – at least since the invention of critical historiography, in which, as Ricoeur says, following Marc Bloch, the "struggle with the document" is taken as given.[14] The problem in ITS is the sheer size of the archive and thus the complexity of struggling with the documents. Although the problem of forgeries or fakes (Valla's exposure of the *Donation of Constantine* marks the birth of modern source critique) is one that need not detain us with respect to the documents in ITS, the question of voluntary or involuntary errors, fraudulent, self-interested statements, and identifying the unlikely or implausible is crucial for research in ITS. How many survivors gave false information about their names, age or nationality to those tasked with registering displaced persons? How many death march routes and identifications contain errors? Understandable they may be in their context, but the researcher needs to be able to identify them or at least to be aware of the likelihood of such errors.

With these preparatory thoughts in mind, taking into consideration the disadvantages of ITS for historical research and attending to the need for a critical approach that seeks to avoid positivism, we are now in a position to consider the uses of ITS. With a focus on the topics of sub-camps, death marches and liberation, I hope to show that ITS can be used, with care, for the purpose of uncovering untold narratives, and of discovering information about little-known sites and experiences of the Holocaust about which one finds out little by relying only or primarily on documents created by the perpetrators. ITS, in other words, allows one to follow the trajectories of individuals and to situate them into bigger patterns of Nazi criminality. This social history of the Holocaust, or Nazism from the perspective of its victims, is one of ITS's main advantages and it provides an important counterpart to a perpetrator-centric narrative. The latter is no less necessary for understanding the pattern of Nazi crimes, but for a rounded history (or

---

14 Paul Ricoeur: *Memory, History, Forgetting*, trans. Kathleen Blamey and David Pellauer, Chicago: University of Chicago Press, 2004, 172.

an *integrated history*), one which is attuned to the effects of the crimes on the victims as well as to the mechanics of the crimes, ITS is indispensable.

Sub-camps

Take, for example, the topic of sub-camps, which in English language historiography at least, remains underdeveloped. By the end of 1944, there were over 1,000 sub-camps attached to the SS's main camps – this is not to include labour camps run by firms, local councils, or other countries within the Axis.[15] Although sub-camps had been part of the history of the concentration camp system from the start, the majority were created late in the war when the pressure on the German war economy led the SS and German firms to use concentration camp inmates – including Jews – as slave labour. For large numbers of Jews, especially Hungarian Jews, this development prevented them from being murdered and, thanks to the vagaries of the war, saved their lives (one should be clear here: these were people destined to die and, given the horrific conditions in most of the sub-camps, large numbers did die, but the fact that they were in sub-camps meant that considerable numbers were still alive in the spring of 1945).

The ITS files provide immense amounts of detail about the lives of the inmates in the sub-camps in ways that one cannot find in perpetrator documents. Here one finds material describing their relationships, food, shelter, medical care (or lack of all three), their interaction with guards and civilian workers, their experience of violence, gender and work. The case of Auschwitz-Monowitz is a good one, since the documents are especially rich. By the summer of 1944, there were 11,000 inmates at Monowitz, mostly Hungarian Jews, but also Jews from other European countries as well as a small number of Roma. Almost all were men with the exception of 10 to 20 women who became forced sex workers.[16] The camp commandant, Heinrich Schwarz, was an important man not just because he remained in his post until the camp was evacuated at the start of 1945 (when he became commandant of Natzweiler), but because as of November 22, 1943, Monowitz was designated the main administrative headquar-

---

15 On which see Joseph R. White and Mel Hecker (eds.): *United States Holocaust Memorial Museum Encyclopedia of Camps and Ghettos 1933–1945, Vol. III: Camps and Ghettos under European Regimes Aligned with Nazi Germany*, Bloomington: Indiana University Press, 2018.
16 I will not use the term *prostitute*, which suggests a degree of volition, or carries a negative implication with respect to the women's morals. The camp *brothels* should be understood as being a labour detail like any other, with those in it being selected for the task and in no way volunteering for it.

ters for all of the Auschwitz sub-camps. The inmates worked either in the *Farben* factory or were subcontracted to other companies, working mostly in construction or in methanol production, some details of which were extremely brutal and dangerous, such as carrying sacks of cement or logs. Only as of 1944 were inmates put to work in specialised details such as chemical laboratories, with Primo Levi being the most famous.

For example, Robert Elie Waitz, a captured member of the French Resistance in the Auvergne, one of some 1,200 Frenchmen who were deported to Auschwitz in October 1943, was among a group of about 230 who were immediately sent on to Monowitz. After the war, when he became the president of the *Amicale d'Auschwitz* – a French survivors' organisation – he testified about his experiences there. The first striking thing Waitz claimed was that he "quickly realised that Monowitz was an extermination camp" (*Vernichtungslager*) – not in the sense of Birkenau where people were gassed, but in the sense that the strenuous work led to the decline of their physical and psychic defences, "whose conclusion was, for most, the gas chamber." Thus, Monowitz was not a camp where people were led immediately to be killed; rather, once they became too weak to work, they would then be taken to Birkenau and killed. "The goal", as Waitz put it, "was unequivocally clear: the total exhaustion and finally the annihilation of the hard-worked IG Auschwitz inmate." Indeed, he claimed to have heard an SS officer say to the Monowitz inmates: "You are all sentenced to death; the carrying out of your sentence is just being extended a little."

Furthermore, Waitz correctly observed that *IG Farben* paid attention neither to how the inmates' productivity could be rationally exploited nor to how the workforce could be sustained. As an example of this disregard, he noted how the inmates' clothing was completely inadequate and that they were freezing to death whilst they were supposed to be working. In summer, by contrast, cases of dysentery broke out thanks to the poor sanitary conditions. The inmates' food contained no protein and the bread was "terrible" (*fuerchterlich*).[17] The "hospital" lacked medicine and sanitary facilities and was, in any case, for most who ended up there, a holding station for selection for Birkenau. There was no toilet, just a pail in the room, "which gave off an evil stench", until the inmates themselves "organised" and built toilets with running water. Furthermore, the inmates were at the mercy of the guards who shot them "like spar-

---

17 Robert Elie Waitz, Testimony to US War Crimes Commission, 12.11.1947, 1.1.2.0/82350522– 82350524/ITS Digital Archive, Wiener Library. ["Das eindeutige Ziel trat klar zu Tage: endgueltige Entwertung und schliessliche Vernichtung des in IG Auschwitz eingesetzten Haeftlings."] See also Waitz's T/D file at 6.3.3.2/713031/ITS Digital Archive, Wiener Library.

rows", as Stefan Budziazek noted of the period when he was in Monowitz, from February to September 1942.[18]

The so-called "hospital" (*Krankenbau*) in Monowitz exemplifies the absurdity of the slave labour operations. With no regard for the inmates' health, it seems surprising that a hospital existed at all, yet we know that this institution – a mockery of a real hospital – existed in most Nazi concentration camps.[19] Berthold Epstein, formerly professor of paediatrics in Prague, and a nurse (*Pfleger*) in Monowitz, explained after the war the various illnesses that resulted from the awful conditions and the relentless work, accompanied by beatings, poor food and inadequate clothing: pneumonia, "phlegmonen", blood poisoning, hunger oedema und extreme emaciation as well as many cases of work-related injuries, caused by falling machinery and raw material and a lack of protective clothing. In winter, there were many severe cases of frostbite and there were always inmates in the hospital who had been beaten by kapos or guards whilst at work. The dysentery block was especially feared by the inmates since there was only a slim chance of leaving it except to be transported to Birkenau.[20] Epstein and his colleagues did what they could, but their appointment as doctors was also a mockery, for they were not supplied with any of the necessary equipment, medicine or sanitary facilities to heal the sick and injured. *IG Farben* also sponsored medical experiments, and SS doctor Hellmuth Vetter, who was commissioned by his former employer, Farben, to test drugs on inmates at Dachau and Mauthausen, did the same at Monowitz.[21]

Monowitz is fairly well known, at least as a name. But in ITS one also finds accounts of little-known sub-camps, for example those attached to Gross-Rosen. Gross-Rosen was founded in 1940 as a sub-camp of Sachsenhausen, the concen-

---

[18] Stefan Budziazek, Testimony to US War Crimes Commission, Frankfurt am Main, 27.10.1947, 1.1.2.0/82350515 (sparrows), 82350517 (toilets)/ITS Digital Archive, Wiener Library.
[19] See, for example, the essays in Michael A. Grodin (ed.): *Jewish Medical Resistance in the Holocaust*, New York: Berghahn Books, 2014.
[20] Berthold Epstein, Testimony to US War Crimes Commission, Prague, 3.3.1947, 1.1.2.0/82350534–82350535/ITS Digital Archive, Wiener Library.
[21] Paul Weindling: *Victims and Survivors of Nazi Human Experiments: Science and Suffering in the Holocaust*, London: Bloomsbury, 2015, 105. Epstein was also later forced to assist Josef Mengele with experiments on treatments for *Noma*, a form of gangrene that was caused by malnutrition; see ibid., 130. For a photograph of Epstein and other inmate physicians who also worked after the liberation caring for survivors, see Jacek Lachendro: *Auschwitz after Liberation*, Oświęcim: Auschwitz-Birkenau State Museum, 2015, 70. On Vetter, see also Henri Desoille, L'Assassinat systématique de prisonniers malades par les médecins Nazis, n.d., c. 1945, 1.1.2.0/82346057–82346061/ITS Digital Archive, Wiener Library. Desoille was an inmate doctor in Auschwitz and Professor of Medicine in Paris after the war.

tration camp near Berlin founded in 1936, when the quarry there was acquired by the *German Earth and Stone Works* (*Deutsche Erd- und Steinwerke*, or DEST). Like Neuengamme near Hamburg and Natzweiler in Alsace, which both became autonomous camps in 1940 and 1941 respectively, Gross-Rosen became an autonomous camp in June 1941 and its original inmates, who were registered at Sachsenhausen, were transferred to the control of Gross-Rosen. They included 255 German *professional criminals*, Poles, German and Czech political prisoners, and a group of *asocials*, that is to say, people identified as beggars, vagrants, or other social outsiders who threatened the Third Reich's image of orderly and clean streets.[22] Thereafter the camp grew enormously, so that by the end of 1944 almost 77,000 inmates were held at Gross-Rosen and its more than 100 sub-camps. The majority of them were Polish and Soviet citizens, but there were inmates from a further 24 countries. Some 45.6% of them, or about 57,000, were Jews, mostly from Poland and Hungary. With some 10.9% of the total concentration camp population, Gross-Rosen was second in size only to Buchenwald. In the last five weeks of the camp's existence, a further 7,100 inmates were transferred to Gross-Rosen from Auschwitz and transports from prisons in the *General Government* (the bulk area of Nazi-occupied Poland not incorporated into the Reich) were also sent to the camp, which became severely overcrowded.[23] The number of inmates includes some 26,000 women, almost all Jews, who were sent directly from the main camp to the sub-camps. Where before 1944 there were no women among Gross-Rosen's inmates, by 1945 it was the fourth-largest camp for women, after Ravensbrück, Stutthof and Buchenwald.

In some ways it is hardly surprising that it has taken a long time for historians and the wider public to gain knowledge of the Gross-Rosen sub-camps. Many were small and the inmates themselves sometimes had little sense of where they were. In her report on Mittelsteine, for example, the former inmate Sara Michałowicz explained, in a mixture of Yiddish and German, that: "Wo war di genaue Lage fun lager Mittelstein kan ich nicht wissen, wajl wir haben ni di frajhejt gezejn" ("I cannot know the exact location of the Mittelsteine

---

22 See Leslaw Braiter: "Gross-Rosen Main Camp", in Geoffrey P. Megargee (ed.): *Encyclopedia of Camps and Ghettos, Vol. I, Part A*, Bloomington: Indiana University Press, 2009, 694. There is a copy of the order creating Gross-Rosen as an autonomous camp in ITS: see 1.1.11.0/82111505/ITS Digital Archive, Wiener Library.
23 Alfred Konieczny: "Das Konzentrationslager Groß-Rosen", in *Dachauer Hefte 4 – Die vergessenen Lager,* Munich 1994, 20–21.

camp, because we never saw freedom").²⁴ Nevertheless, survivors could often provide quite detailed descriptions of their living conditions in the camps.

In 1950, ITS sought to obtain information from survivors about the sub-camps. Writing to the DP camps and elsewhere, they provided a template which asked survivors to provide, where possible, details of the camps they were in, how many inmates there were and where they were from, what work they did and for which firms, and to provide details of any noteworthy occurrences and names of survivors. Some of the respondents simply filled in the form with which they were provided, others wrote their own letters, though these also mostly followed the ITS format. Individually, many of these reports are quite mundane, but taken together, the results add up to quite a detailed picture of the nature of the camps.

For example, writing in the Föhrenwald DP camp after the war, Pesa Srebnik-Heuschowicz described the conditions at Mittelsteine and Weisswasser. In front of both, she writes, stood a watchtower, and both camps were surrounded by barbed wire, which at Weisswasser was electrified, and at night were illuminated by spotlights. The guards at both camps were female SS. At Mittelsteine there were 200 Polish and 200 Hungarian women; at Weisswasser, some 500 to 600 Jewish women from various countries. They wore civilian clothing, but with a red stripe on the back and an inmate number on the chest, and a blue and white prisoner cap. According to Srebnik-Heuschowitz, Mittelsteine was opened on August 23, 1944 and evacuated at the end of March 1945; she and her colleagues (she uses the second person "we" here) were then transferred to Weisswasser, where they were freed by "the Russians" on May 9, 1945. In Mittelsteine, she recalled, the women were housed in a room with triple bunk beds, on which the women shared straw sacks and a blanket. Rations were 150 g of bread per day, and a thin kohlrabi soup, which "was like water." On Sundays, they received 10 g of margarine, a bit of sugar and sometimes some sausage – better rations than at Auschwitz. Still, compare this to the official "menu" that was produced for the Gross-Rosen inmates, and the latter immediately takes on the air of a fiction:

The fact that such a thing as a menu – signed off by three senior members of the camp administration, including the camp doctor – even existed, might seem surprising. Yet, even if it is not exactly appetising, it is quite clear that the inmates did not receive the three meals a day advertised here, many of which were supposed to contain beef (*Rindfleisch*) or vegetables (*Gemüse*). The notice at the bottom that the menu was provisional and subject to change (*Änderungen*

---

24 Sara Michałowicz, ITS Ermittlungsblatt betr. des Lagers Mittelsteine, 26.2.1950, 1.1.0.7/87764788/ITS Digital Archive, Wiener Library.

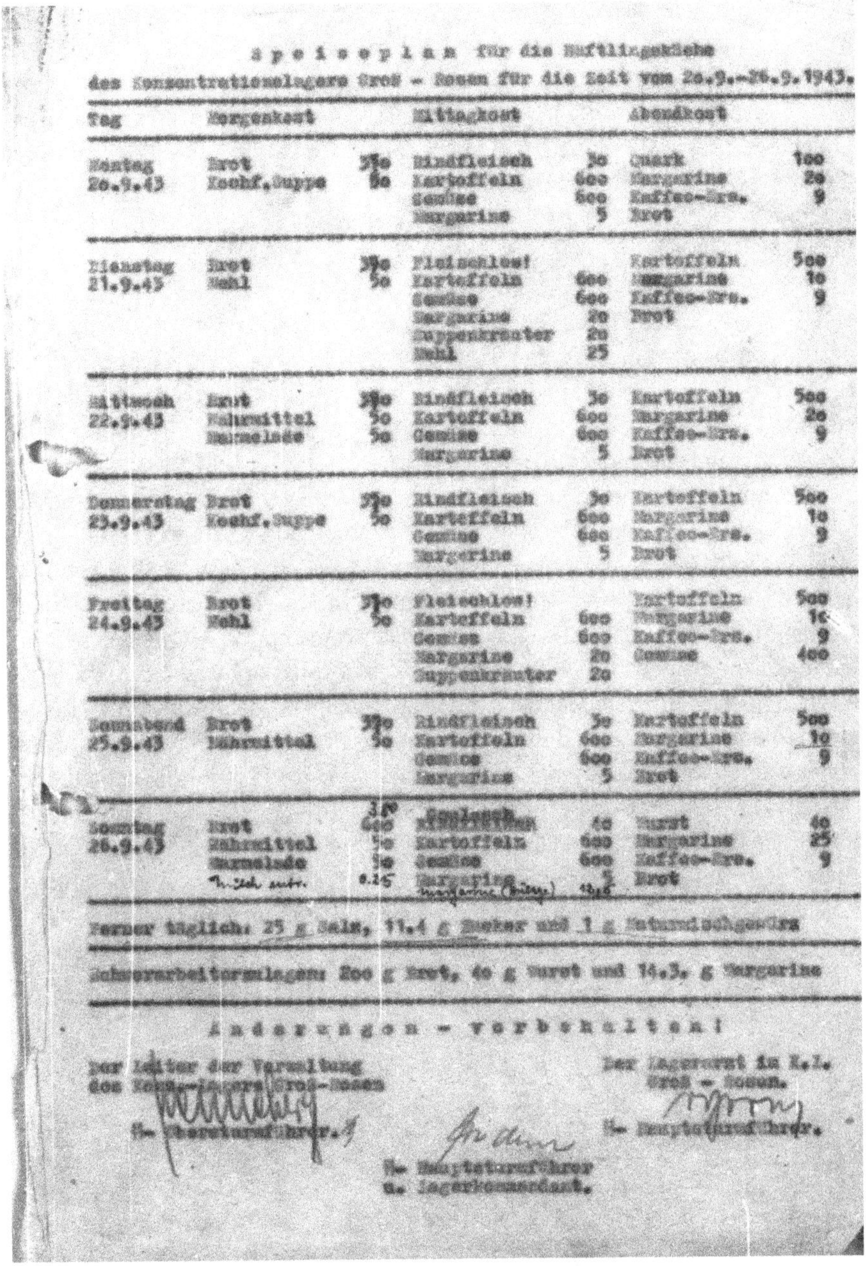

Fig. 1: Menu for Gross-Rosen inmates, 20–26.9.1943 (1.1.11.0/82111176/ITS Digital Archive, Wiener Library)

– *vorbehalten!*) seems like a mocking reminder that in the world of the Nazi camps appearances bore no relationship to actuality.

The women worked twelve hours a day, one week during the day and the next week during the night. Srebnik-Heuschowitz's work involved producing boiler lids (*Kesseldeckel*), 150 per day or else she would not receive the next day's bread. She was not able to name the firm for which she worked, however she did recall that the guard was named Klein, and that he was tall, thin and blond. In Weisswasser, her work involved checking the products, which were spare parts, though she could not say what they were for.[25]

Another survivor, Golda Plutno, wrote from the Landsberg DP camp, giving details of her internment in Sandomierz, Ostrowiec, Auschwitz, Gabersdorf and Georgenthal. With the exception of Auschwitz, these are not well-known Nazi sites and such reports as this are invaluable in expanding our knowledge of the camps and the movements between them. After Auschwitz, in November 1944, Plutno was transferred to Gabersdorf, a former *Schmelt* camp (a group of labour camps under the control of special plenipotentiary Albrecht Schmelt, answerable only to Himmler) now administered by Gross-Rosen, and in February 1945 to Georgenthal, where she was liberated in May 1945. Georgenthal, or St Georgenthal, was already the site of a men's sub-camp run by the Flossenbürg camp, so the new women's camp, which was devoted to dismantling damaged aircraft in the *Rott Company's* factory, was named St Georgenthal II. Plutno's claim to have been liberated there confirms the USHMM *Encyclopedia's* tentative conclusion that Hungarian and Polish Jewish women were freed there by the Soviets in May 1945.[26] Of the camps, she writes that the extreme conditions under which she lived and worked left her unable to think about the sort of information that ITS wanted, such as to which main camp the sub-camps belonged. As she says, "I was yearning for my freedom, I was unable to take an interest in that." Like other survivors still in the DP camps in 1950, Plutno requested that the ITS should send her certificate of incarceration as quickly as possible so that she could take it with her when she emigrated for the US, which she was hoping to do soon.[27]

---

[25] Pesa Srebnik-Heuschowitz, letter to ITS, betr. Ausk. in Mittelsteine & Weisswasser, 23.3.1950, 1.1.0.7/87764790/ITS Digital Archive, Wiener Library.

[26] Hans Brenner: "Gebhardsdorf (aka Friedeberg)", in Geoffrey P. Megargee (ed.): *Encyclopedia of Camps and Ghettos, Vol. I, Part A*, Bloomington: Indiana University Press, 2009, 735. On St Georgenthal, see also the report from *Central Office* Ludwigsburg, 28.6.1972, 5.1/82314053–82314057/ITS Digital Archive, Wiener Library.

[27] Golda Plutno, letter to ITS, 9.5.1950, 1.1.0.7/87764683/ITS Digital Archive, Wiener Library.

What is clear from this brief glimpse into the ITS documents is that when we change our viewpoint and, instead of perpetrator-produced documents, we look at victim-produced accounts, a vast gulf opens up between the bureaucratic, matter of fact nature of the former – even when it is reporting on unpleasant facts – and the brutal reality of daily life in the camps for the inmates.

Death Marches

When it comes to death marches and the liberation of the camps, ITS is rich in testimonies. Ricoeur notes that

> [t]hanks to a reiterable character that confers upon it the status of an institution, testimony can be taken down in writing, deposited. This deposition, in turn, is the condition of possibility of specific institutions devoted to the collecting, conserving, and classifying of documentation with an eye to its subsequently being consulted by qualified personnel.[28]

And he goes on, more significantly for our purposes: "That history should have recourse to testimony is not fortuitous. It is grounded in the very definition of the object of history."[29] But where Ricoeur refers to *testimony*, he in general means any written trace of the past, what we would normally refer to as a document (although for Ricoeur, the *testimony* becomes a *document* when the historian approaches it armed with research questions). In the case of "certain fundamentally oral testimonies", in particular those emanating from the Holocaust, their being placed in an archive is problematic. Why? Because the limited experiences described therein exceed the knowledge of most people and seem therefore incongruous when placed in repositories of everyday experience such as an archive, because archiving appropriates a text, renders it accessible and domesticated. Nevertheless, as Ricoeur goes on to explain, survivors do testify and thus "it is within the same public space as that of historiography that the crisis of testimony after Auschwitz unfolds."[30]

Examining some of the first attempts to investigate the routes taken by the so-called "death marches", one does indeed quickly become aware of what is meant by the "crisis of testimony": the term "unspeakable" here means not that one cannot speak at all – the outpouring of words put paid to that notion – but that even with all of the words, there is an excess, something that exceeds

---

28 Ricoeur: *Memory, History, Forgetting*, 167.
29 Ibid., 169.
30 Ibid., 176.

comprehension.³¹ Indeed, the absurd, surreal nature of the death marches is perhaps their defining characteristic. I will give just two examples.

The first eye-witness, Dr Rolf Busch-Waldeck, captured this aspect of the death marches with particular clarity, in his description of the march from Wiener-Neudorf, a sub-camp of Mauthausen, to the main camp in April 1945:

> It is a Dante-esque, uncanny column of marchers. In the middle the inmates slowly drag themselves along, packed tightly together. Here or there on the street already lies a blanket, a piece of bread, some tinned food, lost or thrown away by one of the 1,900 marchers. You think about what that means. People, some of whom had turned to eating human flesh in the camp out of hunger, are now carelessly throwing food away out of fear of being shot. And left and right, alongside this ghostly procession, march SS men, on one arm their machine pistols at the ready, on the other arm a tarted-up, made-up, powdered, giggling demimondaine, who for her part in her free hand casually leads a dog trained to tear apart human flesh. And more and more shot inmates on the street. The SS man and the demimondaine step laughing over the corpses, the dog growls every time with the hair of the back of its neck standing on end, sniffs the dead, and gets dragged along again.³²

The second example is Leon Kamerfuks, an inmate of Buchenwald. In his postwar report, written in October 1945, he tells how on April 4, 1945, the Jewish inmates were separated from the "Aryans"; two days later, they were sent out on evacuation marches. Kamerfuks was among the first group of 1,650 Jews. They were marched out in rows of five, with at the head of the column an Obersturmführer in a horse-drawn wagon, three further horse-drawn wagons containing food, the SS's weapons and luggage, then four more wagons, each pulled by twelve inmates; at the back were guards with dogs, and further guards were posted all along the column. Anyone who was too exhausted to continue was placed in the "death wagon", drawn by eight inmates, which brought up the rear and, at the next woods the march reached, taken out and shot. The guards also shot inmates as they marched, the first shooting taking place no more than 200 m from the gates of Buchenwald. According to Kamerfuks, "the street was a sea of blood.

---

31 See Saul Friedländer (ed.): *Probing the Limits of Representation: Nazism and the "Final Solution"*, Cambridge: Harvard University Press, 1992, 19–20.
32 Dr Rolf Busch-Waldeck, Bericht über den Aufbau, Tätigkeit und Auflösung des KZ-Wr. Neudorf mit Dokumentenabschriften 1943–1945, 1.1.26.0/82119479/ITS Digital Archive, Wiener Library. The term Busch-Waldeck uses is *Halbweltdame*. His full, long report is at 1.1.26.0/82119406–82119595/ITS Digital Archive, Wiener Library, and see also Bertrand Perz: "Der Todesmarsch von Wiener Neudorf nach Mauthausen: Eine Dokumentation", in *Jahrbuch des Dokumentationsarchiv des österreichischen Widerstandes*, 1988, 117–137. For more on Wiener Neudorf, see Christian Dürr and Ralf Lechner: "Wiener Neudorf", in Geoffrey P. Megargee (ed.): *Encyclopedia of Camps and Ghettos, Vol. I, Part B*, 955–956.

It was indescribable, like a battlefield." After a relatively short march, 80 inmates had been killed and the rest spent the night in barns, prevented by the guards from being fed by "kind-hearted farmers". Over the next two days, the inmates were marched from 6am to 4pm, on the first day with a small piece of bread and on the second without food altogether. When they complained and asked for a rest they were threatened with the "death wagon" and the promise of "eternal rest". Many were murdered on the way, with Kamerfuks giving the example of a father and son walking together; when the father could go no further, the guards' dogs were set on him and, as the son bent over him, they were both shot on the spot. Several days later, the reduced columns reached Flossenbürg. On being told there was no room for them, the inmates marched on again, now into the Bavarian forest. Because the Americans were now nearby, the guards no longer wanted to use their guns, which would give their presence away, so they began killing inmates with daggers and bayonets. When the columns reached the Danube they were taken across by ferry; some of the inmates were thrown into the water and drowned. Shortly before reaching Dachau at the end of April, where the inmates hoped the march would end, they received the order to turn back, and the column now headed in the direction of Salzburg, with the inmates suffering terribly from exhaustion, starvation, and frostbite. On May 3 they were delivered to the former women's camp of Lebenau. 168 of those who set off from Buchenwald were still alive. "We were really amazed", says Kamerfuks, "that we were received in a very friendly way here." The Americans were very close and the SS soon disappeared, leaving the inmates behind, to be found by the Americans on the 4th.[33]

Liberation

As Kamerfuks' account reveals, for many survivors, *liberation* is a concept that needs to be unpacked. Some camp inmates experienced moments of elation as Allied troops arrived at the gates and freed them. But even in those circumstances, a substantial proportion of inmates were too ill either to celebrate or even fully to understand what was happening. And like Kamerfuks, many survi-

---

[33] Leon Kamerfuks, "Ausmarsch von Buchenwald", 12.10.45, 5.3.3/84625594–84625597/ITS Digital Archive, Wiener Library. I examine Kamerfuks' testimony and postwar trajectory in a chapter of my forthcoming book on ITS, *Fate Unknown: Tracing the Missing after the Holocaust and World War II*, Oxford: Oxford University Press, forthcoming 2021.

vors discovered they had been "liberated" more by virtue of the absence of guards than by the arrival of Allied troops.[34]

That is not to say that some of the inmates were unable to appreciate what it meant to see the Americans, even in situations like at Nordhausen, one of the sub-camps in the Dora complex, where many of the dying inmates suffered even more when American bombs landed on the camp at the start of April. One survivor, the Belgian Christian Guy, provided testimony to the Americans on April 14, explaining his trajectory from Gross-Rosen to Nordhausen in February on a journey on which 800 died: "It was the most horrible sight I have ever seen because the people were trying to get their clothes off before the dying were dead."[35] On April 4 his building was bombed and between 1,600 and 1,700 of the 2,000 inmates were killed. Starving and unable to walk, Guy crawled on his hands and knees to search for food: "I ate the raw brains of a horse and it was not bad." The next days are somewhat confusing but it appears that the SS had fled because he and some other comrades were fed by a group of Frenchmen who had stolen food from the German kitchens. Then, on April 11, the leader of this French group disappeared with all the food, which Guy said "was not nice of him but that is alright because he fed us for a week." Then that morning everything changed:

> On the 11th in the morning one of the boys came in and like a mad man called, "There is an American with a car against the gate." All the comrades in the cell started yelling and weeping. They were like mad. I could not move at the moment or believe it. I was astonished but a few hours later I had to accept it. The day after this we were taken away to city houses and then I was evacuated to this American File Hospital. I am glad you arrived and wish you all success and hope that you get as many Germans as you can. I am sorry I cannot help you boys to do my part.[36]

In Vaihingen, a sub-camp of Natzweiler which held about 800 inmates, including a number of well-known, eminent individuals, among them a French archbishop, high-ranking Russian soldiers and the chairman of The Hague tribunal Adrian Bommasijn, the arrival of Allied troops, in this case French, was greeted

---

34 For further discussion, see Dan Stone: *The Liberation of the Camps: The End of the Holocaust and its Aftermath,* New Haven: Yale University Press, 2015.
35 Testimony of Christian Guy, taken at 51st Field Hospital, 14.4.1945, 1.1.27.0/82121869/ITS Digital Archive, Wiener Library.
36 Ibid., 1.1.27.0/82121870, ITS Digital Archive, Wiener Library.

with uproar. As the French arrived on April 7, "the joy was immense."[37] The camp had been brutal, with vastly insufficient clothing, food and sanitary facilities, especially in the winter months, when many died every day through the SS's deliberate neglect. After the liberation, the French troops buried the dead who were laid out in the camp – some 1,650 – and the French sanitary corps and nurses

> began a very energetic, difficult and self-sacrificing task. They disinfected the camp and did everything possible to help the unfortunate inmates. On their own shoulders the French soldiers carried all the corpses, who had died of typhus and other infectious illnesses and which were crawling with millions of lice, and buried them.[38]

The ill French, Belgian and Dutch inmates were then sent to Speyer and Baden-Baden to recuperate, whilst those able to do so returned home. The remaining 350 Poles, Jews and Russians were sent to Neuenbürg near Bruchsal (Baden-Württemberg), where, the local inhabitants having been thrown out of their houses by the French military, they were cared for once more: "Here too the French military administration's doctors and nurses, led by Dr Deramaix, did everything they could with extraordinary love and care to help the people. We will hold that in our memory forever."[39] Such scenes have become quite familiar to Anglo-American audiences in the context of the liberation of Dachau, Buchenwald and Bergen-Belsen, but in ITS one sees that many different experiences of the end of Nazi rule were had by survivors all across Nazi-occupied Europe.

---

37 Szlam Horowicz, Konzentrationslager Natzweiler: SS Arbeitslager Vaihingen/Enz, 12.8.1946, 5.3.3/84630472/ITS Digital Archive, Wiener Library. Horowicz was a former inmate of Vaihingen now working for the Documents and Tracing Bureau in Stuttgart.
38 Ibid.
39 Ibid. On Szlama Horowicz, see Manfred Scheck: *Zwangsarbeit und Massensterben: Politische Gefangene, Fremdarbeiter und KZ-Häftlinge in Vaihingen an der Enz 1933 bis 1945*, Berlin: Metropol, 2014, 118 and 189. Scheck also cites Horowicz's report quoted here, but from the Vaihingen Archive (Archiv der KZ-Gedenkstätte Vaihingen/Enz) rather than ITS. On the local inhabitants, see Scheck: *Zwangsarbeit und Massensterben*, 188 and Olga Wormser-Migot: *Quand les alliés ouvrirent les portes ... Le dernier acte de la tragédie de la déportation*, Paris: Robert Laffont, 1965, 247. And on the death marches from Natzweiler and its sub-camps, which took place over a relatively long period, from September 1944 to April 1945, see Arno Huth: "Die Auflösung des KZ Natzweiler und seines Außenlagerkomplexes: Eine Übersicht", in Jean-Luc Blondel, Sebastian Schönemann, Susanne Urban (eds.): *Freilegungen: Auf den Spuren der Todesmärsche*, Göttingen: Wallstein, 2012, 184–197.

Conclusion: ITS beyond Positivism

The greatest challenge to the historian using ITS is positivism. It is easy to be overwhelmed by the size of the archive and to fall into the trap of thinking that the way to proceed is to read the documents as if all that then remains to be done is to "write up" what is there. Positivism implies that the archive is a neutral, empty holder of documents that are simply waiting for a historian to bring them to light. But the reality is of course different. Archives have their own biographies and politics, and this is clearly the case for the ITS collections, whose history is complex, contested and, in some ways, mysterious. Historians approach archives with research questions and, even if they spend time sifting through documents that do not – at first glance, at any rate – appear to answer those questions, they nevertheless shape the material they find into narratives and analyses of specific problems and topics. With respect to ITS, there is, for the time being, a positivist component to research that is unavoidable: historians are only just starting to familiarize themselves with the archive, its history and its contents, and thus a preliminary stage of research requires scoping exercises, processes of discovery. But that is insufficient for constructing narrative analyses of the past which offer meaningful substitutes for the past in the present, which is what history is.

As I have suggested, much of the material in ITS can be helpful for producing a social history of the Holocaust and its after-effects. But historians need to do more than simply reproduce documents or place them in chronological sequence. They need too to understand how the documents came to be in ITS, and then need to consider how they can be used in order to intervene in ongoing dialogues – historiographical debates – in order to offer interpretations of the past that contribute to developing our understanding of the past. It is at the level of interpretation that history acquires and offers meaning, and this level is one of imagination or poetics that exceeds the content of documents. The ITS collections have many disadvantages, not least the difficulty of negotiating them and the challenge of being overwhelmed by the amount of material available. But the benefits of grappling with these problems are considerable: ITS offers unparalleled opportunities for uncovering aspects of Nazi criminality – not only the Holocaust – about which we know relatively little. Most important, the historian's endeavour, when attuned to the aims of those who set up and administered ITS from its beginning, can be considered an act of ethical repair: seeking to recover the fates of individuals who would otherwise remain unknown and thus rehumanising them, salvaging something from the wreckage brought about by the "Third Reich". In 1947 one of the child search officers, John Troniak, wrote: "The reuniting of the child with family is not only the best humanitarian work of our mission, but also the best rehabilitation of any allied country and nation."[40] His words could be applied to ITS in general and not just to child search. Tracing could be a deeply depressing affair, since so many people being sought were never found. But it also provided some of the few moments of reprieve in an otherwise bleak landscape and served – and still serves – as a reminder of the Allied countries' aspiration to reverse some of the evils of Nazism and to create a more just post-war world.

---

40 John Troniak, Removal of Allied Unaccompanied Children from German Children's Home 'Schloss Hubertus' in Oberlauringen, Kr. Hofheim (Sister Gertrud Zimmer in Charge), 12.5.1947, 6.1.2/82487852/ITS Digital Archive, Wiener Library.

From Early Tracing Activities to Information for Descendants

Christian Höschler, Isabel Panek
The (Early) Search for Missing Nazi Victims

Historical Precedents, Organizational Frameworks, and Methods

Abstract: This chapter aims mainly to provide an overview of the early history of the search for victims of Nazi persecution from 1944 to the early 1950s (though an outlook regarding later developments will also be provided). At the core of this increasingly centralized process was the creation of the *International Tracing Service* (ITS) – later to become the *Arolsen Archives* – by the Allies. The focus will be on the organizational framework of tracing and documenting based on historical precedents while also looking at the use of different methods that were devised by the Allies for the sake of clarifying individual fates of Nazi victims during this time. These have, to date, received little attention from historians.

Introduction

In 1943, on behalf of the *International Labor Office*, Russian-American sociologist Eugene M. Kulischer authored *The Displacement of Population in Europe*. A seminal work in the context of preparing the world community for a new post-war order, it analyzed the myriad instances of civilian mass migration in Europe against the background of the Second World War. Refugees, evacuees, deportees, prisoners, forced laborers: how many individuals – both German and non-German – could the Allies expect to find outside their home countries by the end of the war? Kulischer, using as much statistical material as was available at the time, calculated that a staggering 30 to 40 million individuals would be in need of humanitarian support in order to facilitate their repatriation or resettlement.[1]

However, despite his mathematical determination, Kulischer cautioned that the events of the war were still ongoing and, for now, rendered any definite assessment of future challenges impossible:

---

[1] Eugene M. Kulischer: *The Displacement of Population in Europe*, Montreal: International Labor Office, 1943, 176–177. Available at: https://archive.org/details/displacementofpo031323mbp/page/n3. Last accessed: 26.7.2019.

OpenAccess. © 2020 Christian Höschler, Isabel Panek, published by De Gruyter. This work is licensed under the Creative Commons Attribution-NonCommercial-NoDerivatives 4.0 License.
https://doi.org/10.1515/9783110665376-004

> It is obvious that the number and whereabouts of all those who will have to be redistributed and resettled cannot be determined until the war is over. For the time being, every passing month merely complicates the problem still further. Workers are being snatched from their homes in thousands and tens of thousands; families are disintegrated; whole groups are separated from their national community and scattered or regrouped in distant places.[2]

What Kulischer predicted, then, was unprecedented migratory chaos – a challenge, as the author noted, that could only be solved through a coordinated effort at the international level.[3]

In retrospect, these assumptions proved to be true. During the immediate post-war years, the Allies felt overwhelmed by the challenges they encountered on a continent in disarray. The liberation and (partial) occupation of Europe, the urgent task of supplying food, goods and shelter to populations devastated by the final chapter of the war, all of this constituted a monumental task in its own right. Then there was the care for millions of survivors of Nazi persecution, the so-called Displaced Persons (DPs). They had been defined by the Allies as "civilians outside the national boundaries of their country by reason of war" and "desirous but unable to return home or find homes without assistance".[4] Essentially, the DPs were the former forced laborers, concentration camp inmates, and other victims of Nazi crimes, now scattered across all of Europe, but mainly situated within the territories of the defeated German Reich.[5]

The search for missing persons was of utter urgency and importance not only to those who had endured persecution, but also to their friends and families, as well as the governments of countries who were now determined to have their citizens return, not least for the sake of post-war reconstruction. However, in the immediate months following the end of the war, there was no single and coordinated effort to organize the search for the missing, or the gathering of relevant information necessary to perform this task. As a result, a broad spectrum of individual activists, small initiatives and well-established organizations formed the basis for early tracing and documentation. Characterizing this as a

---

2 Ibid., i.
3 Ibid., 171.
4 Administrative Memorandum 39: Displaced Persons and Refugees in Germany, 18.11.1944, WO 204/2869, The National Archives, Kew.
5 As an introduction to the topic of DPs in post-war Europe, see Mark Wyman: *DP: Europe's Displaced Persons, 1945–1951*, Philadelphia: Balch Institute Press, 1989. The most important overview published in German remains Wolfgang Jacobmeyer: *Vom Zwangsarbeiter zum Heimatlosen Ausländer: Die Displaced Persons in Westdeutschland 1945–1951*, Göttingen: Vandenhoeck & Ruprecht, 1985.

flaw of Allied planning, historian Jenny Edkins has aptly pointed to the "disorder of tracing services" as a reflection of the "'primeval Chaos' into which the European continent had dissolved".[6] Eventually, from the late 1940s onward, the Allies put more centralized frameworks and procedures into place. Going hand in hand with this was the rapid development and sometimes improvised use of different strategies in the search for missing individuals. Finally, with varying needs regarding tracing and documentation emerging in different phases of the postwar era, the nature of this work changed considerably over time.

Historical Precedents of Tracing and Documentation

The Second World War, while unparalleled in its specific events, was not the first crisis that resulted in large-scale search operations regarding missing individuals. Hence, the professional field of search and documentation was also not a tabula rasa. At the beginning of the First World War, the *International Committee of the Red Cross* (ICRC) in Geneva founded the *International Prisoners-of-War Agency*, probably the most significant institution of its kind to play a formative role in this field. The organization's task was to provide a central point of enquiry regarding missing individuals from all belligerent states. It rendered its services to military personnel and civilians alike, e.g. by documenting the current location of POWs or wounded soldiers, as well as casualties in the theatre of war. This information was forwarded to family members seeking reassurance regarding the current whereabouts and/or health of their loved ones.[7] Pioneering methods – such as the creation of a name index referring to relevant materials within other collections, e.g. lists of POWs who found themselves displaced throughout camps all over the world – drew heavily upon the support of volunteers.[8]

There are irrefutable similarities between the activities of the ICRC at the time and the work of institutions that would later play a central role in tracing after the Second World War. As we shall see in a later portion of this chapter,

---

[6] Jenny Edkins: *Missing: Persons and Politics*, Ithaca: Cornell University Press, 2016, 59.
[7] For a brief overview, see International Committee of the Red Cross: *The International Prisoners-of-War Agency: The ICRC in World War One*, Geneva: International Committee of the Red Cross, 2017. Available at: https://www.icrc.org/en/doc/assets/files/other/icrc_002_0937.pdf. Last accessed: 26.7.2019.
[8] Gradimir Djurović: *The Central Tracing Agency of the International Committee of the Red Cross*, Geneva: Henry Dunant Institute, 1986, 43–48.

knowledge transfer would eventually even take place at the staff level. Still, historical research has yet to investigate in more detail to what extent experiences gained in previous conflicts actually had an impact on challenges of a similar nature in the immediate years following the defeat of the Nazis.

Neither Silent nor Passive: The Role of Survivors

In recent years, historians like Laura Jokusch[9] have challenged the long-held notion that survivors of Nazi persecution remained silent and/or passive objects after liberation and the end of the Second Wold War. There is ample proof that the very opposite was the case, with survivors such as Simon Wiesenthal launching their own initiatives[10] to document Nazi crimes.

Managing records pertaining to Nazi persecution was not only important in terms of chronicling historical events. Instead, information about the atrocities committed by the Germans also became a decisive resource in a different context: the search for, and provision of information about, missing victims of Nazi persecution. Again, survivors played a crucial role in this. As we shall discuss in more detail later, the Allies had underestimated and subsequently felt overwhelmed by the scale of Nazi persecution. Because of this, they failed to prepare sufficiently for the task of tracing missing individuals while the war was still ongoing. However, many of those who themselves had witnessed and endured the crimes committed by the Nazis took matters into their own hands by actively engaging in and hence shaping the field of postwar tracing and documentation. Some did this by joining pre-existing relief organizations that were now involved in the search for missing persons. For instance, the *American Jewish Joint Distribution Committee* (AJDC), with its own global network of offices processing search cases at the international level, employed Holocaust survivors for this very task.[11] For a long time, post-war historiography has neglected such activities. In recent years they have started to enter into the wider collective memory, too.[12]

---

[9] Laura Jockusch: *Collect and Record! Jewish Holocaust Documentation in Early Postwar Europe*, Oxford: OUP, 2012.
[10] See, for example, the chapter by René Bienert on Simon Wiesenthal in this volume.
[11] See the chapter by Linda Levi in this volume.
[12] For example, a 2019 exhibition produced by the *Wiener Library* in London documented the tireless zeal of various Holocaust survivors to assemble evidence regarding the hitherto unparalleled crimes of the Nazis and support the legal prosecution of individual perpetrators. The exhibition featured, among other individuals, Emmanuel Ringelblum and Rachel Auerbach,

A particular case in point, which we will explore in more detail here, is that of the *International Information Office* (IIO) in Dachau, Germany. This initiative came into existence in early October 1945, i.e. five months after US troops had liberated the camp during the final days of the war. While the IIO was a newly created body with its own specific agenda, it did fit into a pre-existing structure of self-governance that former inmates had established on the grounds of the camp, all under the jurisdiction and protection of the American occupational forces. The activities of the IIO were manifold: on the one hand, the office supported former prisoners and their families by arranging for donations as well as the provision of clothing, food tickets and other goods that they desperately needed during the post-war struggle. On the other hand, going beyond material aid, the IIO also provided a growing number of enquirers with information about individual inmates of the Dachau concentration camp. The IIO also issued certificates of imprisonment. For this purpose, staff members of the IIO (who were former prisoners themselves) drew upon official SS records that the Germans had failed to remove or destroy before the liberation of the camp.[13] Among these were registration forms for individual prisoners containing a variety of information, such as personal details, arrival and release dates, reasons for arrest and incarceration, and more.[14] While the IIO exerted a degree of agency that may seem surprising in that it defies the previously held conception of helpless victims,[15] the work of the former prisoners in Dachau did in fact have its limitations. What illustrates this well is the correspondence surrounding one particular case in the summer of 1946. Ilse Voigt, a German national, had previously received a certificate from the IIO, showing that her father, Otto Riebe, had previously been a prisoner of the Dachau concentration camp. However, this information was not enough for her. She penned a follow-up letter to the IIO asking for the exact reason why the Nazis had arrested her father. In this letter Voigt indicated that in

---

known for creating and preserving a clandestine archive documenting everyday life within the Warsaw Ghetto. For more information, see The Wiener Library: *Crimes Uncovered: The First Generation of Holocaust Researchers.* Available at: https://www.wienerlibrary.co.uk/crimes-uncovered. Last accessed: 26.7.2019.

13 Sebastian Schönemann: "Das Namensregister als Zeugnis: Zur kommemorativen Funktion früher Überlebenden-Suchdienste", in Rebecca Boehling, Susanne Urban and René Bienert (eds.): *Freilegungen: Überlebende – Erinnerungen – Transformationen,* Göttingen: Wallstein, 2013, 201–203.

14 For more information on the scope of individual concentration camp records and the information they provide, see Arolsen Archives: *e-Guide.* Available at: https://eguide.arolsen-archives.org. Last accessed: 26.7.2019.

15 Katharina Stengel and Werner Konitzer (eds.): *Opfer als Akteure: Interventionen ehemaliger NS-Verfolgter in der Nachkriegszeit,* Frankfurt/New York: Campus Verlag, 2008.

the past she had been subject to some sort of political ostracism surrounding her father's persecution.[16] Polish national Walter Cieślik, a former political prisoner of the Dachau concentration camp who at the time was head of the IIO,[17] replied to Voigt that he did not have authorization to provide her with this information. Only the local municipal concentration camp prisoner support office (*KZ-Betreuungsstelle*) responsible for Voigt was entitled to enquire about the details of her father's arrest.[18] Ilse Voigt then quickly turned to the city of Rostock that dispatched its own request regarding Otto Riebe to Dachau.[19] This resulted in the provision of the desired arrest reason, namely that the Nazis had imprisoned Otto Riebe on the grounds of *police protective custody*.[20] This placed him within the group of so-called *professional criminals*, a victim group that was not eligible for relief services and faced continued discrimination for decades to come.

Although the Allies generally granted the IIO permission to perform its work, it was limited in terms of what information it could disclose. This may have been a means of negotiating authority on the part of the US authorities, and interestingly, the IIO ceased to exist as an independent unit in September 1946. Staff and records were incorporated into the Munich branch of the *United Nations Relief and Rehabilitation Administration* (UNRRA) tracing and documentation department.[21] This too is an indicator of how highly the Allies regarded the tracing work carried out by survivors. However, at the same time, the Allies removed the survivors' autonomy in favor of an increasingly centralized process of tracing and documentation, as will become clear in the next section of this chapter.

Through its work, although only short-lived, the IIO became an integral part of the early search for missing individuals as carried out by those who had shared a similar fate at the hands of the Nazis. The correspondence of the IIO with both inquirers and other authorities, as well as the individual camp records the IIO used for its work, ultimately found their way into the collections of today's *Arolsen Archives*. The provision of information based on documents from

---

16 Letter from Ilse Voigt to the IIO, 12.6.1946, 1.1.6.0/82098503/ITS Digital Archive, Arolsen Archives.
17 Schönemann: Das Namensregister als Zeugnis, 202.
18 Letter from Walter Cieślik (IIO) to Ilse Voigt, 28.6.1946, 1.1.6.0/82098502/ITS Digital Archive, Arolsen Archives.
19 Inquiry from the Victims of Fascism Committee (Rostock City Council) to the IIO, 18.7.1946, 1.1.6.0/82098501/ITS Digital Archive, Arolsen Archives.
20 Response from Walter Cieślik (IIO), 12.8.1946, 1.1.6.0/82098500/ITS Digital Archive, Arolsen Archives.
21 DaA A 2011/2.6.37/41983, Dachau Concentration Camp Memorial Site Archive.

Fig. 1: Walter Cieślik, former Polish political prisoner of the Dachau concentration camp and head of the IIO, at his desk, 5.6.1945 (DaA F 1832/33281/KZ-Gedenkstätte Dachau)

the Dachau concentration camp thus builds, to this day, on the dedicated work that survivors of Nazi persecution performed in the aftermath of their own ordeal.[22]

Creating Larger Structures: The Establishment of the *International Tracing Service*

In terms of developing a centralized system – or, as it would initially come into existence, a coordinated network – of tracing in postwar Europe, the beginnings lie in the United Kingdom in 1944. This was where the European headquarters of UNRRA were located. Officials from the *British Red Cross* (BRC), representatives of the ICRC and UNRRA itself first discussed the issue of large-scale tracing activities to take place after the end of the war.[23]

---

[22] Sub-collection 1.1.6.0: General Information on Dachau Concentration Camp, ITS Digital Archive, Arolsen Archives.
[23] See the chapter by Christine Schmidt in this volume.

Although it appeared evident that millions of people would be searching for millions of friends and relatives, the *Supreme Headquarters, Allied Expeditionary Force* (SHAEF), downplayed the importance of agreeing on an appropriate plan. Instead, the Allies prioritized military operations. They feared that the DPs (estimated to number around 11 million) would clog up roads and jeopardize the advance of Allied troops into mainland Europe. Preventing such circumstances was, from the point of view of SHAEF, more important than the anticipation of social human needs, i.e. enabling DPs to obtain information about missing loved ones. With the war still raging, the success of military efforts against Germany and the principle of limiting assistance to a bare minimum (shelter and food) was the priority.[24]

Because of this rather sobering outlook, larger tracing operations, for now, centered on the *British Red Cross Foreign Relations Department*. It increasingly processed inquiries from all liberated territories in Europe and dispatched staff into the field where they would actively search for missing persons and Nazi documents which might provide information about their whereabouts.[25] Once the Allies realized how urgent the tracing issue was for DPs and others who were searching, they hastily devised a plan to set up a large tracing structure within occupied Germany in the summer of 1945.[26] As a result, the *Central Tracing Bureau* (CTB) was established within the US Zone of Germany. UNRRA agreed to run the CTB in Frankfurt-Höchst, but this proved to be only an interim solution, for the CTB moved to Arolsen in Northern Hesse in January 1946. There were a number of reasons for the move,[27] one of which was the fact that the premises in Frankfurt lacked adequate facilities and equipment.[28] As a result, in terms of getting on with the tracing work, "progress was painfully slow".[29] The chief mission of the CTB was

> to search for missing [...] persons of United Nations nationalities and establish the fate of those who would not be found; to locate, collect and preserve all available records regard-

---

24 Edkins: *Missing*, 60–62.
25 Ibid., 65–66.
26 Ibid., 67.
27 See Henning Borggräfe, Christian Höschler and Isabel Panek (eds.): *A Paper Monument: The History of the Arolsen Archives, Exhibition Catalogue*, Bad Arolsen: Arolsen Archives, 2019, 62–63.
28 International Refugee Organization: Historical Survey of Central Tracing Activity in Germany, 1945–1951: The Tracing of Missing Persons in Germany on an International Scale with Particular Reference to the Problem U.N.R.R.A., Geneva: International Refugee Organization, 1951, 20–21.
29 Ibid., 21.

ing refugees and displaced persons in Germany; and to serve as a link to bring interested persons into communication with each other.[30]

In reality this meant that the CTB joined a network of national tracing bureaus officially representing a number of different countries.[31] These would forward search requests concerning their respective nationals to the CTB, which in turn went about processing the cases within occupied Germany. However, the CTB never assumed a role as central as its name would have suggested, for the Allies also established tracing offices in the individual occupation zones in Germany, the so-called zonal tracing bureaus. They were the ones ultimately processing the inquiries and securing relevant records that would facilitate this work under the jurisdiction of the occupational authorities.[32] The CTB, on the other hand, acted more as a clearinghouse for the enquiries, serving as a hub between the national tracing bureaus producing cases and the zonal tracing bureaus processing them in the field.

In early 1947 the *International Refugee Organization* (IRO) agreed to continue the tracing work in its role as successor agency to UNRRA. In preparing for the takeover, efforts were made to optimize the search for missing persons and thus solve some of the problems that the CTB had been battling with because of the prevailing, decentral structure. The IRO formally assumed responsibility for the CTB and at the same time changed its name to *International Tracing Service* (ITS) at the beginning of 1948.[33] The first director of the newly established ITS, the Swiss national Maurice Thudicum, had previously been involved in the reorganization process as a consultant to UNRRA and the IRO. His expertise was of particular value since he was a former senior staff member of the *International Committee of the Red Cross* (ICRC) in Geneva. Here, then, the link between historical precedents of tracing and the handling of new challenges after the Second World War became evident at the leadership level. The realignment of the work carried out by the ITS involved the step-by-step centralization of all activities in Arolsen.

---

30 The International Tracing Service, Brief Review of its History and Activities (Submitted by the Director-General), 16.3.1951, 6.1.1/82493196/ITS Digital Archive, Arolsen Archives.
31 This volume features two chapters by Christine Schmidt and Maren Hachmeister, dedicated to national postwar tracing activities in Great Britain as well as Poland and Czechoslovakia, respectively.
32 The International Tracing Service, Brief Review of its History and Activities (Submitted by the Director-General), 16.3.1951, 6.1.1/82493196/ITS Digital Archive, Arolsen Archives.
33 Edkins: *Missing*, 82.

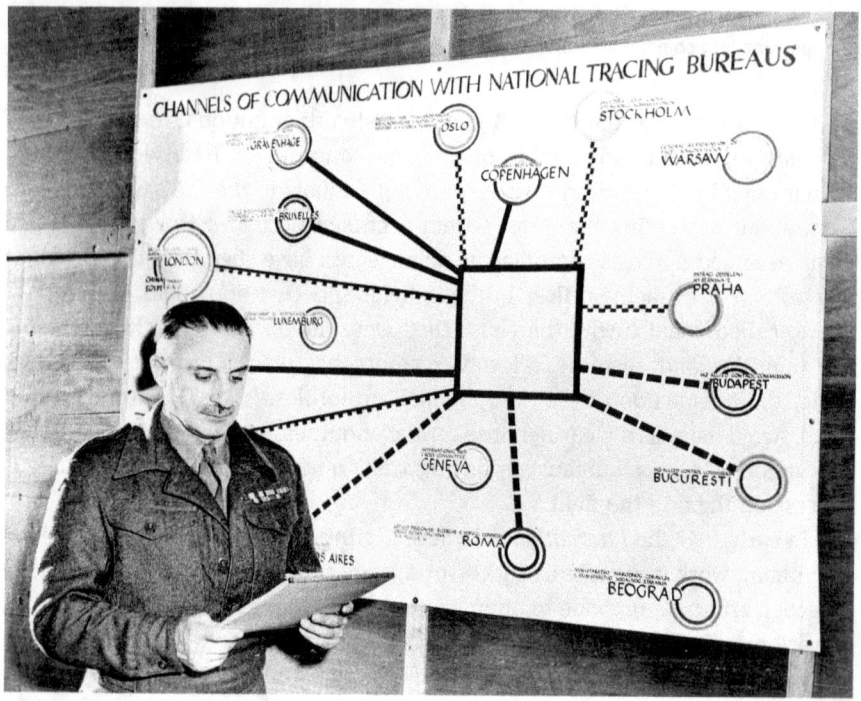

Fig. 2: John R. Bowring, head of the CTB, standing in front of a chart showing communication channels between the CTB and national tracing bureaus, Frankfurt-Höchst, 1945 (S-1058–0001–01–00082/United Nations Archives)

There, the ITS headquarters gradually became the central place for

> all policy planning, liaison with NTB [National Tracing Bureaus] and tracing agencies, and the direction and supervision of zonal field offices, [...] individual tracing activities [...]; and the processing, distribution and preservation of documents from other agencies or collected in the field.[34]

In the end, the Allies closed the zonal tracing bureaus and transferred their respective staff and records to Arolsen. The Allies gathered the aforementioned documents, which became the archival collections of the ITS and today's *Arolsen Archives*, in multiple contexts. Some had been retrieved from liberated concentration camps or compiled through interrogations of Nazi perpetrators. Other ma-

---

[34] The International Tracing Service, Brief Review of its History and Activities (Submitted by the Director-General), 16.3.1951, 6.1.1/82493197/ITS Digital Archive, Arolsen Archives.

terials included lists of forced laborers created by local German authorities during the war, and records from the missions of UNRRA and the IRO, most notably the registration of individual DPs and paperwork regarding their repatriation or resettlement abroad.[35] We will now look at how exactly the search for missing victims of Nazi persecution was organized by the CTB/ITS in the second half of the 1940s.

The Search for Missing Persons in the Post-War Period: Methods and Challenges for the CTB and its successor, the ITS

As described above, the ITS and its predecessor, the *Central Tracing Bureau*, were able to draw in part on knowledge and techniques that had previously been applied by other established tracing services, such as the ICRC or the AJDC, and use them for their own day-to-day work of tracing children, adolescents and adults.[36] However, the Second World War was on a greater scale than any of the previous wars of the twentieth century and new tracing methods had to be developed to cope with the mass deportation, abduction and murder of millions of people. These methods were primarily derived from practical experience, from the need to act; they were tried out and developed further and some were then rejected. The following tracing methods soon established themselves at the CTB: a search in a *Central Name Index* (CNI) with related research in the documents on Nazi crimes that had been rescued, an active search in the field and cooperation with local authorities, and finally, mass tracing efforts utilizing the media.

Work on setting up a *Central Name Index* first started at the CTB in the autumn of 1945. This involved staff transferring all the important information contained in the tracing inquiries onto index cards, most particularly personal details and information about the fate of the persecutees. They then put the cards into alphabetical order and sorted them into the CNI. The idea was that

---

35 Ibid., 7–9. For more information on the creation of the archival collections and their contents, see the paper by Henning Borggräfe and Isabel Panek in this volume.
36 The present chapter concentrates on the search for adults. A special department was set up to trace children and adolescents, see Julia Reus: "'Everywhere where human beings are, we can find our children': On the Organization of the ITS Child Search Branch Files", in Henning Borggräfe, Akim Jah, Steffen Jost, and Nina Ritz (eds.): *Freilegungen: Rebuilding Lives – Child Survivors and DP Children in the Aftermath of the Holocaust and Forced Labor*, Göttingen: Wallstein, 2017, 41–49.

```
Name: ALHADEFE Violetta                    No.: T.        727
Nee:                                        Nat: Italian Jew
B. D.:   29th November 1925                X Ref:
B. P.:   Rodi
Address:        -
Occupation:     -
                Transferred from Dachau to Bergen-Belsen
Last news:
Date:           17th December 1944.
Enquirer's name:    British Red Cross, London.
Address:            c/o Austrian Red X.Peregringasse 2,
Relation: Brother.  Vienna IX. o/b: Mr. Alhadef.
                    Enq;dated 12.12.46.
```

Fig. 3: Inquiry Card for Violetta Alhadefe, 1946 (0.1/13095518/ITS Digital Archive, Arolsen Archives)

the inquiry cards of people who were trying to trace others and the inquiry cards of those who were being traced would come together during this sorting process. At the ITS, this was known as a *meeting of cards*, as it subsequently enabled the tracing bureau to put both parties in touch with each other. However, *meetings* were only possible in a small number of cases, as many of those missing had not submitted an inquiry themselves or were no longer alive to do so. This is why the documents from the concentration camps and the records collected in connection with the Allies' efforts to trace foreign nationals constituted a second cornerstone for the creation of the Name Index.[37] These documents contained information about a person's path of persecution and often provided clues as to the last location of a missing person. Starting in 1946, this type of personal information was also transferred to reference cards and these too were added to the CNI. This procedure continued for decades and was known at the ITS as *carding*.

Despite the fact that the inquiry cards and reference cards were filed alphabetically, mistakes were sometimes made when the cards were sorted and it was not uncommon for information to disappear without a trace. In order to make the card index less vulnerable to errors of this kind, an alphabetic-phonetic system was introduced in 1949. Previously used in the index of prisoners-of-

---

37 See the chapter by Henning Borggräfe and Isabel Panek in this volume.

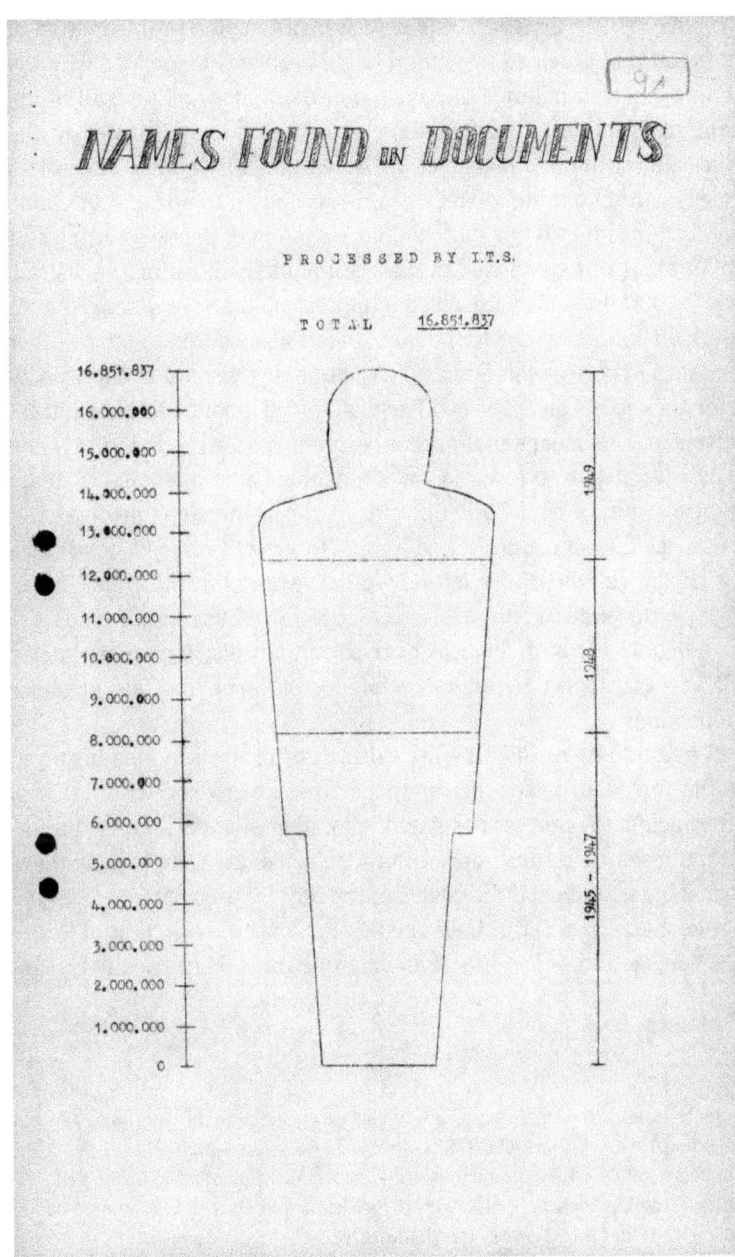

Fig. 4: The chart shows how many names were collected through "carding" from 1945 until 1949 (6.1.1/82505898/ITS Digital Archive, Arolsen Archives)

war created by the ICRC in Geneva[38], this new system took the pronunciation of names into account and provided a solution to the problems associated with the different variants and misspellings of names that often arose as a result of the many different nationalities of the victims of persecution registered by the Nazi authorities and of the DPs registered by Allied administrations. Regardless of how a name is written, all the reference cards pertaining to one and the same individual are filed together to this day.[39] Implementation of the new sorting system began in May and was completed in the autumn of 1949. During the restructuring process, 20,000 previously unsolved inquiries could be answered.[40] Parallel to their work on setting up the Name Index, staff also started to create other indexes. Separate indexes of this kind, each containing several million documents, exist for documents on Displaced Persons, forced laborers and concentration camp prisoners. This means that once a search has been made in the Name Index, other indexes also need to be consulted, as there are no references to the information they contain in the CNI. Because of the many steps involved, research was and is time consuming and prone to error. Cramped conditions were another challenge which affected day-to-day work with the Name Index in the early days: the index grew at a rate of several thousands of cards per month, from 1,976,499 cards in 1948 to over 10 million just two years later.[41] Today, the CNI contains over 50 million reference cards on the fate of about 17.5 million individuals.

In 1947, in addition to *carding* the inquiries, staff in Arolsen also began to open a case file for each person being traced, these were known as *T files*. The *T* stood for tracing, the process of searching for a missing person. All the correspondence and research results concerning a person's fate were kept in these files. At the same time, staff used the covers of the files for an overview of all the steps which were taken in order to trace the person concerned: Action of Correspondence Section, Action of Records Branch, Field Trace, Map Location, Mass

---

38 The International Tracing Service, Brief Review of its History and Activities (Submitted by the Director-General), 16.3.1951, 6.1.1/82493200/ITS Digital Archive, Arolsen Archives.
39 For example, there are 849 different spellings of the surname *Abrahamovic* in the CNI.
40 The International Tracing Service, Brief Review of its History and Activities (Submitted by the Director-General), 16.3.1951, 6.1.1/82493200/ITS Digital Archive, Arolsen Archives.
41 At the beginning, the CTB, and its successor, the ITS, were not accommodated at a single, central location in Arolsen. Most of the facilities available were too small for the card indexes to be stored neatly on shelves. In 1949, following the move to the former barracks in Arolsen, the buildings which used to house military personnel provided enough space for the documentary holdings which were growing day by day.

Trace. If another inquiry about the same person was received later on, the file was continued.[42]

If neither a search in the Name Index with the associated search in the documentary holdings nor contact with the staff of the NTBs yielded any information about the whereabouts of a missing person, the case was forwarded to the zonal tracing bureaus which conducted an active search in the field for the missing person and for documents which could deliver information about their fate. Field searches usually started at the last place where the missing person was known to have resided. This might be a previous place of detention and persecution, but could also be a DP camp or some other place of residence after liberation. Knowledge about Nazi crimes was fragmentary in the immediate postwar period. Many of the camp locations were not known to the staff, who had to use maps and old gazetteers in order to locate them. It was important for staff to find out the correct location in order to be able to forward subsequent inquiries to the right zonal bureaus and local authorities. The zonal bureaus started off by searching their own documentary holdings before turning to local mayors, company owners or other survivors for information on the whereabouts of a missing person. The case of Polish national Stanisław Mróz is a good illustration of just how difficult it was to put the various pieces of the puzzle together. In 1944 the Germans deported him to Germany to perform forced labor. After the war his wife submitted an inquiry as to his whereabouts to the ITS.[43] His last known place of residence was Amorbach which was located in the American zone. Because of this the zonal tracing bureau in the American zone of occupation was assigned the task of tracing Stanisław Mróz. Tracing staff went straight to Amorbach and checked various German Registration Offices located there, interviewing three Polish DPs and numerous companies as well. They described their efforts to trace him in a report to the ITS Headquarters:

> Checks made at Amorbach with the various German Registration Offices failed to reveal any trace of person sought. There are 3 Polish Nationals still living at Amorbach (been in Amorbach all during the War) but none of them ever heard of a Mróz, Stanisław living in Amorbach. Gathering the names all employers [sic!] in Amorbach who at a time had employed, and are still employing foreign nationals, we checked each place but without success.[44]

---

42 Since 2018, all new files have been kept in digital form only.
43 Tracing inquiry from Maria Mróz, 28.1.1949, in: T/D file Stanislaw Mróz, 6.3.3.2/90584857/ITS Digital Archive, Arolsen Archives.
44 Tracing Report, 15.6.1949, in: T/D file Stanislaw Mróz, 6.3.3.2/90584853/ITS Digital Archive, Arolsen Archives.

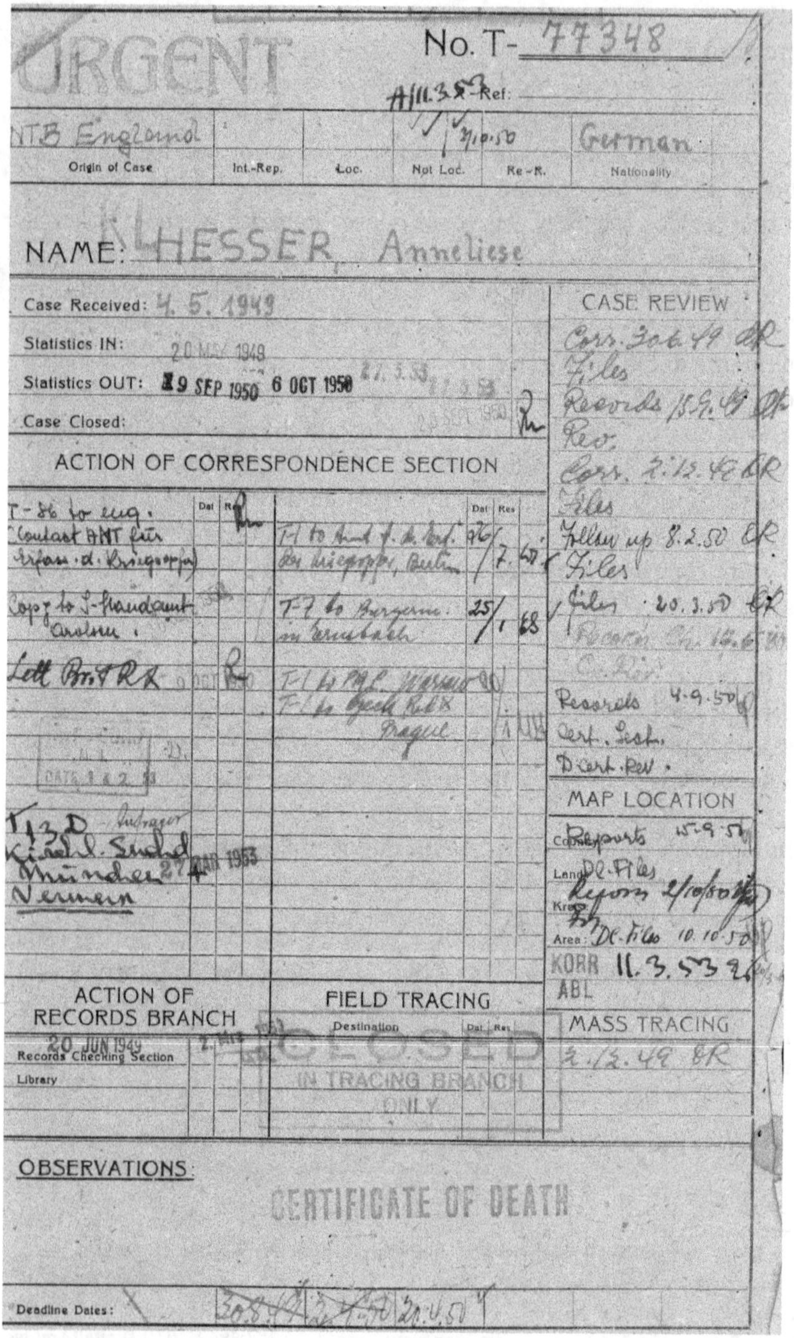
URGENT No. T- 77348

A/11.3.53 Ref:

NTB England | | | 7/10.50 | | German
Origin of Case | Int.-Rep. | Loc. | Not Loc. | Re-R. | Nationality

NAME: HESSER, Anneliese

Case Received: 4. 5. 1949

Statistics IN: 20 MAY 1949

Statistics OUT: 29 SEP 1950 6 OCT 1950

Case Closed:

ACTION OF CORRESPONDENCE SECTION

CASE REVIEW

MAP LOCATION

ACTION OF RECORDS BRANCH

20 JUN 1949

Records Checking Section

Library

FIELD TRACING

Destination | Dat | Res

CLOSED IN TRACING BRANCH ONLY

MASS TRACING

OBSERVATIONS:

CERTIFICATE OF DEATH

Deadline Dates:

Fig. 5: Correspondence File, or *T File*, for Anneliese Hesser, 1949 (6.3.3.2/84699577/ITS Digital Archive, Arolsen Archives)

As well as questioning people locally, the staff of the zonal tracing bureau also checked the index of the Wildflecken DP camp, one of the largest DP camps for Polish DPs in the American zone. This research revealed that Stanisław Mróz had been at Wildflecken for a short time after liberation. The tracing inquiry was then forwarded to the tracing team there.

Successful field searches were dependent on a number of factors: first, the ITS needed personnel with knowledge of various different languages, as shown by the above example involving knowledge of German and Polish. At the same time, staff needed to work in a structured, analytical manner in order to recognize interrelationships during the course of investigations and be able to understand them without assistance. One of the practical challenges which had to be faced was how to provide enough vehicles to be able to travel from camp to camp and from authority to authority. The staff of the zonal tracing bureaus wrote numerous letters complaining about the constant lack of vehicles, which put severe restrictions on their day-to-day work. Another obstacle to investigations was the short period of time spent by DPs in DP camps. This was due to the fact that many DPs set off to search for their relatives themselves or left the camps in order to be repatriated. Good cooperation with the German authorities was therefore indispensable. This is why targeted press campaigns were launched in an attempt to inform the public about how necessary and how difficult it was to trace missing persons as well as to encourage active public support.

At the same time, the media were also involved in mass tracing. This step in the tracing process was started "to search en masse for missing persons when there is too little information to institute individual search or when all other forms of search have failed."[45] For this purpose, staff compiled lists of the names of missing persons, which they published in the media. The following key information was important for mass tracing campaigns: surname, first name, age, place and date of birth, last known address, and nationality. The search lists were sorted alphabetically and by nationality. The ideal procedure for mass tracing, which was not always strictly adhered to, consisted of three steps: first of all, staff sent the lists to the National Tracing Bureaus, tracing agencies, and DP camps, which put them on public display or broadcast them over loudspeakers. From June 1948 onwards, Jewish missing persons were registered on separate lists that were sent to Jewish relief organizations, such as the

---

45 Central Tracing Bureau, Brief Progress Report on the Mass Tracing Division, 15.2.1946, 6.1.1/82500734/ITS Digital Archive, Arolsen Archives.

American Jewish Joint Distribution Committee (AJDC), or to Jewish communities.[46] If the first step did not produce any results, the ITS moved on to the second step, which was to send the search lists to national and international newspapers. They were usually published wherever there was most hope of readers being able to provide information, for example in the place where the missing persons used to live. About 115 German newspapers and 30 DP newspapers received more than 140 search lists for publication per week.[47] If this too failed to produce any information about the fate of a missing person, the third step was to broadcast the search lists on the radio. The lists were usually read out live initially, so hardly any recordings have survived.

One of the few recordings that still exist is an appeal that was broadcast by the BBC in August 1946. The program attempted to find relatives of children and adolescents who were believed to be in England. The program began with the following words: "Captive Children, an appeal from Germany." As well as broadcasting the personal details of the child survivor, the radio program also gave information on his or her path of persecution:

> I call Katz, Salma Katz, who may be living in London. I call her on behalf of her 16-year-old cousin Hela Bergman, born in Poland, who was separated from her family at the age of 12 and made to work in an ammunition factory. Her father, mother, sister and brother were sent to Treblinka extermination camp.[48]

Radio stations in the zones of occupation were used for radio searches as well as radio stations in those countries with which there was close cooperation. The search lists were also broadcast on the ICRC's tracing program on *Radio Geneva* or on *Vatican Radio*. Between 1947 and 1950, about 5101 missing persons were found through mass tracing. At the beginning of 1948 about 190 people were being found every month. From 1949 onwards the number dropped month by month until at the beginning of 1950, about 80 people were still being found per month. Involving the public in tracing activities was a key search strategy that helped to integrate people from all over the world in the tracing process.

---

[46] 6.1.1/82505802/ITS Digital Archive, Arolsen Archives.
[47] In 1949, as well as being sent to German newspapers, the search lists were also sent to one Polish newspaper in London, two Polish newspapers in Paris and one Jewish newspaper in the USA, see: International Tracing Service of IRO. Annual Report of the Director, 1949, 6.1.1/82505887/ITS Digital Archive, Arolsen Archives.
[48] In 2014/2015, Axel Last traced the fate of 12 "child survivors" named in the 1946 broadcast. BBC Archive, London. Available at: https://www.bbc.co.uk/programmes/b0616npl/episodes/player. Last accessed: 1.7.2019.

German authorities too were to be encouraged to make an active contribution, as the opening credits of the UNRRA tracing broadcast show:

> We call all Allied and German agencies and authorities, we call the German police and all those who want to help us. We are appealing for information about the whereabouts of the people we are searching for as well as about the location of any documents or other records concerning foreigners which have not yet been requisitioned by the appropriate German authorities and forwarded to us. This UNRRA tracing service is only responsible for United Nations nationals, people who were forcibly deported and victims of political persecution. [...] Today's search list now follows. [49]

However, mass tracing did not only provide information on missing persons who survived, it also provided information on missing persons who had been murdered. On January 13, 1949, the *Berliner Tagesspiegel* newspaper published an appeal for information listing 39 names of missing Jewish men and women from Berlin. Josef Sander, a dentist in Berlin, wrote a letter to the ITS on the very same day explaining that he had read the appeal for information and had recognized a former patient, Charlotte Nachmann. He wrote: "The most important point I have to convey is the fact that, as a result of the barbaric measures taken by Hitler, the lady concerned is no longer alive because she was deported to the East in a transport of Jews back then."[50] Mass tracing was often the last means staff had recourse to, while for many relatives it was the last hope they had of finding information about the whereabouts of a missing person. A letter from Irmgard Reicher, dated 30 October 1946, expresses this very vividly:

> I have learned that my husband arrived in Auschwitz and suppose [sic] to have died there in August 1944. I cannot believe it. Therefore I kindly request you, from the bottom of my heart to have his name broadcasted in order learn the present whereabouts of my good husband. [...] The Radio Tracing Service of Radio Frankfurt/ Main I hear daily at 23.00 hours.[51]

Because the search for missing persons was often also a search for the dead, the town of Arolsen set up a *special registry office* in 1949 to issue death certificates for deceased concentration camp prisoners.[52] Death certificates are still issued to

---

49 UNRRA tracing broadcast, Radio Stuttgart, 20.11.1946, F834411012, NDR, Hamburg.
50 Letter to the ITS from Josef Sander, 13.1.1949, in: T/D file Charlotte Nachmann, 6.3.3.2/92161085/ITS Digital Archive, Arolsen Archives.
51 Letter to the CTB from Irmgard Reicher, 30.10.1946, in T/D file Karl Reicher, 6.3.3.2/91699432/ITS Digital Archive, Arolsen Archives.
52 Activities of the International Tracing Service during the second fiscal year (1st July 1948 – 30 June 1949), 6.1.1/82505800/ITS Digital Collection, Arolsen Archives.

relatives to this day if a death that took place in a concentration camp can be documented on the basis of archival material from the *Arolsen Archives* or through research in registry offices and memorial sites.

Standardization and Bureaucratization: Changes in the Way Information was Provided by the ITS

Parallel to the search for missing persons, allied authorities also turned to the ITS in search of information for immigration and emigration proceedings in the postwar period. A marked change in working practices began to occur in the 1950s, when many of the inquiries concerned certificates of imprisonment or certificates of residence for West German compensation claims.[53] The Federal Republic of Germany's policy on compensation and the critical analysis of Nazi crimes within German society were mirrored by the fluctuating waves of inquiries received by the ITS in the decades that followed. After a rise in inquiries related to compensation claims in the 1950s and 1960s, the ITS was deluged by a second major wave of inquiries which began in the late 1980s in the context of late debate in society on the Second World War and on victim groups which had not received compensation to date. This was particularly evident after the end of the Cold War, when it first became possible to enforce German compensation of victims of Nazi persecution from East-Central and Eastern Europe. Starting in 2000, there was a massive rise in inquiries in connection with payments made to former forced laborers under the Nazis through the Foundation "*Remembrance, Responsibility and Future*" (German acronym EVZ).

Responding to this type of inquiry relied more heavily on searching the ITS archive for documents related to specific individuals. If the information gleaned from the documentary holdings was not sufficient, staff would sometimes contact other bodies, such as insurance companies or local registration offices, for example. At the beginning of the 1950s, in close consultation with German compensation authorities and the legal representatives of former victims of Nazi persecution, the ITS developed a standardized procedure which was to be used for decades to come. In order to deal with the hundreds of thousands of inquiries connected with compensation or pension claims, the ITS created

---

[53] Active field searches and mass tracing were discontinued in 1950. In 1954, inquiries pertaining to compensation amounted to 62.4% and thus exceeded the number of tracing inquiries. See: Achter Erfahrungsbericht des Internationalen Suchdienstes, 25.3.1955, 6.1.1/82508414/ITS Digital Archive, Arolsen Archives.

standardized inquiry and response forms, one of which was the so-called certificate of imprisonment, for example. For the purposes of issuing these standardized certificates, a search was made in the ITS archive and the details contained in the Nazi documents were copied onto the certificates word for word, but the information given was not put into its historical context. Particularly in the 1950s and 1960s, this was problematic for many former persecutees, as the *German Federal Law for Compensating Nazi Victims* (German acronym BEG) stipulated that only those persons were entitled to receive a payment who had been "victims of violent National Socialist persecution for reasons connected with political opposition to National Socialism, race, religion or belief."[54] The information from Arolsen often provided the authorities with the grounds to exclude Sinti and Roma, homosexuals or so-called *anti-social elements*, and almost all non-German victims of Nazi persecution from receiving compensation. Up until 1955, the ITS still mentioned the problematic nature of the prisoner categories in the accompanying letters they sent out. In April 1955, the accompanying letters were discontinued, but the arbitrary nature of the assignment of prisoner categories was drawn to the attention of the Federal German authorities for the last time:

> In many cases, concentration camp inmates were registered as 'professional criminals' as a consequence of criminal prosecutions on the basis of laws which have since been repealed. On the basis of the documents held by the ITS, it has been established that in many cases prisoners were registered as 'professional criminals' contrary to the provisions of Section 20a of the German Criminal Code.[55]

The changes in the search process itself and in the provision of information in response to inquiries were also reflected in the new name given to the *T files*, which were now known as *T/D files* – T/D denoting *Tracing* and *Documentation*.

Following the enactment of the *Final German Federal Law for Compensating Nazi Victims* in 1965, the number of inquiries received by the ITS continually declined. It was not until the late 1980s that there was another large increase in the number of inquiries. This resulted in an enormous backlog and waiting times that sometimes lasted years. To facilitate the search for information in the archive, a CNI fast-track procedure was introduced and digitization of the documentary holdings began. But despite these measures, the long waiting times re-

---

[54] Federal Law for the Compensation of the Victims of National Socialist Persecution (Bundesentschädigungsgesetz BEG), 18.9.1953, section 1 (1). Available at: https://www.gesetze-im-internet.de/beg/BEG.pdf. Last accessed: 2.7.2019.
[55] Achter Erfahrungsbericht des Internationalen Suchdienstes, 25.3.1955, 6.1.1/82508415/ITS Digital Archive, Arolsen Archives.

mained a major problem for the survivors, who were very elderly by then, and were widely criticized in the media at the time.

Most of the inquiries received today – around 20,000 per year – come from the descendants of former victims of Nazi persecution, primarily from Poland, Russia, Germany, the USA, France and Israel, who want to find out more about the fate of their relatives and reconstruct their family history. In order to answer their questions, research is conducted in the archive and digital copies of the archival documents are sent out together with explanatory information. But even today, new tracing cases are still sometimes opened and families are still being reunited.[56]

---

[56] For information on the way information is provided today and on how the Tracing department of the *Arolsen Archives* provides support to people searching for information as well as on the type of inquiries submitted by the descendants of former victims of Nazi persecution, see the chapter by Ramona Bräu, Kerstin Hofmann and Anna Meier-Osiński in this volume.

Linda G. Levi
Family Searching and Tracing Services of JDC in the Second World War Era

Abstract: JDC HQ and local offices worked unstintingly to rescue and provide relief for Jews fleeing Nazi Europe. The organization's prior experience and relationships with local communities and international and local agencies were advantages that helped JDC galvanize aid where possible. Prior family tracing and search activities laid the groundwork for its extensive networking efforts in the Second World War era with US relatives of refugees in Europe who required assistance and survivors searching for their families. These efforts helped reunite families. JDC and *Central Location Index* staff pursued family search with expertise, empathy, and a sense of personal and communal mission, collaborating with the IRC and UNRRA. Discussions beginning in 1947 about establishing a centralized *International Tracing Service* made CLI and JDC leaders uneasy. Would a more distant and standardized ITS have the necessary knowledge, expertise, and sense of urgency? Nevertheless, JDC leaders cooperated with efforts to establish the IRO *International Tracing Service*. Beginning in August 1948, JDC began closing its tracing bureaus and transferring records to the ITS. In May 1949, the CLI ceased operations.

Introduction

The *American Jewish Joint Distribution Committee* (commonly known as "the Joint" or JDC), established in 1914 in response to the devastation caused by the First World War, began rescue and relief work in Europe at that time and continued its involvement both in Europe and in a total of 70 countries across the globe during the interwar years. Thus, even before the rise of Nazism in Germany, JDC had an understanding of the local context in Europe and had established contacts and relationships with Jewish communities and other NGOs on the ground in Europe and elsewhere. This experience proved useful as the JDC became deeply involved in rescue and relief programs before, during, and after the Second World War. JDC's activities included family searching and tracing services from the perspective of seeking out US-based family members to assist their European relatives with affidavits and other emigration assistance, to assist worried overseas relatives seeking news on the whereabouts of family in Europe during and after the war, and to help survivors with their search for relatives in

OpenAccess. © 2020 Linda G. Levi, published by De Gruyter. [CC BY-NC-ND] This work is licensed under the Creative Commons Attribution-NonCommercial-NoDerivatives 4.0 License.
https://doi.org/10.1515/9783110665376-005

the period immediately after the war. JDC's network of offices in Europe and elsewhere communicated closely on such family searches and worked closely with the *Central Location Index*, which it helped to establish in New York in 1944, and with UNRRA's *Central Tracing Bureau* and later the *International Tracing Service* when it was established in 1948.

Context and Background

The conflicts and pogroms that took place during and after the First World War brought disease, famine, and dislocation to hundreds of thousands of Jews in Central and Eastern Europe, especially in Poland. In response, JDC provided food to hundreds of towns and villages, dispatched delegations of doctors, public health experts, and social workers, set up soup kitchens, rebuilt hospitals, and opened orphanages. To foster independence, JDC sponsored a network of self-help Jewish organizations, cultural and religious institutions, and vocational training centers.

During the First World War and in the years following the war, JDC was extensively involved in networking activities between families in the US and relatives in Europe. During the war years, family members overseas were no longer able to send remittances to their relatives in Eastern Europe. JDC established a transmission bureau[1] whereby they could ensure that financial assistance from relatives in the US and elsewhere deposited with JDC would reach family members impacted by the war in Europe. This relationship worked in both directions in that JDC field workers in Europe would transmit requests for assistance from family in Europe to relatives in the US via the JDC. Similarly, JDC worked with *Landsmanschaften* in the US that sought to get funds to their landsmen in Europe.

During the interwar period, JDC was assisting vulnerable Jewish communities worldwide. As such, it had established on-going relationships with Jewish communities in 70 countries around the world. Thus, given its widespread presence across the globe, JDC was uniquely able to help trace relatives during the Second World War era.[2]

---

[1] JDC Archives, Records of the New York office of the American Jewish Joint Distribution Committee, 1914–1918, Folder #3.2, Minutes of the Executive Committee, 16.11.1916; http://search.archives.jdc.org/notebook_ext.asp?item=165.

[2] For further background, see Avinoam Patt, Atina Grossmann, Linda G. Levi, and Maud S. Mandel (eds.): *The JDC at 100: A Century of Humanitarianism*, Detroit: Wayne State University Press, 2019, chapters 1–3.

JOINT DISTRIBUTION COMMITTEE, NEW YORK

Send through
Messrs.-Warburg Co.,
Hamburg, Germany

REMITTANCES FOR POLAND

NO.	PAYEE	AMOUNT	REMITTER	DISPOSITION
2376	Beile Koss, Store Mossor-Kovel, Uyeso, Wolhyn Gub.	$14.00	Louis Koss, Kings Park L.I.	January 25,1916
2565	Chana & Wolf Gurman Pultusk, Warsaw	30.00	Mendel Silberstein, 33 Attorney St. New York City	"
2568	Sarah Sussman c/o Morduch Slabogwosky, Pashebsk, Pultusk, Warsaw	6.25	Sam Sussman 12 W. Dedham St. Boston, Mass.	"
2789	Leah Reisel Plutsky, Wisni- Lomza Lomza Gub.	5.00	Meyer Plutsky, c/o Machover, 239 Front St., New York City	"
3045	Kadisha Shalman or Moses Rosenthal, Balwershischk, Kreis Mariampol, Post Olito, Kovno St. #96	100.00	Philip Goldberg 1017 Trinity Ave., Bronx, N.Y.	"
3128	Chaem Levensbaum for Chae Itta Soskes, Vladimir, Wolhyn Gub.	20.00	Harry Soskes, c/o Rozenzweig 113 Broome St., New York City	"
				April 3, 1916.
3204	Pluma Levita, Dom Chime Levita Pinsk, Minsk.	20.00	R. Levita, 57 Cherry St., Waterbury, Conn.	"
3205	Merka Hitinsky, Dom Chaskel, Ogulnik, Pinsk, Minsk	20.00	I. Hutinsky c/o R. Levita 57 Cherry St., Waterbury, Conn.	"
3207	Mary Mioduszewski, Tojno, Szczucyn, Lomza	60.00	J. F. Mioduszewski, H.F. Henry, Roman Catholic High School, Phila., Pa.	"

Fig. 1: List of remittances for Poland, 25.1.1916 (JDC Archives, Records of the New York Office of the American Jewish Joint Distribution Committee, 1914–1918, folder #36, Remittances for Poland, 1915–1917; http://search.archives.jdc.org/notebook_ext.asp?item=3303)

JDC Efforts during the Second World War Era

Germany

With its overseas headquarters based in Berlin, JDC had a close vantage point to view the early impacts of the Nazi party on German Jewish life. In 1933, the organization moved its headquarters operations to Paris in response to a threat against its office. However, a small office was retained in Berlin, and close rela-

Fig. 2: People line up in a JDC transmission office to send funds to family abroad, New York, c. 1917 (JDC Archives Photograph Collection, NY_03488)

tions with the Jewish community continued. JDC provided assistance during the 1930s as the German Jewish community responded to the Nuremberg Laws and the restrictions placed on Jews. It also assisted with the development and funding of retraining programs as Jews were excluded from certain professions, established more Jewish schools (as Jewish children were no longer accepted in public schools), funded welfare programs for the needy, and provided emigration assistance.

As Jews began to leave Germany and Austria, JDC worked to identify countries that would accept Jewish refugees either on a temporary or permanent basis. JDC archival records include many lists of people assisted during this period; these lists, which date from the late-1930s and extend throughout the Second World War, were often useful in tracing family members. Lists such as the passengers of the *St. Louis* and the countries to which the 907 stranded passengers were taken after being denied entry into Cuba[3] or lists of over 18,000 refugees assisted in Shanghai[4] are but two examples of the thousands of such lists within the organization's text collections.

JDC provided relief assistance to Polish Jews who were expelled from Germany between 1938 to 1939 to the no-man's land areas at the border with Poland. These efforts were led by Emanuel Ringelblum, who was already serving on the staff of the JDC Warsaw office. A 127-page list from 1938 and 1939 with the names of 1,542 refugees assisted in Zbaszyn and in other no-man's land towns (such as Kolomyja, Jaroslaw, Stanislawow, Drohobycz, Jablonow, and others) is included in the JDC Archives and has been indexed in the JDC Archives Names Index.[5] These lists include the names and addresses of relatives in the US so that JDC New York could contact family members to inform them of the whereabouts and the needs of their relatives who had been expelled from Germany.

Poland

On September 1, 1939, Nazi Germany invaded Poland, and the Second World War commenced. Of the 3.3 million Jews living in Poland in 1939, several hundred thousand fled eastward into Soviet territory, but the vast majority found themselves under Nazi rule. The economic impact was immediate: Jewish enterprises were destroyed, property was confiscated, and Jews were subjected to forced labor. Food shortages were acute, and disease was rampant, especially after the establishment of ghettos in Warsaw, Lodz, and elsewhere.

Thousands of Polish Jewish refugees fled to Vilna, where JDC, working with the local community, assisted refugees with food kitchens, refugee assistance, and emigration including funding passage on trains across the Soviet Union to the Asian areas and to Vladivostok and from there to Japan and Shanghai. One JDC Archives list includes names of over 9,000 Polish Jewish refugees

---

3 JDC Archives, Records of the New York Office of the American Jewish Joint Distribution Committee, 1933–1944, Folder #384, MS *St-Louis* Passengers and their Distribution, 18.7.1939; http://search.archives.jdc.org/notebook_ext.asp?item=444078.
4 JDC Archives: see "Lists from the Nazi Period and Its Aftermath" at https://archives.jdc.org/our-collections/names-index/lists-in-the-names-index/.
5 JDC Archives, Records of the New York Office of the American Jewish Joint Distribution Committee, 1933–1944, folder #879, Lists of Refugees at Zbaszyn, 1938–1939; http://search.archives.jdc.org/notebook_ext.asp?item=509854.

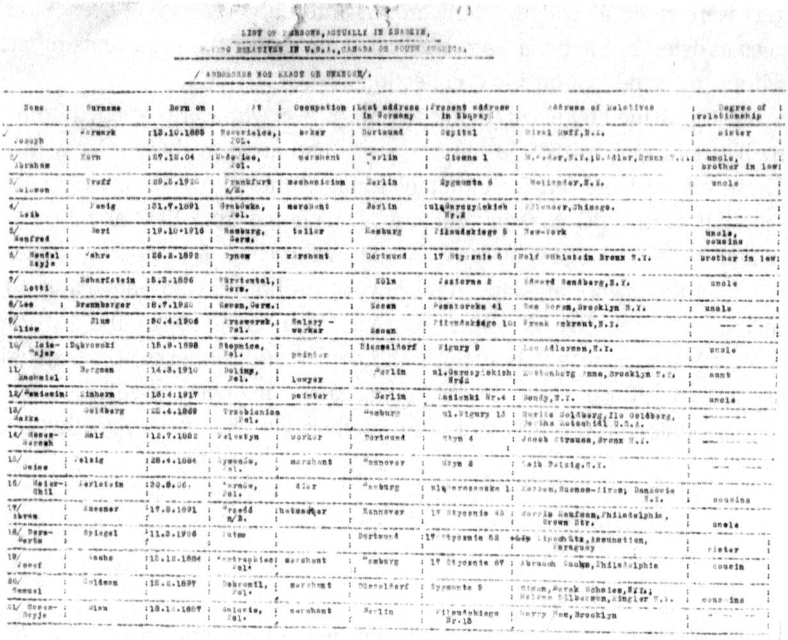

LIST OF PERSONS, ACTUALLY IN ZBASZYN,
HAVING RELATIVES IN U.S.A., CANADA OR SOUTH AMERICA.

/ ADDRESSES NOT EXACT OR UNKNOWN/.

Name	Surname	Born on	At	Occupation	Last address in Germany	Present address in Zbaszyn	Address of Relatives	Degree of relationship
1/ Joseph	[illegible]rmark	13.10.1885	Nowosielce, Pol.	baker	Dortmund	Szpital	Mirel Huff, N.Y.	sister
2/ Abraham	Korn	27.12.04	[illegible], Pol.	merchant	Berlin	Ciemna 1	M. [illegible]der, N.Y.; U. Adler, Bronx N.Y.	uncle, brother in law
3/ Salomon	Treff	29.5.1920	Frankfurt a/M.	mechanician	Berlin	Zygmunta 6	Hollander, N.Y.	uncle
4/ Leib	[illegible]enig	31.7.1891	Grabówka, Pol.	merchant	Berlin	ul. Gerczyńskich Nr. 2	[illegible]lenser, Chicago.	—
5/ Manfred	Beri	19.10.1916	Hamburg, Germ.	tailor	Hamburg	Pilsudskiego 5	New-York	uncle, cousins
6/ Mendel Sayje	[illegible]ahre	26.2.1892	Dynow	merchant	Dortmund	17 Stycznia 5	Wolf [illegible]hlstein Bronx N.Y.	brother in law
7/ Lotti	Scharfstein	5.3.1896	Fürstental, Germ.		Köln	Jeziorna 2	Edward Sandberg, N.Y.	uncle
8/Lee	Brennberger	8.7.1920	Essen, Germ.		Essen	Pensatorska 41	Sam [illegible]en, Brooklyn N.Y.	uncle
9/ Elias	Blum	30.4.1906	Przeworsk, Pol.	Salary-worker	Essen	Pilsudskiego 10	Frank [illegible]akraut, N.Y.	—
10/ Icie-Majer	Dąbrowski	15.9.1898	Stopnica, Pol.	painter	Düsseldorf	Figury 9	Leo Adlerman, N.Y.	uncle
11/ Rachmiel	Bergman	14.3.1910	Dolina, Pol.	lawyer	Berlin	ul. Gerczyńskich Nr. 2	[illegible]enberg Anna, Brooklyn N.Y.	aunt
12/ Beniamin	Einhorn	18.4.1917		painter	Berlin	Łazienki Nr. 4	Bondy, N.Y.	uncle
13/ Malka	Goldberg	25.4.1869	Trzebinia Pol.		Hamburg	ul. Figury 13	Moritz Goldberg, Ilo Goldberg, Bertha Rotschild U.S.A.	—
14/ Moses-Baruch	Wolf	12.7.1882	Palestyn	worker	Dortmund	Rynek 4	Jacob Strauss, Bronx N.Y.	—
15/ Osias	Pelzig	28.4.1884	Rymanów, Pol.	merchant	Hannover	Rynek 2	Leib Pelzig, N.Y.	—
16/ Meier-Chil	Perlstein	30.8.06.	Tarnów, Pol.	tailor	Hamburg	ul. [illegible] 1	[illegible], Buenos-Aires; Dankowicz N.Y.	cousins
17/ Abram	Kessner	17.8.1891	Przedbórz n/B.	hatmaker	Hannover	17 Stycznia 43	Morris Kaufman, Philadelphia, Brown Str.	uncle
18/ Dora-Berta	Spiegel	11.3.1906	Putna		Dortmund	17 Stycznia 52	[illegible] Lipschütz, Assunction, Paraguay	sister
19/ Josef	Sachs	15.12.1884	[illegible], Pol.	merchant	Hamburg	17 Stycznia 67	Abraham Sachs, Philadelphia	cousin
20/ Samuel	Goldman	15.2.1897	Dobromil, Pol.	merchant	Düsseldorf	Zygmunta 9	Simon, Perak Scheies, N.Y.; Helene Silberman, Kingler N.Y.	cousins
21/ Moses-Beyle	Blau	18.12.1887	Kolbuszowa(?), Pol.	merchant	Berlin	Pilsudskiego Nr. 13	Harry [illegible], Brooklyn	—

Fig. 3: List of Jewish refugees in Zbaszyn having relatives in the US, Canada, or South America (JDC Archives, Records of the New York Office of the American Jewish Joint Distribution Committee, 1933–1944, folder #879, Zbaszyn, 1938–1939, Lists of Refugees at Zbaszyn; http://search.archives.jdc.org/notebook_ext.asp?item=509854)

being helped by JDC in 1940 in Vilna.[6] The JDC Archives includes 73 lists detailing 6,300 names and addresses of recipients of free parcels sent to Polish Jewish refugees who fled east to the Soviet Union.[7]

6 JDC Archives, Records of the New York Office of the American Jewish Joint Distribution Committee, 1933–1944, folder #876, Vilna Refugees 1940, List of Refugees, 4.2.1940; http://search.archives.jdc.org/notebook_ext.asp?item=509518.

7 JDC Archives, Records of the New York Office of the American Jewish Joint Distribution Committee, 1933–1944, folder #428, Lists of JDC Beneficiaries Being Sent Packages in the USSR #1–73, 27.6.1944; http://search.archives.jdc.org/notebook_ext.asp?item=449962. For further background, see Atina Grossmann: "'Joint Fund Teheran': JDC and the Jewish Lifeline to Central Asia", in Avinoam Patt, Atina Grossmann, Linda G. Levi and Maud S. Mandel (eds.): *The JDC at 100: A Century of Humanitarianism*, Detroit: Wayne State University Press, 2019, 205–244.

Fig. 4: Polish Jewish refugees. Vilna, Lithuania, 1939 (JDC Archives Photograph Collection, NY_06661)

Warszawa--New Jork U.S.A.
Warscheu--New Jork U.S.A.

Prośba o pomoc.
Gesuch um Hilfe.

14.V.40

Nr.10550. Berta Mochorowska, W-wa, Waliców 5 m.6.
- do
Simon Zimermen, 506 Fort Washington Aven. New Jork.

Nr.10551. Rubin Mochorowski, W-wa, Waliców 5 m.6.
- do
Louis Morrison, 79 Fifth Aven. New-Jork.

Nr.10552. Rubin Mochorowski, W-wa, Waliców 5 m.6.
- do
Abe Morrison, 1864 West 4-th St. Broklyn N.J.

Nr.10553. Natan Wertman, W-wa, Leszno 47 m.6.
- do
Francy Sperling, 165 Suffolk str. New-Jork, City.

Nr.10554. Izaak Nadel, W-wa, Targowa 53.
do
P.L.Fajgenbaum, 62 Irejer Str. Rochester New-Jork.

Nr.10555. Elżbieta Szrejder, W-wa, Elektoralna 31 m.11 u p.Orbach.
do
Samuel Kenn, 160 Brodway , New-Jork.

Nr.10556. Moszek Lancman, W-wa, Zamenhofa 29 m.30.
- do
Sarah Elstein, 309 E.Houston str. New-Jork.

Nr.10557. Małka Goldberg, W-wa, Wolińska 4 m.16.
do
Sarah Elstein, 309 E.Houston str. New-Jork.

Nr.10558. Estera Branfeld, W-wa, Zamenhofa 21 m.81.
do
Majer Brannfeld for Machle Branfeld, 180 Orchard str. New-Jork.

Fig. 5: Calls for help from Polish Jews to US relatives sent via JDC, 14.5.1940 (JDC Archives, Records of the Warsaw Office of the American Joint Distribution Committee, 1939–1941, Folder #164; http://search.archives.jdc.org/notebook_ext.asp?item=2629793)

When the Nazis entered Poland, JDC-Warsaw, which was already working extensively in Poland, expanded its relief efforts in response to the emergency situation across the country and shifted its focus from reconstruction back to relief and financial assistance to communities. From September 1939 until the US entered the war in December 1941, JDC worked assiduously to save lives. By 1941, it supported 650 soup kitchens that served tens of thousands of meals daily, built temporary shelters for refugees, supported 200 hospitals and clinics, and provided childcare assistance – more than 2,000 institutions and agencies – in more than 408 locales. Although JDC struggled to provide aid in the face of dwindling funds, its efforts helped sustain many.

With the US entry into the war, the legal existence of JDC Warsaw came to an end, along with American allocations. Local JDC representatives continued their activities underground.

Evian Conference and the Dominican Republic

JDC Vice-Chairman Jonah B. Wise attended the *Intergovernmental Conference for Refugees from Germany* in Evian in 1938 as JDC's representative and tried to lobby for more countries to accept Jewish refugees.[8] When the Dominican Republic agreed to accept Jewish refugees, JDC began negotiations that resulted in the establishment of the *Dominican Republic Settlement Association* (DORSA), an agricultural settlement of German and Austrian Jews in Sosua in the Dominican Republic, financed by JDC.[9]

France

With the influx of many refugees to France, JDC worked with local Jewish child care organizations such as OSE (*Oeuvre de Secours aux Enfants*), to establish children's homes for orphans and unaccompanied children who had been sent to France, and extended relief assistance to refugee families. Once France was

---

[8] JDC Archives, Records of the New York Office of the American Jewish Joint Distribution Committee, 1933–1944, folder #255, Jonah B. Wise, American Joint Distribution Committee Statement to the Intergovernmental Conference on Refugees, Evian, July 1938; http://search.archives.jdc.org/notebook_ext.asp?item=426835.
[9] See Marion A. Kaplan: *Dominican Haven: The Jewish Refugee Settlement in Sosua, 1940–1945*, New York: Museum of Jewish Heritage – A Living Memorial to the Holocaust, 2008. For further information, see https://archives.jdc.org/our-collections/finding-aids/dorsa-collection/1939-1977.

occupied by the Nazis, JDC, in close collaboration with the *American Friends Service Committee*, provided food and clothing for Jewish internees in transient and detention camps such as Gurs, St. Cyprien, and Camp des Milles in southern France.

Spain and Portugal

Later, when the Nazis entered southern France, many Jewish refugees crossed the Pyrenees to reach Spain, and JDC established an office in Barcelona and a wartime headquarters in Lisbon, the last outpost for those attempting to reach the Atlantic. The services extended by JDC in Spain included protection or intervention on the refugees' behalf, financial support, and assistance with their departure from Spain. JDC arranged for the evacuation of groups of children to the US, helped refugees communicate with friends and family, and provided medical care where possible.

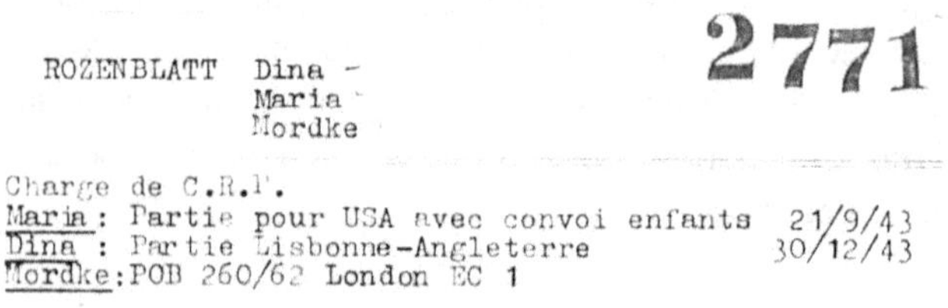

```
ROZENBLATT  Dina -                       2771
            Maria
            Mordke
Charge de C.R.I.
Maria: Partie pour USA avec convoi enfants  21/9/43
Dina : Partie Lisbonne-Angleterre           30/12/43
Mordke: POB 260/62 London EC 1
```

Fig. 6: Index Card for Rozenblatt Family, JDC Barcelona Office, case cards, 1943 (http://search.archives.jdc.org/notebook_ext.asp?item=133248)

More than 100,000 refugees passed through Portugal during the war years en route to overseas lands, and JDC provided care and maintenance and emigration assistance to most of them and operated children's homes there. JDC financed or shared in the financing of dozens of sailings from Lisbon and nearby ports using large ships such as the *Nyassa* for trans-Atlantic crossings and voyages to North Africa and Palestine. The *Serpa Pinto* carried between 700 to 800 passengers per sailing, and in the course of the Second World War, it bore more refugees across the Atlantic than any other single transport. Between 1941 and 1944, JDC financed or shared in the financing of over a dozen *Serpa Pinto* sailings, which brought Jewish refugees from Lisbon and Spain via Morocco and Tangier to Jamaica, Cuba, and the US. JDC archival records include lists of passengers whose fares were subsidized by JDC.

Jewish refugees were permitted to stay in Spain and Portugal only temporarily, and JDC sought to identify new emigration possibilities for the refugees. Overall, JDC needed to base its emigration plans on the refugees' countries of origin, depending on which nationals each country was ready to accept, either on a temporary or permanent basis. Polish Jews were taken to Gibraltar and England. Czechs were transferred to England. Many were taken to Tangier, an international city, and later from there to other countries, including Canada and the US. JDC's guarantee of care and maintenance costs often facilitated the refugees' acceptance.

Cuba and Shanghai

In Cuba, JDC established a refugee committee and worked closely with the local community to assist the many Jewish refugees who came to Cuba between 1938 and 1945. Likewise, JDC developed an extensive refugee assistance program in Shanghai, the only free port in the world ready to accept Jewish refugees without passports, to which approximately 20,000 Jewish refugees from Germany and Austria and later from Czechoslovakia and Poland escaped. The majority were destitute or nearly so, and JDC provided food and other services to over 16,000.[10]

Hungary

JDC worked in Hungary to develop children's homes and welfare programs to assist needy Hungarian Jews impacted by the entry of the Nazis into Hungary in March of 1944. JDC, as a primary funder of the US War Refugee Board, was involved in sending Raoul Wallenberg to Hungary and the funding of his operations there. JDC's office in Istanbul sought to channel refugees from the Balkans to Palestine and to assist the many refugees arriving in Turkey, a neutral country.

---

10 For further background, see Zhava Litvac Glaser: "Laura Margolis and JDC Efforts in Cuba and Shanghai: Sustaining Refugees in a Time of Catastrophe", in Avinoam Patt, Atina Grossmann, Linda G. Levi and Maud S. Mandel (eds.): *The JDC at 100: A Century of Humanitarianism*, Detroit: Wayne State University Press, 2019, 167–204.

Thus, both prior to and during the Second World War, JDC was active in a large number of countries, both in Europe and beyond. The organization's experience from its work in the aftermath of the First World War, its longstanding relationships with Jewish communities across Europe, and its pre-existing partnerships with other nonsectarian agencies, enabled JDC to create early-on systems to collect and disseminate information on individuals that it assisted that would later facilitate family tracing and search efforts. JDC began preparing lists of refugees receiving JDC assistance even before the official outbreak of the Second World War and developed systems to share these lists with other JDC offices and other NGOs. JDC's know-how and the networks it had established made it well-positioned to lead efforts to help survivors and refugees after the war.

Role of JDC in the *Central Location Index*

Even before the end of the war, there was a need for a central clearinghouse in the US for inquiries from family members desperate to learn the whereabouts and fate of their relatives in Europe. With the outbreak of the war, communications were limited, and with the desperate attempts of European Jews to escape to other countries, it was increasingly difficult for family members to know where their relatives had gone. Those with family members in Europe frantically turned to a number of Jewish and non-sectarian organizations that were working in Europe to attempt to receive information. JDC played a central role in initiating a series of meetings during 1943 with other US agencies regarding the setting up of a US-based central location file for refugees.[11]

These organizations came together to create a *Central Location Index* (CLI), chartered on May 27, 1944, that was initiated by seven founding US organizations actively engaged in servicing US residents' inquiries for location of their relatives and friends: *American Committee for Christian Refugees, American Friends Service Committee, American Jewish Joint Distribution Committee, Hebrew Immigrant Aid Society, International Migration Services, National Council of Jewish Women, National Refugee Service.* Later they were joined by several additional organizations: *Unitarian Service Committee, International Rescue and Relief Committee,*

---

11 JDC Archives, Records of the New York Office of the American Jewish Joint Distribution Committee, 1933–1944, folder #23, Moses A. Leavitt, Report of the Secretary to the Executive Committee Meeting of the Joint Distribution Committee, 27.10.1943, 4–5; http://search.archives.jdc.org/notebook_ext.asp?item=401367.

Canadian Location Service, and *American Federation of International Institutes*.[12] The CLI proved to be of great value in the difficult task of family reunification and eliminated duplication of inquiries and effort.

The CLI, established while the Second World War was still raging, beginning in May 1944, was a clearinghouse for all inquiries originating with the member agencies, and served as a channel to secure information from government-sponsored registration centers abroad. Utilizing a standardized CLI application form, each stateside organization would forward requests for information to CLI Headquarters in New York where the agency's request was filed in the CLI, and a central location file and index card were created for each refugee. Then an *International Red Cross* card was made out for each member of the dispersed family and sent to Geneva,[13] and the CLI Headquarters would channel these requests to Europe. These procedures were established and already in operation by the autumn of 1944 as reported by Moses Leavitt to the *Emergency Administration Committee* of the *Joint Distribution Committee* on October 10, 1944.

In December 1945, the *US War Refugee Board* designated the CLI as the sole agency in the US to cooperate with UNRRA *Central Tracing Bureaus* in Germany and Austria. The CLI cleared its inquiries and information with the *International Red Cross*. Lists of Displaced Persons gathered by JDC and other overseas agencies in neutral and liberated countries and occupied areas were registered in the file and served as an additional source of information. These resources were the basis for checking inquiries by relatives in the US. The CLI sought to match names and help to locate the American relatives and friends sought.

JDC's primary work was overseas, and it did not service US relatives in the same way as US-based organizations with a mandate to service populations in the US. JDC, however, had an interest in creating this index in relation to its work overseas and the cooperation that its overseas staff could provide. JDC was the primary funder of the CLI, and the CLI president was Moses Leavitt, JDC Secretary from 1940 to 1946 and Executive Vice-Chairman from 1947 to 1965. Etta Deutsch served as CLI executive director from its founding in 1944 until November 1948, and Carolin Flexner served thereafter for the last six months until the organization closed down. They led a staff of 75 trained searchers.

---

12 "Agency to Find Relatives in Liberated Europe Established in New York", August 9, 1944, Jewish Telegraphic Agency, JTA Archives.
13 JDC Archives, Records of the New York Office of the American Jewish Joint Distribution Committee, 1933–1944, folder # 63, Minutes of the Emergency Administration Committee of the Joint Distribution Committee, 10.10.1944, 21–22.

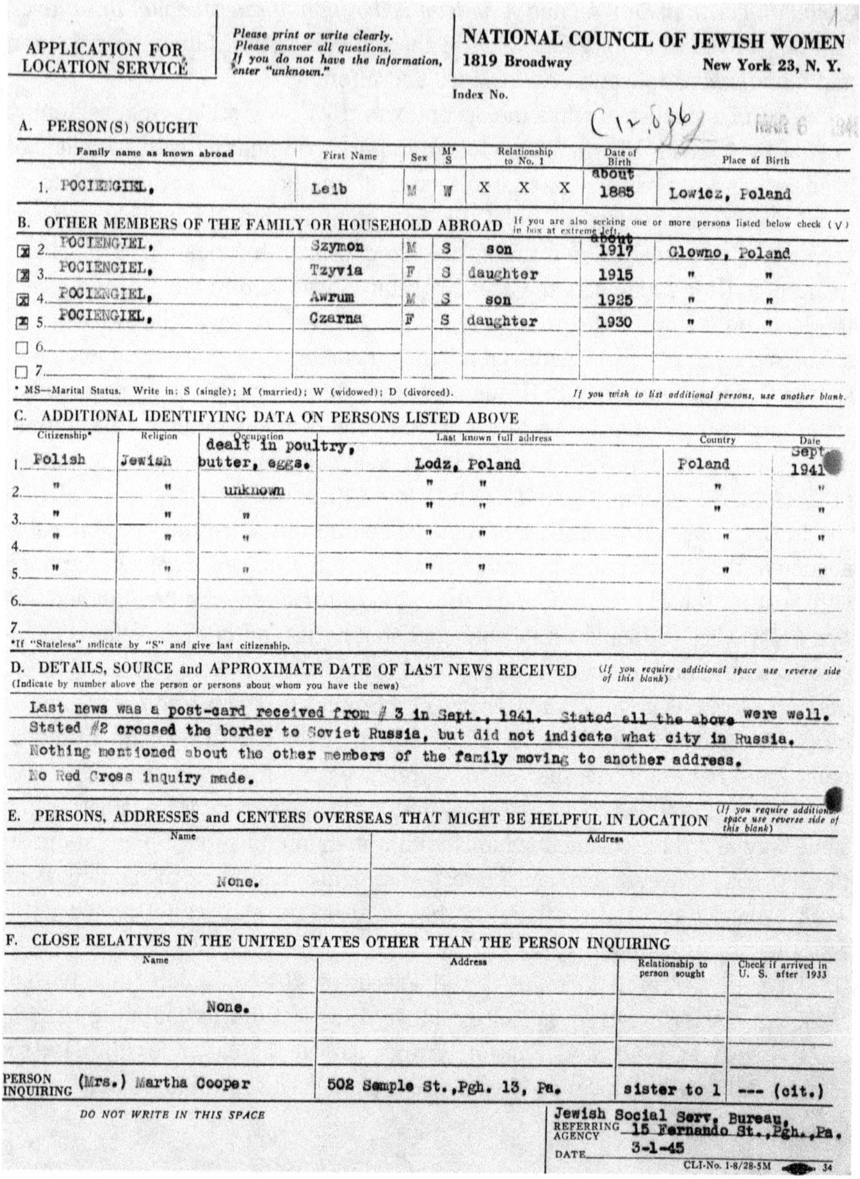

APPLICATION FOR LOCATION SERVICE

Please print or write clearly. Please answer all questions. If you do not have the information, enter "unknown."

NATIONAL COUNCIL OF JEWISH WOMEN
1819 Broadway **New York 23, N. Y.**

Index No. C12,836

A. PERSON(S) SOUGHT

Family name as known abroad	First Name	Sex	M* S	Relationship to No. 1	Date of Birth	Place of Birth
1. POCIENGIEL,	Leib	M	W	X X X	about 1885	Lowicz, Poland

B. OTHER MEMBERS OF THE FAMILY OR HOUSEHOLD ABROAD (If you are also seeking one or more persons listed below check (√) in box at extreme left.)

☒ 2. POCIENGIEL,	Szymon	M	S	son	about 1917	Glowno, Poland
☒ 3. POCIENGIEL,	Tzyvia	F	S	daughter	1915	" "
☒ 4. POCIENGIEL,	Awrum	M	S	son	1925	" "
☒ 5. POCIENGIEL,	Czarna	F	S	daughter	1930	" "
☐ 6.						
☐ 7.						

* MS—Marital Status. Write in: S (single); M (married); W (widowed); D (divorced). *If you wish to list additional persons, use another blank.*

C. ADDITIONAL IDENTIFYING DATA ON PERSONS LISTED ABOVE

	Citizenship*	Religion	Occupation	Last known full address	Country	Date
1.	Polish	Jewish	dealt in poultry, butter, eggs.	Lodz, Poland	Poland	Sept. 1941
2.	"	"	unknown	" "	"	"
3.	"	"	"	" "	"	"
4.	"	"	"	" "	"	"
5.	"	"	"	" "	"	"
6.						
7.						

*If "Stateless" indicate by "S" and give last citizenship.

D. DETAILS, SOURCE and APPROXIMATE DATE OF LAST NEWS RECEIVED (Indicate by number above the person or persons about whom you have the news) *(If you require additional space use reverse side of this blank)*

Last news was a post-card received from # 3 in Sept., 1941. Stated all the above were well. Stated #2 crossed the border to Soviet Russia, but did not indicate what city in Russia. Nothing mentioned about the other members of the family moving to another address. No Red Cross inquiry made.

E. PERSONS, ADDRESSES and CENTERS OVERSEAS THAT MIGHT BE HELPFUL IN LOCATION *(If you require additional space use reverse side of this blank)*

Name	Address
None.	

F. CLOSE RELATIVES IN THE UNITED STATES OTHER THAN THE PERSON INQUIRING

Name	Address	Relationship to person sought	Check if arrived in U. S. after 1933
None.			
PERSON INQUIRING (Mrs.) Martha Cooper	502 Semple St., Pgh. 13, Pa.	sister to 1	--- (cit.)

DO NOT WRITE IN THIS SPACE

REFERRING AGENCY Jewish Social Serv. Bureau, 15 Fernando St., Pgh., Pa.
DATE 3-1-45

CLI-No. 1-8/28-5M 34

Fig. 7: Application for Location Service, 1.3.1945 (JDC Archives, Records of the Warsaw Office of the American Joint Distribution Committee, 1945–1949, Folder #873; http://search.archives.jdc.org/notebook_ext.asp?item=2274927)

The CLI received cables from Europe in February 1945 with names of 1,200 people rescued from Theresienstadt who had arrived in Switzerland. CLI staff were able to match many of these individuals with inquiries in the CLI records, demonstrating the benefits of a central index. This unexpected development led to great excitement. Thus began an active process whereby lists of liberated internees from the various concentration camps were sent to the CLI which immediately sought to make matches with their inquiry records.[14]

Already in October 1944, Moses Leavitt reported to the JDC *Emergency Administration Committee* about the CLI work in the US and his concerns about the inadequacy of tracing efforts of the *International Red Cross* system overseas. He stressed the need for a local service in every country. Since most location inquiries would be Jewish requests, Leavitt proposed that JDC had a major contribution to make in this regard. He indicated that UNRRA agreed about the need for national tracing offices but was not itself interested in establishing local national tracing offices. UNRRA efforts would only be temporary as UNRRA would be closing down its operations. Joseph Schwartz, JDC Director of Overseas Operations, noted that refugees want first and foremost assistance with finding their family. The committee authorized Dr. Schwartz to study how JDC might establish local tracing and family search offices in Europe with local staff which would work in consultation with local organizations such as Red Cross chapters or municipalities.[15]

From 1944 to 1949, the *Central Location Index* processed appeals for aid in locating 750,000 people. They were able to find 50,000 persons in postwar Europe for relatives inquiring from all over the world. Of these, 40,000 persons were alive, and information on their whereabouts was shared with their relatives. Deaths or deportations of 10,000 individuals were confirmed. To do this, the CLI maintained 1.2 million file cards and files. Lost and orphaned children were a particularly difficult problem. The total cost of this operation was $450,000.[16]

---

14 JDC Archives, Records of the Geneva Office of the American Jewish Joint Distribution Committee, 1945–1954, folder #ORG.320, Etta Deutsch, History of the Central Location Index, Inc., May, 1949, 5; http://search.archives.jdc.org/notebook_ext.asp?item=2143458.
15 JDC Archives, Records of the New York Office of the American Jewish Joint Distribution Committee, 1933–1944, folder # 63, Minutes of the Emergency Administration Committee of the Joint Distribution Committee, 10.10.1944, 21–25.
16 JDC Archives, Records of the Geneva Office of the American Jewish Joint Distribution Committee, 1945–1954, folder #ORG.320, Etta Deutsch, History of the Central Location Index, Inc., May, 1949; http://search.archives.jdc.org/notebook_ext.asp?item=2143458. See also JDC Archives, Records of the New York Office of the American Jewish Joint Distribution Committee, 1945–1954, folder #1541, Press release: "Central Location Index Ends Missing Persons' Hunt", 12.5.1949; http://search.archives.jdc.org/notebook_ext.asp?item=607207.

As JDC local offices in countries around the world received inquiries, these local offices would seek information from local contacts and institutions on the subject of the inquiry and respond to the inquiring office with copies to other offices around the world. In this way, many times, an individual might be found in Poland, but a sibling might be found in Belgium. With this broad communication, JDC was successful in reconnecting many relatives. JDC staff members themselves were often personally affected. For example, A. Malamoud of JDC Warsaw wrote to JDC Brussels on February 29, 1948, expressing thanks for information on the whereabouts of his cousin, Karola Eisenberg, who was now in Stockholm.[17]

Often, relatives in the US did not know all the names of family members in Europe. So, for example, the ITS final report quotes a letter from JDC Warsaw: "We were fortunate enough to locate the brother of the sought Morris. He is Chaim M. aged 27. born at Jasniowska, distr. Bialystok. His parents: Abram and Lejka, maiden name K. Mr. M. stated that he is the only survivor of his whole family and that he is a brother of Morris. His present address is Warsaw, Roznanska 38/14."[18]

In the years immediately following the Second World War, the various offices of the organization worked tirelessly to trace family members of survivors, collaborating closely with the CLI. Many lists of survivors or emigrants assisted by the Joint or refugees seeking relatives were produced and disseminated, some of which included names and addresses of relatives in the US. After the CLI was disbanded, the documentation was stored by JDC in New York; in 1957, this documentation was transferred to *Yad Vashem* in Jerusalem. Copies of the CLI registration cards were shared with the *International Tracing Service* when it was established.

---

17 JDC Archives, Records of the Warsaw Office of the American Joint Distribution Committee, 1945–1949, folder #1162, letter from A. Malamoud of JDC Warsaw to JDC Brussels, 19.2.1948; http://search.archives.jdc.org/notebook_ext.asp?item=2312390.

18 JDC Archives, Records of the Geneva Office of the American Jewish Joint Distribution Committee, 1945–1954, folder #ORG.320, Etta Deutsch, History of the Central Location Index, Inc., May, 1949, 7; http://search.archives.jdc.org/notebook_ext.asp?item=2143458.

JDC during the Immediate Post War Period

Displaced Persons Camps in Germany, Austria and Italy

When Saly Mayer, JDC representative in Switzerland, made his first visit from May 26 to 28, 1945, to the Displaced Persons camps in Germany, he cabled JDC New York outlining his observations and conclusions. The following two points were among the priority action points: "THREE: All most anxious to find out if and where missing members of their family are living FOUR: They are most anxious that their relatives abroad are informed of their being still alive and of present address."[19] Several days after receiving Mayer's June 6 and 8 cables, Harold Trobe, JDC Representative in Vienna and Prague, in a handwritten note to Joseph Schwartz and Moses Leavitt, wrote:

> Lists with incomplete data seem to circulate all over Europe without much rhyme or reason. Can the Int. Red Cross handle the whole job or must there be a Jewish location index as well? [...] I know how difficult the task is. It will take all the ingenuity of the Int Bus Machine people plus many others whose hearts are in the task.[20]

By late 1945, tens of thousands of European Jews, aided by underground networks of guides, had flooded into the US and British occupation zones in Germany and Austria. They crowded into Displaced Persons camps that were hastily set up by the Allies to house the hundreds of thousands of people displaced by the war. The *United Nations Relief and Rehabilitation Administration* (UNRRA) was responsible for the basic needs of refugees. It became immediately apparent that the Jewish inhabitants had very different needs, and the devastation to their communities was more complete. They also needed protections from their fellow inhabitants who were often hostile to them.

Joseph Schwartz accompanied Earl Harrison, President Truman's Special Envoy, on his official tour of the camps. As a result of this visit and the report submitted, separate camps were established for Jewish DPs. JDC received permission from UNRRA and the US Army to work within the DP camps supplementing

---

[19] JDC Archives, Records of the New York Office of the American Jewish Joint Distribution Committee, 1945–1954, folder #323, Cable from Saly Mayer in St. Gallen to American Joint Distribution Committee New York, 8.6.1945; http://search.archives.jdc.org/notebook_ext.asp?item=674481.

[20] JDC Archives, Records of the New York Office of the American Jewish Joint Distribution Committee, 1945–1954, folder #1051, letter from Harold Trobe to Joseph Schwartz and Moses Leavitt, 14.6.1945; http://search.archives.jdc.org/notebook_ext.asp?item=624304.

the meager aid provided by UNRRA. In addition to providing food, clothing and healthcare, JDC opened schools and developed cultural and religious activities within the Displaced Persons camps. The JDC Emigration Service in Munich and Vienna assisted Jewish refugees with information, applications, visas, papers, and help to fund their emigration. A file was created for each family, and a card index was maintained of all individuals. These cards have been indexed in the JDC Archives Names Index.

In Italy, as well, JDC provided assistance to the many refugees in Rome and in smaller camps including ten children's homes in Selvino, Campolecciano and elsewhere, a TB rehabilitation center in Grottaferrata, and vocational training programs at Ostia, Fano, and elsewhere. The JDC Rome Emigration Service assisted Jewish families with emigration.

Poland

In Poland, JDC embarked upon a massive assistance program for shattered survivors in the immediate postwar period. It shipped vital supplies to the needy, promoted economic activity, supported a network of schools, homes, hospitals, and cultural institutions, and assisted tens of thousands to emigrate to Israel and other countries, including many children who were retrieved from the families and churches who had hidden them during the war. Many of these children no longer had parents, and the search for their relatives was a complicated endeavor.

JDC Warsaw worked extensively to prepare applications to the *Conseil Interoeuvre d'Aide aux Immigrants et Transitaires Juifs* in Paris for the emigration of Jewish children to France. Many of these children ultimately continued to Israel. The JDC *Warsaw Emigration Service* maintained family files and a card index for each individual. What remains of this card index has been digitized and is searchable in the JDC Archives database.

Children in France

Following the war, in 1945, there were over 15,000 Jewish children in France, 11,000 of them needy and receiving assistance from JDC. Over 9,000 children were in Jewish childcare institutions operated by OSE and other local organizations. All of these institutions were supported primarily by JDC. JDC was also providing relief support to 2,000 children via their families and Jewish children placed in foster homes by OSE and other organizations. Among these children were many orphans including 535 Buchenwald child survivors admitted temporarily en route to Palestine,[21] and children of Jewish refugees streaming in from Soviet-occupied countries including Poland and other East European countries.

Shanghai

Between the resumption of emigration in 1946 and 1953, JDC helped 16,000 Jews, mostly living in Shanghai, leave China for other lands. Approximately 6,700 were admitted to the US. The remainder went to Israel, Europe, Australia, Latin America, and Canada.

Fig. 8: Dining hall of an OSE children's home in France, c.1947 (JDC Archives Photograph Collection, NY_07983)

---

21 JDC Archives, Records of the Istanbul Office of the American Jewish Joint Distribution Committee, 1937–1949, folder #IS.181, Orphan Children from Buchenwald Now in Paris: Enfants Venus d'Allemagne—Convoi du 8 Juin 1945 à Écouis, 8.6.1945; http://search.archives.jdc.org/notebook_ext.asp?item=875790.

When the communist government took over in China, it became clear that JDC would need to leave. It closed its offices in 1949, and it became imperative for the refugees to leave. JDC assisted the refugees to find temporary and permanent immigration solutions and helped to fund the travel for the needy. For some, there was no recourse other than leaving China and returning to Austria and Germany via the US, which would not permit entry to those without US visas. In some cases, refugees had to travel from Shanghai to San Francisco and from there across the country in sealed trains to New York to board ships and planes back to Austria and Germany.

JDC Tracing Services in the Post-War Period

Initially, there was no mail service in the military zones of Germany and elsewhere. This made communication often impossible. JDC began to develop local tracing bureaus in localities where it was working. The methodology was to create lists of survivors and card indexes with their names. JDC assisted Jews in searching for relatives, served as a liaison with the *Central Location Index* in New York and other JDC offices, placed newspaper ads, and pursued inquiries with other organizations.

Beginning in June 1945, JDC established the JDC *Tracing Service* in the US Zone of Germany. The first step was to encourage the survivors themselves to create lists of survivors. The *Central Committee of Liberated Jews*, established in June 1945, prepared lists of Jewish survivors in Germany. JDC supported this effort financially. JDC created a card index and assisted Jewish survivors in the search for their relatives. By September 1946, 14,313 individuals had requested assistance with the tracing of relatives from the JDC *Tracing Service* in the US Zone of Germany.[22] If addresses of US families were not known, tracing staff utilized telephone directories from large US cities or turned to the CLI and other JDC offices. The JDC *Tracing Services* placed ads in newspapers and made inquiries with other organizations. By January 1947, the JDC Tracing Service in the US

---

[22] JDC Archives, Records of the Geneva Office of the American Jewish Joint Distribution Committee, 1945–1954, folder #GER.63, Memorandum from Leo W. Schwarz to Dr. Joseph Schwartz, Subject: Summary Analysis of AJDC Program in the U.S. Zone of Occupation, Germany, 13.1.1947, 19–20; http://search.archives.jdc.org/notebook_ext.asp?item=2057018.

Zone of Germany had assigned 14 staff to tracing work, and during 1947, it had 29,037 inquirers and 15,054 positive results.[23]

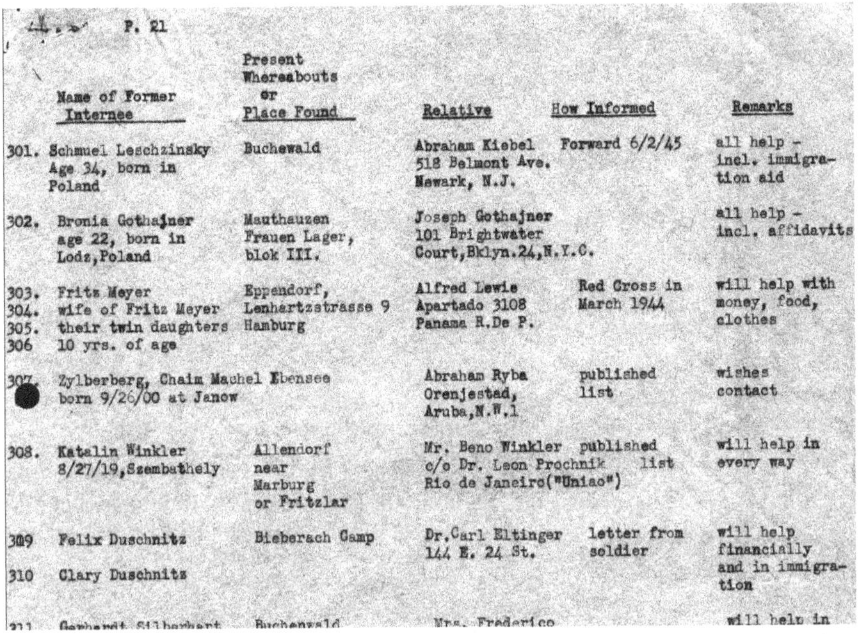

P. 21

	Name of Former Internee	Present Whereabouts or Place Found	Relative	How Informed	Remarks
301.	Schmuel Leschzinsky Age 34, born in Poland	Buchewald	Abraham Kiebel 518 Belmont Ave. Newark, N.J.	Forward 6/2/45	all help - incl. immigration aid
302.	Bronia Gothajner age 22, born in Lodz, Poland	Mauthauzen Frauen Lager, blok III.	Joseph Gothajner 101 Brightwater Court, Bklyn. 24, N.Y.C.		all help - incl. affidavits
303. 304. 305. 306	Fritz Meyer wife of Fritz Meyer their twin daughters 10 yrs. of age	Eppendorf, Lenhartzstrasse 9 Hamburg	Alfred Lewie Apartado 3108 Panama R.De P.	Red Cross in March 1944	will help with money, food, clothes
307.	Zylberberg, Chaim Machel born 9/26/00 at Janow	Ebensee	Abraham Ryba Orenjestad, Aruba, N.W.I	published list	wishes contact
308.	Katalin Winkler 8/27/19, Szembathely	Allendorf near Marburg or Fritzlar	Mr. Beno Winkler c/o Dr. Leon Prochnik Rio de Janeiro("Uniao")	published list	will help in every way
309	Felix Duschnitz	Bieberach Camp	Dr. Carl Eltinger 144 E. 24 St.	letter from soldier	will help financially and in immigration
310	Clary Duschnitz				
311	Gerhardt Silberhart	Buchenwald	Mrs. Frederico		will help in

Fig. 9: Portion of a page from a list of survivors, 7. 8. 1945 (JDC Archives, Records of the New York Office of the American Jewish Joint Distribution Committee, 1945 – 1954, folder #1051, Survivor Lists: General, 1944 – 1945; http://search.archives.jdc.org/notebook_ext.asp?item=624286)

In Berlin, the JDC Berlin Search Bureau was established based on information gathered from the *Gestapo Deportation Index*, which included the names of 126,000 Jews deported from Berlin and a card index of 140,000 Dutch Jews who were deported. This index was shared with the Dutch Jewish Community and with the CLI.[24]

---

23 JDC Archives, Records of the Geneva Office of the American Jewish Joint Distribution Committee, 1945 – 1954, folder #GER.81, Report of Activities in the United States Zone of Occupation for the Year 1947, 25; http://search.archives.jdc.org/notebook_ext.asp?item=2057329.

24 JDC Archives, Records of the Geneva Office of the American Jewish Joint Distribution Committee, 1945 – 1954, folder #GER.783, Larry Lubetsky, A Report on the Activities of the AJDC Berlin Tracing Office, January 1 thru March 31st, 1947, April, 1947, 1 – 2; http://search.archives.jdc.org/notebook_ext.asp?item=2101170.

In the British Zone, JDC established the *Belsen Joint Tracing (Search) Department*. Resources included the lists of survivors prepared by the camp committee and UNRRA registers. A card index was prepared using lists of people in the British Zone, including those from all communities and *Gemeindes*, and three DP camps.[25]

JDC Opens Local Tracing Bureaus in Europe and Elsewhere

Elsewhere in Europe, most Jewish refugees returned first to their hometowns to seek family and news of those who had survived. Most were devastated to realize the enormity of the loss of family and friends, and to the Jewish people as a whole. JDC offices in Europe opened local tracing bureaus to assist survivors of all ages, some of whom had been separated from spouses and children during the war. Following the disappointment of not finding loved ones, they often proceeded on the journey to the Displaced Persons camps in Germany, Austria, and Italy.

The search for family not only emanated from overseas family members in the US and elsewhere. Survivors themselves were seeking family members and requested assistance in tracing their overseas relatives. With so many family members having been lost in the war, tracing overseas relatives was seen as their salvation for a better future. Another area of activity for JDC local tracing bureaus was putting surviving relatives in touch with each other. Often, the parties did not know of each other's survival.

In the post-war period, all JDC offices in Europe, and in other countries where the organization was involved with large refugee programs, established local tracing bureaus to assist survivors to reconnect with their family and friends and to connect with overseas relatives. The tracing bureaus communicated with local groups, UNRRA tracing bureaus, and the Red Cross to seek information and corresponded with other JDC offices around the world and with the CLI to seek information in the search for relatives.

The JDC Overseas Headquarters moved back to Paris immediately after the war and established a vital, bustling location and tracing service. For a period in July 1947, there was an experiment to make JDC Paris the headquarters for all JDC location and tracing services. The Paris office transferred to the *Interna-*

---

25 JDC Archives, Records of the New York Office of the American Jewish Joint Distribution Committee, 1945–1954, folder #301.1, undated memorandum from Belsen Joint Tracing Department; http://search.archives.jdc.org/notebook_ext.asp?item=671932.

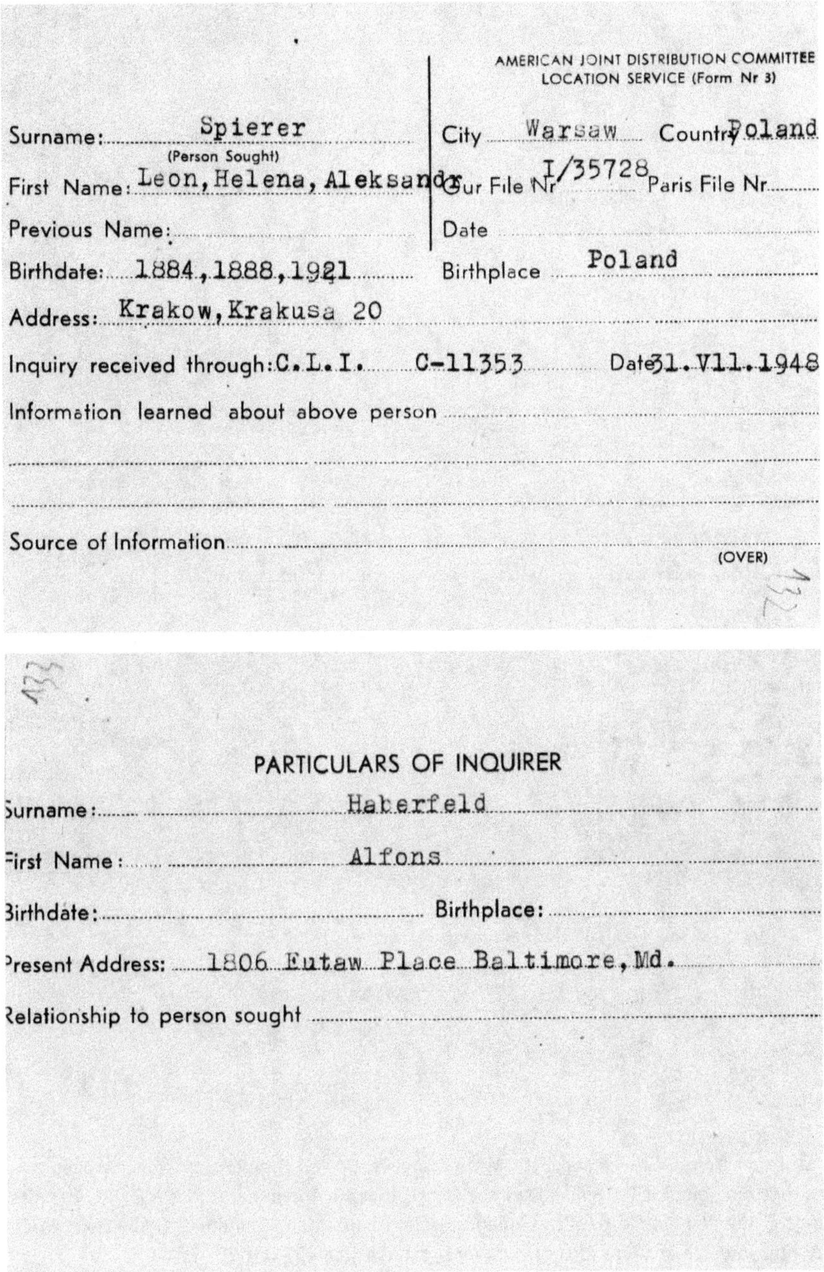

AMERICAN JOINT DISTRIBUTION COMMITTEE
LOCATION SERVICE (Form Nr 3)

Surname: Spierer (Person Sought)
City: Warsaw Country: Poland
First Name: Leon, Helena, Aleksander
Our File Nr: I/35728 Paris File Nr:
Previous Name:
Date:
Birthdate: 1884, 1888, 1921 Birthplace: Poland
Address: Krakow, Krakusa 20
Inquiry received through: C.L.I. C-11353 Date: 31.VII.1948
Information learned about above person

Source of Information
(OVER)

PARTICULARS OF INQUIRER
Surname: Haberfeld
First Name: Alfons
Birthdate: Birthplace:
Present Address: 1806 Eutaw Place Baltimore, Md.
Relationship to person sought

Fig. 10: Front and back of a JDC Location Service index card for inquiry received from the *Central Location Index*, 31.7.1948 (JDC Archives, Records of the Warsaw Office of the American Joint Distribution Committee, 1945–1949, folder #1023; http://search.archives.jdc.org/notebook_ext.asp?item=2292715)

```
                                                      September, 10th    8
        L/35444, L/35521,
    File: 24606/421


    To - Asociacion Filantropica Israelita  -  BUENOS AIRES

            The following are inquiries of persons in Poland looking
            for their relatives in Argentina
    ----------------------------------------------------------------------
    sons sought              Age    Address       Inquirer         Age    Address
    ----------------------------------------------------------------------
    ELBERGER Josef, from      52 y.  Buenos Aires  HALPERN MN Elberger    Szczecin,
    Horodenka, cousin, em.1935                      Berta, from Horodenka Słowackiego 11

    STOLAR vel Stolarz I      1887   Buenos Aires  KULIK MN Chai- 1895   Niemcza, pow.
    voto Wajeman Szprynca                           mowicz Szoszka        Dzierzonów,
    daught. of Szlejma and                          daught. of Izrael-    "Dom Starców"
    Irma, her husband                               Iser, Chana MN Szwarc, Dworcowa 16
    Salomon, em.1921 from                           from Rokitno Wol.
    Białystok, cousin

    OT MN Enkier Renata       32 y.  Buenos Aires  SZWALBENFELD Lila 35  Wałbrzych,
    from Lwów, daughter of                          daught. of Wilhelm    Mickiewicza 28
    ax, Luga, her husband                           and Teresa MN Feld,   assumed name:
    liasz, bookeeper in a                           from Lwów             Pietraszkiewi
    icycles' factory, em.1937,
    ousin

    TARKHAND Boruch, son of   60 y.  Argentina     FAJNBERG MN Sztark-97 Warszawa,
    ordka, Sara, from Warsaw                        hand Chana, daugh. of Chmielna 130/
    ousin, until 1936 was in                        Tane and Chaja MN     /26, assumed
    Anheim, Germany, wherefrom                      Grincajg, from Warsaw name: Lewan-
    migrated to Argentina                                                 dowska


            Looking forward to an early report about your findings, we
            thank you for your cooperation


                                        Very sincerely yours

                                        AMERICAN JOINT DISTRIBUTION
                                                 COMMITTEE

                                            J. Gitler-Barski
                                            Secretary General
```

Fig. 11: Letter from J. Gitler-Barski, JDC Warsaw, to *Asociacion Filantropica Israelita*, Buenos Aires, regarding inquiries of Polish Jews seeking relatives in Argentina, 10.9.1948 (JDC Archives, Records of the Warsaw Office of the American Joint Distribution Committee, 1945–1949, folder #618; http://search.archives.jdc.org/notebook_ext.asp?item=2231260)

tional Tracing Service over 30,000 emigration service cards from its emigration service.

JDC offices maintained lists and card indexes of survivors and helped in the painstaking search for friends and relatives of the survivors. JDC Warsaw records from 1945 to 1949 reveal relentless activity to assist survivors to find their relatives. A file entitled "Correspondence: Thank you letters for help in locating missing persons" includes 70 documents, most of them in Polish and Yiddish. A September 1946 letter from the *Jewish Search Centre* in London to JDC Warsaw notes: "not only we but the enquirers as well are most grateful to you for your excellent search-work and the valuable assistance you gave us. May G-d bless your welfare work in 5707, and we wish you leshonah tauvoh." A March 13, 1947, letter from the *Canadian Jewish Congress* location service thanks JDC Warsaw for finding Mendel Wiseman-Wajsman, the relative of Mrs. Mandelbaum in Windsor, Ontario. A March 12, 1947, letter from a house painter in New York expresses thanks for locating the sender's nephew, Izzi Kempler, in Poland, and notes that he has already heard from Kempler.[26]

JDC Warsaw established its location department in October 1945, and JDC Rome's *Location Service Bureau* was established in January 1946. In Warsaw, a card index was prepared with 30,000 names of persons sought. Tracing activities were conducted in cooperation with other JDC offices. Ads were placed in the Polish/Yiddish press.[27] Between October 1945 and September 1946, the JDC Warsaw office received 22,148 letters, wrote 16,963 letters, was successful in locating 3,450 cases in Poland, and contacted 1,095 persons abroad. During this period, it placed 30,882 search ads in newspapers.[28]

The Warsaw office made extraordinary efforts to search for children and financed the redemption of Jewish children from Polish families, established and supported orphanages, provided health care, granted scholarships, and prepared children for emigration.[29]

---

26 JDC Archives, Records of the Warsaw Office of the American Joint Distribution Committee, 1945–1949, folder # 1162, Correspondance: Thank you letters for help in locating missing persons.
27 JDC Archives, Records of the Warsaw Office of the American Joint Distribution Committee, 1945–1949, folder #642, Newspaper clippings from "Dos Naye Lebn" (The New Life; Lodz) and "Nowym Życiu" (New Life; Wroclaw) with the lists of names of persons sought. See, for example, page 30 of the document in this folder.
28 JDC Archives, Records of the New York Office of the American Jewish Joint Distribution Committee, 1945–1954, folder #734, Report January – September 1946, AJDC Poland, 7.10.1946, 13–14.
29 See finding aid for JDC Archives, Records of the Warsaw Office of the American Joint Distribution Committee, 1945–1949; https://archives.jdc.org/our-collections/finding-aids/warsaw/1945-1949/.

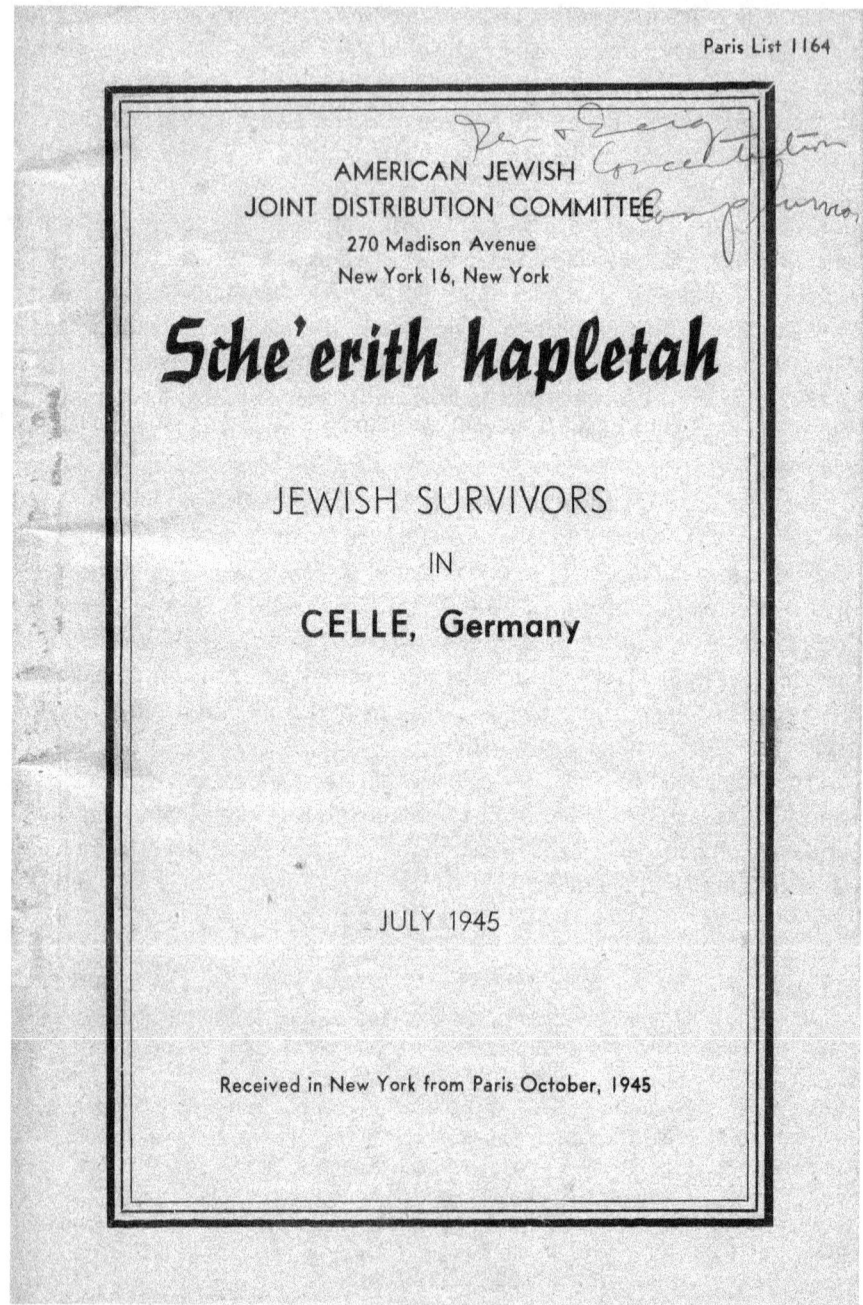

Fig. 12: *Sche'erith Hapletah* (The Surviving Remnant): *Jewish Survivors in Celle, Germany,* New York: American Jewish Joint Distribution Committee, July 1945 (JDC Archives, Records of the New York Office of the American Jewish Joint Distribution Committee, 1945–1954, folder #1057; http://search.archives.jdc.org/notebook_ext.asp?item=624387)

Fig. 13: Jewish refugees in Shanghai look for names of relatives and friends who may have survived the war. Shanghai, China, 1946 (Photograph: Arthur Rothstein. JDC Archives Photograph Collection, NY_17434)

JDC's *Central Location Service* in Rome maintained offices in Rome and Milan and was the sole organization in Italy dealing with large-scale tracing of Jews. It created a card index with 82,000 cards of Jews who fled to Italy, passed through Italy, or were deported from another country. In addition, 866 search lists were created. Over 13,000 cases were handled in 20 months.[30]

In places where refugees congregated, such as the Lutetia Hotel in Paris or in Shanghai, for example, bulletin boards posted lists of united families and missing persons. Booklets and books with lists of survivors from certain localities, e. g. Jewish Survivors in Celle, Germany, published in July 1945, or a two-volume book listing survivors in Slovakia published by JDC in New York based on information received from overseas offices and shared with the CLI in New York and with the JDC office in Jerusalem. In Palestine, names of Holocaust survivors on

---

[30] JDC Archives, Records of the New York Office of the American Jewish Joint Distribution Committee, 1945–1954, folder #627, Louis D. Horwitz, Location Service Bureau Quarterly Report July – September 1947, Rome; http://search.archives.jdc.org/notebook_ext.asp?item=701980.

these lists were read daily on Kol Israel radio, to inform new immigrants who eagerly awaited word of living family members.[31]

Complexity of Location and Tracing

Despite good will and good intentions, lists of survivors could often be problematic. These lists indicated where a person was at a particular point in time. During a period of havoc and emergency, many people were on the move. Thus lists of survivors don't reveal information on where these survivors went, whether they are still alive, etc. In addition, the lists often do not contain sufficient identifying data. There might be a number of people with the same name, and how could a family member ascertain that the person on the list was his/her relative? There may be a list of names but where could these individuals now be found? Many lists contained out-of-date addresses. Even when a family member was found on a list, painstaking work still needed to be done to try to ascertain whether the person was still alive and where they might be. Sometimes, relatives may have had contact and were known to be alive, but their whereabouts were unknown. This was prevalent particularly among those who moved from the East to the West.

Tracing relatives of children who were alone, often without a request from an inquirer, was particularly difficult. Often overseas relatives may not have known of the existence of the child or may not have known the child's name. Children did not have knowledge of their overseas relatives.

Background on the *International Tracing Service*

In February 1946, UNRRA accepted responsibility for tracing persons eligible for UNRRA care, including those receiving UNRRA care in Germany, eligible people not yet receiving care, and those technically eligible but no longer living. The *Central Tracing Bureau* (CTB) headquarters was established in 1946 at Arolsen, Germany, at the UNRRA headquarters.[32]

> The objectives [...] [of the CTB] were to search for missing military and civilian persons... and establish the fate of those who could not be found; to locate, collect, and preserve

---

31 JDC Archives, Records of the New York Office of the American Jewish Joint Distribution Committee, 1945–1954, folder #1051, *Reshimot Nitzolim* (Lists of Survivors).
32 See the article by Christian Höschler and Isabel Panek in this volume.

all available records regarding refugees and displaced persons in Germany; and to serve as a link to bring interested persons into communication with each other.[33]

Zonal tracing bureaus were to be operated under the military commanders in each zone. In addition, individual UN member countries were encouraged to open national tracing bureaus that would receive initial inquiries concerning their own nationals and initiate tracing and search activities in their respective zones. The CTB was to operate as a central clearing house between zonal and national bureaus.

With plans to cease UNRRA operations in Arolsen on June 30, 1947 and to transfer UNRRA headquarters to Paris, the future of the *Central Tracing Bureau* was reviewed. Beginning in February 1947, individual and child tracing services were decentralized to the zonal tracing bureaus. The UNRRA CTB in Arolsen retained the central records office and mass tracing through newspapers and radio.

On July 1, 1947, with the closing down of UNRRA operations in Arolsen, the *Provisional Committee of the International Refugee Organization* took over the UNRRA *Central Tracing Bureau* with "three main functions: 1) collective search, 2) formation of a library and catalogue, and 3) tracing on an international scale."[34] In addition, the CTB was to coordinate work of the national tracing bureaus. To carry this out, the help of the *International Committee of the Red Cross* (ICRC) was enlisted, and the ICRC senior tracing expert, Mr. Maurice Thudichum, was seconded to help convert the *Central Tracing Bureau* into an *International Tracing Service*. The mandate of the ITS was "to include [...] the tracing of all non-German nationals, and of such German nationals as would be eligible under the constitution of IRO, who have disappeared by reason of the War."[35]

The *International Tracing Service* began operations on January 1, 1948. All governments and voluntary organizations involved in tracing work were invited to relate their activities to the work of the ITS and make arrangements to exchange information. The zonal tracing bureaus were to be subsumed within the ITS.

---

[33] JDC Archives, Records of the Geneva Office of the American Jewish Joint Distribution Committee, 1945–1954, file #ORG.430, Report submitted by the Director-General of the Seventh Session of the International Refugee Organization General Council entitled "The International Tracing Service. Brief Review of Its History and Activities," March, 1961, 3; http://search.archives.jdc.org/notebook_ext.asp?item=2146841.
[34] Ibid., 5.
[35] Ibid.

```
                                                              PLaza 7-7875

              CENTRAL LOCATION INDEX, Inc.
              165 WEST 46TH STREET, NEW YORK 19, N. Y.

OFFICERS                    MEMBER AGENCIES                    DIRECTORS
MOSES A. LEAVITT,   American Federation of International Institutes   ISAAC L. ASOFSKY,
   President        American Friends Service Committee         MRS. EDITH T. BREMER
RUTH LARNED,        The American Jewish Joint Distribution Committee, Inc.   MRS. HELEN H. BROWN
 Vice-President     Church World Service Committee on Displaced Persons   FRANCES C. BUTLER
ISAAC L. ASOFSKY,   Hebrew Sheltering and Immigrant Aid Society   RUTH LARNED
   Treasurer        International Social Service               MOSES A. LEAVITT
MRS. HELEN H. BROWN United Service for New Americans, Inc.     ANN S. PETLUCK
   Secretary                                                   ETTA DEUTSCH
                                                               Executive Director
In reply please refer to:            June 25, 1948

ROMANKIEWICZ, Estera, L-90785
62548: LR
                              RE: Estera ROMANKIEWICZ, born
                                  1/1/13 in Kosow, now living
Location Division                 at 28 Rue Rogier, Brussels,
American Joint Distrib. Committee Belgium.
Chocimska 18
Warsaw, Poland

Gentlemen:

Please refer to our inquiry of May 20, 1948 (a copy of which we
are enclosing for your convenience), concerning the possible rela-
tionship of the above-named to the following persons:

     Blima LEJZEROWICZ, in Dzirzoniow, Poland
     Estera ROMANKIEWICZ, under UNRRA Care in Germany
     Eliasz ROMANKIEWICZ, registered in Bedzin, Poland in 1945

We have just heard from the Aide Aux Israelites Victimes de la
Guerre in Brussels that Estera ROMANKIEWICZ in Belgium (see address
above) is indeed the cousin of all the above-mentioned persons.
She was given the address of Blima LEJZEROWICZ in Dzirzoniow, but
she would like to be put in contact with her cousins, Estera and
Eliasz.

Would you please send us the addresses of these people as soon as
possible. We are sending copies of this letter to the I.T.S. Germany
and the Central Committee of Liberated Jews in Munich.

In the event that Eliasz and Estera are no longer to be located,
would you please inform us so that we may continue the search for
them.

                                Sincerely yours,

                                Etta Deutsch
LR/lr                           Executive Director

cc: International Tracing Service, Germany
    Central Committee of Lib. Jews, Munich
```

Fig. 14: Letter from Etta Deutsch, Central Location Index, to JDC Location Division, Warsaw, regarding relatives of Estera Romankiewicz, now living in Brussels, Belgium, 25.6.1948 (JDC Archives, Records of the Warsaw Office of the American Joint Distribution Committee, 1945–1949, folder #1006; http://search.archives.jdc.org/notebook_ext.asp?item=2290048)

Given the non-permanent character of the *International Refugee Organization* (IRO), the ITS was intended to be a temporary function for a 2 to 3 year period. Work would be organized so as to facilitate a future transfer of remaining tracing functions from the IRO to a more permanent body, as yet not determined.

Under Maurice Thudichum's leadership, a three-year plan was designed beginning in 1948 for the reorganization, consolidation and coordination of tracing work. The greatest results were attained in 1949 when the child service bureau was expanded. The ITS master card index expanded from 1,976,499 cards in January of 1948 to 10,538,358 cards by the end of 1950.[36]

As of March 1950, individual tracing was ended, and responses to inquiries were based only on ITS information (and not sent to national tracing bureaus). From 1948–1950, the ITS handled 220,303 individual tracing requests from 100 countries. It was able to positively establish the fate of 26,797 individuals and tentatively establish the fate of a further 18,997. In addition, the records of tracing agencies that had ceased activity (such as the CLI and JDC tracing activities) were integrated into the files of the ITS.[37]

JDC and the *International Tracing Service*

In January 1948, Maurice Thudichum wrote to organizations involved with tracing services soliciting feedback. Etta Deutsch responded with a long letter describing the CLI; inquiring how JDC field offices could get maximum benefit from ITS services in cases where their local search is not successful; and asking what mechanism would be worked out with ITS local and central. Deutsch concluded that the CLI would be happy to cooperate and referred the ITS to JDC Overseas Headquarters in Paris to discuss these questions.[38]

By August 1948, JDC transferred the Berlin tracing records to the ITS and closed its Berlin location tracing office.[39] The JDC Paris headquarters Emigration Service registration cards were shared with the ITS, as were lists of survivors and

---

36 Ibid., 7–16.
37 Ibid., 12.
38 JDC Archives, Records of the New York Office of the American Jewish Joint Distribution Committee, 1945–1954, folder #ORG.431, Letter from Etta Deutsch to Mr. M. Thudichum, 12.1.1948; http://search.archives.jdc.org/notebook_ext.asp?item=2146882.
39 JDC Archives, Records of the Geneva Office of the American Jewish Joint Distribution Committee, 1945–1949, folder #SM.940, memorandum from Dorothy Levy of Location Service, Paris to All Country Directors and Field Offices regarding Transfer of Location Service from Berlin, Paris, 12.8.1948; http://search.archives.jdc.org/notebook_ext.asp?item=2545627.

```
Search Dept.
   I/24774                                    Sept. 8, 1948
File: 24617/3


To - International Tracing Service Headquarters - Germany.


                                 RE: Motel KWIATKOWSKI, b. 1911


       Dear Sirs,
              We find in the lists of the survivors of the Camp
       Libenau the name of Motel Kwiatkowski, born 1911 in Grodno;
       Miss Minnie Kwiatkowska, born 1924, daughter of Isaac and
       Rachel, at present Transit Camp in Bari, Italy, stated that
       the above named is her cousin and that she would like to get
       into contact with him.

              Therefore we shall greatly appreciate if you will
       find the present address of Motel Kwiatkowski liberated 1945
       at Kamp Libenau.

              Thanking you for your cooperation in advance, we are

                                         Very sincerely yours

                                         American Joint Distribution
                                                 Committee

                                                J. Gitler-Barski
                                                Secretary General


BM/fk
```

Fig. 15: Letter from J. Gitler-Barski, JDC Warsaw, to *International Tracing Service* Headquarters – Germany, regarding an inquiry from someone in a transit camp in Bari, Italy, about her cousin, whose name appeared on a list of survivors, 8.9.1948 (JDC Archives, Records of the Warsaw Office of the American Joint Distribution Committee, folder #618; http://search.archives.jdc.org/notebook_ext.asp?item=2231249)

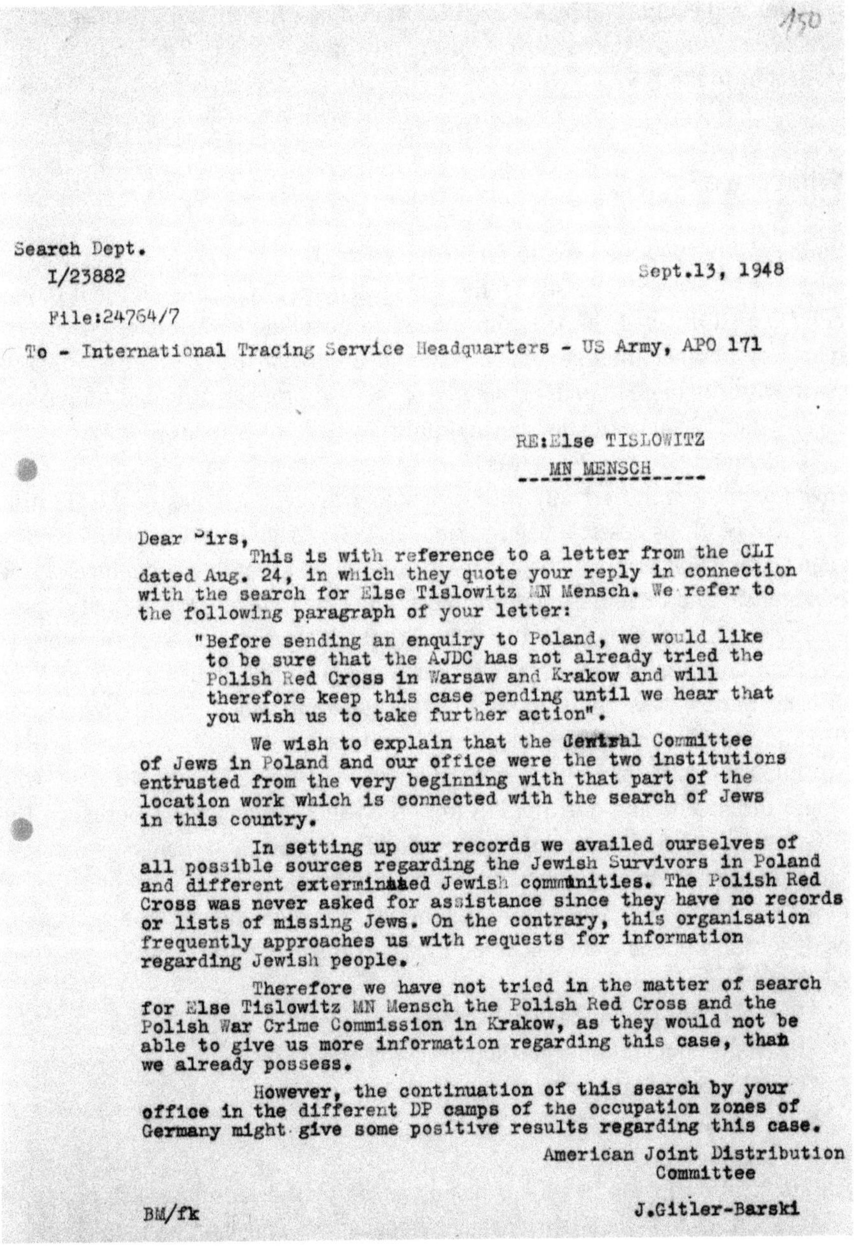

Search Dept.
I/23882

Sept.13, 1948

File:24764/7

To - International Tracing Service Headquarters - US Army, APO 171

RE: Else TISLOWITZ
MN MENSCH

Dear Sirs,
      This is with reference to a letter from the CLI dated Aug. 24, in which they quote your reply in connection with the search for Else Tislowitz MN Mensch. We refer to the following paragraph of your letter:

> "Before sending an enquiry to Poland, we would like to be sure that the AJDC has not already tried the Polish Red Cross in Warsaw and Krakow and will therefore keep this case pending until we hear that you wish us to take further action".

      We wish to explain that the Central Committee of Jews in Poland and our office were the two institutions entrusted from the very beginning with that part of the location work which is connected with the search of Jews in this country.

      In setting up our records we availed ourselves of all possible sources regarding the Jewish Survivors in Poland and different exterminated Jewish communities. The Polish Red Cross was never asked for assistance since they have no records or lists of missing Jews. On the contrary, this organisation frequently approaches us with requests for information regarding Jewish people.

      Therefore we have not tried in the matter of search for Else Tislowitz MN Mensch the Polish Red Cross and the Polish War Crime Commission in Krakow, as they would not be able to give us more information regarding this case, than we already possess.

      However, the continuation of this search by your office in the different DP camps of the occupation zones of Germany might give some positive results regarding this case.

American Joint Distribution Committee

BM/fk

J.Gitler-Barski

Fig. 16: Letter from J. Gitler-Barski, JDC Warsaw, to *International Tracing Service* Headquarters – US Army, APO 171, regarding search procedures and location work in Poland, 13.9.1948 (JDC Archives, Records of the Warsaw Office of the American Joint Distribution Committee, folder #618; http://search.archives.jdc.org/notebook_ext.asp?item=2231121)

refugees and emigration lists from JDC local offices. In May 1949, the *Central Location Index* closed down in New York, and copies of the CLI registration cards were sent to the ITS.

What Next?

By the fall of 1949 the need to find a successor to handle ITS activities was urgent. The IRO was scheduled to terminate its activities in June 1950. The IRO General Council directed the Director-General to negotiate with interested governments or another international or inter-governmental body. Discussions took place with the *International Committee of the Red Cross* and yielded no positive result. The ITS was extended beyond June 30, 1950, on a reduced scale.

In March 1950, a decision was taken to enter into negotiations with the *Allied High Commission* in Germany with a view to arrange a takeover of the ITS from the IRO as early as possible before March 31, 1951. As of January 1, 1951, the *Allied High Commission* assumed responsibility and set up a working committee of British, French, and US representatives to negotiate the transfer. Operational responsibility was assumed as of April 1, 1951, with the IRO seconding tracing experts to the *High Commission* in Germany for 6 months. In April, 1951, the *International Tracing Service* was transferred from the *International Refugee Organization* (IRO) to the Allied High Command in Germany.

Intensive discussions then ensued among governments and NGOs on who would ultimately take over the ITS from the Allied Command in Germany. The JDC Archives includes extensive correspondence among Jewish organizations around the world trying to determine what the best alternatives for the auspices of the ITS would be for the Jewish community. The advantages and disadvantages of several options were discussed in this correspondence:

- Germany?
- International Committee of the Red Cross?
- UN High Commissioner for Refugees and DPs?
- US Library of Congress?
- The Claims Conference?

JDC archival records reflect the concerns raised by the various Jewish organizations, attempts to build a consensus preference, and consultation among organ-

izations and with government officials.[40] These letters and memoranda highlight the concerns of the Jewish community, which focused on the following issues:
- The preservation of the records needed to be assured.
- Nazi victims needed to turn to these records to prove entitlement to indemnification.
- Recognizing the role of the international governing body to be established, Jewish organizations were eager to ensure that Israel would be represented on the governing body.
- The attitudes of the Director of the body were critical, and the Jewish groups sought to ensure that the selected director would not be antisemitic or biased.

In 1955, an *International Commission* was established as the supervising body of the ITS, which remained in Arolsen, Germany. The *International Commission* today includes representatives from eleven member states, including Belgium, France, the Federal Republic of Germany, Greece, Israel, Italy, Luxembourg, the Netherlands, Poland, the United Kingdom, and the United States of America. The Federal Republic of Germany agreed to fund the operating costs of the ITS. In June 1955, Nicolas R. Burchhardt assumed the newly established position of ITS director. Burckhardt was affiliated with the ICRC which covered the ITS director's salary. Some of the concerns raised by Jewish groups came to haunt the ITS in subsequent years.

Conclusion

JDC Headquarters and its local offices around the world worked unstintingly to rescue and provide relief services for Jews fleeing Nazi Europe. The organization's prior experience and its relationships with local communities and with international and local agencies were advantages that helped JDC to galvanize aid where possible. JDC's prior experience with family tracing and search activities dating back to the First World War laid the groundwork for its extensive networking efforts in the Second World War era with US relatives of refugees in Europe who required assistance with affidavits and funds for visas and transportation. Likewise, these networking activities helped to reunite families in the US with their European relatives. JDC workers pursued these family search and tracing

---

[40] For examples of this correspondence, see: JDC Archives, Records of the Geneva Office of the American Jewish Joint Distribution Committee, folders #ORG.430 and #ORG.431.

activities with passion, expertise, empathy, and a sense of personal and communal mission, collaborating closely with the *International Red Cross* and with UNRRA *Central Tracing Bureaus*. Discussions that began in 1947 that envisioned the establishment of a more centralized *International Tracing Service* made *Central Location Index* and JDC leaders uneasy. They wondered whether a more distant and standardized ITS would have the knowledge, expertise, and sense of urgency that JDC local offices and the CLI staff had. Nevertheless, JDC leaders sought to cooperate with efforts to establish the IRO *International Tracing Service* and copied the ITS on all tracing correspondence. Beginning in August 1948, JDC began gradually closing down its tracing bureaus and transferring records to the ITS. In May 1949, the CLI ceased its operations.

The longer-term permanent fate and auspices of the *International Tracing Service* became political questions. In the decades following the establishment of the ITS in Arolsen, Germany, as an independent body with an international board, some of the concerns of Jewish agencies proved to be well-founded.

Christine Schmidt
Those Left Behind

Early Search Efforts in Wartime and Post-War Britain

Abstract: This chapter examines early search efforts in Britain, particularly the creation of the *United Kingdom Search Bureau* for German, Austrian, and Stateless Persons from Central Europe (UKSB), within the context of Jewish refugee migration to Britain and the history of Anglo-Jewish responses to the Holocaust. It will consider the early involvement of the *British Red Cross Society* (BRCS) in the search and the foreshadowing of its later exclusion from centralised search machinery established in post-war occupied Germany. It also briefly analyses how tracing might have been instrumentalised for purposes other than strictly humanitarian ones, reflecting wariness on the part of the British government to resolve the position of refugees in Britain. By examining the organisation of search efforts in Britain as early as 1943, precedents for and complexities of search efforts developed at the end of the war in Continental Europe can be more fully elucidated. The history of searching in Britain reveals both the British and transnational elements of tracing as well as the confrontation with loss and move toward recovery after the Holocaust, and more specifically, how Jewish refugees in Britain and the communities that interacted with them made sense of the Holocaust as greater understanding of the extent of destruction materialised.

Introduction

"I am sorry to have to inform you that we have not been able so far to trace your parents, who were indeed last inhabitants of the Theresienstadt camp. Although we think we may expect bad news…there is still a little hope that they might turn up in the near future," wrote Dr B. Mogendorf, a friend of the Gross family in the Netherlands, to Dorothea Gross in Birmingham, England in July 1945.[1] Originally from Breslau, the Gross family had become separated by the Nazis' persecution of the Jews, with the children of the family fleeing to England and the parents remaining behind on the Continent. The reply Dorothea Gross received from Dr Mogendorf is all too familiar to those who have engaged in examining the history

---

1 Dr BEM Mogendorf, Herzogenbush, to Dorothea Gross, Birmingham, 30.7.1945. Gross family document collection, 1183, Wiener Library Archive.

ϴ OpenAccess. © 2020 Christine Schmidt, published by De Gruyter. [CC BY-NC-ND] This work is licensed under the Creative Commons Attribution-NonCommercial-NoDerivatives 4.0 License.
https://doi.org/10.1515/9783110665376-006

of the *International Tracing Service* (ITS) and the post-war search for the missing, as well as to those who have assisted families in tracing the fates of their relatives. The archives of the ITS, now *Arolsen Archives*, particularly within the largely unexplored depths of the *Tracing and Documentation files*, abound with myriad similar examples of uncertainty, allusions to last sightings and rumours about the whereabouts of loved ones, and the desperate attempts of survivors to learn their ultimate fates. In some cases, intimations about individual fates were revealed to family and friends through correspondence between a variety of communal and voluntary organisations, agencies and international bodies that worked to find and reunite missing people after the Holocaust, although these groups did not all share the same motivation in carrying out their work and their cooperation was far from neatly aligned. The case of Dorothea Gross and her family is one of millions like this, but in many ways it embodies Jewish refugee experiences in Britain and their fragile link to the Continent via the search for family members. It also points to the history of burgeoning Holocaust victim search efforts created in Britain, which in some ways were a forerunner of later centralised searching organised in liberated Europe.[2]

The Gross family were assimilated middle class German Jews living in Breslau at the time the Nazis rose to power – Dorothea's father Wilhelm was a professor of engineering, and her mother, Gertrud Gross-Sachs, the daughter of wealthy industrialists. Due to anti-Jewish laws, Wilhelm was deprived of his professorship and deported to Buchenwald following the events of the November Pogrom (*Kristallnacht*) in November 1938. He was released five weeks later on the proviso that he and his family, which included Gertrud and their three children, Dorothea (aged 18), her older brother Karl, and Klaus, the youngest (aged 10), would leave Germany. Wilhelm and Gertrud managed to arrange for their children to find refuge in Britain, whilst they fled to the Netherlands in 1939 to wait for visas for the United States. The Nazi occupation caught up with them there. At various points, the family received assistance from relatives abroad, professional networks and the *Society for the Protection of Science and Learning* (later known as the *Council for At-Risk Academics*, or CARA). The children maintained contact with their parents in Roermond via Red Cross telegrams until these messages ended abruptly in early May 1944. The *Dutch Red Cross Society* replied to Karl that Wilhelm and Gertrud were no longer in the Westerbork transit camp and that they had been potentially transferred to Theresienstadt. It explained that it was unable to forward further messages on. Indeed, as was con-

---

[2] With thanks to Elizabeth Anthony, Ben Barkow, Gábor Kádar, Jan Lambertz and Dan Stone for their comments on and discussion of this chapter.

firmed to their children in 1946, Wilhelm and Gertrud were deported via Westerbork to the Theresienstadt ghetto in January 1944, and in October 1944 to Auschwitz, where they are presumed to have perished.[3]

A significant part of the Gross family's document collection, which was deposited at *The Wiener Holocaust Library* in London in 1993, recounts Dorothea and Karl's efforts to uncover their parents' fates and to maintain tenuous relationships with surviving relatives and friends, who had fled to the United States or who had remained on the Continent. Dorothea and Karl Gross wrote to as many contacts as possible, and the correspondence gradually reveals information about the fate of their parents. Amidst the letters related to tracing is prewar correspondence from Wilhelm Gross, which illustrates his determination to secure passage for his children first before he or his wife could escape. Wilhelm's letters were salvaged by neighbours and brought to Dorothea Gross in 1946, along with Wilhelm and Gertrud's few remaining possessions that had not been stolen or destroyed.

In many ways, the contours of the Gross family's story reveal the history of the search for missing Jewish relatives from Britain, as those who had become separated from their families due to Nazi persecution were met by restrictive and selective British immigration policies and tried to maintain contact, where possible, with those left behind. Although correspondence usually (and necessarily, due to wartime censorship) carried only the faintest outlines of the experiences of those persecuted in Europe, the severing of this connection often prompted Jewish refugees in Britain to return to the same organisations and agencies that had assisted them with their passage to Britain to begin their search. The quickly accumulating requests compelled representatives of these various organisations to establish a centralised search effort in 1943 in what came to be known in 1944 as the *United Kingdom Search Bureau* for German, Austrian and Stateless Persons from Central Europe (hereafter, UKSB). The UKSB was affiliated with the Foreign Relations department of the *British Red Cross Society* (BRCS), which had been set up in May 1940 and which already had formed a tracing service. The Foreign Relations department dealt with queries beyond Displaced Persons, allied nationals or persecuted Jews. The UKSB bureau was established in London to work with the Foreign Relations department of the BRCS.[4] The name and focus of the UKSB, which dealt extensively with Jew-

---

[3] Tracing and Documentation File 5819 for Wilhelm Gross, 6.3.3.2/90692062–90692086/ITS Digital Archive, Wiener Library; Tracing and Documentation File 5820 for Klara Anna Gertrud Gross-Sachs, 6.3.3.2/90692089–90692108/ITS Digital Archive, Wiener Library.
[4] Jenny Edkins: *Missing: Persons and Politics*, New York: Cornell University Press, 2011, 65. See also PG Cambray and GGB Briggs: *The Official Record of the Humanitarian Record of the Human-*

ish missing persons, is a reflection of the context of Jewish refugee migration to Britain, as it sought to fulfil what it identified as a need to trace individuals who did not fall within the scope of work of other tracing operations, including the national Red Cross agencies in Europe. The work of the UKSB to trace Jewish missing persons from its base in London is the focus of this article.

By examining the organisation of search efforts in Britain as early as 1943, precedents for and complexities of tracing and searching organised at the end of the war in Continental Europe can be more fully elucidated. The history of the early search in Britain reveals both the British and transnational elements of tracing as well as the confrontation with loss and move toward recovery after the Holocaust, and more specifically, how Jewish refugees in Britain and the communities that interacted with them made sense of the Holocaust as greater understanding of the extent of destruction materialised. While this chapter cannot treat the entirety of this topic and reflects research still in progress, the core of the present work derives from a recent exhibition, entitled *Fate Unknown*, co-curated with Dan Stone (Holocaust Research Institute at Royal Holloway, University of London) and shown in 2018 at *The Wiener Holocaust Library* in London.[5] The history of the Library itself, an institution initially created by German Jewish refugees and involved in the collection and dissemination of early Holocaust documentation and research (though not specifically active in post-war tracing efforts), is inexorably linked to the history of early searching in Britain, not least because the creation of its person-related archival collection derives in part from families' search for missing relatives. Family document collections of German-speaking Jewish refugees and their descendants form a significant part of the Library's repository, particularly as the Library turned in the 1950s and 1960s to a more "victim-centred" approach in its research and collections strategy.[6] The *Fate Unknown* exhibition examined the search for the missing

---

itarian Services of the War Organisation of the British Red Cross Society and Order of St. John of Jerusalem, 1939–1947, London, 1949, 473. For the complexities and ambiguities of tracing wounded and disappeared servicemen and the notification of relatives during World War I, which in many respects served as a model for later civilian tracing efforts, see Eric F. Schneider: "The British Red Cross Wounded and Missing Enquiry Bureau: A Case of Truth-Telling in the Great War", in *War in History,* 4, 1997, 296–315; and Jay M. Winter: *Sites of Memory, Sites of Mourning,* Cambridge: Cambridge University Press, 1995, 35–42.

5 Christine Schmidt and Dan Stone: *Fate Unknown: The Search for the Missing after the Holocaust,* North Charleston: KDP/Createspace, 2018.

6 Ben Barkow: *Alfred Wiener and the Making of the Holocaust Library,* London: Vallentine Mitchell, 1997. See also EHRI Document Blog: Christine Schmidt: "Visualising Methodology in the Wiener Library's Early Testimonies' Project". Available at: https://blog.ehri-project.eu/2018/01/16/wiener-librarys-early-testimonies/. Last accessed: 25.9.2018.

after the Holocaust, with a focus on the history of the ITS and the foundations of these efforts in Britain and elsewhere, which later coalesced into centralised tracing in Arolsen.

This chapter will situate the history of early search efforts in Britain within the context of Jewish refugee migration to Britain and by extension, the history of Anglo-Jewish responses to the Holocaust. Beyond the scope of this analysis is an extensive consideration of Jewish refugee experiences of searching and how they made sense of that search, although this study will point to new findings in this area.[7] It will consider the early involvement of the *Red Cross* in aspects of searching for German, Austrian and stateless persons from Britain and how its involvement foreshadowed the reasons for its later exclusion from centralised search machinery established in post-war occupied Germany. It will also briefly consider how tracing might have been instrumentalised for purposes other than strictly humanitarian ones, both on the Continent and in Britain, reflecting wariness on the part of the British government to resolve the position of refugees who had settled in Britain.

Anglo-Jewish and Government Responses to Refugees

The history of the search for the missing during and immediately after the war in Britain is intertwined with Jewish migration to Britain in the 1930s, and by extension, the relief efforts and humanitarian responses of the Anglo-Jewish community. The community formed the predominant bodies that lobbied for and facilitated Jewish immigration in response to the Nazis' persecution of the Jews in Germany, Austria and Czechoslovakia in the 1930s. An extensive body of literature treats the topic of Jewish migration from the Continent to Britain from a variety of angles, including accounts written by contemporaries as the events unfolded, on the rash decision of the government to intern refugees in 1940, on the ambiguities and complexities of British and Anglo-Jewish attitudes towards Jewish refugees, on xenophobia and antisemitism within Government and in British society more broadly, on the *Kindertransport* scheme, as well as the cultural, so-

---

[7] See Jan Lambertz: "Vermisstenschicksal und jüdische Erfahrung: Das Wissen vom Holocaust in Briefen aus der Nachkriegszeit", in Frank Bajohr and Sybille Steinbacher (eds.): '... *Zeugnis ablegen bis zum letzten*': *Tagebücher und persönliche Zeugnisse aus der Zeit des Nationalsozialismus und des Holocaust*, Göttingen: Wallstein, 2015 and Jan Lambertz: "Early Post-War Holocaust Knowledge and the Search for Europe's Missing Jews", in *Patterns of Prejudice*, 53, 2019, 61–73.

cial and economic impact of Jewish refugees in Britain.[8] However, scant attention has been paid to the history of tracing and search efforts from Britain and its relationship to burgeoning post-war international efforts, especially as a distinct element of relief extended by the already overstretched charities of the Anglo-Jewish community. Early tracing in Britain of Holocaust victims is most often referenced, albeit briefly, in connection to the 'origins' story of the *International Tracing Service*; the ITS is often described as having its roots in search efforts conceived and developed in London in 1943, but generally not further elaborated.[9]

Britain, like other countries in Europe, did not consider itself a final destination for immigrants, which as many historians have argued, provides context for the restrictive and selective nature of its immigration practices and policies in

---

[8] See, among others, Norman Bentwich: *The Refugees from Germany, April 1933 to December 1935*, London: G. Allen & Unwin, Ltd., 1936; François Lafitte: *The Internment of Aliens*, Harmondsworth: Penguin Books, 1940; AJ Sherman: *Island Refuge: Britain and Refugees from the Third Reich, 1933–39*, Abingdon: Routledge, 1973; Bernard Wasserstein: *Britain and the Jews of Europe*, London: Leicester University Press, 1979; Tony Kushner: *Persistence of Prejudice: Antisemitism in British Society during the Second World War*, New York: Manchester University Press, 1989, and *The Holocaust and the Liberal Imagination*, Cambridge, MA: Blackwell Publishers, 1994; Richard Bolchover: *British Jewry and the Holocaust*, Liverpool: Liverpool University Press, 1993; Ronald Stent: "Jewish Refugee Organisations", in Werner Mosse and Julius Carlebach, et al. (eds.): *Second Chance: Two Centuries of German-Speaking Jews in the United Kingdom*, Tübingen: JCB Mohr, 1991; David Cesarani: *Britain and the Holocaust*, London: Holocaust Educational Trust, 1998; Amy Zahl Gottlieb: *Men of Vision: Anglo-Jewry's Aid to Victims of the Nazi Regime, 1933–1945*, London: Weidenfeld & Nicolson, 1998; Louise London: *Whitehall and the Jews, 1933–1948*, Cambridge: Cambridge University Press, 2001; Pamela Shatzkes: *Holocaust and Rescue: Impotent or Indifferent? Anglo-Jewry, 1938–1945*, London: Palgrave Macmillan, 2002; Marion Berghahn: *Continental Britons: German-Jewish Refugees from Nazi Germany*, New York: Berghahn Books, 2007; and Anthony Grenville: *Encounters with Albion: Britain and the British in Texts by Jewish Refugees from Nazism*, Taylor & Francis, 2017.

[9] For instance, see Suzanne Brown-Fleming: *Nazi Persecution and Postwar Repercussions: The International Tracing Service Archive and Holocaust Research*, Lanham, MD: Rowman & Littlefield, 2016, 3; Jennifer Rodgers: "From the 'Archive of Horrors' to the 'Shop Window of Democracy': The International Tracing Service and the Transatlantic Politics of the Past", Phd Diss., University of Pennsylvania, 2014; Silke von der Emde: "Women in the Archive: Locating the International Tracing Service in German Memory Work", in *Seminar: A Journal of Germanic Studies*, 53, 2017, 202–18; Jenny Edkins: "Chapter 3: Tracing Services", in *Missing: Persons and Politics*, Ithaca: Cornell University Press, 2011, 58–83; Dan Stone: *Fate Unknown: Tracing the Missing after the Holocaust and World War II*, forthcoming (Oxford: Oxford University Press, 2021). See also Maurice Thudichum's history of the ITS, The Tracing of Missing Persons in Germany on an International Scale with particular reference to the Problem of UNRRA, 6.1.1/82492860–82492908/ITS Digital Archive, Wiener Library; History of the International Tracing Service, 1945–1951, 6.1.1./82492910–82493152/ITS Digital Archive, Wiener Library.

the 1930s and their impact on Jewish migration. Nevertheless, the history of Britain during the Holocaust is ultimately bound up with Jewish migration and transmigration. Between 1933 and 1939, approximately 90,000 refugees were admitted to Britain, with approximately 85 to 90 per cent being Jews or those fleeing due to anti-Jewish laws, including at least 70,000 Jewish refugees by the outbreak of war in 1939.[10] With the arrival of Jewish refugees in 1933, pro-active leaders of the Anglo-Jewish community negotiated in support of incoming refugees' permission to remain temporarily in the country by guaranteeing, on behalf of Britain's Jewish community, that the community would bear expenses associated with maintaining and accommodating refugees. This assured the government that no Jewish refugee from Nazi Germany would become a charge on public funds, despite their being permitted in only exceptional cases to take up employment upon their immigration (for example, women who worked as domestic servants or, in fewer numbers, were permitted to work as nurses).[11] The acceptance of Jewish refugees in Britain was predicated on the assumption that most Jewish refugees would ultimately transmigrate to other countries.[12]

Consisting of representatives from various communal organisations, the *German Jewish Refugees Committee* (JRC; later temporarily called the *German Jewish Aid Committee*), was thus created in March 1933 to orchestrate the reception, accommodation and, from 1938 with the introduction of visas, the selection and approval of German and Austrian Jewish refugees. In March 1936, the *Council for German Jewry*, which worked closely with the *American Jewish Joint Distribution Committee* (JDC, or commonly known as the Joint) was established. When the JRC began to cooperate with the Council, it tapped into an international framework for assisting Jewish refugees. The JRC also cooperated with the *Central British Fund for German Jewry* (CBF, which would later become *World Jewish Relief*), which provided "spiritual, financial and organizational aid for German Jewry from the very beginning of the Nazi regime".[13] As historian David Silber-

---

[10] For a discussion of the difficulties in reaching precise figures of incoming refugees and those who transmigrated, see London: *Whitehall*, 11–12 and AJ Sherman: *Island Refuge*, 269–272. This is due in part, according to Sherman and others, to under-reporting during the pre-war period as well as according to London, the "Home Office's loss of control over the details of the influx."
[11] Jillian Davidson: "German Jewish Women", and Tony Kushner: "An Alien Occupation: Jewish Refugees and Domestic Service in Britain, 1933–1948", in Julius Carlebach et al. (eds.): *Second Chance: Two Centuries of German-Speaking Jews in the United Kingdom*, Tübingen: J.C.B. Mohr, 1991, 533–552, 552–578.
[12] Louise London: "British Government Policy and Jewish Refugees, 1933–45", in *Patterns of Prejudice*, 23, 1989, 28.
[13] David Silberklang: "Jewish Politics and Rescue: The Founding of the Council for German Jewry", in *Holocaust and Genocide Studies*, 73, 1993, 333–371, here 334.

klang has emphasised, Jewish organisations that supported Jewish emigration from Nazi-dominated territory, whether they were Zionist-oriented like the *Jewish Agency*, or non-Zionist, like the CBF or *Council for German Jewry*, which focused on helping Jews emigrate to Palestine as well as other destinations, were dependent "upon governments and international bodies, be they British, German, or American governments, or the League of Nations."[14]

The assessment in the historiography of the nature and effectiveness of Anglo-Jewry's response to events in Nazi Germany and the help provided to German-speaking Jewish refugees has ranged from celebratory to critical. Some historians have offered more positive assessments of these organisations' work on behalf of refugees, citing the practical accomplishments of communal leaders such as Otto Schiff, Leonard Montefiore, Anthony de Rothschild and others in creating networks of assistance, leveraging limited resources and private donations in wartime and providing an effective intercessory role with the British government authorities, even though these efforts did little to change government policy.[15] Other scholars argue that some of the work of Anglo-Jewish bodies "strengthened the restrictionist slant of [government] policy in the pre-war period."[16] They maintain that the JRC and its chairman, Otto Schiff, supported government favouritism toward Jewish refugees who were more easily able to assimilate or re-emigrate, and children and young people were prioritised over others because they were more likely to assimilate or could be prepared for ultimate emigration to Palestine. Likewise, Jews from outside Germany and Austria who wished to flee did not benefit initially from the work of the JRC. This line of criticism emphasises that Schiff and the JRC operated with the constant fear of inflaming domestic antisemitism, one of the same reasons that British officials and politicians cited for maintaining restrictive policies.

By 1938, the Évian conference had confirmed that no country was willing to take in a significant number of Jewish refugees. And while Britain slightly opened its borders, its visa application procedures remained complicated with long wait times, which translated into a painfully slow response to the Nazis' increasingly violent actions against Jews in the Reich. After *Kristallnacht*, a ground swell of humanitarian and public outcry prompted the British government to relax some of its policies, after which numbers of refugees potentially climbed to nearly 80,000 – with 90 per cent of these being Jewish refugees from Germany, Austria and Czechoslovakia. Pre-selection of refugees prior to their arrival in Brit-

---

14 Ibid., 347.
15 Sherman, Gottlieb, Shatzkes, and Grenville.
16 Here, London: "British Government Policy", 29.

ain was undertaken by the voluntary and relief organisations. The terms of immigration were especially alleviated around the intake of children, provided they were sponsored and maintained, so that some 10,000 unaccompanied children were permitted entry into the UK on what came to be known as the *Kindertransporte*.[17] With the outbreak of war, several thousands of Jewish refugees further migrated to the United States and elsewhere. Fearing a "fifth column", the British government interned "enemy aliens" in 1940, including many Jewish refugees, and deported some 8,000 to Canada and Australia. Admission policy during the war again became very strict, although some refugees still managed to enter. With the outbreak of war, all visas granted to "enemy nationals" were invalidated. War refugees were admitted at a trickling pace, and only when it suited the Home Office. Moreover, emigration to Palestine was restricted in response to the Arab Revolt.[18]

By March 1939, representatives of most pro-refugee aid organisations were headquartered in Bloomsbury House in London, which became known colloquially as "heartbreak house". At the time of the *Anschluss*, there were some 11,000 clients registered with the *Jewish Refugees Committee* at Bloomsbury House alone, a number that does not reflect those who had emigrated to Britain and who did not need sponsorship or assistance. By September 1939, the number had climbed to 60,000.[19] The resources of Anglo-Jewish aid organisations committed to helping at least some Jewish refugees were overstretched in part due to delays in re-emigration; in December, the government agreed to inject some public funding into refugee assistance schemes. This state of affairs prompted considerable criticism of the voluntary organisations because they became even more selective about their assistance; resulting in accusations of favouritism and inefficiency.[20] With the outbreak of war, re-emigration was largely stymied, further admissions restrictions were introduced, and mass internment in 1940 began.[21]

---

17 See, among others, Jennifer Craig-Norton: "Contesting the Kindertransport as a 'Model' Refugee Response", in *European Judaism*, 50, 2017, 24–33.
18 See London: *Whitehall*, and "British Government Policy".
19 AJ Sherman and Pamela Shatzkes: "Otto M Schiff (1875–1952), Unsung Rescuer", in *Leo Baeck Institute Year Book*, 54, 2009, 262.
20 Pamela Shatzkes, *Holocaust and Rescue*, 257–258.
21 Sherman and Shatzkes, 265; London, *Whitehall*, 131–140. See also Rachel Pistol: *Internment during the Second World War*, London: Bloomsbury Academic, 2017.

The *UK Search Bureau* and the *British Red Cross Society*

In the midst of wartime constraints, in 1943 a committee was formed from many of the same voluntary organisations that had been providing refugee assistance. They met initially in November to discuss the creation of a central search office (at first called the *Central Search Bureau*) to handle the accumulation of a high volume of enquiries that had been submitted to the various organisations. In many respects, supporting communication and searches for lost relatives was a natural extension of the assistance already being provided to refugees. Chaired by Otto Schiff and administered by his secretary, Joan Stiebel, and later, Anita Wolf-Warburg, the groups represented at the first meetings in November and December 1943 included the *Jewish Refugees Committee, Austrian Centre, Czech Trust Fund, Refugee Children's Movement, Friends Committee for Refugee* (Quakers), *Polish Jewish Refugee Fund, Association of Jewish Refugees and Women's Voluntary Services*, and the *Foreign Relations Department of the British Red Cross Society* (of which the Search Bureau became a section), among others that would later affiliate with the Bureau, including the aforementioned *Society for the Protection of Science and Learning*. Eventually, some fifty-seven different organisations became affiliated with the Search Bureau. The initial meeting minutes of the Committee acknowledged that all of the organisations represented had received enquiries and had begun to conduct searches for missing persons independently, usually via the *British Red Cross*, which had created a tracing service in cooperation with the *Red Cross* in Geneva.[22] However, the Committee recognised that there were gaps in the populations being served by their efforts. It also realised that as enquiries flowed in, there were considerable inefficiencies and overlap in their endeavours to trace missing people, owing in part to the fact that enquirers submitted requests to more than one organisation. With limited resources, the committee felt it was necessary to have a centralised clearing-house in Britain for queries.[23] The Committee began to explore the possibilities of creating a central index of all refugees in Britain who might wish to be reunit-

---

[22] Minutes of Meeting to Discuss Establishment of Centralised Search Bureau Held at Bloomsbury House, London, W.C.1. on Friday, 17th December, 1943, at 2.30 p.m. and Notes of meeting held at Bloomsbury House on 25 November 1943, dated 8 December 1943, HO 294/169, National Archives, Kew; Edkins: *Missing*, 63–65.

[23] Minutes of Meeting to Discuss Establishment of Centralised Search Bureau, 17th December, 1943, HO 294/169, National Archives, Kew.

ed with relatives or friends on the Continent and also to assist in answering the quickly accumulating enquiries.

The question of who would be served by the Bureau remained of prime concern. The plan that developed for the *United Kingdom Search Bureau* (as the *Central Search Bureau* came to be called in May 1944 upon the prompting of the *British Red Cross*[24]) notes that although the *British Red Cross* already was accepting and registering enquiries that had been forwarded to Geneva, "in the case of all the Aliens in the United Kingdom, there exist Red Cross organisations who collect enquiries from their own Nationals for their own Nationals". The Committee went on to justify the need for the UKSB because "this is not the case with German, Austrian and Stateless persons from Central Europe"; there was a need for a search body that would specifically assist these populations.[25] Looking ahead to the end of hostilities in Europe, the UKSB conceived their index as a first stage, until a larger, pan-European index could be created. The UKSB's index would later assist the fledgling *United Nations Relief and Rehabilitation Administration* (UNRRA), formed in 1943, in its task of registering Displaced Persons, who would undoubtedly seek to be reunited with relatives and would submit enquiries for information about missing family.[26]

During these first meetings the Committee debated who would and would not be indexed centrally by the UKSB. By the December 1943 meeting of the UKSB, the Foreign Office was represented by Major Eyre Carter. Dr Gustav Kullman, the deputy of Sir Herbert Emerson, the High Commissioner for Refugees and director of the *Intergovernmental Committee on Refugees*, was also present. Foreshadowing the challenge of so-called "hard core" DP cases, Kullman felt that any register "should be confined to long-term refugees, i.e., those who could not return to their country of origin, now resident in countries not covered by any existing organisations, i.e., Great Britain, the Iberian Peninsula, Sweden, Switzerland, Turkey and the Western Hemisphere." Carter countered that the registration should be all-inclusive, "with indexing of names to be carried out geographically in each country, since it would be impossible to determine who at

---

[24] Minutes of Meeting of the United Kingdom Search Bureau for German, Austrian and Stateless People from Central Europe, Held at Bloomsbury House, Bloomsbury Street, WC1 on Monday, May 15th, 1944 at 2:45pm, HO 294/169, National Archives, Kew.
[25] United Kingdom Search Bureau for German, Austrian and Stateless Persons from Central Europe. Bloomsbury House, Bloomsbury Street, London WC1. 1944. FO 371/42801; HO 294/169, National Archives, Kew.
[26] On the history of UNRRA, see Jessica Reinisch: "Auntie UNRRA at the Crossroads", in *Past and Present*, 218, Supplement 8, 2013, 70–97; and Reinisch: "Internationalism in Relief: the Birth (and Death) of UNRRA", in *Past and Present*, 2011, 258–289.

first instance was a long-term refugee." This aim for inclusivity was presumably one of the driving factors for the Committee to assume that the *British Red Cross* would be a key partner in its work, since it already had experience with large-scale registration and tracing and by 1944, had instituted a full-fledged service under the direction of Sydney Jeanetta Warner.[27] However, by the following summer, it was clear that other motivations and priorities would supersede the largely humanitarian intentions of the voluntary organisations, including the *British Red Cross*.

Before moving on to a consideration of these shifting priorities, however, it's important to also examine briefly the role of the *British Red Cross* and the *International Red Cross* in early search efforts in Britain. For the foundations of the *UK Search Bureau* confirm that the *Red Cross* seemed to be the natural partner for future tracing work and would lead in convening centralised efforts. At the December 1943 meeting, the *Red Cross card file* was held up as a model for future tracing work. Because tracing relied on maintaining lines of communication, the Committee recognised that the ICRC was the "only agency at present able to maintain contact between all belligerents".[28] The meeting on December 1943 concluded that the *Central Office for Refugees* at Bloomsbury House would act as a Clearinghouse in Britain for all the different organisations working to search on behalf of refugees. Individual agencies should supply to the clearinghouse triplicate cards for each case, based on the card provided by the IRC and printed by the *Central Office* for the agencies'.[29] Warner confirmed that the BRCS would largely act as a centre of transmission at this point because it had decentralised its search activities to various Allied Red Cross societies; she stated: "The British Red Cross were perfectly willing to offer their services as such a distributing centre, to whom the military, UNRRA and other bodies could send messages for forwarding through the appropriate bodies." Warner further emphasised that "the cloak of the Red Cross would be thrown over everyone as long as war conditions lasted."[30] At the meeting in May 1944, some populations were specifically excluded from the UKSB's index; for example, Warner declined to include Hungarians and Romanians because "there were many Balkan nationals in the country

---

[27] Minutes of Meeting to discuss establishment of Centralised Search Bureau, held at Bloomsbury House, London WC1 on Thursday, November 25 [1943] at 3pm, HO 294/169, National Archives, Kew.

[28] Ibid.

[29] Minutes of Meeting to discuss establishment of Centralised Search Bureau, held at Bloomsbury House, London WC1 on Friday, 17th December 1943 at 2:30pm, HO 294/169, National Archives, Kew.

[30] Ibid.

who were not refugees".[31] The UKSB Committee aimed for the BRCS to treat its Bloomsbury House headquarters "as an Allied Red Cross Society".[32] In April 1944, the parameters of the UKSB were agreed, including how Polish and Czech citizens would be traced in cooperation with the *Polish Jewish Refugee Fund* and the *Czech Refugee Trust*. There was still fear on the part of those whose families remained behind in occupied territories that they would endanger their relatives by enquiring after them.

The Network and Resources of the UKSB

A significant challenge faced by the UKSB was a persistent lack of resources and shortages in supply, including paper and index cards.[33] They operated with limited staff and financial capacity, but managed to leverage the work of both paid and voluntary staff, who worked for the Bureau but also fielded enquiries within the affiliated organisations in Britain and abroad. By the end of 1944 the network had grown. Chairman Otto Schiff and Anita Wolf-Warburg made connections via in-person visits to organisations that had begun to establish their own tracing indexes outside of Britain, for example, the *Central Location Index* in New York.[34] They also agreed to cooperate with the *World Jewish Congress*, which had a section in London and which had begun to compile lists of individual survivors, primarily Jewish, throughout the Continent based on information from multiple sources, including remnants of local Jewish communities, military chaplains, and relief workers in the field.[35] The Committee also exchanged

---

[31] Minutes of Meeting to discuss establishment of Centralised Search Bureau, held at Bloomsbury House, London WC1 on Wednesday, May 3rd, 1944 at 3:00pm, HO 294/169, National Archives, Kew. For more on Warner's role in developing the BRCS's search mechanisms and her involvement in developing centralised searching in post-war Europe, see Caroline Moorehead: *Dunant's Dream: War, Switzerland and the History of the Red Cross*, London: HarperCollins, 1999; Edkins: *Missing*, 2011 and Evelyn Bark: *No Time to Kill*, London: R. Hale, 1960.

[32] Minutes of Meeting to discuss establishment of Centralised Search Bureau, held at Bloomsbury House, London WC1 on Friday, 17th December 1943 at 2:30pm, HO 294/169, National Archives, Kew.

[33] Minutes of Meeting of the United Kingdom Search Bureau for German, Austrian and Stateless People from Central Europe, Held at Bloomsbury House, Bloomsbury Street, WC1 on Monday, May 28th [1945] at 3pm, HO 294/169, National Archives, Kew.

[34] Anita Wolf-Warburg to Melville Goldstein, AJDC (Paris), 21.3.1947, JDC Archives, G 45–54 / 4 / 8 / 48 / GER.791, Germany: United Kingdom Bureau – Berlin. 1947.

[35] Minutes of Meeting of the United Kingdom Search Bureau for German, Austrian and Stateless People from Central Europe, Held at Bloomsbury House, Bloomsbury Street, WC1 on Monday,

lists and information with the *Relatives Information Service* set up in Johannesburg by the *Jewish Board of Deputies*.[36]

The question of who would finance the work of the UKSB was a point of recurring discussion in the meeting minutes and reports, and Schiff and other leaders of the refugee organisations continued to intercede with government to attempt to raise additional support. As we have already seen, by 1939, the resources of the organisations involved in refugee assistance were strained.[37] In the minutes of the UKSB meeting of April 24, 1944, Schiff declared his intention to ask the *Home Office* whether its work could be eligible for 75 per cent grant under the Government scheme, with the remaining 25 per cent of their operating budget being covered by the *Christian Council for Refugees* and the *Central Council for Jewish Refugees*.[38] Communication between Otto Schiff and representatives of the Foreign Office indicates the result of these appeals, as well as some intimation of how tracing efforts might be viewed not solely as a humanitarian effort, but a means to an ends by the Refugees department of the Foreign Office: a registration index could be used not only to reunite families but to prompt them to resettle elsewhere. Requests for funding by Schiff to support search and tracing efforts met with some resistance by Foreign Office officials because they were reluctant to devote specific resources to aid Jews, a sentiment that scholars like Tony Kushner have identified in other areas of government response to Jewish immigration.[39] Their response also reflected an ongoing concern that Britain was not to become a final destination for immigration and that refugees should further emigrate, another potential happy outcome of successful search and reuniting efforts.[40] Lady Cheetham of the Refugees Department of the Foreign Office remarked in her notes:

May 28th [1945] at 3pm, HO 294/169, National Archives, Kew. World Jewish Congress, British Section, Report to Members of the National Council, 1 December 1945, HO 294/169, National Archives, Kew.

36 Minutes of Meeting of the United Kingdom Search Bureau for German, Austrian and Stateless People from Central Europe, Held at Bloomsbury House, Bloomsbury Street, WC1 on Monday, November 6th, 1944 at 3pm, HO 294/169, National Archives, Kew.

37 Gottlieb: *Men of Vision*, 1998.

38 Minutes of Meeting of the United Kingdom Search Bureau for German, Austrian and Stateless People from Central Europe, Held at Bloomsbury House, Bloomsbury Street, WC1 on Monday, April 24th, 1944 at 3pm, HO 294/169, National Archives, Kew.

39 See, for example, Kushner: *The Persistence of Prejudice*, 1989.

40 Otto Schiff to Mr Randall, Establishment of a Search Bureau in United Kingdom for German, Austrian and stateless nationals, 5.7.1944, FO 371/42868, National Archives, Kew.

> If the Search Bureau is to be financed by the ICA [Jewish Colonization Organisation], it will become mainly a Bureau for Jews and not for German Austrian and Stateless Refugees in general. I think we might ask Sir H. Emerson to consider at the next executive meeting of the IGC whether a grant might not properly be made by the [*Intergovernmental Committee on Refugees*, IGC] for the financing of the Bureau.

She goes on to assert that

> [t]he Bureau might well become the means by which the IGC could get a 1.) preliminary idea of the number of refugees who wish to return to their countries of origin or former countries of residence 2.) to seek new countries of domicile. Both categories of refugees will be the concern of the Intergovernmental Committee, and their return will be one of the Intergovernmental Committee's functions.[41]

Correspondence between Foreign Office representatives dated 19 July 1944 agreed that "it seems undesirable for the Bureau to be financed by ICA, for it might mean its becoming mainly a Jewish affair [...]".[42] As Louise London has emphasised with regard to the Foreign Office, "the role of these [Refugee Department] officials was...largely reactive: they deflected pressure and defended inaction. The alleged need not to discriminate was their standard justification for opposing proposals for the rescue of Jews exclusively".[43] The government eventually provided some funding for the Bureau's work via the IGC, but activities in 1946 were primarily financed by the *Jewish Colonization Organization* (known as the ICA or IKA) and the *Central British Fund*.[44]

---

41 Cover sheet, Otto Schiff to Mr Randall, *Establishment of a Search Bureau in United Kingdom for German, Austrian and stateless nationals*, 5 July 1944, National Archives, Kew, FO 371/42868.
42 Otto Schiff to Mr Randall, Establishment of a Search Bureau in United Kingdom for German, Austrian and stateless nationals, 5.7.1944, FO 371/42868, National Archives, Kew.
43 London: *Whitehall*, 206.
44 See Summary of Receipts and Payments for the Year ended 5 June 1945, and Summary of Receipts & Payments for the Period 6 June 1945 to 31 December 1946; Central British Fund for World Jewish Relief Archives, UK Search Bureau, MF Doc 27/19/95, Wiener Library. In this latter period, the CBF provided the majority of funds (9500), with supplementation from the *Jewish Colonization Association* (4000), and to a smaller extent, the *Inter-Governmental Committee on Refugees* (1500) and *Friends Committee for Refugees and Aliens* (150). See also Theodore Norman: *An Outstretched Arm: A History of the Jewish Colonization Association*, London: Routledge & Kegan Paul, 1985.

Leveraging Humanitarianism

The Foreign Office was not the only body that saw tracing machinery as a useful tool to achieve other goals. Forward planning for postwar relief efforts can be understood within the context of a general aim for more far-sighted policy for humanitarian intervention, which was developed after the experience of the First World War.[45] But the UKSB Committee underestimated the extent to which their ambitious plans for post-liberated Europe could be realised logistically and did not take into account how tracing mechanisms might later be leveraged as a means to control population movement during military operations.[46] The Bureau assumed, for example, that as "Continental countries are liberated UNRRA will take the first available opportunity of making a complete register of all aliens discovered there and would refer, amongst other places, to the index in London to discover if anybody in this country was enquiring on behalf of any of the persons named".[47] Some on the Committee, such as the representative of the *Czech Refugee Trust*, recognised the potentially impractical nature of this idea, noting that a geographical register was a "useful plan, even though one might foresee that it will never operate perfectly. Nobody has made an estimate of what it would cost to establish and run such an office, nor has any thought been given to where the money is to be found."[48] The ideas reflect at least some lack of understanding of the extent of the devastation and massive uprooting of people that would confront Allied militaries and the UNRRA after the war, as well as the extent to which the movement of populations would clash with logistical military priorities and other urgent matters of relief.

As the international body organised in 1943 to provide relief and support for the repatriation of refugees, UNRRA laid out its priorities for Displaced Persons in a paper based on a June 1944 meeting in London of the *British Red Cross*, UNRRA and the IRC: specifically, the two future goals would be repatriation and ensuring that Displaced Persons obeyed the 'stand still' orders of military authorities. The paper notes that "to attempt to answer [...] queries, or to trace the exact whereabouts of the displaced persons newly liberated, would clog the repatriation machinery and slow down the process of sending displaced per-

---

45 Johannes-Dieter Steinert: "British Humanitarian Assistance: Wartime Planning and Postwar Realities", in *Journal of Contemporary History* 43, *Relief in the Aftermath of War*, 2008, 421–435.
46 Edkins: *Missing*, 64.
47 Minutes of Meeting of the United Kingdom Search Bureau for German, Austrian and Stateless People from Central Europe, Held at Bloomsbury House, Bloomsbury Street, WC1 on Monday, April 24th, 1944 at 3pm, HO 294/169, National Archives, Kew.
48 Ibid.

sons home."⁴⁹ The DPs were to be induced to register their enquiries using *Red Cross* postcards, but for this they would be required to enter Assembly Centres (i.e. DP camps). Obviously, for militaries, tracing would be one concern among a host of many other pressing issues, but Jenny Edkins' assertion that "military planners wanted to control refugee movements and focused on military objectives—for them civilians were largely in the way" is largely correct.⁵⁰

The *British Red Cross Society* already had staff assigned to tracing on the Continent and had begun to search and locate missing people from an office in Bari, Italy in 1944.⁵¹ The UKSB maintained close cooperation with the *British Red Cross Society* throughout 1944 and 1945, and the UNRRA representative to UKSB meetings continued to reassure the Bureau that as soon as national tracing bureaux were set up in liberated territories, the Bureau would be notified.⁵² But the creation of a centralised search bureau in liberated Europe was anything but straightforward, and as Edkins remarks, the chaos of post-war Europe was reflected in the disarray of the different bodies vying for control of search and tracing efforts.⁵³ As Edkins notes, "It was the voluntary agencies, together with some in the military, who insisted on the visibility of missing persons and the audibility of the voices of those who searched for them. The occupying authorities finally acknowledged the importance of tracing services, albeit on their own terms."⁵⁴ The *Supreme Headquarters Allied Expeditionary Force's* (SHAEF) primary concern was military necessity and to plan for the "control, care and disposition of refugees and displaced persons."⁵⁵ In November 1944, these plans expanded to including fighting disease, ill-treatment, and facilitating repatriation, but did not include the search for missing family members.

---

49 UNRRA, Communication between Displaced Persons and their families-Enquiries, Tracing, and Registration of Missing Persons, 22 August 1944, HO 213/1071, National Archives, Kew. See also Edkins: *Missing*, 59–60.
50 Edkins: *Missing*, 59. See also Dan Stone: *The Liberation of the Camps: The End of the Holocaust and its Aftermath*, New Haven/London: Yale University Press, 2015.
51 Thudicum, and Evelyn Bark, *No Time to Kill*. See also PG Cambray and GGB Briggs, 471.
52 Minutes of Meeting of the United Kingdom Search Bureau for German, Austrian and Stateless People from Central Europe, Held at Bloomsbury House, Bloomsbury Street, WC1 on Monday, November 6th, 1944 at 3pm, HO 294/169, National Archives, Kew; Minutes of Meeting of the United Kingdom Search Bureau for German, Austrian and Stateless People from Central Europe, Held at Bloomsbury House, Bloomsbury Street, WC1 on Monday, May 28th [1945] at 3pm, HO 294/169, National Archives, Kew. See also Central British Fund for World Jewish Relief Archives, UK Search Bureau, MF Doc 27/19/95, Wiener Library.
53 Edkins: *Missing*, 59.
54 Ibid., 58.
55 Ibid., 61.

The Marginalisation of the UKSB

By July 1945, militaries had been receiving multiple tracing enquiries and had taken a greater interest in coordinating these activities. The *British Red Cross Society* was ready to respond to all enquiries, no matter the nationality of those submitting them, but this inclusivity did not reflect the goals of UNRRA and the military; in other words, so-called enemy nationals were not within the remit of their plan for a centralised search bureau.[56] Neither was the *International Committee of the Red Cross* satisfactory as a lead in centralised search efforts because it was unacceptable to the Soviet Union, which was suspicious of its neutrality. The *Red Cross* was thus gradually excluded from tracing because of the question of nationality of the displaced. Moreover, as Edkins notes, "The overriding aim of the Allied tracing services was political—or biopolitical—not humanitarian: the control of populations, and their repatriation or resettlement in line with the wishes of the member governments of UNRRA."[57] According to Edkins, Warner was extremely frustrated by the sidelining of the BRCS in the creation of the *Central Tracing Bureau*. Nevertheless, it forged ahead under the supervision of the *Combined Displaced Persons Executive* (CDPX) and UNRRA, moving from Frankfurt to Arolsen in 1946, and was renamed the ITS in 1948, when it was transferred to the successor organisation of UNRRA, the *International Refugee Organization* (the PCIRO, or Preparatory Commission for the IRO, until early 1948).[58]

By 1946, the UKSB was considering its eventual closure. By this time the Bureau had shrunk from 40 full-time staff/8 part-time staff at the end of 1945, to 22 full-time and 6 part-time. In the first six months of 1946, the work of the UKSB "changed considerably". Despite the inefficiencies in fielding their enquiries, answers were starting to return to the UKSB from queries sent to liberated territories. However, the UKSB voiced some frustration with the process:

> Each country on the Continent took its time to organize Search Bureaux and the co-operation of these various Search Bureaux only developed later. As there is a great lack of co-operation between the Committees on the Continent, the UKSB sent Mrs Wolf-Warburg

---

56 Ibid., 72.
57 Ibid., 64.
58 On the early work of the ITS, publicity about its work and circulation of knowledge about its work within British circles, see Dan Stone: "'The Greatest Detective Story in History': The BBC, the International Tracing Service, and the Memory of Nazi Crimes in Early Postwar Britain", in *History & Memory* 29, 2017, 63–89.

to Switzerland and France in order to ascertain that enquiries sent to these countries were really getting all the attention called for.[59]

The report goes on to describe the persistence in difficulties associated with spotty postal service and communication networks, but notes that cooperation with the *Central Location Index* based in New York (which primarily received requests from the American zone of occupation) along with the *Jewish Agency* in Palestine had been fruitful. The UKSB felt it was extremely important to maintain good contact with the various Search Bureaux to ensure that its enquiries were being answered. It noted with more than a hint of frustration:

> The Bureaux on the Continent are so involved in their own work and so preoccupied with their own technical difficulties and possessed by the aims and ambitions of their own little organizations, that they fail to see or to know of the Search Bureaux abroad and their problems and, therefore, without taking up these personal contacts, it is difficult to establish cooperation [...] As long as this muddle exists, one has to reckon with it and deal with the consequences.[60]

The report concluded that the UKSB hoped to create further closer cooperation with the *Jewish Relief Unit*, the operational arm of the *British Jewish Committee for Relief Abroad* (JCRA), which was already characterised positively. Finally, the Bureau still felt that a small staff needed to remain in place "as long as 2,000 families are being informed each month of the fate of their loved ones".[61]

The UKSB wound up most of its operations by 31 October 1947. As of November 1947, it estimated that it had sent 2,200 postal messages to the Continent via the *British Red Cross Society* and over 16,000 enquiries, which concerned missing persons of nationality other than German or Austrian, or Stateless Persons from Central Europe, were forwarded to the Other Nationalities Department of the *British Red Cross*. The index of the UKSB comprised more than 160,000 cards, which covered the records of German, Austrian and Stateless persons from Central Europe. Altogether 88,000 enquiries were received, and out of these, the fate of 49,000 persons could be ascertained, no small accomplishment for a relatively short-lived operation.[62] The *Jewish Refugees Committee* continued to maintain

---

59 UKSB, Report on the work from 1ˢᵗ January to 1ˢᵗ July, 1946, 1ˢᵗ July 1946. Central British Fund for World Jewish Relief Archives, UK Search Bureau, MF Doc 27/19/95/12–13, Wiener Library.
60 Ibid.
61 Ibid.
62 Circular signed by A Wolf-Warburg, dated received 29 November 1947, HO 294/169, National Archives, Kew.

a small tracing department thereafter to field correspondence from outstanding enquiries.[63]

Conclusion

The work of the UKSB and its cooperation with the *British Red Cross Society* form part of the messy foundations of later searching on the Continent, which eventually centralised in the work of the *International Tracing Service*. It suggests the outlines of debates and differing motivations that led to the exclusion of the *Red Cross* from running the ITS, and how humanitarian aims gave way to other priorities, including the rejection of "neutral humanitarianism", control of population movement and the push toward repatriation, the latter being two of the main concerns of military authorities and UNRRA after the war.[64] Inducing temporarily displaced or resettled refugees to move onward or to return home is mirrored in the post-war reluctance of the British government to resolve the position of refugees who had settled in the country from the 1930s. The government attempted to prolong its control over the length of time that refugees could remain and permanently settle in Britain, and took a cautious approach to admitting Jewish refugees after the war.[65] Additional research is needed to examine the extent to which, if at all, the British government leveraged search mechanisms to encourage further emigration of refugees after the war.

Likewise, further research about the contours and effectiveness of tracing work conducted by the UKSB and other similar groups is also needed. Did the UKSB's tracing efforts reflect some of the criticisms levied against Anglo-Jewish aid organisations? Were certain enquiries prioritised over others and if so, along what criteria? Documentary sources on this question are fragmented and dispersed; the most obvious body of evidence are records of family searches and correspondence with various search agencies affiliated with the UKSB, which the *Wiener Library* holds in large number, and of which the Gross family documents are but one example. Also revealed in this correspondence are the ways in

---

[63] It is unclear whether any of the UKSB records, such as indexes, beyond the administrative documents and correspondence held at the UK National Archives HO 294/169 and scattered in other collections, such as the Wiener Library and JDC archives, have survived.

[64] Historically, access to the vulnerable has been one of the motivating factors behind the ICRC's claim to neutrality. See Barbara Ann Rieffer-Flanagan: "Is Neutral Humanitarianism Dead? Red Cross Neutrality: Walking the Tightrope of Neutral Humanitarianism", in *Human Rights Quarterly* 31, 4, 2009.

[65] London: *Whitehall*, 252–271.

which survivors made sense of and reacted to information exposed by their search efforts, as well as their early assumptions about what transpired during the Holocaust.⁶⁶ As Jan Lambertz has concluded, efforts to find Jewish survivors began long before tracing became linked to relief in liberated Europe and before it was taken over by larger international agencies.⁶⁷ Lambertz has found that correspondence derived from searching confirms that "a rapidly widening gulf opened up between those who were subjected to extreme oppression and those who were out of the reach of the Nazi empire".⁶⁸ That gulf is plainly evident in a 1946 letter to Dorothy Gross from one of the family's friends in Roermond who had last seen her parents before their deportation, who remarked: "What a sad, sad thing it is your dear parents did not come safely through this war. Again and again you ask yourself: could they not have hidden themselves? But it seems, especially your father would not do that, though he had several opportunities". ⁶⁹

An enquiry letter to then ITS-director Maurice Thudicum dated June 22, 1948 from solicitors based in Basel reveals additional layers and impetus for the Gross children's search for the ultimate fate of their parents. Gertrude Gross's uncle, Carl Sachs, had been a well-known art collector, and he left an inheritance to his niece. However, without a definitive certificate for Gertrud's death date and location, it was impossible for the solicitors to pass her inheritance on to the children. The ITS issued a certificate of incarceration about Gertrude Gross-Sachs' time in Westerbork and her transfer to the Theresienstadt ghetto, but it was unable to issue a death certificate because there was no documentary evidence of her fate in Auschwitz. The files at the *Wiener Library* and the ITS are silent about the outcome of the legal query regarding the inheritance.⁷⁰ As Lambertz has rightly noted and as the archives of the *Wiener Library* show, time and again, correspondence related to the search for the missing reinforces the tremendous loss and uncertainty that surrounded the lives of survivors in the aftermath of the Holocaust.

---

66 Lambertz: "Vermisstenschicksal", 105.
67 Ibid., 102.
68 Juergen Matthaeus, Emil Kerenji, Jan Lambertz and Leah Wolfson (eds.): *Jewish Responses to Persecution*, vol. III, *1941–1942*, Lanham, MD: AltaMira, 2013. See Lambertz, fn 31.
69 Nelly Smeets Verbunt, Roermond, to Miss Dorothea Gross, Birmingham 8 March 1946. Gross family document collection, 1183, Wiener Library Archive.
70 Tracing and Documentation File 5820 for Klara Anna Gertrud Gross-Sachs, 6.3.3.2/90692074–90692075/ITS Digital Archive, Wiener Library.

Maren Hachmeister
Tracing Services in Poland and Czechoslovakia after 1945

Between Humanitarian Principles and Socialist Ideology

Abstract: This chapter introduces the national Red Cross societies of Poland and Czechoslovakia as initiators of tracing services after the Second World War. The tracing services of the *Polish Red Cross* (PRC) and the *Czechoslovak Red Cross* (CSRC) were central places to go for all individuals seeking others or being sought in these two countries. Furthermore, they were located in a network of international tracing agencies, such as UNRRA and ITS. The chapter presents the tracing activities of both organizations in the context of *socialist humanitarianism*.

Introduction

This chapter introduces two organizations that operated tracing services in Central Eastern Europe after 1945: The *Polish Red Cross* (PRC) and the *Czechoslovak Red Cross* (CSRC). These national Red Cross societies were founded shortly after the end of the First World War (1918) as humanitarian organizations. They understood themselves as international and non-political organizations, and ever since their formation they have been members of the international humanitarian Red Cross movement and maintained contact with the *International Committee of the Red Cross* (ICRC) in Geneva.

Both organizations are characterized by a remarkable organizational continuity: They outlasted the Second World War, survived the coming into power of Communist parties, and survived the democratic transition of the 1990s. This chapter will examine more closely their involvement in national and international search and tracing activities after 1945,[1] and will focus on three questions. First, under which conditions did they initiate their tracing services? Sec-

---

[1] Both tracing services are academically under-researched. Introductions can be found in the following volumes: Joanna Szymoniczek, *Działalność Biura Informacji i Poszukiwań Polskiego Czerwonego Krzyża*, Wybrane zagadnienia (German-Polish Yearbook), 2007, 125–143 and: Zora Mintalová: *Červený kríž na Slovensku v rokoch 1939–1947*, Martin/Bratislava: Vydavateľstvo Matice slovenskej, 2005, 7.

OpenAccess. © 2020 Maren Hachmeister, published by De Gruyter. This work is licensed under the Creative Commons Attribution-NonCommercial-NoDerivatives 4.0 License.
https://doi.org/10.1515/9783110665376-007

ond, what form did the work of these tracing services take? And third, what influence did the socialist state exert on them? All three questions will lead to a better comprehension of PRC and CSRC in general. Significantly more sources were available for the Polish case and so the chapter focuses on it slightly more.

Furthermore, the chapter aims to illustrate how tracing activities helped international and non-political agents survive while Communist parties liquidated most forms of civic engagement in their countries. It is indeed remarkable that PRC and CSRC both managed identification and registration processes in states that were simultaneously creating surveillance societies. Jane Caplan and John Torpey have explained how registration is related to surveillance:

> Registration and documentation of individual identity are essential if persons are to "count" [...]; they ease mobility and communication as well as controlling these activities; and they enhance public security at the same time as they expose everyone to [...] official surveillance.[2]

Thus, political agendas might have influenced tracing activities in post-war Poland and Czechoslovakia – in particular the resources which were provided for the tracing and documenting of victims of Nazi persecution. Keith Breckenridge adds that the socialist state in particular has an interest in the registration of individuals (or collectives), first, in order to eliminate so-called dangerous classes and, second, in order to equally distribute wealth. In his opinion the ideological predisposition of the state must be brought into the picture, because registration is always motivated either politically or ideologically. He thus describes registration as both an instrument of oppression, as in Nazi Europe, and an instrument to promote liberation and equality.[3]

The tracing activities of PRC and CSRC after 1945 have changed the lives of thousands of Displaced Persons after the Second World War. Both cases reflect a certain post-war order. The next section introduces the Polish case.

Tracing in the PRC

From 1945 till 1955 the PRC established itself as the officially recognized tracing service with a central office in Warsaw and subordinated branches in other

---

[2] Jane Caplan and John Torpey: Documenting Individual Identity. The Development of State Practices in the Modern World, Princeton: Princeton University Press, 2001, 6.
[3] Keith Breckenridge and Simon Szreter (eds.): Registration and Recognition. Documenting the Person in World History, Oxford: Oxford University Press, 2012, X.

Polish cities. Both those seeking others and sought-after individuals in Poland used the PRC. As the PRC had experienced staff and had already started building up a professional card file, the Polish Government and also international tracing agencies quickly acknowledged it as the most important local contact. An agreement between the PRC and the *United Nations Relief and Rehabilitation Administration* (UNRRA) from March 1946 confirms that the organization was to be regarded as a National Tracing Bureau (NTB) for Poland. The document states that since this date all documents and records which concerned Polish citizens had to be sent "exclusively" to the PRC in Warsaw. The agreement specified the following:

> This will be done through the intermediaire of Mme Los – Chief Tracing Officer of the Polish Red Cross, attached to the CTB as the representative of the Polish National Tracing Bureau in the Coordinating Committee.[4]

The quotation shows that the PRC had been in contact with UNRRA and the *Central Tracing Bureau* (CTB) in Arolsen, i.e. the predecessor of the *International Tracing Service* (ITS), very shortly after the end of the Second World War. Apparently, such international cooperation was of great importance for the identification of the PRC at that time. In the same year the organization invited the leaders of all NTBs to Warsaw. With regard to that meeting, the PRC chairman addressed a letter to the director of UNRRA to German territory. The letter reads as follows:

> During the past six months the Polish Red Cross, which is the National Tracing Bureau, received precious records and documents giving concrete news about nearly two thousand Polish people who were deported to German concentration camps. We feel that news about missing persons is as important to families as the help received in food and clothing. This country was particularly affected by the war, as nearly every family lost someone and often has no news. We feel that the International Meeting of the Chiefs of the N.T.B.'s which we have organised to be held in Warsaw from 26 to 29 June will greatly help a better and more complete co-ordination between N.T.B.'s and the C.T.B. in this humanitarian work."[5]

This quotation is particularly interesting, because it uses a narrative that could be found very often until the middle of the 1950s, namely that Poland was in particular affected by the war. In the PRC self-image this statement extended from Displaced Persons to Red Cross activists. A PRC booklet from 1956 stated:

---

4 Agreement PRC-UNRRA, 1946, 6.1.1/82518959/ITS Digital Archive, Arolsen Archives.
5 Letter by Kostkiewicz to General Morgan, 1946, 6.1.1/82500069/ITS Digital Archive, Arolsen Archives.

> During the war years the occupant twice burned the files of the Polish Red Cross which contained millions of cards on prisoners of war, concentration camp inmates and those deported for slave labour. Thousands of P.R.C. workers themselves were sent to prisons and camps where many of them perished. In spite of these repressions the P.R.C.'s humanitarian work embraced, from year to year, ever larger numbers of prisoners of war, camp inmates, invalids and children. Thanks to the patriotism and devoted work of hundreds of thousands of its members, the Polish Red Cross fulfilled its duties honourably in the years so difficult for our nation.[6]

One can probably spot some socialist rhetoric in this quotation. In the years of Nazi occupation the PRC continued working under the authority of the *German Red Cross* (GRC) in most cases. Archival documents do not speak of thousands of arrested Red Cross activists. Actually, the only identified PRC activist to be arrested is Maria Bortnowska, who was head of the PRC Tracing Bureau from 1939 to 1942 and again from 1945 to 1947. The Nazi regime arrested her because she had helped Jews and Polish prisoners of war. After the end of the war she was again arrested, although by the Communist regime. She was then accused of collaboration with the Nazis. Bortnowska remained in jail in the Polish People's Republic until 1956, i.e. until after Stalin's death.[7]

The number given above of hundreds of thousands of activists who supposedly helped in tracing activities more likely refers to the total number of PRC members. According to PRC documents the organization had about 700,000 members in 1938.[8] In the 1960s socialist mass recruitment became a reality and the PRC gathered approximately 5,150,000 members.[9] When reading contemporary PRC publications one therefore needs to bear in mind that there were no reliable records of numbers of members for the post-war period. Besides search and tracing, the PRC maintained various other activities, i.e. blood donation, medical services, nursing schools, youth activities, and so forth. Knowing exactly how many members contributed to PRC tracing activities at a specific point of time in a specific place is hard to tell. However, the case of Maria Bortnowska shows that tracing activities were closely monitored by the different authorities. With regard to this chapter, the previous quotation provides an additional piece of information: The PRC registered prisoners of war, camp inmates and forced laborers. How did the PRC Bureau for Information and Search (*Biuro informacji i Poszukiwań*) work in practice?

---

6 The Polish Red Cross: *The Polish Red Cross 1944–1956*, Warsaw, 1956, 6.
7 Jadwiga Boryta-Nowakowska: *A chciałam być tylko aktorką*, Warsaw: Prokop, 1995, 195–202.
8 Irena Domańska: "The Work of the Red Cross in Poland", in *International Review of the Red Cross*, 9/95, 1969, 59.
9 Ibid., 69.

The Information Bureau was located in Warsaw and thus experienced the Warsaw uprising in August 1944. The original name index of missing Polish individuals was then lost during the fighting. A photograph from the ICRC Audiovisual Archives (ARR) shows the remains of the former office. Notes with information were posted on the front wall, covered with wire-mesh fence for protection, but pasted up with more notes on the outside.[10] The photograph shows quite plainly that tracing activities in Warsaw were based on paperwork, trust and improvisation as well as the commitment of PRC employees.

The Information Bureau started cooperating with international agencies, such as UNRRA and the *International Refugee Organization* (IRO) in the first years after the war had ended. From 1948 the Information Bureau worked in close collaboration with the ITS in Arolsen. It was the central place to go in Poland for all individuals, seeking or sought-after. There were of course state institutions in charge of repatriation, for instance the Ministry of Foreign Affairs (*Ministerstwo Spraw Zagranicznych*) and the State Repatriation Office (*Państwowy Urząd Repatriacyjny*). Still, nearly all communication regarding repatriation went through the PRC Information Bureau. One can retrace this arrangement, especially from the beginning of the 1950, when the People's Republic of Poland dropped diplomatic relations with the Federal Republic of Germany. In 1948 the PRC and GRC had taken turns supervising so-called transports that carried Germans from Poland to Germany. Usually PRC members accompanied trains up to the border of the Soviet occupation zone. In the British occupation zone, GRC members took over.[11] This routine was disturbed in November 1949 immediately after the establishment of the German Democratic Republic (GDR). A correspondence between the ITS and the PRC chairwoman Irena Domańska speaks of several trains carrying German children from Poland to Germany who arrived without any identification documents. Domańska explained in her letter that they had certainly left Poland with documents but that they had probably been withheld at the inner German border, because from now on the Polish government intended to resolve all repatriation affairs only with the GDR.[12]

Such types of politically highly sensitive communication often occurred via national Red Cross societies or international tracing agencies. The Polish vice minister of foreign affairs, Marian Nazskowski, justified this procedure using a

---
[10] V-P-HIST-02988–31 A, 1945/ICRC Audiovisual Archives (ARR). Available at: https://avarchives.icrc.org/Picture/10692. Last accessed: 25.6.2019.
[11] Letter from ITS to PRC, 1949, AAN 2/284/0/9 and AAN 2/284/0/9/50, Archiwum Akt Nowych, Warsaw.
[12] Letter to Irena Domańska, 1950, AAN 2/284/0/9, Archiwum Akt Nowych, Warsaw.

very clever argument. In November 1954 he stated in front of the Polish Communist party that the *Soviet Red Cross* also cooperated with the *German Red Cross*. If even the Soviet Union relied on the Red Cross in such delicate matters as repatriation, it must be alright for Poland to do the same.[13] Consequently both Poland and Germany let representatives of their national Red Cross societies negotiate bilateral search and repatriation activities. The first transport of individuals with German nationality, who happened to have relatives in West Germany, could leave Poland on December 14, 1954. In January 1955 two more transports followed, carrying 341 passengers. The Polish historian Dariusz Stola remembers this as a first breakthrough for German nationals who were still in Poland and emphasizes the role the PRC and GRC played here. The GRC had been adjudged a Nazi synchronized organization until shortly before that time. Now the GRC and PRC were jointly working on the repatriation of Nazi victims.

Being involved in political affairs challenged the apolitical status of the PRC in Poland and drew attention to the organization's international relations. The following example illustrates that tracing activities were no longer just a humanitarian commitment, but also depended on the current political agenda and thus affected the situation of registered individuals.

In 1949 the Liaison Officer van Banning led a delegation from the ITS to Poland. The main objective was to recover and copy files that were located at the PRC Information Bureau. It possessed identification cards, lists of former prisoners and lists with numbers and death records. When the delegation arrived in Warsaw, they were again in close contact with Irena Domańska. Unfortunately, she had received official instructions not to hand over any material unless van Banning brought a so-called "clearance" from the Polish government. After the delegation had returned to Germany, a second conference of NTBs took place in Arolsen from September 1 to 3, 1949. At this conference van Banning reported on his mission to Poland as follows:

> [T]his mission has done everything possible to get the clearance necessary to work in Poland. [...] My personal feeling is that the success or failure of this mission was a question of politics, I was received very kindly by the National Tracing Bureau [...] they were willing to [...] give me documents. All depended, however, on clearance with the Government and therefore this is a matter of politics between IRO and the Polish Government.[14]

---

13 Dariusz Stola: *Kraj bez wyjścia? Migracje z Polski 1949–1989*, Warsaw: Instytut Pamięci Narodowej, 2010, 111.
14 ITS Mission to Poland, 1949, 6.1.1/82510271/ITS Digital Archive, Arolsen Archives.

Cooperation between the PRC and international tracing agencies improved significantly when the PRC started sending some of its personnel to Germany, where they worked in the framework of UNRRA and later ITS. The case of Roman Hrabar is particularly interesting. In 1947 he had been nominated Plenipotentiary for the Vindication of Polish Children at the IRO. In 1948 he worked in the *Child Search Division* of the ITS in Esslingen. A report from 1947 comments as follows about his function:

> The plenipotentiary [...] [is] responsible primarily to the Division of Labor and Social Welfare, Poland, and secondly to the PRC. [He has] a quasi-diplomatic status, and responsibility for search in the British and French Zones, as well as investigations in other countries, such as Switzerland. [The] function includes investigating and expediting return of children who are technically accompanied and therefore not IRO responsibility, but whose repatriation has been requested by the Polish Government. The Plenipotentiary's position needs further description because it has been a most helpful relationship and suggests the form which liaison with other countries should take in regard to the Tracing Service as a whole. He interprets to Poland the needs and findings in Germany, and promotes the development of required services there. He gives the program here the Polish thinking [...][15]

A personnel evaluation file on Roman Hrabar dated from September 1947 describes him as "cooperative, responsible and competent". In his role as plenipotentiary representative for searching for Polish children in Germany, he was considered "a lawyer and a tower of strength to the Child Search programme" with an excellent "objective judgement".[16]

The same Roman Hrabar published a book in 1962 in which he documents his work in Germany. The book gives us an insight into how Polish activists perceived international tracing activities. He describes his situation in a rather pessimistic manner:

> Several organizations and social institutions are accredited via the UNRRA, they are called voluntary agencies. The Polish Red Cross is the most strongly represented. There are more Polish affairs here than affairs of all the others altogether. The working conditions in Heidelberg are fatal. The main offices are located in the military area. It is cramped; there is no place for files or typewriters. Getting used to work methods and orienting yourself is difficult. Let alone the organizational apparatus. Accommodation, meals, transport, communication, telephone lines – everything runs like clockwork. There is no space here for our 'art of improvisation'. We lack the basis for acting as an independent mission. We are not treated like UNRRA-personnel, thus the Polish Red Cross remains a voluntary agency. We stay at our own expense.[17]

---

15 Child Search and Tracing, 1947, 6.1.1/82506219/ITS Digital Archive, Arolsen Archives, 13.
16 Personnel evaluation Roman Hrabar, 1947, 11.21/B 6/2–1/ITS Archive, Arolsen Archives.
17 Roman Hrabar: *Jakim prawem?*, Katowice: Śląsk, 1962, 24–25.

Besides political and cultural obstacles the Polish case proves that there were also language barriers. The correspondence of the ITS with the PRC in 1951 illustrates how severe these barriers were even after several years of cooperation. The ITS usually communicated only in English, French and German. This was reasonable, because it ensured standardized and quick communication and helped with standardized registration procedures. But the PRC representative in Germany explained the matter from a different point of view. He argued that the PRC in Warsaw did not have enough qualified personnel anymore in order to answer letters in English. Employees who spoke foreign languages had since 1946 been sent step by step to UNRRA and ITS. In her letter from June 1951, Vera Samsonoff explains the situation:

> Our experience has proved that letters addressed to the Polish Red Cross in Warsaw, if written in Polish, received better and quicker attention. Last year in Esslingen, Mr. Bikart, Chief of the Polish Red Cross in Germany, told me that they have no competent staff in the Polish Red Cross in Warsaw, who could quickly and precisely translate letters from English into Polish, and requested that all letters addressed to Warsaw should be written in Polish. [...] This is easy to understand; we cannot expect a Polish person, who perhaps lives in some remote village in Poland, to speak foreign languages. [...] I believe the Board will readily understand the anguish of a mother, or wife, who receives news from abroad concerning her next of kin. She can read the name, but cannot understand the contents of the letter, and to have same translated, she may have to send the news received some few miles away and await anxiously the reply. As far as Tracing Branch is concerned, letters written in Polish do not delay our action, as we have Polish employees, who can easily draft, or even type reports themselves.[18]

In addition, names of places and names of individuals could be transcribed or declined differently. Thus, the content of card files depended greatly on either the skill or the nationality of the person who filled out the cards. When looking at records of the post-war period, we should therefore keep in mind individual backgrounds, such as the following of the PRC recruited correspondent Maria Bolesta:

> Miss Bolesta has proved an invaluable worker. Her work is accurate, neat and well-organized. She has considerable speed in typing Polish and types rather more slowly in English. Prior to being displaced to Germany by reason of the war, she had 3 years of commercial school at Lwow. She has considerable poise, a pleasing personality, and is a young woman of integrity. Her ability to speak English has improved remarkably in the past six

---

18 Office Memorandum, 1951, 6.1.1/82507423–82507424/ITS Digital Archive, Arolsen Archives.

months. She is being terminated by this Organisation for the purpose of resettlement in Canada.[19]

Language barriers can also be found in the *Tracing/Documentation files (T/D)* in the Arolsen Archives. In *T/D* cases involving the PRC one finds different languages and different spellings for the *Polish Red Cross*.[20] Some of the cards have been reviewed regularly. One card was recorded in 1958 and marked again in 1977 and 1998.[21] The *T/D* cases up to the present day demonstrate what a huge bureaucratic challenge the PRC Information Bureau and its employees have faced. Indeed, German sociologist Martin Abraham understands the history of organizations as the history of individuals. Who really acts is not the organization as a body, but the individuals in it.[22] This applies to the history of the PRC Information Bureau.

To sum up some characteristics of the PRC Information Bureau, after the end of the Second World War the PRC initiated a tracing service that became recognized by national and international institutions. It functioned as the NTB for Poland but drew its human resources and funding primarily from the PRC. Between 1946 and the early 1950s the PRC sent employees to international agencies such as UNRRA, IRO and ITS. There they participated in international search operations and assisted in the search for and documentation of Polish citizens, activities that were funded by the state. Furthermore, the Polish government entrusted those employees with a quasi-diplomatic status, which allowed them to make decisions on behalf of the state. At that point of time, the Polish government was particularly interested in the search and repatriation of Polish children.

Despite the socialist environment, the Polish tracing service stayed in contact with international, especially Western agencies. It did so in three ways: first, it sent staff to Germany, second, it hosted an international conference of NTBs in Warsaw in 1946, and third, it welcomed delegations of the ICRC and delegations of UNRRA and ITS to Warsaw. This influenced how the state treated the PRC in general. The need for tracing operations legitimated the need for a Red Cross society, and the tracing service is one of the projects that the PRC always

---

19 Letter of Recommendation for Maria Bolesta, 1948, 11.21/B 6/2–1/ITS Archive, Arolsen Archives.
20 i.e. Pl. Czerwony Krzyz Zarzad Glowny, Biuro Inform. i Poszukiwan, Polski Czerwony Krzyz, Zarzad Glowny, PRK, Warszawa, Poln. R. Kr. Warschau, P.R.K. Warschau, (Name) üb. PCK Warschau, PCK Warschau für (Name), Polish Red Cross, Polish Red Cross, Warsaw ul. Mokotowska 14 Poland.
21 Card file, 1958, 0.1/52659583/ITS Digital Archive, Arolsen Archives.
22 Martin Abraham: *Einführung in die Organisationssoziologie*. Wiesbaden: VS Verlag für Sozialwissenschaften, 2009, 27.

liked to present as a success. Irena Domańska was one of the protagonists who have most strongly shaped the history of the PRC after 1945. In an interview from 1976, Domańska commented on PRC activities as follows:

> Your readers, especially young people, have no idea how terribly destroyed our country was – not to compare with France. The need of people was boundless. I was then nominated vice-president of the Polish Red Cross. I coordinated relief from Sweden, Switzerland, the American Polonia and the Soviet Union, relevant and altruistic help. In contrast to that parcels from UNRRA had to be paid. Our organization tried hard to help those who returned to the country, the resettlers and repatriates. Our tracing bureau engaged actively in the search of families and family reunification. Let us not forget that even in the year 1974 the bureau contained 7 million cards and determined the fate of 6,000 individuals.[23]

Domańska explains that the Information Bureau was for a long time one of the PRC's most essential activities. The socialist environment did influence Red Cross activities after 1945, but it also encouraged the PRC's tracing service as a humanitarian assignment. Therefore, the PRC sought international (Western) networks and participated in efforts at so-called "family reunion" until the 1970s. The next section introduces tracing activities in neighboring Czechoslovakia.

Tracing in the CSRC

The tracing services in Poland and Czechoslovakia were principally very similar. They were both established in a post-war Europe, where (among others) the national Red Cross societies initiated and pursued means of searching and documenting. Both tracing services were located in the respective capitals, i.e. Warsaw and Prague. The CSRC also sent members to UNRRA and ITS in Germany, though in contrast to members of the PRC they were only financed by their home organization.

Due to the fact that search and documentation was mostly carried out by a delegation of the ICRC between 1945 and 1948, the CSRC tracing service began working effectively only after 1948. Miloslav Hlach, chairman of the CSRC (1969–1979)[24], understood the allocation of tasks between the CSRC and the ICRC as follows:

---

[23] Article by Janina Pałecka in Zwierciadło, 1976, AAN 2514/2/275, Archiwum Akt Nowych, Warsaw.
[24] Josef Švejnoha: "Svěží jubilant doktor Miloslav Hlach", in *Noviny Červeného kříže*, 19, 39, 1.2012.

> It is the duty of each country to take care of its own territory and its own citizens. It cannot help those who are in the hand of the enemy on the other side of the front. To whom do those citizens belong? They are mainly the wounded, the captured on the battlefield, the fleeing and eventually some groups of civilians, mainly citizens of the occupied territory and civilian internees. It is the International Committee that acts on behalf of them.[25]

When it came to tracing activities, Hlach promoted the ITS as a valuable problem solver. He described the ITS as the most important information center for those who were either deported or resettled in Germany or in the German occupied countries during the Second World War. He thus understood the close contact of ITS and Red Cross societies as a matter of course:

> In 1955 the ICRC was entrusted with the direction of that service [ITS]. Its card index contains 25 million cards. Since the year 1951 it received 2 million inquiries.[26]

This information was made available only in 1975. Until then (other than the PRC) the CSRC had treated tracing activities with utter secrecy. Having experienced the strict regime of the 1950s and the Prague Spring in 1968, the formally apolitical organization avoided making daring political statements for a long time. Not only was communication about tracing activities in public restricted, but also communication inside the organization. Thus, documents and correspondence about tracing activities in the CSRC are very rare. On the official website the *Czech Red Cross* (CRC) today looks back on the post-war period as follows:

> In the first years after World War II the CSRC continued in the spirit and tradition of the First Republic. It renewed the education of nurses and paramedics as well as the ambulance service. A huge challenge awaited the tracing service of the CSRC that was overwhelmed with thousands of inquiries.[27]

The ITS reported only briefly on a successful cooperation with the CSRC in 1951, and referred to relations with Eastern European countries in general:

> Many attempts were also made, all through the years, to get some kind of cooperation in the field of pure tracing from the National Tracing Bureaux from the Eastern countries. But again, the results remained practically nil. [...] Only from Czechoslovakia did the ITS,

---

25 Miloslav Hlach: *Mezinárodní Červený kříž*, Prague: Čes. ÚV ČSČK, 1975, 12.
26 Ibid., 23.
27 Český červený kříž: "Marek Jukl: *Činnost ČSČK po druhé světové válce*". Available at: http://www.cervenykriz.eu/cz/historiepovalce.aspx. Last accessed: 27.3.2019.

early in 1951, receive quite an important number of valuable replies to enquiries which had been sent to Prague during 1949 and for which all hope had been given up.[28]

The author of this statement was obviously ignorant of the political restrictions which the CSRC faced in the early socialist state. After the communist take-over in 1948, the CSRC struggled for survival without having to abandon the principles of the international humanitarian Red Cross movement. In addition, only a small circle of the top-ranking CSRC leaders knew about particular tracing activities. In 1956, for instance, the CSRC secretary Josef Švarc drafted a speech on the occasion of the Second National Congress of the CSRC in Prague. Among other things he mentioned the tracing service:

> In terms of the humanitarian principles the CSRC contributed to the reunion of several thousand foreign citizens with their families abroad. At present we help in all possible ways to carry out the repatriation of our own citizens abroad, in order to bring them home. Even if our international activity was relatively rich, we must admit self-critically that the PÚV[29] has not sufficiently informed the ÚV[30] and the lower organs of members about events and actions and the acquired experiences.[31]

It is very unlikely that Josef Švarc got to speak these words at the National Congress because Eduard Tůma (CSRC chairman from 1952 to 1956) marked the entire passage literally as *secret*. Such interventions certainly influenced the (political and public) recognition of war victims and affected tracing and documenting practices in the CSRC.

Despite such obstacles the CSRC communicated with tracing agencies and other institutions in the early 1950s, for instance the State Office for Compensation Baden Württemberg (*Landesamt für die Wiedergutmachung Baden-Württemberg*). In November 1951 that State Office hoped to obtain information from the CSRC on certain individuals who had supposedly been internees in a camp in Chrastava near Liberec. The response read as follows: "The camp in Chrastava was established in 1944, it was a camp for Jews. On May 5, 1945 the inmates were freed by the Red Army. No indices of names have been preserved."[32]

Such fragments of information can be found in the ITS Digital Archives and several Czech archives. Still, those archival documents hardly allow any estima-

---

[28] Report on relations with Eastern European Countries, 6.1.1/82493049/ITS Digital Archive, Arolsen Archives.
[29] PÚV = *Předsednictvo Ústředního výboru* (Board of the Main Committee).
[30] ÚV = *Ústřední výbor* (Main Committee).
[31] Hlavní referát, 1956, NA, ČSČK Praha, ka. 12b II, Národní archiv v Praze, Prague.
[32] Transcription, 1951, 1.1.11.0/82111424/ITS Digital Archive, Arolsen Archives.

tion of registered and completed cases, card files, or involved CSRC members. However, those documents tell us about individual CSRC representatives in Germany. Cornelia Heise, Chief of the ITS Child Search and Tracing Section, wrote a confidential report in November 1947. The report spoke of three CSRC members and specified their relation to the Czechoslovak government:

> Mr. Ondracek and Mrs Hrubcova of the Czech Red Cross reported on November 11th, on their return from Czechoslovakia, that the government had decided to continue child search activities in Germany, on a reduced scale for one year. It was specified that three persons would be retained in Germany, specifically Mr. Ondracek, Mr. Vondracek, and a third who had not been specifically named. Mr. Ondracek was of the opinion that more persons might be retained in Germany if a specific request was made. He felt that a strong representation would need to be made to retain Captain Pumperka, since there seemed to be an element in the home government who felt that he should not continue.[33]

This quotation confirms that tracing activities were an issue for the CSRC in the post-war period, but that they were handled in closed sessions. The CSRC only began formally documenting tracing activities in the 1970s. It then recorded 4,000 cases in 1971, 3,600 cases in 1972, 3,500 cases in 1973 and 700 cases in the first quarter of 1974. According to a report of tracing activities in 1973 the CSRC tracing service had relations with both socialist and capitalist countries, mainly with the Soviet Union and the Federal Republic of Germany. In the same year, the CSRC tracing service found documents concerning arrests in concentration camps, documents about the state of health, proof of military service, or death certificates in 350 cases. In 2,700 cases it searched for people who had been separated from their families during the Second World War or experienced other kinds of displacement. The CSRC furthermore identified 257 dead individuals and took over official functions in 123 cases.[34]

Although early tracing activities were scarcely documented in the socialist environment, one can conclude that the CSRC maintained a tracing service very similar to the PRC Information Bureau. Under the impression of the so-called normalization period that followed the Warsaw Pact invasion of Czechoslovakia, Miloslav Hlach pictured the *Soviet Red Cross* (SRC) as a role model for tracing:

> The Soviet Red Cross, together with the help of Soviet citizens and foreigners, has continued searching relatives of those, whose traces were lost as a consequence of Word War II. In

---

33 Czechoslovakian Red Cross participation in Child Search, 1947, Rotes Kreuz/Institutionelle Ablage 11.21, Ordner: B 6/2–1, ITS Bad Arolsen.
34 Statistická ročenka, 1974, NA, ČSČK Praha, ka. 18, Národní archiv v Praze, Prague.

the years 1969 to 1972 the Soviet Red Cross located 28,847 individuals. This humanitarian endeavor required the cooperation of the Soviet Red Cross with national societies in 72 countries and with the International Committee of the Red Cross.[35]

With or without the example of the *Soviet Red Cross* (SRC), both the Polish and the Czechoslovak national Red Cross societies faced problems with standardized registration procedures. *T/D* cases involving the CSRC (like *T/D* cases involving the PRC) used different languages and different spellings.[36]

To sum up some characteristics of the CSRC tracing service, after the end of the Second World War the CSRC initiated a tracing service in Prague that became widely recognized by national and international institutions. Like the PRC, the CSRC had representatives in international search and tracing agencies (UNRRA, ITS). However, in contrast to the PRC Information Bureau, the CSRC tracing service did not start operating until 1948. Due to political concerns – being an apolitical organization in a socialist state with close contacts to the capitalist world – tracing activities were considered highly confidential until the 1970s. In the first post-war years the tracing activities of the CSRC were to some extent covered by international cooperation.

Conclusion

When dealing with the tracing services of the PRC and CSRC it is essential to consider the fact that they operated under state socialist conditions. Both organizations arranged themselves within a framework of *socialist humanitarianism* which allowed a day-to-day routine, combining socialist ideology with humanitarian principles. Still, both Red Cross societies were located in surveillance societies where the searching and collecting data had a different connotation than in Western Europe. Accordingly, the international relations of PRC and CSRC are a remarkable exception. The tracing activities of the PRC and CSRC can thus be recognized as humanitarian efforts that changed the lives of thousands of Displaced Persons after the Second World War and partly substituted state responsibilities in the field of registration and documentation. Unfortunately, both tracing services have been subject to (surprisingly) little research to date.

---

[35] Miloslav Hlach: *Mezinárodní Červený kříž*, Prague, 1975, 54.
[36] i.e. Ceskoslovensky Cerveny Kriz/federalni Vybor, Ceskoslovensky Cerveny Kriz, Prag, Czechoslovakian Red Cross, Ustredni Seretariat Praha, Slovensky Cerveny kriz, Slovak Red Cross.

René Bienert
Survivors Helping Survivors
Simon Wiesenthal and the Early Search for Nazi Criminals in Linz

Abstract: This chapter explores the early years of Simon Wiesenthal's post-war activities which so far have not received much attention. Immediately upon his liberation from the Mauthausen concentration camp, Wiesenthal began – in Linz, Upper Austria – to search for Nazi perpetrators. However, this early search is closely linked to Wiesenthal's active support for Holocaust survivors. The temporary presence of survivors who lived in assembly centers, waiting for a chance to emigrate, was seen as an opportunity to systematically question them as witnesses, and indeed this approach was successful: hundreds of witnesses were, in this way, involved in investigations and court proceedings carried out by the US, and soon also by Austrian authorities. This combination of help for survivors on the one hand, and help from survivors on the other, only occurred for a short period of time, due to mass emigration taking place from 1948 onwards. Still, attempting to reconstruct these events not only provides insight into the foundation of Wiesenthal's later, lifelong activities, but also helps better understand the history of his archive.

Introduction

On starting to study the holdings of the archive of the *Vienna Wiesenthal Institute for Holocaust Studies* (VWI) and learning about their history, it is fascinating to see how closely the beginnings of Simon Wiesenthal's activities after 1945 are interwoven with the history of Jewish Displaced Persons. Not only is this close relationship linked to numerous aspects, including early attempts to (judicially) deal with and come to terms with Nazi crimes and the beginnings of the Cold War, oftentimes it is also linked to the question of how the survivors themselves – Wiesenthal among them – dealt with the resulting challenges immediately after 1945. The present chapter is an attempt to characterize this relationship as a reciprocal one, which can be described on the one hand as help for survivors, and on the other hand as help from survivors – either as witnesses or as workers. If this relationship is seen as a history of professionalization and institutionalization at the same time, then it becomes clear that as far as Wiesenthal's search for Nazi criminals is concerned, it worked quite well – it created a model for success, so to speak, and last but not least, it laid the foundations for his life's work. To this end, this chapter will outline Wiesenthal's early years in Linz, of which still little is known, and will focus on reconstructing his working methods. The aim is not least to make a contribution to the history of the *Simon Wiesenthal Archive* in Vienna, as not insignificant parts of it date from or build upon the Linz period. However, there is one obstacle that needs to be overcome: most of the documents from these first years of his activity, i.e. the very documents which are of most interest here, are not located in Vienna but in *Yad Vashem*, where Wiesenthal himself – for reasons I will discuss below – sent them in the mid-1950s.

Tracking down Nazi Criminals in the Morning, Helping Survivors in the Afternoon

Shortly after his liberation from the Mauthausen concentration camp, Wiesenthal handed the Americans a list of the names of Nazi criminals he could still remember.[1] The representatives of the *War Crimes Office* which had been set up in the liberated camp were presumably impressed not only by the information on all 91 perpetrators, but also by the persistence with which Wiesenthal repeatedly expressed his desire to help them apprehend Nazi criminals. Returning to his former life as an architect in Lviv was certainly not an option for Wiesenthal – his family and friends had been murdered. Instead, the task of seeking justice on behalf of the victims promised a sense of mission as well as new meaning.

However, the abovementioned list was not just his "entry ticket" to the *War Crimes Branch*, as Winfried Garscha[2] put it, it can also be seen as the prototype for his future approach, which was based on questioning survivors (systematically) about their memories of Nazi perpetrators. When the Americans even took him with them shortly afterwards when first arrests were made, not only did this mark the start of a quasi-cooperative relationship (Garscha), most importantly, it enabled Wiesenthal to make valuable contacts which would be of use to him later on.

---

[1] Wiesenthal to the US Camp Commander of the liberated Mauthausen concentration camp, 25.5.1945, II.1., A-I.6.1, Vienna Wiesenthal Institute – Simon Wiesenthal Archive (VWI-SWA).
[2] Winfried Garscha: Simon Wiesenthal's contribution to the prosecution of Nazi criminals in Austria, [presentation given at a conference titled "Österreichs Umgang mit der NS-Täterschaft" held on the occasion of the ninetieth birthday of Simon Wiesenthal, Vienna 2/3 December 1998]. Available at: https://www.doew.at/cms/download/6kqis/garscha_wiesenthal.pdf. Last accessed: 22.6.2019.

Because the liberated Mauthausen concentration camp was located in an area which was soon to become part of the Soviet zone, the Americans moved their offices to Linz. Wiesenthal followed them, as did many other survivors from Mauthausen. On June 8, 1945, he began to work there in the relocated office of the *War Crimes Branch*[3] and he seems to have done such a good job that shortly afterwards he also started working for the *Counter Intelligence Corps* (CIC)[4] and the *Office of Strategic Services* (OSS).[5] However, cracks soon started to appear in his cooperative relationship with the Americans. Not only did competition and wrangling over responsibilities between the various bodies for which Wiesenthal now worked make cooperation more difficult, changes in the personnel deployed by what was now the occupying force also had a role to play: those who had fought in Europe and liberated the concentration camps were gradually replaced by newcomers who often lacked empathy for the experiences and the situation of the survivors. Moreover, the ban on fraternization between members of the occupying forces and the local population was lifted in the autumn of 1945. Later, Wiesenthal would refer to this laconically as the "Fräulein factor"[6]. Many a time, it was responsible for ensuring that Nazi criminals who had only just been put under arrest were already freed the next day, thanks to the intercessions of a younger sister or daughter.[7]

As well as searching for Nazi criminals, Wiesenthal, who never seemed to sit still, also began to involve himself in the issues which faced the survivors.[8] Shortly after his arrival in Linz in June 1945, he became active in the *Jewish Committee* founded by survivors.[9] This laid the first foundations for combining the two areas of activity. Speaking of his memories of this period later on, Wiesenthal used the following words to describe this period: "I spent the mornings in the office tracking down war criminals and the afternoons at [the] committee."[10]

One of the central tasks of committees like the one in Linz was to support survivors in their search for relatives and loved ones as well as for information

---

3 Simon Wiesenthal: *Ich jagte Eichmann. Tatsachenbericht*, Gütersloh: Bertelsmann Lesering, 1961, 24.
4 CIC Detachment Travel Pass 13.7.1945, II.1., A-I.1.6, VWI-SWA.
5 OSS Authorization Linz 20.8.1945, II.1., A-I.1.6, VWI-SWA.
6 Alan Levy: *Die Akte Wiesenthal*, Wien: Ueberreuter, 1995, 76.
7 Interview between Herbert Rosenkranz and Simon Wiesenthal, 1.12.1986, M.9, 837, 18, Yad Vashem Archive.
8 Certification from the Headquarter Land Upper Austria Area Command U.S. Army, 3.2.1947, II.1., A-I 1,VWI-SWA.
9 Certification from the Military Government Displaced Persons Office, 18.6.45, II.1., A-I.1.6, VWI-SWA.
10 Simon Wiesenthal: "Doch die Mörder leben", in *Der Spiegel*, 33, 1967, 52–65, here 55.

about their fate and whereabouts – for most survivors, this was one of the most important questions after liberation. However, in view of the massive destruction of infrastructure and communications in the immediate post-war period, this posed a real challenge. In order to tackle the task, lists of survivors were first compiled in one place and then passed on to comparable organizations – which were emerging all over liberated Europe at the time – as *search lists* in transcript form. Copies were soon being circulated worldwide. Conversely, transcripts of lists of this kind were also constantly arriving in Linz from other countries and other places.

For example, a register compiled by the Committee in Linz contains information on some 1,700 Polish Jews who had previously been liberated (most of them from the Mauthausen concentration camp and its sub-camps), among them Wiesenthal himself. For the purposes of identification and location, the register includes names, dates of birth, last place of residence, place of liberation and current whereabouts.[11] *Search lists* created on the basis of this information finally also reached the organization that was later to become the ITS after comparison with the data held by the central tracing bureau of the JOINT and the *Central Location Index* (CLI) in New York up until November 1945.[12] Wiesenthal later described this work in detail:

> The first thing we did at the committee in Linz was to draw up lists of the survivors. Any one who came to us to ask after somebody else was always asked where he came from. [The] name was put onto the list for the town or village concerned. Gradually, the lists grew, people from Poland, Czechoslovakia and Germany brought us their lists. We gave them copies of ours. We worked into the night transcribing these lists. Because the first people would arrive early in the morning, wanting to look through the names, some of them waited all night until they were allowed to come in. As soon as the first one had finished, the next in line was already waiting to take a look at the list which could mean hope or desperation for him.[13]

Wiesenthal – who had, by his own account, lost almost all of his relatives and friends in the Holocaust – initially had doubts as to the efficacy of the lists

---

11 The register was discovered by chance after the VWI moved into the new institute building in Vienna thanks to my colleague Barbara Grzelak, who found it amongst boxes which had been packed for the library and put into the archive, Register of Names Committee of Polish Jews, [Linz], [circa July 1945], V I.7., VWI-SWA. For more information on the register, see also: Interview between Rosenkranz and Wiesenthal, 18.
12 Poles and German Refugees at Gut Hart near Linz/Austria, 3.1.1.2/78806502/ITS Digital Archive, Wiener Library.
13 Simon Wiesenthal: *Doch die Mörder leben*, München: Dromer-Knaur 1967, 67.

and this laborious work.¹⁴ However, all this changed in the summer of 1945 when he found his wife Cyla, whom he had previously believed dead, with the aid of one of these lists.¹⁵ This too motivated him to continue the work he was doing in the interests of the survivors. The committee was certainly the right place for it. The contacts he had made during his time with the Americans helped him to make his voice heard, while his imposing appearance lent him authority. As of September 1945, he was "permitted to enter the building of the 26th Division Headquarters at any time to see the Displaced Persons officer"¹⁶, and he was soon one of the leading representatives of the Linz committee.¹⁷ The committee soon became a point of contact and a center for the exchange of all kinds of different information. In the autumn of 1945¹⁸, he already had an office at the *Displaced Persons Information Center* at Goethestraße 63 in Linz, where representatives of DPs of other nationalities were also based.¹⁹

The committee's everyday work was not limited to cooperation with other tracing bureaus. In fact, it became the point of contact for a range of different issues: the members assisted survivors in their dealings with the (Austrian) authorities²⁰ or issued certificates of imprisonment, for example. Wiesenthal was also a strong advocate of survivors being given identity papers and for restrictions on their freedom of movement being lifted.²¹ In the spring of 1946, he organized events to mark the first anniversary of the liberation of the Mauthausen concentration camp.²²

Relief activities for survivors also included a remarkably early attempt to collect information for compensation payments. In the summer of 1946, former Jewish forced laborers in Bindermichl and other DP camps were questioned directly about the nature and duration of their forced labor and about the companies in-

---

[14] Ibid. and Levy: *Akte Wiesenthal*, 71.
[15] For detailed information, see Tom Segev: *Simon Wiesenthal. Die Biografie*, München: Siedler, 2010, 94–95.
[16] Certification from the Headquarters of the 26th Infantry Division, 18.9.1945, II.1., A-I.1.6, VWI-SWA.
[17] Wiesenthal: *Eichmann*, 25.
[18] Letter to the Amt für Wirtschaftsförderung [Business Development Office] of the city of Linz, 26.11.1945, M.9, 10, 124, Yad Vashem Archive.
[19] For information on the various agencies, see also Vincent Odierna's dedication book, 2.1.7., Archive of the Mauthausen Memorial.
[20] For example, for many survivors who were living outside the DP camps as "free living DPs" and who needed certificates of allocation from the local housing departments in order to do so. See interview between Rosenkranz and Wiesenthal, 17.
[21] Wiesenthal to the Federal Chancellery, Vienna, 15.7. 1946, M.9, 10, 72, Yad Vashem Archive.
[22] Minutes of the meeting, 18.4.1946, M.9, 16, 6, Yad Vashem Archive.

Fig. 1: *DP Information Center* at Goethestraße 63, Linz, which later also accommodated the office of the *Jewish Historical Documentation Center* for some years, 1946 (Archive of the City of Linz)

volved. The aim was to use the information collected in this way to make claims for outstanding wage payments. One of the points covered in the questionnaire concerned the DPs' state of health: "lung problems", "T.B.C." or "physical weakness" were the entries made most frequently, but "heart problems", "loss of a little finger" or "water in the feet" can also be found.[23] The companies mentioned include *Amstetten Sägewerke*, *Austro Daimler Puch Werke* and *Wiener Elektrizitätswerke*, to mention just a few examples. A reply received from the city of Vienna serves as proof of the fact that efforts really were made to contact the companies concerned. The city authorities had obviously been asked about forced labor in a *Steinbruch Wien* (stone quarry Vienna), but they put the ball firmly back in the court of the Linz committee by requesting more detailed infor-

---

[23] For more information, see the entire file labeled "Questionnaires of the Central Jewish Committee in Linz, upper Austria, filled out by Jews who had been forced laborers in 22 camps", M.9, 20, Yad Vashem Archive.

mation.²⁴ Because of the small number of surviving questionnaires, though, the question of what became of this project must remain unanswered at this point.

Making the Most of the Time in the Waiting Room: Recruiting Survivors as Witnesses

However, what this example already points to is the need to proceed more systematically when collecting information. This also applied to that other task, which – as described above – played a recurring role for Wiesenthal:

> One day I was visited by a married couple. [...] The two of them were looking for surviving relatives and had come to our office to look at the lists of refugees which we had received from all over liberated Europe. We took the opportunity to question them routinely about their experiences and how they had managed to survive the Nazi period and we asked whether they could remember the names of any of the people who had persecuted them.²⁵

What Wiesenthal describes here as routine questioning of survivors is not only reminiscent of how he himself had gone about things in May 1945 with the list of the 91 names he could still remember. It is also a good example of the combined approach referred to in the present chapter as *Survivors Helping Survivors*. And it was precisely this combined approach that was soon to become typical, the use of questionnaires in particular, making it possible to go about things systematically (as shall be shown).

Systematization was also important because Wiesenthal and his helpers realized that the presence of thousands of survivors was an opportunity they did not want to miss. As Wiesenthal put it in 1947, it was a matter of "making the most of the time they spend here in the Austrian waiting room"²⁶ and recruiting the survivors in the DP camps as witnesses before they left Austria and emigrated all over the world. The time available was often very short – especially once the *International Refugee Organization* (IRO) had taken over the care of the DPs in mid-1947 and established a resettlement program. Not to mention the many additional survivors, most of them from Poland, who arrived in Austria from

---

24 Wiener Magistratsabteilung [Vienna Municipal Department] 21 to the Central Jewish Committee, 9.11.1946, M.9, 20, 64, Yad Vashem Archive.
25 Simon Wiesenthal: *Recht nicht Rache, Erinnerungen,* Frankfurt/Main: Ullstein, 1989, 54.
26 Simon Wiesenthal: Die Rolle der Jüdischen Historischen Documentation bei der Verfolgung und Bestrafung der Kriegsverbrecher (Das Beispiel Österreich), 25.11.1947, I.1., Mappe Jüdische Historische Dokumentation (JHD), Unterlagen zum Verein Jüdische Historische Dokumentation, 1, VWI-SWA.

1946 onwards to flee Europe with the assistance of the Jewish organization *Bricha*, which used the infrastructure of the DP camps to smuggle them illegally via a number of routes, some of which led through Upper Austria.[27] What is more, it was important to force the pace of the creation of such a systematic basis "as long as the memories of the eyewitnesses were still fresh enough."[28]

Jewish Historical Documentation

The aim was also to institutionalize the process of systematization by founding[29] an organization that was as independent as possible – unlike comparable survivors' initiatives of the same period, which had, however, a similar focus. Later in 1947, Wiesenthal himself put it like this: Instead of "limiting itself to work of a purely historical nature," the *Jewish Historical Documentation Center* (JHD) in Linz aimed to "fight for atonement for the crimes of the war years [and] assume the role of a reminder to the conscience of the immediate Jewish past [as well as] using compelling facts to force the authorities to prosecute and punish Nazi criminals."[30]

Evidence was to be collected and evaluated with the aid of a central office in Linz and a network of staff in the DP camps. The work rested "mainly on the shoulders of former concentration camp prisoners; together with our representatives in various refugee camps, between 20 and 30 people were active at any one time, the number fluctuated constantly."[31] At first, the monthly budget of 50 dollars provided by Abraham Silberschein had to suffice to finance most of the running costs – to cover postage and telephone calls, for example. Silberschein had emigrated to Switzerland from Poland before the war and had built up the RELICO refugee relief organization in Geneva, where Wiesenthal became acquainted with him in 1946 and got him interested in his idea.[32]

---

27 For information on the cooperation between Wiesenthal and Asher Ben-Nathan (or Arthur Pier), the Bricha Commander for Austria, see: Michael John: "Zwischenstation Oberösterreich", in Thomas Albrich (ed.): *Flucht nach Eretz Israel*, Innsbruck: Studienverlag, 1998, 67–92, here 76, and Asher Ben-Nathan and Susanne Urban (eds.): *Die Bricha. Aus dem Terror nach Eretz Israel*, Düsseldorf: Droste, 2005, 236.
28 Joseph Wechsberg: "Der Mann und seine Aufgabe", in Wiesenthal: *Doch die Mörder leben*, 19.
29 Approval for the foundation of the Jewish Historical Documentation association from the Directorate of Security for Upper Austria, 12.2.1947, I.1., Mappe JHD, VWI-SWA.
30 Wiesenthal: Die Rolle der Jüdischen Historischen Documentation, 2, I.1., Mappe JHD, VWI-SWA.
31 Wiesenthal: *Eichmann*, 58.
32 Segev: *Wiesenthal*, 102–103.

In June 1947, the Linz office had eight staff, not counting Wiesenthal himself, while 17 others worked as so-called correspondents in the DP camps in Upper Austria.[33] Up until now, it has only been possible to identify a small number of the staff by name: Josef Weissmann served many years as "secretary-general", while Mordechaj Schorr was the head of the archive.[34] Helene Fucksmann, the only female member of staff identified so far, was the correspondent responsible for the Ebelsberg DP camp.[35]

Wiesenthal was probably influenced by a number of role models when he founded the JHD. However, the origins of these ideas and influences cannot be identified with any real certainty in the present chapter. Wiesenthal made mention of the fact that the key inspiration came to him in the autumn of 1946 during a visit to the *Central Committee of Liberated Jews* in Munich.[36] It is also conceivable that the role model was imported from Poland, so to speak, and came to Linz in the person of Mejlech Bakalczuk. Before his arrival, Bakalczuk had been actively involved in a number of projects in Poland, including the establishment of the *Central Jewish Historical Commission* (CZKH, *Centralna Żydowska Komisja Historyczna*) and – fleeing from anti-Semitic pogroms – he left there and came to the Bindermichl DP camp in Linz in the spring of 1946.[37] The documentation center which Tuviah Friedmann set up in Vienna in the summer of 1946 with the assistance of Asher Ben-Nathan and which was soon working closely with Wiesenthal was probably just as influential.[38]

---

33 Wiesenthal to Silberschein, 30.6.1947, M.20,182,126–128, Yad Vashem Archive.
34 Wiesenthal: *Eichmann*, 59–60.
35 See the section below titled "Possibilities and Limitations of the Model".
36 Wiesenthal: *Eichmann*, 50.
37 For more information, see the entry for "Historische Kommissionen" in Dan Diner (ed.): *Enzyklopädie Jüdischer Geschichte und Kultur*, vol. 3, He-Lu, Stuttgart/Weimar: Metzler, 2016, 70–75, here 71, and Laura Jockusch: *Collect and Record! Jewish Holocaust Documentation in Early Postwar Europe*, Oxford: Oxford University Press, 2012, 150.
38 For information on Tuviah Friedmann (1922–2011), a survivor of the Holocaust who came from Radom, and his work with Wiesenthal, see: John: *Zwischenstation Oberösterreich*, 76, as well as Ben-Nathan and Urban: *Bricha*, 236 and also Jockusch: *Collect and Record!*, 152, and Stephan Stach: "Praktische Geschichte. Der Beitrag jüdischer Organisationen zur Verfolgung von NS-Verbrechen in Polen und Österreich in den späten 40er Jahren", in Katharina Stengel and Werner Konitzer (eds.): *Opfer als Akteure. Interventionen ehemaliger NS-Verfolgter in der Nachkriegszeit*, Frankfurt/New York: Campus, 2008, 242–262.

Questionnaires and Card Indexes as the Basis for Further Work

Initially, questionnaires were the primary means which were put to use in order to find witnesses and collect information on Nazi crimes; they were distributed in the DP camps of the American zone and filled out with the aid of the correspondents. Distribution of the more than 3,000 questionnaires created in this way started as early as in November 1946 (even before the JHD had officially been founded). Survivors were requested to provide information which included personal data and details of their path of persecution as well as of any functions which they performed. This information was to be authenticated by two witnesses.[39] The majority of the questionnaires – about 2,500 of them – had probably been returned to the JHD in Linz by August 1947.[40] A few hundred latecomers trickled in during the years that followed and by the autumn of 1952 at last, 3,295 questionnaires had been returned – an impressive number. However, the work did not stop at the questionnaires. In order to be able to use the data and the information collected in this way as quickly as possible, the completed questionnaires were successively evaluated and gradually made accessible by means of a number of card indexes. It seems that this process had already begun in the winter of 1946/47 as in one of his monthly reports to Silberschein Wiesenthal announced in March – perhaps rather prematurely – that work on the card file was nearly complete.[41] In fact, the JHD developed quite a sophisticated card index system for this purpose, which – as is also the case with the questionnaires themselves – no one has yet made efforts to reconstruct. One ob-

---

[39] These questionnaires are a very interesting source. First conceived in 1946 in response to plans to hold elections for representatives to the *Jewish Central Committee*, they were originally intended to prevent former Jewish collaborators from putting themselves up for election or taking on any official functions in future. This topic cannot be covered in greater detail here. The author of the present paper is currently working on a publication which deals with the subject – including a look at the so-called honor courts held in Jewish DP camps. For the latest research on the topic, please see Laura Jockusch and Gabriel N. Finder (eds.): *Jewish Honor Courts: Revenge, Retribution, and Reconciliation in Europe and Israel after the Holocaust*, Detroit: Wayne State University Press, 2015.

[40] See the descriptive information for the questionnaires, accommodated in 16 files, which includes the earliest and latest date of creation. According to this information, the majority of the questionnaires were filled out between the beginning of November 1946 and the spring of 1947. M.9, 122–137, Yad Vashem Archive.

[41] His original words were "The file of all witnesses living in Austria is almost completed." See the transcripts of Wiesenthal's letters to Silberschein, 21.4.1947 and 31.3.1947, RG 1347, 4, YIVO.

stacle that will have to be overcome is the fact that the various card indexes that Wiesenthal later gave to *Yad Vashem* have not been indexed yet, let alone made available online, which is why only a rough outline of the way they functioned can be given here.[42] However, one thing is certain: the card indexes made it possible to connect the information given in the questionnaires regarding the places where crimes were committed and the perpetrators who committed them with the (data of the) witnesses concerned, so that the latter could be found at a later date – in order to give evidence in court, for example. It seems that a pivotal point of the whole card index system was possibly a card index of places which contained around 1,000 entries in the end, including concentration camps, labor camps, ghettos and other sites where crimes had been committed. Similar to the way a database query works today, specific information could be compiled from this card index, such as a register of perpetrators who had committed crimes in a specific place. A register titled *Liste der Kriegsverbrecher aus Radom, laut der Kartei* [List of war criminals from Radom, according to the card index] contains the names and ranks of 70 individuals, for example.[43]

The card index of places also provided the basis for comprehensive directories. Probably in the late summer of 1947, for example, the JHD created a version of the provisional *Directory of concentration camps, labor camps, ghettoes and localities in the territories occupied by the Germans* (*Verzeichnis der KZ-Lager, Arbeitslager, Ghettos und Ortschaften in den durch die Deutschen besetzten Gebieten*). The cover page of this directory includes an additional text which also summarizes the way it worked: "The people listed in the card index of the Jewish Historical Documentation Center can testify about the conditions in the camps mentioned here and about the people who worked there. (more to follow)."[44] The lists, registers and directories generated with the aid of the questionnaires and card indexes were soon made available to other institutions, as Wiesenthal summed up at the end of 1947: "Each and every department of the People's

---

42 See "The Wiesenthal Collection," in *Yad Vashem Bulletin*, 1, April 1957, 28–29. In addition to the card index of places, other card indexes are mentioned here, which, however, require further research. Mention should be made of just one further card index which is particularly noteworthy because of the content-related evaluation which was apparently already planned at the time: "A lexicon of terms dealing with the life of Jews under the Nazi regime, indicating the number of the relevant questionnaires from which these terms are derived." Available at: http://www.simon-wiesenthal-archiv.at/02_dokuzentrum/01_geschichte/img/YadVashemBuletin.pdf. Last accessed: 22.6.2019.
43 Liste der Kriegsverbrecher aus Radom, laut der Kartei, [undated, probably summer 1947], M.9, 812, 53, Yad Vashem Archive.
44 Verzeichnis der KZ-Lager, Arbeitslager, Ghettos und Ortschaften in den durch die Deutschen besetzten Gebieten [undated, probably late summer 1947], RG 1347, 4, YIVO.

Court, the State Police and the American, English and French offices for war crimes have our directory of localities and use it. Our services are much in demand from these authorities who are sending us letters and inquiries all the time."[45]

In fact, not only had the JHD started evaluating the data quickly, the information gleaned from the questionnaires was also put to good use right from the start. For example, in the winter of 1946/47 already, the JHD was able to find numerous witnesses for the military court proceedings held by the US army in Dachau at this time and this must also have impressed the *War Crimes Group* when they attested in February that Wiesenthal had provided "invaluable assistance to this organization in securing evidence for use in the Mauthausen Concentration Camps case".[46] Shortly afterwards, in his monthly report to Silberschein for March 1947, Wiesenthal's self-confident introduction reads as follows: "We have got hold of 249 witnesses to be present in the process in Dachau against the SS men from Mauthausen, Ebensee, Melk, Steyr and other concentration camps in Austria. The witnesses – each group consisting of 30 people – are leaving for Germany. The first group has just returned."[47] During the course of the preliminary investigations for the trials, the witnesses made statements, identified individual perpetrators at identity parades and finally gave evidence at the actual trials. In fact, it would be very interesting to take a new step and make a concrete comparison of the obviously successful search for witnesses with the court documents. Because it may well have been an exaggeration when, in connection with the *Dachau trials*, Wiesenthal argued elsewhere that "70 percent of all the witnesses for the prosecution come from Austria and were organized through us."[48]

"ATTENTION former concentration camp prisoners [...]!": Notices and Appeals for Information

However, the questionnaires were not the only means by which information and testimonies were generated, collected and then made available to others. Numerous notices and appeals for information also played a role later on. Once Wiesen-

---

[45] Wiesenthal: Die Rolle der JHD, 2, I.1., Mappe JHD, VWI-SWA.
[46] Certificate of the War Crimes Group of the U.S. army for Wiesenthal, 5.2.1947, II.1., A-I.1.6, VWI-SWA.
[47] Wiesenthal to Silberschein, 30.3.1947, RG 1347, 5, YIVO.
[48] Wiesenthal: Die Rolle der JHD, 5, I.1., Mappe JHD, VWI-SWA.

thal had been successful in finding important witnesses for the *Dachau trials*, he received photos from there in return, depicting Nazi criminals who were already in detention but against whom the American investigators did not have any or did not have enough incriminating material. By putting the photos on display in DP camps, it was possible to gather more "evidence against a few hundred criminals who were shortly to be released and send the witnesses to the Dachau trial."[49] If and how this really made it possible to prevent the release of any perpetrators who were about to be set free and what concrete role the witnesses provided by the JHD played in trials like this would have to be examined in greater detail here as well.[50] The example below serves to illustrate what the aforementioned notices looked like. It concerns the search for witnesses to testify against two guards from the Melk concentration camp, a sub-camp of the Mauthausen concentration camp. The following words can be seen above the photos and the details of the two men: "<u>ATTENTION former concentration camp prisoners from the MELK CONCENTRATION CAMP!</u> Anyone who knows anything about the behavior and the deeds of the people shown below is requested to pass this information on, either orally or in writing, to the Jewish Historical Documentation Center, [Linz], Goethestraße 63."[51]

Many of these notices have survived and they do not only cover the locations which belonged to the camp system of the Mauthausen concentration camp or the Buchenwald or Flossenbürg concentration camps and which were the focus of the *Dachau trials*.[52] One, for example, bears the heading: "ATTENTION

---

49 Cf. Wiesenthal: Die Rolle der JHD, 3, I.1., Mappe JHD, VWI-SWA. The suggestion that the investigations of the war crimes in Dachau were speeded up in order to prevent impending releases is also corroborated by other sources. See, for example, the transcript of the interview with George Czuczka in the Austrian Heritage Archive (AHA), Vienna. Available at: http://austrianheritagearchive.at/de/interviews/person/74. Last accessed: 22.6.2019.
50 As far as I know, no research papers have yet been published on the here mentioned process of providing these witnesses to courts like in Dachau or later to Austrian People's Courts. The testimonies against Karl Horvath, the former prisoner functionary (*"Kapo"*) in the Gusen II sub-camp of Mauthausen, which were collected in the Bindermichl and Ebelsberg DP camps, for example, could provide a way of approaching the subject. See among other things: Fucksmann to Wiesenthal, 3.2.1948, M.9, 49, 83, Yad Vashem Archive and Wolfgang Freitag: *Der Fall Karl Horvath. Ein Loiperdorfer "Zigeuner" vor dem Linzer Volksgericht*, Vienna: Mandelbaum 2019, 64, and Christian Rabl: *Der KZ-Komplex Mauthausen vor Gericht*, Dissertation, University of Vienna 2017, 161.
51 Call for witnesses to provide information on Albert Gillenberger and Kurt Hirsche, [undated], emphasis in the original, M.9, 53, 70, Yad Vashem Archive.
52 Appeal for witnesses, undated, M.9, 53, 102, Yad Vashem Archive.

JEWS from LODZ!" and appeals for witnesses who can provide information about a guard who worked at the ghetto of the same name.[53]

Although these notices did not lead to witnesses being found for the *Dachau trials* alone, this approach does seem to have been particularly successful – in purely numerical terms – in that case: at the end of November 1947, Wiesenthal gave Silberschein a summary of the "services provided for the trial against the SS Mauthausen and subcamps before the military court in Dachau" and concludes that "the witnesses which the J.H.D. was able to provide to the court by displaying photos and carrying out further research gave testimony which resulted in a total of 36 death sentences, 19 life sentences, 498 years of imprisonment."[54]

In addition to the notices, newspapers and the press also published repeated appeals. This is mirrored by many of the documents from the Linz period which are held by *Yad Vashem*. DP publications were used as well as domestic newspapers, for example. This was an ideal solution in Linz, which was home to a

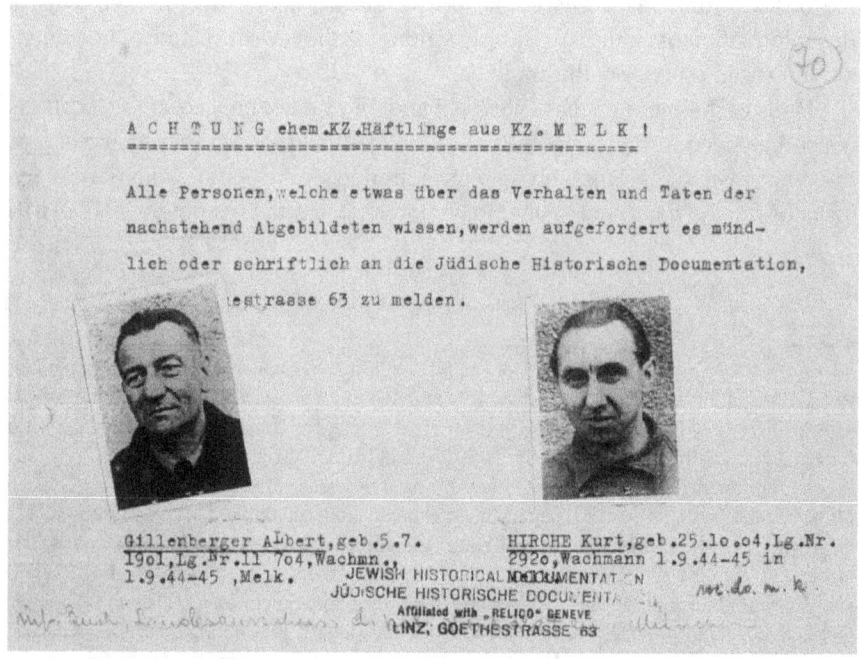

Fig. 2: Copy of the notice addressed to former prisoners from Melk which was distributed to all DP camps and Jewish communities in the US zone, probably in 1947 (Yad Vashem Archives)

---

53 Appeal for witnesses re. Anton Slezak, undated, M.9, 53, 3, Yad Vashem Archive.
54 Wiesenthal to Silberstein, 20.11.1847, RG 1347, 4, YIVO.

number of DP camps at the time – as well as Bindermichl, there was, among others, also Ebelsberg (Star of David) and the Wegscheid transit camp (Camp Tyler) – and can, according to Michael John, certainly be regarded as a center of the Jewish press.⁵⁵ One such publication was *Ojfgang*, which appeared in Bindermichl and published various appeals, including one in April 1948 calling for witnesses able to testify against Nazi criminals in Latvia.⁵⁶ Appeals were also published in foreign newspapers, for example in Hungary, leading to a certain Hirsch Lajos contacting the JHD from there in April 1948 after the Budapest newspaper *Új élet* had published an appeal directed at former prisoners from the Mauthausen concentration camp calling for witnesses who could testify against Albert Matuschke.⁵⁷ This approach too – involving the press and creating publicity – is one which Simon Wiesenthal was to fall back on again and again throughout his life, by the way.

Expanding the Successful Model

As the approach described above had proved its worth, the JHD began to act proactively and offered its material to other authorities too. The following argument – which makes mention of the successful involvement in the *Dachau trials* – is found in a letter addressed to the *Innsbruck People's Court* written in August 1947, for example:

> As recently those war criminals who were surrendered to the Austrian authorities and various regional courts in the Glasenbach internment camp, [are now available] we suggest that the People's Court avail itself of our card index or give us a list of the names of the war criminals with details of the site of their activity and we will use the card index to find the witnesses, <u>if they are in Austria</u>, and make them available to the People's Court.⁵⁸

The idea was to exploit the circumstance that many Nazi criminals were still in Allied captivity at the time. And above all, to do so while most of the witnesses were still in the DP camps. Hence lists created from the material were not only

---

55 Quoted from Sandra Knopp: "Erinnern, berichten, bewahren. Zeitungen jüdischer DPs in Deutschland und Österreich," in Danielle Spera and Werner Hanak-Lettner (eds.): *Displaced in Österreich. Jüdische Flüchtlinge seit 1945*, Innsbruck/Vienna/Bozen: StudienVerlag 2015, 100 – 110, here 104.
56 Letter to the editors of *Ojfgang*, 14.4.1948, [in Yiddish], M.9, 246, 1, Yad Vashem Archive.
57 Hirsch Lajos to JHD, 3.4.1948, M.9, 679, 3, Yad Vashem Archive.
58 Wiesenthal to the Innsbruck People's Court, 6.8.1947, M.9, 45,7, Yad Vashem Archive, grammar and emphasis in the original.

sent to the authorities in Austria, but also to "all the Allied authorities, the Americans, British, French and Russians, as well as to the Hungarian, Polish, Czechoslovakian and Yugoslavian government and before long the Documentation Center was playing an important role."[59] The following example shows how far news of the JHD's methods had spread in the meantime – and that they were even being applied in other countries and zones. In November 1948, the war criminals department of the *Central Committee of Liberated Jews* in Munich acting on behalf of the Leipzig public prosecutor's office asked the JHD to send witnesses from the Bindermichl and Ebelsberg DP camps in Linz to testify at the HASAG trial which, was to begin a few days later:

> We have now received a list from Leipzig. The Leipzig public prosecution service has sent the invitations to the witnesses by telegram. It turns out that not 3 but 9 witnesses are expected from you. [...] No doubt you have obtained the necessary inter-zonal passes for these witnesses by now. Now we only have to agree on the travel arrangements.[60]

Wiesenthal was not alone in envisioning the creation of an international network to improve cooperation at international level. With this in mind, he made the following suggestion at a conference attended by representatives of comparable survivors' initiatives which took place in Paris in December 1947: "A European office of the Jewish Historical Documentation Center should be set up [and] special war crimes departments should be established at all the branches of the J.H.D. or other similar historical committees. A joint European card index should be set up for the purpose of sharing the experience gained so far."[61] In the spring of that year, the JHD had already invited comparable institutions in Europe to proceed in the same way and had encouraged them to work together and exchange information. The institutions concerned also included Jewish communities in Paris and Madrid, to mention just two examples.[62] In fact, a *Comité Européen de Coordination* was indeed successfully established, but cooperation was not intensified any further because – as Laura Jockusch shows – not only

---

59 Simon Wiesenthal: report, untitled [1972], 5, I.1., Mappe JHD, VWI-SWA.
60 Central Committee of Liberated Jews, Munich to JHD, 12.11.1948, M.9, 45, 158, Yad Vashem Archive. The HASAG, or Hugo Schneider AG, profited among other things from forced labor carried out by concentration camp prisoners who were deployed via sub-camps of the Buchenwald concentration camp in the Leipzig area.
61 Wiesenthal: Die Rolle der JHD, 25.11.1947, 6, I.1., Mappe JHD, VWI-SWA. This manuscript which has already been cited several times is probably the manuscript for the talk that Wiesenthal gave at the conference in early December 1947 in Paris.
62 Letters to the communities in Paris and Milano, May 1947, M.9, 19, 39 and 35, Yad Vashem Archive.

did the focus of financial support shift towards Israel, which was just coming into being, but cooperation between organizations in the West and in the East was also becoming increasingly difficult as the Cold War got underway.[63]

Possibilities and Limitations of the Model

However well the model may have worked, in many cases it also proved to have limitations. For example, although it was perfectly possible to create lists with names of perpetrators for a great number of places, problems were encountered when it came to quite a lot of localities in Eastern Europe, which were often small in size: "We are in the difficult situation of usually having no more than one or two testimonies against these persons, as the Latvian Jews were completely wiped out in many villages."[64]

Another challenge was the fact that more and more individual survivors reacted to the appeals with disinterest. One of the reasons for this was probably that many people believed the Austrian judiciary to be too lenient and, if the perpetrators were convicted at all, they were often released shortly afterwards.[65] Survivors also had to cope with the fact that the reports they had submitted in quite large numbers since 1945, which had initially been received with interest, now frequently met with denial.[66] And last but not least, even many of themselves now wanted to look to the future and leave the years of persecution behind them. Often, however, the notices put up in the camps were simply covered up by posters announcing cultural events or the like which were soon pasted over them, for example.[67]

Despite all of this, Wiesenthal was still keen to push on with the work. This was probably due in no small part to the fact that it could also function as a means of helping people to help themselves, as he had found out for himself when his work for the War Crimes Office in the liberated Mauthausen concentra-

---

[63] See, in more detail, Jockusch: *Collect and Record!*, 160–185.
[64] Wiesenthal to World Jewish Congress and the National Community Relations, 1.12.48 und 8.2.1949, III.1., Büro Linz, 1945–50, Buchstabe W und N, VWI-SWA.
[65] Jockusch: *Collect and Record!*, 152.
[66] Peter Novick: *Nach dem Holocaust. Der Umgang mit dem Massenmord*, Stuttgart/Munich: Deutsche Verlags-Anstalt, 2001, 184.
[67] The further above mentioned Helen Fucksman from the Ebelsberg DP camp is one of the correspondents who provides Wiesenthal with regular, detailed reports on the response to the appeals and passes on information about witnesses. See M.9, 49, 89, Yad Vashem Archive and, for more detailed information and different examples, Jockusch: *Collect and Record!*, 152.

tion camp gave him a mission and helped him find new meaning in life. He argued as follows:

> No one can really imagine or appreciate how the camp inmates feel when they hear it reported that a person who murdered or tortured members of their family has been arrested. These reports are much more important for them and for their rehabilitation than food parcels and extra calories. We have reawakened people's interest in the subject and have revived their search spirit.[68]

What is more, instead of continuing to reduce survivors to the status of victims or passive recipients of assistance, the JHD involved them actively in its work. This probably also had a positive impact on the survivors as it gave them self-efficacy and enabled them to experience themselves as actively engaged agents.[69] Years later, Wiesenthal still remembered what this work meant to survivors, as it did not only provide them with an opportunity to participate in the establishment of justice, but also gave them a means of coming to terms with and coping with their experiences. Both of these things are absolutely essential if people are to gain any ability to look forward and build a new life:

> Material compensation and parcels of food and clothing will not be enough to encourage the survivors of this terrible bloodbath to settle down to a normal life. What they need is the certainty that the world will punish such criminals [like Eichmann], and that this punishment will remain a warning for all time, so that such abominations will never be repeated.[70]

In the late summer of 1947, the JHD had already launched a remarkable campaign to remind the survivors of the importance of this work and to increase their motivation: "is entitled to wear our *'Einen Mörder entlarvt'* [a murderer exposed] badge". Together with a number of blank forms and pre-printed documents and various questionnaires, one of the folders in Wiesenthal's archive in Vienna also contains a certificate, which is the source of the quotation above.[71] The certificate and the badge which came with it were intended as a means of motivating people and, as Wiesenthal put it in the above quotation, of reviving their "search spirit" again. At the same time, they were seen as an expression of appreciation for concrete information which had led to a perpetrator being identified and apprehended. One of the few surviving certificates was

---

[68] Wiesenthal: Die Rolle der JHD, 3, I.1., Mappe JHD, VWI-SWA.
[69] See also Stengel and Konitzer (eds.): *Opfer als Akteure*.
[70] Wiesenthal: *Eichmann*, 102.
[71] Certificate, I.1, Mappe JHD, VWI-SWA.

awarded to a certain Mejer Blitz, who received it on 11.10.1947.[72] In the summer, he and another survivor were near the Admont Jewish DP camp – located in the British zone of Austria – because they wanted to exchange the canned goods and chocolate they had received from the British for some poultry as part of their preparations for a feast day. Wiesenthal later described what happened next:

> But the farmers were poor. Most of them got out of the situation by advising them to try asking someone else. And one of the pieces of advice they were given caught the attention of the two young Jews: "Try asking the one up there. He has a big farm and at least two thousand chickens. But he might throw you out. He hates the Jews. People say he was a big Nazi.[73]

On hearing this, the two of them went straight to Linz to see Wiesenthal. He accompanied them to the British zone to inform the local gendarmerie where they learnt that the farmer's name was Franz Murer. Knowing that Murer bore the primary responsibility for the death of countless people in the Vilnius ghetto, they rushed to the Admont DP camp where there were some survivors from Vilnius:

> With the help of the camp committee clerks, we wrote down four witness statements, had the signatures authenticated and went straight to the Gaishorn gendarmerie station together with the witnesses. Two gendarmes immediately left to find Murer and were able to arrest him in time. Somehow he must have been warned; they found him ready to leave with two suitcases full of gold and other valuables.[74]

The British handed Murer over to the Soviets, who sentenced him to 25 years of imprisonment in 1948. However, only a few years later, he was able to return to Austria as a "Spätheimkehrer" [late homecomer][75], where he soon carved out a career in the Styrian ÖVP and the regional farmers' association. The evidence collected against Murer is also remarkable from an archival point of view: when Wiesenthal tried to take Murer back to court at the beginning of the 1960s – he was in Vienna by then – one of the first steps he took was to contact Yad Vashem and ask them to send him copies of more than one hundred witness statements[76] which he had already collected against Murer during his time in Linz. This goes to show how important the evidence collected in Linz really was.

---

72 Certificate for Mejer Blitz, 11.10.1947, M.9, 46,5, Yad Vashem Archive.
73 Cited in Peter Michael Lingens: "Wer ist Simon Wiesenthal?", in Wiesenthal: *Recht nicht Rache*, 13–39, here 30.
74 As cited in Wiesenthal: *Ich jagte Eichmann*, 138.
75 See Garscha: *Wiesenthals Beitrag*, 12.
76 Witness statements, I.1., Mappe Franz Murer (1), VWI-SWA.

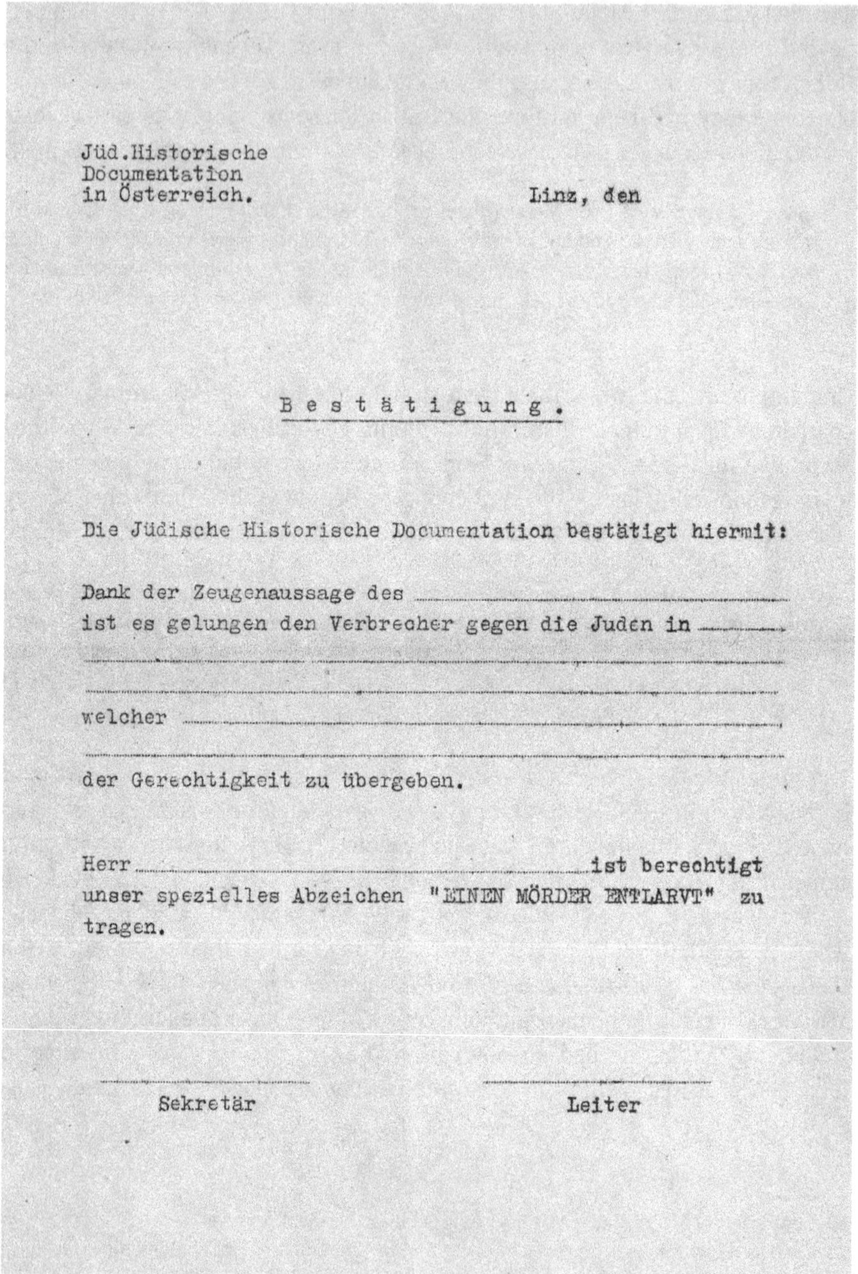

Jüd.Historische
Documentation
in Österreich.   Linz, den

B e s t ä t i g u n g .

Die Jüdische Historische Documentation bestätigt hiermit:

Dank der Zeugenaussage des _____
ist es gelungen den Verbrecher gegen die Juden in _____
_____

welcher _____

der Gerechtigkeit zu übergeben.

Herr _____ ist berechtigt
unser spezielles Abzeichen "EINEN MÖRDER ENTLARVT" zu
tragen.

            Sekretär   Leiter

Fig. 3: Pre-printed certificate awarded for information which led to the apprehension of a Nazi criminal, 1947 (Simon Wiesenthal Archive, Vienna Wiesenthal Institute)

The Beginning of the End of the JHD

Following in particular the foundation of the State of Israel in May 1948 and the American *Displaced Persons Act of 1948* – which was to be emulated in the years that followed by other countries with similar emigration programs – the mass emigration of most of the witnesses, which had now begun, became a problem and heralded the end of the JHD as it had worked up until then. Moreover, once the big American and Allied trials like those held in Dachau (1948) or Nuremberg (1949) had ended, the interest shown by the Americans in carrying out further investigations into Nazi criminals, which had been waning for some time, now became even weaker. Although the People's Courts continued to work until 1955, they still could not fill the gap: a large proportion of the trials had already been completed at that time and, according to Winfried Garscha, almost 80 percent of the investigative proceedings had been initiated before March 1948.[77]

Wiesenthal continued working all the same, despite making plans to leave Linz on a number of occasions and despite having at least one opportunity to do so: when an application for emigration to Israel which was submitted to the IRO for him and his family at the beginning of 1949 was accepted, for example.[78] But Wiesenthal stayed, even though his wife had urged him to leave Austria again and again. We can only speculate about his reasons here. According to Alan Levy, Wiesenthal did not want to leave Linz because he wanted to keep a watchful eye on Eichmann's family, who also lived there.[79] Tom Segev, who authored an impressive and sensitive biography of Wiesenthal, sums it up by saying that Wiesenthal stayed in Austria in the end because he assumed that it must make more sense to search for Nazi criminals there than in Israel.[80]

The end of his documentation center in Linz has already been mentioned; in the mid-1950s, Wiesenthal gave *Yad Vashem* most of the material collected by the center. However, by then, Wiesenthal had already been sitting on packed crates, so to speak, for a number of years. In a letter to Tuviah Friedmann written at the beginning of 1951 he sounds rather monosyllabic and disappointed: "Dear Tadek! I have answered your two letters. Of course, I welcome any cooperation, but I would like to point out that everything is in the process of being wound down here. 95% of the witnesses against the detainees have left." But what is most remarkable here is the fact that the documents of the JHD are already

---

77 Garscha: *Wiesenthal*, 4 and 9.
78 Application for Assistance, 3.2.1.3/80880905/ITS Digital Archive, Arolsen Archives.
79 Levy: *Akte Wiesenthal*, 130.
80 Segev: *Wiesenthal*, 162.

"nailed up in boxes and ready to be taken to Israel."[81] But obviously, nothing came of this plan either. When the financing for a possible continuation of the work of the JHD fell through too on Silberschein's death at the end of 1951, Wiesenthal started to look for alternatives. In March 1952, he tried to set up a business in Israel selling cars no longer needed by the IRO which had also ceased operations in the meantime[82] – however, his efforts were not crowned with success. Wiesenthal seems to have been so frustrated about his search for the financial means he would need to make a new start in Israel that at the end of 1952 he even tried to sell his collection of books and documents to a stamp collector.[83] This too – happily – led to nothing. Only through the mediation of Tuviah Friedmann, who had left Vienna for Israel in 1952, did *Yad Vashem* begin to take an interest in Wiesenthal's documentation. In the spring of 1956, two crates with a combined weight of 436 kg were finally on their way to Israel by ship[84] – Wiesenthal, however, remained in Linz.

Aid to Refugees Continues

Wiesenthal continued working with refugees in Linz until 1960, which – in view of the work he had been doing with survivors from 1945 onwards – demonstrates quite a remarkable degree of continuity. In the spring of 1953[85] already, he worked for the *World ORT Union* (ORT) organizing vocational training for the remaining DPs as well as for other Jewish refugees who soon began to arrive in Austria from various countries of Eastern and Southeastern Europe, including several thousand from Hungary from 1956/1957 on. The aim was to improve the refugees' chances of being able to emigrate by providing them with specialized training and further education in sought-after occupations.[86] Working from the District Office in Linz, he coordinated various courses for car mechanics, courses in metalwork and tailoring and courses for painters and varnishers – in-

---

81 Wiesenthal to Tuviah Friedmann, 2.2.1951, I.1., Mappe JHD, Korrespondenz, VWI-SWA.
82 Wiesenthal to Daniel Segat in Genf, 12.3.1952, III.1., Korrespondenz Varia, 1946–1955_Buchstabe S, VWI-SWA.
83 Wiesenthal to Jaques Rogers, 12.12.1952, III.1., Korrespondenz Varia, 1946–1955, Buchstabe R, VWI-SWA.
84 Wiesenthal to Yad Vashem, 1.3.1956, III.1., SW Büro Linz 1.1.53–31.12.56, Buchstabe X-Z, VWI-SWA.
85 ORT to Wiesenthal, 8.5.1953, II.1., A-I.1.9, VWI-SWA.
86 See "Interview mit Simon Wiesenthal über die Befreiung des KZ Mauthausen und seine Tätigkeit in Linz," in *Arche*, 9 (1995), 8–13, here 12.

itially only in Upper Austria, later in other places such as Innsbruck too, for example. From the mid-1950s onwards he also organized courses for TV repairmen and courses in electrical engineering.[87] It was not until his contracts with the ORT[88] in Linz had expired that Wiesenthal – certainly encouraged by the capture and conviction of Eichmann – left Linz after about 16 years there and opened a new office in Vienna on the invitation of the Jewish communities of Austria in August 1961. Here he dedicated himself completely to the search for Nazi criminals from then on. One of the very first things he did was to obtain copies of some of his earlier documents from the Linz period.[89]

Conclusion

To sum up, it can be said that the model developed by Wiesenthal in Linz worked quite successfully – although a next step would be to examine the figures he quoted in connection with the *Dachau trials* on various occasions. At least it worked as long as the relationship between help for and help from survivors, which has been highlighted here, was still possible. The presence, involvement, active and collective participation of the survivors as witnesses offered the opportunity for a systematic, targeted approach based on concrete information. The years 1946 to 1948 stand out in particular as this was when the two different aspects – gathering information and finding witnesses on the one hand and detaining and prosecuting the perpetrators on the other – interacted and could be combined particularly successfully. Admittedly, what has been described here needs to be looked at in greater detail and other documents need to be consulted, such as the abovementioned card indexes in the *Yad Vashem* archive. Building on this, a broader contextualization would then make sense, including comparison with other survivors' initiatives. So, for example, it would make sense to draw a comparison with the situation in Vienna, where Tuviah Friedmann and Asher Ben Nathan built up their documentation center. And instead of examining the early years in Linz in isolation and focusing only on the two extreme poles constituted by the victims and the perpetrators, so to speak, it seems that another promising approach would be to integrate other groups to a greater extent – the local population and the occupying forces in equal measure

---

87 See the correspondence between Wiesenthal and ORT, III.1., SW Büro Linz 1.1.53–31.12.56, Buchstabe O, VWI-SWA.
88 Certificate of ORT for Wiesenthal, 10.1.1961, II.1., A-I.1.9, VWI-SWA.
89 See, for example, the folder Jüdisches Dokumentationszentrum Simon Wiesenthal, November 1961–Dezember 1963, A/VIE/IKG/III/DZ/2, Archiv der IKG Wien.

– in order to draw a more comprehensive picture of the whole.[90] This broadening of the focus should also be seen in spatial terms: Wiesenthal's activity also needs to be examined against the background of Linz as a divided city, split by the border between the American and Soviet zones. And, last but not least, it would be very interesting to examine if and how this early work - in all its facets - can be seen in the context of what we nowadays understand as Transitional Justice.

---

90 For example, see Atina Grossmann: *Jews, Germans and the Allies. Close Encounters in Occupied Germany*, Princeton: Princeton University Press, 2007, and Adam Seipp: *Strangers in the Wild Place: Refugees, Americans and a German Town, 1945–1942*, Bloomington: Indian University Press, 2013.

Silke von der Emde
Caring for the Dead and the Living
DPs and the Arolsen Archives of Feelings

Abstract: Although Displaced Persons (DPs) made crucial contributions to the organization and operation of the *International Tracing Service* in its early years, their work in the ITS has not been analyzed in any depth. Playing the dual role of archivists who handled the files and subjects whose stories were collected in the files, they were instrumental both in the ITS's mission of tracing the fate of the victims of Nazi persecution and in the creation of a community within the ITS where Displaced Persons could find a safe place of healing. Using archival sources and oral interviews to recover the stories of the DPs in Bad Arolsen not only changes our narrative about Displaced Persons after the Second World War but also reconstructs the ITS as an *archive of feeling*, in Ann Cvetkovich's terminology. Understanding the importance of their work and continuing DPs' efforts to be responsive to the "pain of others" make possible active, multidirectional memory practices that not only look to the past but also to the politics of the now.

Introduction

Jakob Verbitzki's personnel file in the *Arolsen Archives* – the new name for the *International Tracing Service* (ITS) in Bad Arolsen and one of the largest archives of Holocaust documents in the world – contains two certificates of employment from May and August 1949, which he needed in order to apply for a reduced-fare train ticket to visit the grave of his wife in the Ruhr region.[1] Verbitzki, a Displaced Person (DP) from Ukraine who was employed as a janitor in the *International Tracing Service* in 1949, was one of the few DPs who had a physical place that could hold the memories of a dead loved one. The fact that he seems to have taken the long trip repeatedly in times when such travel was difficult and expen-

---

[1] The ITS was first set up as a tracing service to help families of victims receive information about the fate of their loved ones and assist Allies in repatriating the millions of Displaced Persons who were stranded in Germany. Its name has recently been changed to *Arolsen Archives – International Center on Nazi Persecution*. For the sake of convenience, I use the name ITS for most of my examples that occurred when the archive was still named ITS in the time between 1948 and 2018.

∂ OpenAccess. © 2020 Silke von der Emde, published by De Gruyter. This work is licensed under the Creative Commons Attribution-NonCommercial-NoDerivatives 4.0 License.
https://doi.org/10.1515/9783110665376-009

sive testifies to the emotional importance of place for the grieving process. The ITS employees must have understood the heartbreak and pain of mourning because they thought that this detail was important enough to include in Verbitzki's personnel file.[2] Surprisingly, the ITS at that time not only provided a place of employment for many DPs stranded in Germany but also supported them in dealing with their painful memories and coming to terms with the trauma they had experienced.

Although DPs made crucial contributions to the organization and operation of the ITS in its early years, their work in the ITS has not been analyzed in any depth. In a sense, their narratives have been just as displaced in the archive as the people who helped build it. One reason for this neglect is that the ITS was focused on events before 1945 and not on experiences after the war. Furthermore, the stories of DPs' continuing trauma challenge our familiar post-war narrative of redemption in which the Allies liberated the Nazi concentration camps and the survivors embarked on new lives.[3] Rather than easy redemption, however, the stories of the DPs tell of long lasting physical and psychological wounds that stubbornly refused to go away. Because emotions have long been defined as private and feminine, the continuing traumatic experiences of the DPs were deemed neither important nor practical enough to be filing priorities in the ITS.

Long considered women's labor, feelings have often been hidden within the archive and thus overlooked by researchers. Yet, traces of affect and empathy in the records of the ITS show that responding to what Susan Sontag has powerfully termed "the pain of others" actually became a modus operandi in the archives.[4] I argue that focusing on the records of DPs employed in the ITS after the war and reading their records with an eye to the affective content of the documents can reveal how these individuals helped create the *International Tracing Service* as an *archive of feelings* in Ann Cvetkovich's sense of the term.[5] Just as with LBGTQ archives that Cvetkovich analyses, affects are encoded in the ITS documents not only in their content but also in the practices that surround their production and reception. My work with the DP personnel files shows that the presence and work of the DPs in the ITS functioned to keep the affective essence of the millions of documents collected in Arolsen in constant view, bear-

---

[2] ITS Administrative Archives, Personnel File of Jakob Verbitzki, ITS Archive, Arolsen Archives.
[3] Compare Ben Shephard: *The Long Road Home: The Aftermath of the Second World War*, New York: Anchor Books, 2012, and Dan Stone: *The Liberation of the Camps: The End of the Holocaust and Its Aftermath*, New Haven and London: Yale University Press, 2015.
[4] Susan Sontag: *Regarding the Pain of Others*, New York: Farrar, Straus & Giroux, 2003.
[5] Ann Cvetkovich: *An Archive of Feelings: Trauma, Sexuality, and Lesbian Public Cultures*, Durham and London: Duke University Press, 2003.

ing the potential for active, multi-directional memory practices that not only look to the past but also to the politics of the now.

Focusing on and recognizing the value of emotion is a fairly recent development in archival discourse.[6] In this different kind of archival work, archivists become deeply implicated in the relations and ethics of witnessing because, as feminist cultural theorist Sara Ahmed maintains, it is the relationship of witnessing that gives emotions such as pain a life beyond the fragile, vulnerable borders of an individual body and authenticates its very existence.[7] In the case of the ITS, the DPs who helped set up the archive and organized its search tools knew firsthand that "archivists are deeply implicated in webs of affective relations" because they were both the archivists who handled the records and the subjects of these records.[8] In fact, the DPs were ideal participants in this early work because they had the language skills, the understanding of what the victims had gone through, and the motivation to make this archive useful for them and their families. Most importantly, however, they bore the same pain that permeates the records collected in the archive. The archive therefore not only contains facts necessary to document the crimes of the Nazi regime but also contains traces of what the events meant to the people that were affected by them.

Reading the documents with attention to this affective dimension and drawing on feminist and affect theorists such as Marianne Hirsch, Sara Ahmed, and Ann Cvetkovich, I aim to open a space for the consideration of affect, embodiment, privacy, and intimacy as concerns for history.[9] Such a feminist reading can draw attention to the experiences of marginalized groups such as those of the DPs that might otherwise remain absent from the historical record. It can point out how – because of the presence of the DPs for whom private and public often overlapped in the ITS – relational forms of memorial transmission and practices were written into the structure of the archive. This feminist approach can illuminate not only which stories and images were privileged and which forgotten, but also how those stories were told and how these images were constructed. As Hirsch points out, "in its awareness of power as a central factor in the construction of the archive, [...] feminist analysis can shift the frames of

---

[6] It only started as part of the affective turn in the 1990s. See Marika Cifor: "Affective Relations: Introducing Affect Theory to Archival Discourse", in *Archival Science* 16, 2016, 7–31.
[7] Sara Ahmed: *The Cultural Politics of Emotion*, Edinburgh: Edinburgh University Press, 2004, 30.
[8] Marika Cifor: "Affective Relations: Introducing Affect Theory to Archival Discourse", in *Archival Science* 16, 2016, 7.
[9] Marianne Hirsch: *The Generation of Postmemory: Writing and Visual Culture After the Holocaust*, New York: Columbia University Press, 2012.

intelligibility so as to allow new experiences to emerge, experiences that have heretofore remained unspoken, or even unthought."[10] Shifting our attention from the Allied politicians and international players to the DPs busy behind the scenes and deep within the archive itself can give the victims a voice that has up until now been unheard.

This type of feminist analysis can be especially useful in the context of the Holocaust, which has long been regarded as a limit case for memory and memory studies. In fact, it has been somewhat of an orthodoxy among scholars to treat the traumatic experiences of the Shoah as unrepresentable precisely because they reside at the intersection between emotional and social processes, private and public spheres, as well as memory and history. However, rather than focusing on the irrepresentability of traumatic experiences, Ann Cvetkovich insists that we make traumatic memories productive by understanding them as a call to political action. In fact, she maintains that it is vitally important to keep traumatic experiences in view because they can contradict the denial of emotions in atrocities reflected in many of our archives and cultural institutions.[11]

Nevertheless, this affective dimension of documents is often not easily accessible in archives, and the ITS is no exception. Gendered notions of knowledge production in which detachment, objectivity and rationality are valued have often marginalized emotions in archival discourse. Yet, by deploying tools from literary interpretation and cultural studies such as close attention to the language, tone, and context and the use of a broad range of records, including oral history interviews, we can locate some of the affective facets of the documents.[12] In fact, the contrast between the voice of the DPs in the ITS files and the dehumanizing Nazi files about the same people cannot be missed. This contrast makes a powerful point about the humanity of the DPs and international officers working in the ITS, who in contrast to the Nazis' instrumentalization of human beings as objects and raw material for labor camps allowed for feelings to play a role in important decisions.

Evidence of the affective dimensions of the archive resides in different locations in the ITS. First, we find it directly in the documents of the DPs, not only in

---

10 Ibid., 18.
11 Cvetkovich: *An Archive of Feelings*, 2003.
12 Historians such as Dan Stone have begun calling for the use of tools from cultural studies in the historiography of the Holocaust. He argues, "we need to bring the insights of narrativism, with its focus on the text, and rational constructivism, with its focus on the argument and the discursive context, together" in the historiography of the Holocaust. Dan Stone: "Excommunicating the Past Narrativism and Rational Constructivism in the Historiography of the Holocaust", in *Rethinking History*, 21, 4, 2017, 549–566, here 554.

their wartime documents but also in their personnel files from after the war. Second, other types of evidence are also contained in institutional documents, such as official reports and directives but also in letters by and to the personnel manager, the director, and other officials in the institution. Lastly, oral history materials, such as interviews with former employees conducted over the last two years, provide important sources for emotions that are often not directly recorded in institutions like the ITS. Even if locating the emotional essence of the documents is not always easy, rendering it visible can accomplish three important goals: At one level, it complicates our familiar understanding of post-war developments in Germany; at another level, it challenges traditional notions of the archive and the power structures involved in narrating the past; and finally, it makes the affective power of the documents productive for a transformation of collective memory and public culture. In what follows I show that this happened in very small ways in Bad Arolsen itself as well.

Displaced Persons in the ITS

Before turning to the ITS itself, it is important to understand the difficult situation that DPs faced after the liberation of the camps by the Allies. Not only did the Allies have distinct attitudes towards different victim groups from the beginning, but their policies were also shaped by the geopolitics of the Cold War, the debates over the future of Europe, and the unfolding events in the Middle East. Ben Shephard points out that the term "displaced persons" was created by the Allies before the war had ended in order to deal with the humanitarian crisis they foresaw. It encompassed not only Jewish and non-Jewish survivors of concentration camps but also a large number of "displaced persons" mostly from Eastern Europe who had been forced to work as slave laborers in the German war economy. All of these people had diverse and complicated wartime histories for which, as Shephard says, "modern terms, such as 'victims' and 'perpetrators' do scant justice."[13] Often lacking families in the wake of the Holocaust, the DPs had to struggle with intense loneliness, and they were often unwelcome in their hometowns where they were treated as traitors or collaborators. With more than 20 million people on the move competing for scarce resources, the fight for survival was difficult.[14] Even if the individuals succeeded in finding shelter in the

---

13 Shephard: *The Long Road Home*, 5.
14 In addition to the DPs, there were also other groups, including German refugees and expellees crowding into what remained of the former Reich.

DP camps the Allies set up, they had to fight to avoid being forcibly repatriated and be allowed to emigrate to places that offered them a chance at a new beginning. Many of the DPs were stateless without the protection of a passport and a nationality that would give them basic civil rights. Moreover, German women, such as Johanna Kopaniak, the long-serving personnel manager at the ITS, lost their German citizenship when they married a *Heimatlosen Ausländer* (stateless foreigner), a fate that also befell the children of these marriages.

In Arolsen, the small town in Northern Hesse where the ITS was finally set up, the situation was not much better. Although small and somewhat remote, Arolsen was chosen because it was very close to the intersection of three occupational zones, had large intact buildings, a fairly developed infrastructure (ironically because it had been the SS command post for the Fulda-Werra region with an SS officer academy and sub-camp of Buchenwald under the leadership of Higher SS and Police Leader Prince Josias of Waldeck and Pyrmont), and had been spared Allied bombardment.[15] However, because of this problematic history, the same painful interactions between Germans and DPs that took place in other parts of Germany also occurred in Arolsen to an even greater degree. On the one hand, Arolsen civilians were drawn to the ITS and the DP camps as a place of trade and employment. On the other hand, many locals were upset that in contrast to the German refugees, the foreign DPs had Allied protection, were better fed, were placed in confiscated houses, and were able to use their situation as victims to their advantage.[16] Early on, the Arolsers tried their best to get rid of the ITS, but when the tracing service grew into one of the most important employers in the town, they changed their mind and tried their best to keep the archive in Arolsen in the midst of Allied debates about moving it to a bigger city and less remote region. However, even when the ITS had moved to a beautiful new building constructed with Allied funds, empathy with the victims and painful processes of mourning were not readily encouraged in Arolsen

---

15 For more on Arolsen's past, see Gerhard Menk: *Waldeck im Dritten Reich: Voraussetzungen und Wirken des Nationalsozialismus im hessischen Norden,* Korbach: Archiv der Kreisstadt Korbach, 2010; Michael Winkelmann: *"Auf einmal sind sie weggemacht": Lebensbilder Arolser Juden im 20. Jahrhundert. Eine Dokumentation,* Kassel: Jenior und Pressler, 1992 [University Library Kassel, 2008], Anke Schmeling: *Josias Erbprinz zu Waldeck und Pyrmont: Der politische Weg eines hohen SS-Führers,* Kassel: Jenior und Pressler, 1993 [University Library Kassel, 2008], Bernd Joachim Zimmer: *Deckname Arthur. Das KZ-Außenkommando in der SS- Führerschule Arolsen,* Kassel: Jenior und Pressler, 1994 [University Library Kassel, 2008], and my own article: "Women in the Archive: Locating the International Tracing Service in German Memory Work", in *Seminar: A Journal of Germanic Studies,* 53/3, 2017, 202–218.
16 Compare Dan Stone's analysis of the DP situation in Germany in *The Liberation of the Camps,* 24.

– or in post-war Germany, for that matter. For years after the end of the war, the persistence of Nazi ideas and values made it very hard for the DPs to integrate into the life of the town. Newspaper reports documented both the citizens' resentment of the occupation of some of their houses by the DPs, and the constant complaint that German refugees from the East were not supported by the Allies in the same way as DPs. The self-pity and lack of perspective and empathy in early reports during this time are hard to stomach when we read them today. It is no wonder that often the trauma of the DPs did not end with liberation but instead became a systemic and everyday experience in Arolsen and in all of post-war Germany, which was not only unwilling to mourn but also seemed unable to empathize with the survivors and DPs towards whom the Nazis had committed unimaginable crimes.

The Documents' Affective Dimension

While the DPs were clearly marginalized in the town of Arolsen, they found a much friendlier atmosphere in the ITS, a place that not only gave them employment but also a new community with people who had similar experiences. Nevertheless, their voices have largely not been heard and their stories not told. From postmodern and other archivist thinkers we know that accepted institutionalized appraisal frameworks too often (re)enforce the interests of dominant power structures, and exclude the experiences, values, and desires of marginalized individuals and communities from the archival record. This was certainly true for the DPs in Arolsen. Fortunately, however, we can find some of their voices in the affective layer that is hidden in the ITS archive. Aside from reevaluating the important work that the DPs did in the *International Tracing Service* and doing emotional justice to their efforts and experiences, reading these records for their affective value also accomplishes a greater political goal in recognizing the implication and ethics of archives as agents of witnessing. In the best case, our work as researchers can contribute to what Hirsch calls the labor of the generation of postmemory.[17]

---

[17] Hirsch defines postmemory as "the relationship that the 'generation after' bears to the personal, collective, and cultural trauma of those who came before – to experiences they 'remember' only by means of the stories, images, and behaviors among which they grew up". She distinguishes between "familial" and "affiliative" postmemory and shows how the transmission of traumatic experiences occurs not only within families but also across a much wider social field. See Marianne Hirsch: *The Generation of Postmemory*, 5.

The artefacts in the ITS that have the most affective power are the collection of personal effects (belongings taken from prisoners when they arrived in concentration camps), such as watches, letters, personal pictures and wedding bands: all the things that people deemed important enough to take with them on their deportation journey to the camps.[18] The emotional value of these objects, which the ITS is still trying to return to family members today, is obvious. It is perhaps somewhat surprising then, that even the personnel files of the DPs employed at the ITS also contain many emotional documents and constitute an archive of feelings in their own right. In addition to rather typical and mundane documents such as job applications, dates of employments, promotions, insurance notifications, etc. found in other personnel files, they include very personal records, such as a list of belongings saved from a room after the DP camp in the barracks had to be vacated, letters from Frau Kopaniak, the administrative director, to the relatives of an elderly employee who needed help, and even a whole correspondence about funeral arrangements for one DP employee, complete with a description of the flower arrangements and a list of mourners. The abundance of ephemerals and non-traditional documents in the personnel files of the ITS show how the DPs and others who worked in the ITS placed a certain value on records and items that carry feelings and emotional reactions. In contrast to the somewhat hostile environment in Arolsen, the ITS seems to have been a place where emotions were acknowledged and taken into consideration.

Two 1957 postcards from Eugen Alakosow's personnel file are a good case in point.[19] Alakosow, a stateless DP and former chemist from Mariupol, Ukraine was one of the very first employees at the ITS (when it was still run by UNRRA as the *Central Tracing Bureau*, the CTB). From October 1945 until his emigration to the US in 1957 he worked as a case reviewer. Although he did decide to leave the ITS in order to start a new life in the US, the decision must have been a difficult one for he found it necessary to write one of his last goodbyes, shortly before he boarded the ocean liner, to his colleagues in the ITS. The first postcard that he wrote from Bremen shows an impressive ship on the front and hints at the emotional turmoil that goes along with a decision to leave everyone and everything behind to try for a new start in a foreign country. Worried that he was unable to say goodbye to all of his colleagues before he had to leave, he wanted to make sure that the director conveyed his regret to the ITS community he left behind. The other postcard, this one with a skyline of Boston on the front, was

---

18 A description of the *Arolsen Archives*' collection of personal effects has been digitized and can be accessed at https://digitalcollections.its-arolsen.org/010209. Last accessed: 3.7.2019.
19 ITS Administrative Archives, Personnel File of Eugen Alakosow, ITS Archive, Arolsen Archives.

sent shortly after he had arrived in the US and is addressed to personnel manager Johanna Kopaniak. Aside from a request for a piece of documentation, the card again contains greetings to his colleagues and the promise to keep in touch even across the ocean. After 12 years at the ITS, Eugen Alakosow sent his last communication from his old life in Europe and his first one from his new home in the United States to the ITS, the place that had made it possible for him to be part of a new kind of community in which almost everyone was struggling with the same aftermath of displacement and trauma. The human bond between Alakosow and other ITS employees – apparent in the few sentences contained in these postcards and in the fact that the personnel manager cherished them enough to file them – shows the ITS as much more than just a workplace and archive.

Other documents in the personnel files – institutional by nature – also reveal a community that valued the emotional lives of its employees. Even a simple request of incarceration confirmation for restitution claims, like the one written by Witold Malkowski in 1989, reveals a whole narrative about the person who wrote it. The type of language used in the letter, his tone, the metaphors, and the style together with side notes and comments in the margins carry as much meaning as the facts that are conveyed. The impeccably polite letter that begins with a misspelled "very honored ladies and gentlemen" and goes on with a mix of German, Polish and English and often phonetic spelling of German words with a Polish accent (for example "chaben" instead of "haben") includes a ten dollar bill for shipping and a request to send greetings to a "Herrn G." and his old colleagues at the ITS.[20] As much as the letter shows Malkowski's continued attachment to the ITS after he left Germany 38 years earlier, it also demonstrates the connection and responsibility that his ITS colleagues still felt toward him, as witnessed by a hand-written note from one of the employees at the ITS ensuring him that greetings were in fact relayed. Furthermore, in the answer letter, the writer does not forget to mention that Herr G. has retired but is still in contact

---

20 Wording of the original letter: "Sehr geährte Damen und Herrn! Ich möchte sie bitten mier zu senden ein neues Zeugnis und eine Arbeitsbescheinigung wie lange ich bei der Internationalen Suchdienst Stelle gearbeitet chabe, ich brauche einige kopien unterlagen vür den Deutschen Konsulat chier in Buffalo. [...] ich wurde mit andern Polnischen Kamaraden am einen Sontag aus der Kirche von der Deutschen Gestapo rausgeschelt worden, ich wurde unschildigt vür 8 Jahre Zuchthaus verurtelt worden, ich wurde gezwungen mit bedrohung den Haft Protokol zu unterschreiben, das chaben die Gestapo mit allen Polnischen Statsbürger getan, und dan wurde ich mit andere Polische bürger nach West Deutschland verschlept worden in einen Lager unterbrcht, das wahr im Morhgebit in Papenburg Emsland an der Holendische Grenze, dort chagen wier Torf gestochen, [...] " in: ITS Administrative Archives, Personnel File of Witold Malkowski, ITS Archive, Arolsen Archives.

with his colleagues and that they conveyed Malkowski's greetings to him. Reading this simple letter, we can begin to sense what the ITS meant to Witold Malkowski and how he never forgot the ITS contacts that helped him survive the aftermath of the war. In fact, reading his Care and Maintenance (CM/1) file, we know how hard Malkowski fought to be able to emigrate despite the fact that he was sick. Even with parts of the form illegible, we still learn:

> Subject person has been twice hospitalized in Merxhausen. He has a wife and child. Wants to emigrate but has not [been able] to apply for any scheme [?] because of poor health. He has been in Oranienburg and Buchenwald. His wife is healthy, but he himself is under control. Lungs already verheilt [instead of healed].

Malkowski had been arrested in Poland for theft and sentenced to six years slave labor in the moor in Emsland and a warplane factory in Northern Germany followed by a few years in different DP camps before he came to Arolsen in 1949. The ITS seems to have been a safe haven for him because of the way the administration took care of him. We can see evidence of this from a note in his personnel file with a directive to prolong his lunch break for half an hour for him to go home for a good meal to help cure his tuberculosis. The deep humanity that was at work in the ITS on the part of the DPs when they tried to help other victims and on the part of the director, personnel manager and supervisors in the ITS shines through in the details of this astonishing collection of documents.

Emotional Labor and Community in the ITS

We find affect not only in the records themselves but also in how the records were used and what kind of meaning they had for the people who worked in the archive. There are of course heroic stories in the archive that we know from books and films, such as that of Marian Ciepielowski, one of the prisoners who risked his life to sabotage the cruel medical experiments in Buchenwald.[21] But even documents of a quieter heroism have immense affective power. An example is the struggle of two sisters who fought for their sick mother to be ap-

---

[21] For more on Ciepielowski's background as part of the prisoner team that sabotaged the medical experiments in Block 34 in Buchenwald, see my article: "Recovering a Displaced Archive: DP Employees of the ITS in Arolsen", in Christian Höschler and Isabel Panek (eds.): *Two Kinds of Searches. Findings on Displaced Persons in Arolsen after 1945*, Bad Arolsen: Arolsen Archives, 2019; and Arthur Allen: *Fantastic Laboratory of Dr. Weigl: How Two Brave Scientists Battled Typhus and Sabotaged the Nazis*, New York: WW Norton & Company, 2014.

proved for emigration, helped by the director and personnel manager in the ITS who wrote them glowing work recommendations. In addition, the many cases of people who seem to have suffered from post-traumatic stress disorder (PTSD) are heart-breaking, and the examples of the many employees who tried to help these people are even more touching. Against the backdrop of continued trauma, the ITS became an institution that not only documented the history of persecution and helped find lost relatives and family members, but also provided a support system and even a substitute family for many DPs in Arolsen.[22]

The extent to which feelings were taken into consideration in the daily operations of the ITS is also revealed in a 1967 letter to the director Albert de Cocatrix from Gerda Koschuschko, the wife of a long-time employee who was supposed to be laid off because of new retirement laws. The impeccably polite, yet slightly clumsy and very emotional letter displays the woman's deep trust in the leadership of the ITS, who, as she writes, supplied the DPs with new "courage to go on living" [*Lebensmut*], by giving them work and a new noble direction after the war. She writes the letter out of fear for her husband's physical and emotional health because, as she writes apologetically, "he is very sensitive, it's his mentality."[23] The fact that she feels obliged to apologize for the "heightened sensitivity" of her husband and at the same time trusts that the director will not hold this "weakness" against him indicates that her husband's nervousness, depression, and other PTSD symptoms were not unusual in the ITS. In fact, the personnel files of the DPs who worked in the ITS contain a large number of documents that seem to point to the aftereffects of traumatization and signs of PTSD. While psychological problems are not surprising in employees who are survivors of concentration camps, forced labor and displacement, it is surprising how patiently the administration and fellow DPs seem to have reacted to people who had even major behavioral and emotional problems. Rather than giving in to the discourse dominated by medical and pathologizing approaches, the leadership of the ITS together with the DP employees seem to have tried to find other more humanizing solutions.

A good example is the case of Maria Sawczenko, an apparently illiterate DP from the Ukraine who worked in the ITS as part of the cleaning staff. Having been deported from her place of work in the Ukraine to do slave labor in Germany, she seemed to have never gotten over the abuse she suffered from the Nazis. Although her file lists education as none and specifies that she speaks Ukrainian

---

22 For more on the DP employees creating familial or family-like structures in the ITS, see my article "Recovering a Displaced Archive".
23 Gerda Koschuschko, letter to Albert de Cocatrix, 5.2.1967, in: ITS Administrative Archives, Personnel File of Peter Koschuschko, ITS Archive, Arolsen Archives.

and only a little bit of German, she remained employed in the ITS until at least 1972 despite accumulating problems. From 1962 on her file is filled with serious accident reports that mostly seem to document injuries from falls. But there are also numerous complaints against her for being aggressive and even attacking other people. When she is finally sued for her aggressive behavior by an elderly couple in 1977, it is Frau Kopaniak, the personnel manager, who helps her write a response to the lawyer which explains that Sawchenko does not speak much German and did not intend to insult the couple.[24] Instead, she felt persecuted by them. Unfortunately, we do not know what happened to the lawsuit and to Maria Sawchenko. However, the fact that she went to Frau Kopaniak for help, even after she seemingly no longer worked at the ITS, indicates that the ITS became a haven for its employees, even ones who were not always easy colleagues. In stark contrast to the Nazis' treatment of people in forced labor settings and concentration camps where only their work performance was able to prolong their life, the ITS seems to be focused on taking care of members of its community even after their employment had already ended.

Sophie Bernau is another example of an individual that the administration seems to have helped patiently by trying to shift her to other positions after she had many quarrels with colleagues over small details such as whether windows needed to be opened during breaks. Her personnel file contains a handwritten letter to Frau Kopaniak in which she vents about her problems, complains about being sick, and tells Frau Kopaniak who to contact after her death. She even specifies who should get her belongings, specifically a cherished radio, which she wants her granddaughter to have.[25] The style of the letter indicates that Bernau had some sort of emotional disturbance. Despite having been reprimanded, she still trusts the administration enough to write such a personal letter, and the administration seems to have tried its best to figure out solutions for traumatized employees like her. Clearly, many people in leadership positions in the ITS insisted on the power of a community of people who were practiced in acknowledging pain and dealing with it patiently.

---

24 ITS Administrative Archives, Personnel File of Maria Sawczenko, ITS Archive, Arolsen Archives.
25 ITS Administrative Archives, Personnel File of Sophie Bernau, ITS Archive, Arolsen Archives.

Women's Work and the Construction of an *Archive of Feelings*

These types of responses from the personnel manager and the director show that the institution had to be committed at some level to the affective dimension in which emotional engagement and empathy were encouraged. While both men and women performed this emotional labor within the institution of the ITS, women did assume a leadership role in this regard. One of the key figures in this context was Johanna Kopaniak, the personnel manager in the ITS who came to Arolsen as a young woman in January 1946 in order to find work. As one of the first German employees in the ITS, she worked there for almost 50 years until she stepped down in 1984. In the ITS, she met her husband Alexander Kopaniak, a stateless DP who had spent more than five years in POW camps in Germany. Although she lost her own German citizenship when she married him and had a very difficult position in Arolsen as a young working woman with three little children and a "foreigner" husband who continued to suffer from his war wounds and what was probably a mild case of PTSD, she never ceased in her empathy and support of her colleagues in the ITS. The files reveal how well she worked with some of the more successful British, American and Swiss directors of the ITS and how much they trusted the young personnel manager in her decisions about how best to assist different people and mediate conflicts.

Fortunately, the ITS had one director, Albert de Cocatrix, first Deputy director (from 1955 on) and then director from 1970 to 77, who explicitly valued this emotional labor and was committed to creating community both within the ITS and between the ITS and the town of Arolsen. It is no surprise that Johanna Kopaniak found him to be one of the best directors the ITS ever had, an evaluation that scholars such as Isabel Panek and others share.[26] Historians point to the extraordinary period of openness and accessibility that he initiated, and Johanna Kopaniak reinforced this evaluation by emphasizing his personal outreach to people inside and outside the ITS. In fact, under his directorship the archive invited researchers from the outside into the archive and launched several internal research projects, such as research on human experiments, death marches, and, in 1976, the Nazi persecution of homosexuals. De Cocatrix transformed the ITS into an access point for the relevant authorities and supported memory projects of all kinds at a time when memory and responsibility for

---

26 See the chapter by Henning Borggräfe and Isabel Panek in this volume.

the past was only beginning to be acknowledged in Germany at large.[27] According to Johanna Kopaniak, he knew the names of all employees, their spouses and their children, encouraged employees to bring their children into the archive for celebrations and summer job opportunities, and asked about family members who were sick or had other problems. He seems to have been one of the rare but influential men who acknowledged the importance of affect and emotions in making the ITS into an archive that truly advocated for both the dead and the living.[28]

The affective power of the documents of the ITS had the most immediate influence on the people who came in direct contact with the archive, such as the DPs and the international employees who worked there. But this affective power also spilled over to local Germans, especially the young women from Arolsen and the surrounding area who began to be hired when more and more DPs emigrated and the ITS became busier. Most of these affective encounters are not in the archival record in the ITS and need to be accessed instead through oral history interviews.[29] These oral history interviews not only further demonstrate the emotional dimension that made the ITS into the institution it is today, but also do justice to the heritage of the DPs who trained the young German employees. In the stories they tell about their work and the work climate in the ITS, we can trace the emotional connection they had not only to their colleagues but also to the stories contained in the documents themselves. For example, 80-year old Hanna Koeltz spoke about her job as a typist in the ITS as one of the best jobs she ever had, not just because of the good salary and work conditions, but also because of the solidarity among the employees. The work that these women had to do was actually surprisingly stressful because copying over files meant that, as she explained, "one was not allowed to make any, not even the tiniest mistake." Mistakes would inadvertently lead to a visit to the supervisor's office who had to invalidate the mistaken document and authorize a

---

[27] Henning Borggräfe and Hanne Leßau maintain that in the 1970s and under the leadership of de Cocatrix, the ITS became a pioneer for a confrontation with and examination of NS crimes for a second time in its history. Compare their article: "Die Wahrnehmung der NS-Verbrechen und der Umgang mit den NS-Verfolgten im International Tracing Service", in Henning Borggräfe, Hanne Leßau, and Harald Schmidt (eds.): *Fundstücke: Die Wahrnehmung der NS-Verbrechen und ihrer Opfer im Wandel*, Göttingen: Wallstein, 2015, 23–44, here 44.
[28] Borggräfe and Panek emphasize de Cocatrix's advocacy for the victims and survivors. See their chapter in this volume.
[29] For this project I conducted interviews with several former employees and other witnesses who lived through the early years of the ITS. Unfortunately, many of these witnesses will not be with us for much longer and I recommend that such interviews be conducted and added to the archive.

new attempt.³⁰ However, the way that all the women working in the office supported one another, together with their belief and understanding that what they did was important work, alleviated the stress and made them want to stay at the ITS.

Yet it was not only the connection to colleagues that had affective power. The documents themselves touched these women in profound ways and helped them open up to the victims whose stories the Arolser seemed to want to repress. Hanna Koeltz reported that, "when we had time to read and understand what we copied we couldn't help but cry." She and other German women like her were not able to ignore the voices of the victims and instead were deeply touched by them. Even women who began working in later decades were similarly affected. Margret Schlenke, who began working in the ITS in 1970 and was trained by Vilma Anderson, a DP and former slave laborer from Latvia, and who became head of the children's search division, is another good example of the passion and the sense of community that people felt in the ITS.³¹ In an interview from the fall of 2018, Schlenke spoke of the way that the tracing work did not just end when people left the archive at the end of the day, but kept them emotionally engaged at home and in their daily lives.

There are countless examples of people who witness how the work in the ITS effected people emotionally.³² One person I interviewed (name withheld) is the wife of a former employee who was asked to consult for the ITS even after he retired. Her testimony is a good example of how difficult this emotional labor could sometimes be. Herself expelled from the Sudeten area after the war, she felt ambivalent about the ITS. Like Gerda Koschuschko, who was worried about the emotional consternation of her husband, this woman also worried about her husband's health when she saw how deeply the victims' stories touched him. She told me that she wished that her husband could have enjoyed his retirement without continuing to be exposed to these emotional burdens again and again. Clearly, the women and men who performed this emotional labor carried these new experiences outside of their place of work to the people of Arolsen, which could be a painful labor. However, very slowly they were able to contribute to a change of public opinion among the Arolser who, as a group, resisted confronting the past for a long time.

---

30 Personal Interview, 19.7.2015.
31 For a more detailed discussion of Schlenke's role in the ITS see my article "Recovering a Displaced Archive".
32 Personal Interview, 12.10.2018.

The Labor of Mourning and the Future of Memory in the *Arolsen Archives*

The difficult task of acknowledging painful emotions that accompany trauma and guilt seemed in some regards to have been passed on to the second generation. Having grown up in Arolsen in the 1970s, I and most of my peers had little knowledge of what the ITS did, and we were almost completely ignorant about the important documents that were housed there. I overlapped with the Kopaniaks' youngest son Thomas in high school for a year or so and had no idea that he was the son of a DP. Only after I recently told him about my work in the ITS and my interest in the stories of the DPs who worked there did we begin to talk about his and his family's experiences in Bad Arolsen. Obviously one of the reasons for the ignorance of the younger generation was that, except for the period of openness under director de Cocatrix in the 1970s, the archive was closed to the public (and historians) until 2007. But it was also the case that the emotionality of the documents in the ITS and the difficult situation and status of the people who worked there deterred people from fully acknowledging the archive's mission and purpose. A general social intolerance toward a display of emotions and a suspicion toward the feelings of mourning and regret that must have haunted DPs and Germans alike in Arolsen and made it hard for the survivors and even their children to open up about their personal situation. Only by talking about my own interest in the DP narrative did space open up to acknowledge the emotional burdens that followed the DPs into the next generation.

This work of mourning and opening up to the pain of others is still ongoing in the ITS in Arolsen as well. Just as in Verbitzki's case, the labor of mourning is one that needs to be brought back into German communities. By helping Joseph Verbitzki go and visit the grave of his wife, the ITS not only acknowledged his personal pain but also brought him back into a community in which his emotions were respected and his pain was acknowledged. This kind of emotional acknowledgement not only made a big difference to the survivors, helping them cope with the ongoing trauma and sense of displacement, but it also changed the archive itself. The ITS developed from what the Allies and international politicians had planned as a place where facts and knowledge would be stored, into an archive where layers of emotions are also preserved in less obvious but still accessible ways for our own task of restoring the humanity of the victims and making their voices heard. In this way, the affective layers that run through the archive call us as members of the second and third generation to continue the DPs' memory work.

The ITS has seen countless changes and transformations over the course of its history. For a long period of time it was a male-dominated, unapproachable and sealed-off organization. This is especially true of the 1980s after de Cocatrix left Arolsen until the opening of the archive in 2007.[33] Yet, the spirit of openness and outreach that characterized the period under de Cocatrix and Kopaniak in the 1970s and the female directorships starting with Rebecca Boehling in 2013 and continuing with Floriane Azoulay until today needs to be made central going forward. The recent name change of the archive to *Arolsen Archives: International Center on Nazi Persecution* is an encouraging reflection of this new sensibility. In fact, the announcement of the name change on the ITS website for April 2019 speaks to the *Arolsen Archives*' important new goal of reaching out to the younger generation in order to "provide opportunities for people to engage with their hearts and minds" ("Angebote schaffen, die Herz und Kopf erreichen") [author's translation].[34] My own research into the narratives of the DPs and their important emotional labor in the archive is meant as a contribution to this task.

The personnel files together with other documents provide a fascinating glimpse into the lives of DPs after liberation. They complement as well as complicate what Dan Stone termed the "standard template of liberation" after the Second World War and what Werner Sollors refers to as a legendary story of success of bringing a country ruled by a ruthless dictatorship back into the fold of democracy through nation building.[35] While the documents show the difficult and painful emotional labor that the DPs did every day in the archive and in the town Arolsen, they also reveal the remarkable degree of sympathy and genuine care for the victims of Nazi persecution, both dead and living, within the ITS. The tracing service emerges as a community of people who created the conditions for their own recovery and healing by keeping the affective essence of the documents in constant view. Their work included not only tracing people's relatives and helping them gain approval for restitution claims, but also helping people reconstruct and reclaim their own identities. Hardly anyone working in the ITS at that time was unaffected by the documents they handled and organized.

---

33 Johanna Kopaniak tellingly resigned in 1983 after the new director Philipp Züger slowly revealed his strategy of systematically closing off the archive to the public and actively obstructing research. Although it was only three years before her official retirement age, Kopaniak was unable and unwilling to watch Züger destroy the culture of openness and transparency that she and de Cocatrix had built.
34 Website of the *Arolsen Archives*, News: https://arolsen-archives.org/news/its-wird-arolsen-archives/. Last accessed: 21.8.2019.
35 Compare Dan Stone: *The Liberation of the Camps;* and Werner Sollors: *The Temptation of Despair: Tales of the 1940s*, Cambridge, MA: Harvard University Press, 2014.

The DPs, together with a surprisingly high number of women in leadership positions, shifted the emphasis away from disaffected knowledge and facts to an important acknowledgement of pain and mourning. Behind the scenes and almost unnoticed in the context of the turbulent cold war politics, the DPs turned the archive into a place where traditional divisions of affect and knowledge, private and public, margin and center, and power and powerlessness were challenged. By opening themselves up to pain and by allowing affect to play a role in their interactions with the documents and with one another, the employees of the archive constructed the ITS as an archive of feeling with profoundly affective power. Putting these emotions in the foreground continues to offer not only opportunities for recovery but also for affecting real social change. The *Arolsen Archives* have the potential to continue the work that the DPs began and contribute to memory practices that do emotional justice to those who have been overlooked and open people's minds to a broader repertoire for the expression of emotion.

Zvi Bernhardt
Yad Vashem and Holocaust Victim's Search for Family

Abstract: Immediately after liberation, Holocaust survivors started their search for family members who had survived and to learn the fate of family members who had not. This chapter explores the changing role of *Yad Vashem* over time and explains why *Yad Vashem* did not play a major role in this endeavor up to the 1980s and how it became a major center for these searches in subsequent years. It also tries to explain some of the changes in the societal role of searching for Holocaust victims' fate within the framework of Israeli society.

Introduction

The attempts by Holocaust survivors and their descendants to discover information on the fate of individuals can be divided into four periods. The first period starts with the liberation of the victims and ends around the early 1950s with the closure of the DP camps and with most of the victims settling in various countries of immigration. This period includes frantic searching for family members or friends who survived. The second period starts in the 1950s and ends in the early 1970s. While hope still exists in many hearts to find loved ones who survived, the search for the fate of individuals takes on more of a symbolic aspect and seems to be more about making a place in the lives of survivors leave this for those missing. On a more practical level many now search for information about themselves in order to receive reparations rather than searching for those who are missing. The third period, from the 1970s till the mid 1980s showed a lull in the interest in the fate of Holocaust victims and names. The fourth period, a rekindled interest in names and fates, which started around 1984 and continues to this day. In this fourth period *Yad Vashem* came to occupy a central place for those searching for the fate of a Holocaust victim. Even though *Yad Vashem* was established first in the mid-1940s and had started collecting archival material including information on names and fates of individuals, *Yad Vashem* was not a major player in the search for names and fates in the first three periods. Even the re-establishment of *Yad Vashem* as a semi-governmental institution in 1953 by an act of the Israeli parliament did not result in *Yad Vashem* playing a central part in the search for names, nor did its receipt of a copy of most of the ITS collection relating to Jews at the end of that decade.

∂ OpenAccess. © 2020 Zvi Bernhardt, published by De Gruyter. (cc) BY-NC-ND This work is licensed under the Creative Commons Attribution-NonCommercial-NoDerivatives 4.0 License.
https://doi.org/10.1515/9783110665376-010

This chapter attempts to identify some of the reasons why *Yad Vashem* did not play a large role in this endeavor up until the 1980s, and why this changed in that decade.

The First Period: After Liberation

In almost any Holocaust period testimony you can find a description of the search for relatives immediately upon liberation. Three examples are offered here:

Paul Landau was born in Warszawa, Poland in 1922 and his family moved to Paris in 1926. During the war he was in various forced labor camps – some of the time disguised as an ethnic Pole. He was then in Auschwitz and other camps. He was liberated in Ebensee, from where he travelled to Paris. In his testimony he states: "When we arrived in Paris [...] railroad station there were thousands of people there [...] I was still with my stripes [...] Did you meet Duron, John? Did you see so and so? The people were there hoping to have news from somebody"[1]

Stanley Firestone was born in Lodz in 1928 and was deported to Auschwitz in August, 1944. He was liberated in May, 1945 around Mauthausen and was then sent to the Santa Croce Hospital in Italy:

> I started hearing rumors that my mother survived [...] so I escaped from the hospital [in Italy] and made my way north [...] I had no money [...] having gotten to Feldafing [...] I met people that said they saw my mother in Lodz [...] In Germany I joined a group of Polish repatriates and made my way back to Poland [...] In Lodz [...] I went to the Jewish community center and asked [...] they told me [...] my mother and a cousin of mine lived in a small apartment [...] my mother opened the door and started running toward me [...] we both burst out crying.[2]

Eda Reed was born in Humniska, Poland in 1920. She was eventually deported to a camp in Sambor from where she escaped. She acquired false papers as an "Aryan" first in Lublin, then in Regen in Germany where she worked for a German farmer. After liberation she made her way to Augsburg and describes plans she made with two friends: "So we said first we will go to Krakow, to see Rozia Mintz's family [...] And she didn't find anybody [...] I went back to Humniska [...] In every place I went they said: "Well, we didn't hear anybody survived"[3]

---

[1] Testimony of Paul Landau, O.3/7015/Yad Vashem Archives, Jerusalem.
[2] Testimony of Stanley Firestone, O.3/7280/Yad Vashem Archives, Jerusalem.
[3] Testimony of Eda Reed, O.3/10468/Yad Vashem Archives, Jerusalem.

From a very early stage, the *Jewish Agency* played a major role in helping survivors search for relatives. Representatives of the *Jewish Agency* as the official representative body of the nascent Jewish National Home in Palestine had existed around Europe before the war and were quickly re-established with liberation. These offices frequently registered and publicized lists of survivors. The *Bureau for Missing Relatives*, the official central clearing house for all such endeavors, was founded by the agency in June 1945. Books with lists of survivors were published under the auspices of the *Jewish Agency*, and it published *Lekarov Velerahok*[4], a newspaper consisting of various lists of names of survivors and emigrants to Palestine – most of them also survivors. All these publications sold extensively in Palestine and around the Jewish world. As Tehila Darmon shows in her thesis on this bureau[5], the *Jewish Agency* saw the founding of this bureau as one way to encourage the survivors to see their final destination as Palestine at a time when British regulations limited the ability of the agency to actually bring the survivors to Israel. This was seen as particularly important as other non-Zionist Jewish organizations, for instance the *American Jewish Joint Distribution Committee* and HICEM were also active in trying to assist survivors in their search for relatives. The *Bureau* cooperated with these organizations but also saw them as competitors for the hearts of the survivors. Thus even though *Yad Vashem* saw its goal as the collection of names when it was first organized – in 1946 – the *Jewish Agency* was already active in helping people search for information about relatives.

The Second Period: 1950s to 1970s

One of the symbols of the second period, that of continued search but with less hope, is the daily radio broadcast in Israel *Hamador Lehipus Krovim*.[6] This was

---

[4] Published from 5.7.1945 – 17.11.47, altogether 93 issues were published. A full copy of this publication exists in the *Yad Vashem* library. The title is both a play on words: *Lekarov Ulerahok* means both "from near and far" but the word for near is also the word for relative and a biblical quote from Isaiah 57 v. 19 "peace, peace to the far and to the near, (Shalom Shalom La'rahok Vela'Karov) says the Lord, and I will heal him." This verse is part of the reading from the prophets for Yom Kippur, the Day of Atonement.
[5] Tehila Malka (Darmon): *The Search for Surviving Relatives after the Holocaust. The Establishment of the Search Bureau For Missing Relatives in Israel in the 1950s–1960s*, Ben Gurion University of the Negev, 2010, 4. (unpublished M.A. Thesis. [Hebrew]).
[6] I could not find a source for when the program started. It was well established by the mid-1950s. There were definitely predecessor programs broadcasting lists of names starting in the 1940s. Zionist Archives, "Hamador Lehipus Karovim", Available at: http://www.zionistarchives.org.il/AttheCZA/AdditionalArticles/Pages/ChipushKrovim.aspx. Last accessed: 9.7.2019.

sponsored by the above mentioned *Bureau* established by the *Jewish Agency*, and in fact the name of the program was simply the Hebrew name of the *Bureau*. Memoirs from the time and literary references – for example in Chava Alberstein's song *Shaaraliya*[7] – portray this broadcast as a sacrosanct moment in the day where survivor parents listened intently to what was essentially an audio list of names. It seems though that the main impetus for listening to the program was not a real hope to find connections that had been lost but rather a daily recognition of the existence of loss in their lives.

Parallel to this symbolic and commemorative interest in names and fates was the search for proof of an individual's wartime experience in order to receive compensation, which began after the signing of the Reparations agreement in 1952.

Around this time the Israeli Foreign Ministry was involved in the negotiations for putting the *International Tracing Service* on a new legal footage and full Israeli participation in its institutions. Knesset member Cizling raised an official parliamentary question to the Foreign Minister in November 1953 regarding the fear that the ITS documents would be transferred to the Germans.[8] The Israeli delegation supported the proposal to have the *International Red Cross* manage the ITS. The main impetus for this proposal was to ensure that the ITS not be managed by a German governmental agency. The negotiations included attempts to receive a copy of the ITS material to be used by Israel and by Jewish organizations. A meeting on receiving a copy of the ITS material was held in the Israeli Foreign Ministry in 1954 and included representatives of the *World Jewish Congress*. Absent from the meeting – and in fact the whole file – is any mention of *Yad Vashem*.[9]

While *Yad Vashem* was not the initiator of the demand for a copy of the ITS material relating to Jews, and even though the crew headed by Joseph-Kurt Sella that actually microfilmed the materials between 1955 to 1957 was an Israeli Foreign Ministry crew, *Yad Vashem* was heavily involved technically and financially.

---

7 For the text of this song in the original Hebrew: Shironet, *Shaaraliya*. Available at: https://shironet.mako.co.il/artist?type=lyrics&lang=1&prfid=383&wrkid=3137. Last accessed: 20.11.2018.
8 Knesset protocol (Divrei Haknesset) 23.11.1953, 208–210. Available at: https://fs.knesset.gov.il//2/Plenum/2_ptm_250554.pdf. Last accessed: 20.11.2018.
9 Israel National Archives, file ISA-mfa-IsraeliMissionUK-000qv1s. Available at: http://www.archives.gov.il/archives/#/Archive/0b07170680319a2e/File/0b07170680cc9bf7. Last accessed: 20.11.2018.

By 1960 the 5,467 microfilms of this project were available in the *Yad Vashem* archive.[10]

By the mid 1950s *Yad Vashem* had become a quasi-governmental organization, recognized by law as the official state organ for Holocaust remembrance. However, other Holocaust memorial institutions existed. These institutions represented various ideological strains in Israeli society, many of whom represented parties and groups that had existed in European Jewry of the Holocaust period. Each institution aimed to put forward their own agenda on memory as the central prism through which Israeli society would view the Holocaust period. Two central examples were *Beit Lohamei Hagetaot*, the memorial institution at the aptly named *Ghetto Fighter's kibbutz* in the north, founded among others by Tzivia Lubotkin and other veterans of the *Zionist socialist fighters* in the Warsaw ghetto uprising, and the *Chamber of the Holocaust* on Mount Zion near the traditional site of the *tomb of King David*, founded by Rabbi Dr. Shmuel Zanviel Cahana, a leader of the *Mizrahi Zionist-orthodox Party*. Both these institutions were founded in 1949 right after the War of Independence, before *Yad Vashem* was given centrality by law, and in fact at a time that *Yad Vashem* as an institution was more or less moribund. It would be many years before *Yad Vashem*'s preeminence became clear.[11]

Interestingly in the 1960s *Yad Vashem* did attempt to assist individuals in the documentation of their own Holocaust travails and in their research on the fate of their relatives, often using the ITS collection, which was copied in the 1950s. This however was not seen as a central *Yad Vashem* role and its then publication, the *Yad Vashem* bulletin mentions this type of activity only once parenthetically in 1964.[12] However, in the 1970s for reasons I could not ascertain *Yad Vashem*

---

10 Kurt-Sela, Dr. Josef: "The 'ITS' Microfilm Project of Yad Vashem – Guide and Key to the Project. Compiled by Dr. Josef Kurt-Sela former Laison Officer of the Israeli Government to the ITS", Jerusalem, March 1950, 3.
11 Many documents attest to a continued struggle of *Yad Vashem* to be recognized as the central Israeli organ for Holocaust remembrance. In a letter from February 28, 1968 the Prime Minister's office notifies *Yad Vashem* that the Prime Minister will not participate in the Holocaust Memorial Day ceremony in *Yad Vashem* as he will be attending the ceremony in *Lohamei Hagetaot*, see: AM 2.2 318.1/40/Yad Vashem Archives, Jerusalem. In one document from 1975 the *Yad Vashem* directorate discusses moving the main ceremony at *Yad Vashem* from the end of Holocaust memorial day to the beginning so it does not compete with other ceremonies, including at *Beit Lohamei Hagetaot*, see: AM 2.2, 318.3/37/Yad Vashem Archives, Jerusalem.
12 *Yad Vashem* Bulletin March, 1964, in the article "Recent Activities of the Yad Vashem Archives", 67; "[...] these lists may be of great help in the search for missing relatives, and in claims for payment of damages." Compare this short sentence – part of a description of archival acquisitions – with the frequent publication of successful *Yad Vashem* relatives search in *Yad Vashem*'s

changed its policy and would not provide service for the ITS collection and sent inquirers to the ITS in Arolsen and the *Jewish Agency* bureau.¹³

Here it is important to note that the collection of the *Pages of Testimony* – begun in the mid-1950s – was not seen as a way to gather information, but was seen strictly as commemoration. One of the sections in the *Yad Vashem* laws is the direction "4: to confer upon the members of the Jewish people who perished [...] the commemorative citizenship of the State of Israel".¹⁴ As can be seen in this early *Page of Testimony* – some of the first pages were gathered in South America – the aim of the document is presented as a basis for bestowing that citizenship.¹⁵

Close to a million names had been collected in *Pages of Testimony* by 1960 – but they were not indexed until 1968. On May 31, 1968, Mr. Kalish from the department of *Pages of Testimony* noted that as a result of the establishment of the *Hall of Names* building, interest in looking for information from the *Pages of Testimony* was growing and letters were being received – he mentions 100 not yet answered – to look for *Pages of Testimony*, but that the staff was not able to answer them because the pages had not yet been completely arranged.¹⁶

---

current publication: "Yad Vashem Jerusalem", in *Examples*, 82, 2017, 20; Ibid.: *Examples*, 83, 2017, 20; *Examples*, 84, 2017, 17; *Examples*, 85, 2018, 18. All available at: https://www.yadvashem.org/magazine.html. Last accessed: 20.8.2018.

13 One of many examples: AM.4/392/Yad Vashem Archives, Jerusalem: "We can not help you in your search after your brother. We are not a relatives search institute. [...] I suggest that you contact the relatives search institute of the Sochnut, Bezalel str. 18, Jerusalem – maybe your brother arrived to Israel after W.W.II. You can also try to contact the International Tracing Service, Waldeck/Arolsen W. Germany which is the most competent authority for individual documentation."

14 Martyrs' and Heroes Remembrance (*Yad Vashem*) Law 5713, 2.4.1954. Available at: https://www.yadvashem.org/about/yad-vashem-law.html Last accessed: 20.8.2019

15 Note on the bottom it says in Spanish: "Por ello, pido otorgar ciudadania post-mortem del Estado de Israel, al nombre arriba mencionado." In English: "Therefore I ask for post-mortem citizenship of the state of Israel to the person who is written above."

16 AM.4/391/Yad Vashem Archives, Jerusalem: "Letters are being worked on (indexing) and will be finished by the end of July. [...] Since the opening of the Hall of Names (memorial building) we feel [...] a renewed interest in [...] Pages of Testimony [...] both in requests for empty forms and queries about names recorded in the past [...] we have not yet received the boxes which makes answering queries impossible [...] the material is in tied parcels [...] the number of unanswered queries now exceeds 100."

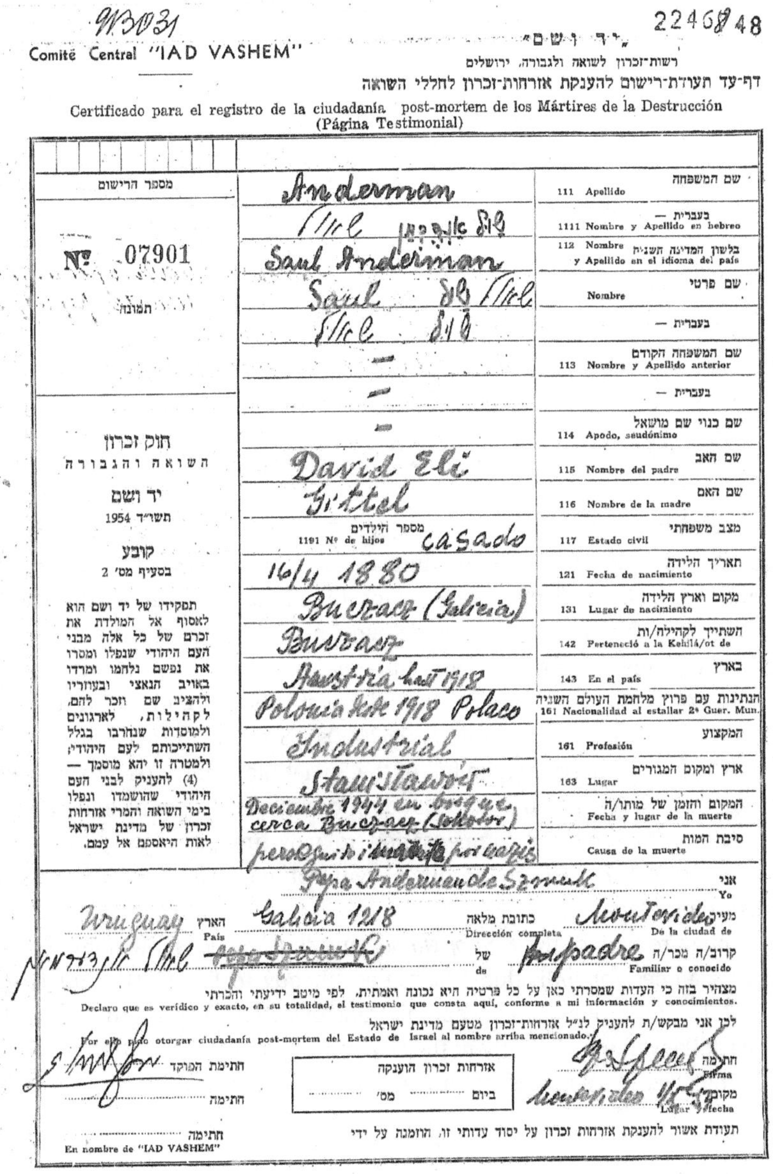

913031 — 2246848

Comité Central "IAD VASHEM"

יד ושם

רשות-זכרון לשואה ולגבורה, ירושלים

דף-עד תעודת-רישום להענקת אזרחות-זכרון לחללי השואה

Certificado para el registro de la ciudadanía post-mortem de los Mártires de la Destrucción (Página Testimonial)

מספר הרישום	Anderman	שם המשפחה 111 Apellido
Nº 07901	שאול אנדערמאן	בעברית — 1111 Nombre y Apellido en hebreo
תמונה	Saul Anderman	בלשון המדינה השניה 112 Nombre y Apellido en el idioma del país
	Saul שאול	שם פרטי Nombre
	שאול	בעברית —
	—	שם המשפחה הקודם 113 Nombre y Apellido anterior
	—	בעברית —
חוק זכרון השואה והגבורה יד ושם 1954 תשי"ד	—	שם כנוי שם מושאל 114 Apodo, seudónimo
קובע בסעיף מס' 2	David Eli	שם האב 115 Nombre del padre
תפקידו של יד ושם הוא לאסוף אל המולדת את זכרם של כל אלה מבני העם היהודי שנפלו ומסרו את נפשם נלחמו ומרדו באויב הנאצי ובעוזריו ולהציב שם וזכר להם, לקהילות, לארגונים ולמוסדות שנחרבו בגלל השתייכותם לעם היהודי; ולמטרה זו יהא מוסמך — (4) להעניק לבני העם היהודי שהושמדו ונפלו בימי השואה והמרי אזרחות זכרון של מדינת ישראל לאות היאספם אל עמם.	Gittel	שם האם 116 Nombre de la madre
	מספר הילדים 1191 Nº de hijos — casado	מצב משפחתי 117 Estado civil
	16/4 1880	תאריך הלידה 121 Fecha de nacimiento
	Buczacz (Galicia)	מקום וארץ הלידה 131 Lugar de nacimiento
	Buczacz	השתייך לקהילה/ות 142 Pertenecío a la Kehilá/ot de
	Austria hast 1918	בארץ 143 En el país
	Polonia desde 1918 Polaco	הנתינות עם פרוץ מלחמת העולם השניה 161 Nacionalidad al estallar 2ª Guer. Mun.
	Industrial	המקצוע 161 Profesión
	Stanislawów	ארץ ומקום המגורים 163 Lugar
	Deciembre 1944 en bosque cerca Buczacz (Sokolov)	המקום והזמן של מותו/ה Fecha y lugar de la muerte
	perseguido por nazis	סיבת המות Causa de la muerte

אני Yo Pepa Anderman de Szwuck

מעיר De la ciudad de Montevideo — כתובת מלאה Dirección completa Galicia 1218 — הארץ País Uruguay

קרוב/ה מכר/ה Familiar o conocido — hija padre — של de

מצהיר בזה כי העדות שמסרתי כאן על כל פרטיה היא נכונה ואמתית, לפי מיטב ידיעתי והכרתי.
Declaro que es verídico y exacto, en su totalidad, el testimonio que consta aquí, conforme a mi información y conocimientos.

לכן אני מבקש/ת להעניק לנ"ל אזרחות-זכרון מטעם מדינת ישראל
Por ello pido otorgar ciudadanía post-mortem del Estado de Israel al nombre arriba mencionado.

חתימת המפקד — חתימה Firma

אזרחות זכרון הוענקה ביום — מס'

חתימה — מקום ותאריך Lugar y fecha Montevideo 1/10 54

חתימה En nombre de "IAD VASHEM"

תעודת אשור להענקת אזרחות זכרון על יסוד עדותי זו, הוזמנה על ידי

Fig. 1: Page of Testimony given to Yad Vashem to commemorate Saul Anderman, signed in Montevideo, Uruguay, 1.10.1954 (Yad Vashem Pages of Testimony collection)

The Third Period: 1970s to 1980s

By the 1970s we reach the third stage, whereby the search for names of Holocaust victims starts losing importance. The symbol of the second period – the radio broadcast of the *Bureau for the Search for Relatives* – is initially moved from a prime broadcast time and then stopped completely.[17] Survivors are seen to have got on with their lives, and internalized the fact that for the most part those they have not found are lost. Commemoration had also been institutionalized. Rather than a daily reminder of the loss, commemoration would take place on Holocaust Memorial day or at designated memorial sites, one of these being *Yad Vashem*.

The Fourth Period: 1980s to today

The renewed interest in searching for names and fates begins in the 1980s – a symbol of this being the first international Jewish genealogy conferences in Jerusalem in 1984. There are many reasons for this change, one being demographic, as by the 1980s many of the survivors had finished rearing their children and were starting to retire and had more time to devote to interest in the past. For many different reasons interest in the Holocaust was rising in the west.

Later on, during the 1990s and early 2000s a series of events – among them the reunification of Germany, the fall of the Soviet bloc, the agreements reached over dormant accounts in Switzerland and dormant insurance accounts – opened new programs for compensation to new groups of people, many of whom turned to *Yad Vashem* and other organizations to find documentation to establish their claims.

Although reports of the *Hall of Names* and the Archive show numerous and growing searches for individuals answered already in the 1980s, *Yad Vashem* also had to go through a conceptual transformation.[18] A standard handout that was still given out regularly in the *Hall of Names* in the early 1990s informed visitors that *Yad Vashem* was not a place for genealogical research.[19]

---

17 Malka: *The Search for Surviving Relatives*, 68, 95.
18 For example: *Hall of Names report of activities for April 1989–March 1990* AM.9/2/ 32/Yad Vashem Archives, Jerusalem.
19 Ibid., 143. "THE HALL OF NAMES IS NOT THE PLACE FOR FAMILY RESEARCH OR FOR LOCATING SURVIVORS OF THE HOLOCAUST" (Capitals in original).

It took some time for *Yad Vashem* to realize that the genealogical search for names was mostly survivors and their descendants still looking for connections over the breach of generations that the Holocaust caused. It should also be noted that although genealogists symbolize the change at *Yad Vashem* and at times facilitated it, most of those who benefitted from a change in *Yad Vashem* attitude geared more toward service to individuals would not have defined themselves as genealogists.

Technology was another factor. By 2000 *Yad Vashem* had an extensive – and ever expanding – database of names and fates, which went online in 2004. Many questions that in the past would have taken much research time were now answered instantly. Of course, the initial major scanning and data-entry program for the *Yad Vashem* names collection was funded by the aforementioned committee on the dormant Swiss accounts in 1999 – showing the interconnection of so many of the factors in this story.

Another factor was also important, namely that in the 1950s the search for individuals frequently included a search for living individuals, a task that *Yad Vashem* was never – and is not today – able to accommodate in most cases. By the 1980s the search for information was concentrated more on the Holocaust period travails and less on the finding of people still alive, a task which the *Yad Vashem* resources were more capable of. Here it should be noted that the *Jewish Agency Search Bureau for Missing Relatives* was officially closed in 1999, and its archives was transferred to the *Central Zionist Archives*.[20]

Numerous organizations still function in Israel covering every aspect of Holocaust commemoration, research and education. However, by the 1990s *Yad Vashem* had established its centrality. A committee was founded to establish the list of officially sanctioned memorial ceremonies recognized by the Israeli government. Only two of the members of the committee were not direct government employees, one of them a representative of *Yad Vashem*.[21] So *Yad Vashem* was now not only central to the commemoration of the Holocaust in Israel – it was also considered an institution with a say in what issues and events the government of Israel would officially commemorate. Of the 30 annual ceremonies approved, two take place at *Yad Vashem* and require the participation of the Prime Minister and the President.[22]

---

20 *Central Zionist Archives* website: http://www.zionistarchives.org.il/familyresearch/GenealogyDatabases/Pages/RelativeSearch.aspx. Last accessed: 28.1.2019.
21 Decision of the committee of ministers for symbols and ceremonies, 5.1.2005. Available at: https://www.gov.il/he/Departments/policies/2005_des3117. Last accessed: 28.1.2019.
22 Ibid. decision 139, 16.11.2008. Available at: https://www.gov.il/he/departments/policies/2008_des4292. Last accessed: 28.1.2019.

To conclude, there were many reasons why *Yad Vashem* was not a central source for information on the fate of individuals in the first decades after the Holocaust, and why that started changing in the 1980s. One is the infrastructure – *Yad Vashem* did not have the archival materials, the organizational abilities or the human resources to give such services in the first critical decades after the Second World War. It is also likely that at the time the search for relatives was a high prestige activity that played a major role in Israeli society, while at the time *Yad Vashem* was an organization with little prestige. The *Jewish Agency* had both the infrastructure and the prestige to play a major role in searching for relatives. Later, as the search for relatives became an issue with less prestige, the *Jewish Agency* would reduce its role, while a more central *Yad Vashem* in Israel would expand its role. *Yad Vashem* opened its doors to new groups interested in people's fate only to find that in fact they were the continuation of groups they had served before. *Yad Vashem*'s repositories – among them the *Pages of Testimony* and archival collections, including the copy of the ITS collection – became major resources for name searches, and along with *Yad Vashem* 's adaptation of new technologies would make it the major player in this area in Israel – and many would say in the larger Jewish world.

Diane Afoumado
ITS Research at the *United States Holocaust Memorial Museum* for Descendants of Holocaust Victims and Survivors

Abstract: Many studies have been published about the children of survivors. Most of them approach the subject from the angle of psychological trauma and transmission, but very few deal with name heritage. For that reason, this paper will focus on what name-related documentation can mean for the second and third generations. The impact of names inherited from Holocaust victims often comes with a heavy moral burden, and with a responsibility to transmit their history. The opening of the *International Tracing Service* (today *Arolsen Archives*) to the public allowed access to relevant information that was not available before. Here, I will demonstrate how ITS materials sometimes help the second and third generations beyond expectations. Case studies will illustrate how combining other sources with the ITS further enhances the impact of our research on users' lives.

Introduction

When the *United States Holocaust Memorial Museum* (USHMM) partnered with Ancestry.com to create the World Memory Project,[1] the late Sol Finkelstein was interviewed with his son Joseph for a promotional video.[2] Jo made a powerful comment about what it means to be "second generation":

> the second generation [...] if you think about it, means that our parents are the first generation and nothing existed before us. And it is not true. We had a whole history, we had a

---

[1] The USHMM partnered with Ancestry.com to index some collections by names and to make them accessible to the public. USHMM: "About the World Memory Project". Available at: https://www.ushmm.org/online/world-memory-project/pages/about-the-project/index.html.
Last accessed: 30.7.2019. Volunteers around the world work on indexing. The names are then searchable through USHMM: "Database of Holocaust Survivor and Victim Names". Available at: https://www.ushmm.org/remember/resources-holocaust-survivors-victims/database-of-holocaust-survivor-and-victim-names. Last accessed: 30.7.2019.
[2] "World Memory Project—Sol Finkelstein". Available at: https://vimeo.com/25239476. Last accessed: 30.7.2019.

OpenAccess. © 2020 Diane Afoumado, published by De Gruyter. This work is licensed under the Creative Commons Attribution-NonCommercial-NoDerivatives 4.0 License.
https://doi.org/10.1515/9783110665376-011

whole world. And my grandfather is just one person in that world, but he existed. He existed before the war and I found him.³

It is as if the world of the children of Holocaust survivors started after the war, as if 1945 was Year One of their very existence. Based on that artificial way of counting, we talk about the second, third, and even fourth generations. All of them link back to the survival of increasingly distant relatives.

Thanks to an effort led by USHMM to open the ITS archives, the Museum eventually received the first batch of the documents in December 2007.⁴ Over 11 years have passed since the opening of the ITS collection at the USHMM and interest in the people therein shows no sign of decreasing. Some thought that the ITS would first pique the curiosity of many because of the publicity surrounding it, and they assumed that this would slow with the passing of the survivors. This could not have been further from the truth. The statistics demonstrate a continued rising interest not only in the United States, but around the world. Survivors were among the first to contact the USHMM for research in the ITS, but they were never the only group.

Here I will first focus on the meaning of name-related research for the second and third generations. I will then describe how the combination of ITS with other resources changed USHMM research services. Finally, using case studies I will show how that research has impacted patrons' lives and how the ITS collection sometimes helps them beyond their expectations.

The Meaning of Name-Related Documentation and 2Gs and 3Gs

Many books on the second generation (2G) have appeared, most focusing on transmission and trauma.⁵ The terms "second generation" or "child of survivors"

---

3 Ibid.
4 Testimony of Paul Shapiro, then director of the *Center for Advanced Holocaust Studies* at the USHMM before the Committee on Foreign Affairs, Subcommittee on Europe: "Opening Up of the Bad Arolsen Holocaust Archives in Germany", 2007. Available at: https://www.gpo.gov/fdsys/pkg/CHRG-110hhrg34481/pdf/CHRG-110hhrg34481.pdf. Last accessed: 16.8.2019.
5 To cite only a few studies about the second generation and trauma, see: Helen Epstein: *Le traumatisme en héritage: Conversations avec des fils et filles de survivants de la Shoah*, Paris: Gallimard, 2012; Yoram Mouchenik, Marion Feldman, Marie-Rose Moro: "Les 'enfants cachés', survivants de la Shoah. Traumatismes et deuils. Études retrospectives", in *L'information psychiatrique*, 89, 7/2017, 523–532; Nathalie Zajde: *Enfants de survivants: La transmission du traumatisme*

have been studied⁶ and thus remain common understandings, so we will not need to develop that topic here. But what is surprising is that not much has been written about the meaning for the second generation of bearing the name of a family member who was murdered during the Holocaust.

In many cultures and civilizations, names have a very strong power. In ancient Egypt,

> the name of an individual was considered one of their most important aspects, both in this life and the next. A name provided identity: without a name, it was thought that a person would cease to exist – the worst possible fate to the ancient Egyptians. [...] Erasing someone's name was considered an effective way to render them nonexistent.⁷

Consequently, "the act of speaking aloud the name of the deceased restored him to life and, if repeated daily, guaranteed his immortality."⁸ In Jewish memorial practice, as Nina Fischer of the University of Edinburgh explains, "the survival of a name [is] the predominant vehicle for carrying the memory of the dead."⁹ She emphasizes that naming those born after the Holocaust after murdered grandparents (or other relatives) became "the most frequent marker of survivor families."¹⁰ "Being named after someone can establish an assumed or ascribed special bond [...] Searching for knowledge about this person can also be [...] memory work process."¹¹ Names often come with a heavy heritage, and therefore a responsibility to pass on family memory to future generations. Many people who contact the USHMM Research service do exactly that since they seek any possible information behind a name, i.e. historical context about a ghetto or a camp, a village in which the name bearer used to live, and so on and so forth. Behind every name lies the story of a life.¹²

---

chez les enfants des juifs, Paris: Editions Odile Jacob, 2005; Nathalie Zajde: *Guérir de la Shoah: Psychothérapie des survivants et de leurs descendants*, Paris: Editions Odile Jacob, 2005.
6 Diane L. Wolf: "What's in a Name? The Genealogy of Holocaust Identities", in: *Genealogy*, 2017, 1(4), 19. Available at: https://doi.org/10.3390/genealogy1040019. Last accessed: 30.7.2019.
7 *Queens of Egypt*, Exhibition, National Geographic Museum, Washington, D.C., 2019.
8 "I know you and I know your names", Spell 144, *Book of The Dead*, see *Toutânkhamon. Le Trésor du Pharon* (Exhibition), Grande Halle de la Villette, Paris, 2019.
9 Nina Fischer: *Memory Work: The Second Generation*, Houndmills: Palgrave Macmillan, 2015, 69.
10 Ibid., 70.
11 Ibid., 79.
12 USHMM: "Behind Every Name a Story". Available at: https://www.ushmm.org/remember/holocaust-reflections-testimonies/behind-every-name-a-story. Last accessed: 31.7.2019.

When people fill out the *United States Holocaust Memorial Museum* online research request form[13] they often include comments that illustrate what the names that they are looking for mean to them: "I am named after (middle name) my 2nd of three deceased uncles and am curious of circumstances surrounding his death" (case 3190). "Next month I am visiting Prague with my daughter who is named after this great aunt" (case 6317). "This person is my grandmother's older brother. I was named after him. I believe he died in Auschwitz" (case 14679). Naming a child born as Second Generation could serve "as a memorial for the entire family."[14] According to Nina Fischer, "Memory work is also self-work."[15] Behind such comments appears the message that research requests are not simply about one person. Why do requesters feel that they have to share this relationship to names with the researchers? Would it be to emphasize that this is not "just a name search" type of request that could be comparable to what genealogists do? Is it to make sure that we understand that the request is beyond information about a person? Often when we conduct individual research with the requester next to us that information emerges early in the interaction without our asking for it. The name embodies a person who was murdered and the requester wants to make sure that we understand that the research is not abstract: we are searching for a person, not just a name. The information we find returns some embodied identity to the victim. Behind every name, there is a story that people feel the need to share with us as if they expected us to become the recipients of the victim's heritage. The recovery of the victim's story becomes a forever-living memorial through the bearer, who can now perpetuate and honor memory of the victim. Sometimes, people bring photographs to show that behind the name they are searching there was a face, a body, a person who existed.

Since the opening of the ITS to the public at the USHMM in December 2007, we have received more than 32,000[16] requests for information about individuals. More than half are from survivors and their families.[17] Beyond the need to learn about a member, families seek "to recreate a family genealogy that crosses temporal and physical distances."[18] The ITS collection offers powerful tools for this,

---

[13] USHMM: "Research an Individual". Available at: https://secure.ushmm.org/individual-research/getting_started.php. Last accessed: 6.8.2019.
[14] Fischer: *Memory Work*, 96.
[15] Ibid., 80.
[16] 32,245 research requests as of February 2019.
[17] 19,553 as of February 2019.
[18] Fischer: *Memory Work*, 89.

but to regard a name search as genealogy would be too reductive. Finding individuals in the ITS is not creating a family tree, it is reestablishing history.

The provenance of requests plays an important role. A majority of our requests come from the 50 states of the United States,[19] but we have received them from 79 countries,[20] among them unexpected ones like Laos. Noticeable differences distinguish requests from the US and Europe. A country of immigration such as the United States inevitably faces the present and the future, and the past seems to fade more rapidly than in the old continent. Not being a physical theater of the Second World War, memory of the Holocaust among the younger generation seems less concrete than in Europe, where the past is in many ways visible, made palpable through physical markers such as commemorative plaques, memorial sites, museums, *Stolpersteine*, and so on. Another factor in the United States is distance. In America it is not rare that families spread out over the country, and children leave for college in a different state, mitigating against family story transmission. Consequently, the "third generation" often knows little about its grandparents. By the time some start to show interest, it might be too late, and often even basic information such as a date of birth may have been lost.

When we travel in North America to present on the ITS, meeting with a 2G is a very different experience than meeting with a 3G. For the 3G (or even 4G), distance acts like a screen, and trauma becomes memory and commemoration. In Fischer's words, they can "remember enough without remaining trapped in the past."[21] We also receive research requests from families who want to know more so they can honor the victim during a bar mitzvah or bat mitzvah, as seen in messages that we have received: "I am sponsoring this child for my bar mitzvah. I got his name from the *Remember Us* project. I would like to see if I could get some more information about him" (case 17134). The Remember Us Project "invites every child who is preparing for bar / bat mitzvah to remember a child who was lost in the Holocaust."[22] "My son is researching this boy to remember him during his bar mitzvah this September 6th and he would like to know as much as possible to honor him properly" (case 7973). In such instances the ITS collection makes information personal and we circle back to the importance and significance of commemorating a name in Jewish tradition. Having

---

[19] 23,066 as of February 2019.
[20] 9,179 as of February 2019.
[21] Fischer: *Memory Work*, 71.
[22] Remember Us: "The Holocaust Bnai Mitzvah Project". Available at: http://www.remember-us.org/. Last accessed: 31.7.2019.

looked at some general points, we can now study how the ITS collection changed USHMM research services.

What did the ITS Change? Changes in the Research Process

Name related searches did not start at the USHMM with the opening of the ITS. Before it was designated the national repository for the ITS digital collection,[23] the USHMM's reference staff employed a large variety of collections and online resources to answer inquiries about individuals. We already had two major name databases, which we continue to enrich every year. The Benjamin and Vladka Meed Registry of Survivors contains more than 209,000 names,[24] and is the only database of both Jewish and non-Jewish survivors in the world (based on the USHMM definition).[25] The Holocaust Survivors and Victims Database (HSV) is the other, capturing data from various archival collections that the Museum has duplicated worldwide, and including all categories of victims (both Jewish and non-Jewish) of the Nazis and their collaborators.

Before we started receiving the ITS digital collection, the number of requests about individuals was not captured as such, and the reference staff did not differentiate between inquiries about names from other kinds of inquiries i.e. about locations, historical questions, and so on. Those general inquiries still arrive daily from the general public, but there is definitely a before and an after ITS. Regarding research on individuals, over 60 percent of our requests are from survivors, their families, and families of victims. On average we receive more than 200 new requests per month, and we complete nearly 300 (we continue to ad-

---

[23] Paul Shapiro: "Opening the Archives of the International Tracing Service (ITS). How did it happen? What does it mean?", in: *Shoah Intervention Methods Documentation*, 2008. Available at: http://www.vwi.ac.at/images/Downloads/SWL_Reader/Shapiro/SWL-Reader-Shapiro.pdf. Last accessed: 31.7.2019. Also see: Kenneth Waltzer: "Opening the Red Cross International Tracing Service, 26 J. Marshall J. Computer & Info. L. 161", in: *Journal of Computer & Information Law*, Fall 2008. Available at: https://repository.jmls.edu/cgi/viewcontent.cgi?referer=https://www.google.com/&httpsredir=1&article=1651&context=jitpl. Last accessed: 31.7.2019.

[24] USHMM: "Holocaust Survivors and Victims Database". Available at: https://www.ushmm.org/online/hsv/person_advance_search.php. Last accessed: 31.7.2019.

[25] USHMM definition of survivors: The Museum honors as survivors any persons, Jewish or non-Jewish, who were displaced, persecuted, or discriminated against due to the racial, religious, ethnic, social, and political policies of the Nazis and their collaborators between 1933 and 1945. See https://www.ushmm.org/remember/the-holocaust-survivors-and-victims-resource-center/benjamin-and-vladka-meed-registry-of-holocaust-survivors. Last accessed: 31.7.2019.

dress an inherited backlog). Every research case generates an exhaustive search that includes not only the ITS and other USHMM databases, but also links to online resources that could complement the research. In February 2019, the largest number of documents for one single case was 257, but the largest number ever sent was 658. This suggests how in-depth our research can be.

We also search our name-related database (Holocaust and Victims database – HSV), and when appropriate, the "list database" (a list of lists)[26] which is similar to the one in *Yad Vashem*.[27] Those databases are constantly growing thanks to the World Memory Project, which is our partnership with Ancestry.com to index some of our digital collections.[28] Since the beginning of that partnership in May 2011, we have added 1,881,791 indexed names to our name-related database.

The arrival of the ITS digital collection corresponded with a new digital era that changed the research process dramatically. Thanks to the digitization campaign undertaken by the National Institute for Holocaust Documentation at the USHMM, we need to consult fewer and fewer paper, microfilm, or microfiche collections.[29] Searching for the names of Jews in the Lodz ghetto for example, we could check the collection of workers cards[30] in addition to the *Lodz-names: list of the ghetto inhabitants 1940–1944* book[31] that can also be found in the last folders of ITS digital sub-collection 1.1.22.1.[32] Although the ITS added to our collections millions of documents about the wartime era, most of that material was not entirely new. We already had records collected for more than 25 years from memorial sites and archival centers in Europe. The French deportation lists,

---

[26] USHMM: "Holocaust Survivors and Victims Database". Available at: https://www.ushmm.org/online/hsv/source_advance_search.php. Last accessed: 31.7.2019.
[27] Available at: https://yvng.yadvashem.org/advanced-search.html?language=en. Last accessed: 21.8.2019.
[28] USHMM: "World Memory Project". Available at: https://www.ushmm.org/online/world-memory-project/. Last accessed: 31.7.2019.
[29] USHMM: "Search our collections". Available at: https://collections.ushmm.org/search/. Last accessed: 31.7.2019.
[30] Przełożony Starszeństwa Żydow w Getcie Łódzkim, 1939–1944/RG-15.083M/USHHM. *The United States Holocaust Memorial Museum* Archives received the first part of the filmed collection from the *Polish States Archives* in Łódź via the *United States Holocaust Museum* International Archives Project in June 2000, and several subsequent accretions between 2001 and 2007. Available at: https://collections.ushmm.org/search/catalog/irn507401. Last accessed: 6.8.2019.
[31] *Lodz – names: list of the ghetto inhabitants 1940–1944*, Yad Vashem, Organization of Former Residents of Lodz in Israel, 1994.
[32] List Material Litzmannstadt, folders 6 to 10, 1.1.22.1/ITS Digital Archive, USHMM.

for example,[33] have long been accessible online at the Mémorial de la Shoah's website.[34] The ITS's Stutthof records were already in the Museum archives[35] (prisoner names are now searchable on the USHMM website through HSV with associated color images via the ITS collections).[36] But ITS post-war sub-collections (mostly DP materials) had not been accessible for researchers for decades up until 2007.

So what exactly did the ITS digital collection bring to name-related research? The short answer is that the ITS materials generally allow us to "zoom in" where before we were able to look only from a distance. By combining the ITS digital collection with archival materials, books, metadata, and other resources, Museum researchers can provide a family member with the precise time of death of a victim, a block number in a concentration camp, a photograph taken in a Displaced Person (DP) camp that helped the individual to re-establish his identity and apply for refugee status. Such detail might make a big difference to family members: knowing that your grandfather died during an Auschwitz death march is not exactly the same as knowing his precise grave location that you might then be able to honor during a memory trip. If such details don't change the world, they change that grandson's world, and for that alone the ITS is invaluable.

But even more significant than granularity, one of the many ITS treasures lies in the post-war sub-collections. First, those documents are materials that researchers have not fully explored. Second, this may be true more in the United States than in Europe, where many descendants of Holocaust survivors and forced laborers live, and many were born in DP camps. Often times they do not even know those documents existed. DP personal files, applications for assistance (Care and Maintenance) files, and lists of DPs in the Allied occupation zones are a gold mine not only for research on individuals, but also for historians and researchers in general. The Tracing and Documentation, or *T/D files*, contain

---

[33] List Material B.d.S. France and List Material Drancy, 1.1.9.1. and 1.1.9.9/ITS Digital Archive, USHMM.

[34] Mémorial de la Shoah: "Recherche de Personne". Available at: http://www.memorialdelashoah.org/le-memorial/qui-sommes-nous/les-services-du-memorial-de-la-shoah.html. Last accessed: 31.7.2019.

[35] Stutthof concentration camp records. Personal files/RG-04.058M/Państwowe Muzeum Stutthof w Sztutowie, USHHM. Officials of the Stutthof concentration camp created the records from 1939 to 1945. *Muzeum Stutthof* filmed the records for the *United States Holocaust Memorial Museum* Archives in 1995. Available at: https://collections.ushmm.org/search/catalog/irn507370. Last accessed: 31.7.2019.

[36] Here is one example: "Karl Kliefoth". Available at: https://www.ushmm.org/online/hsv/person_view.php?PersonId=8269667. Last accessed: 31.7.2019.

information too, even if for a long time they were not considered archival materials in their own right. I recently conducted on-site research for a second-generation requester who wanted to know the names of her maternal grandparents. She had no information at all about them. Her parents were survivors, but never discussed the family they had lost. My only hope was that her mother had previously contacted ITS at Bad Arolsen to open research cases about her parents – and indeed she had! Not only did we identify her maternal grandparents, but reiterating the research for her father's side, we found her paternal grandparents as well. Although *T/D files* cannot (and should not) be considered a fully reliable source because in most cases the information there came from a third party, the basic information can prove useful. That day a 30-minute-search changed that woman's life and she left with the identity of her grandparents on both sides of her family. Although the ITS did not contain any further documents on them, knowing names brought the requester some closure.

Beyond such closure, the 2007 opening of the ITS increases chances to reunite relatives around the world. The Sol Finkelstein case mentioned above illustrates this. Sol had been deported with his father to Auschwitz and was able to remain with him until the death march on which they became separated. For his whole life Sol experienced a sense of guilt for having "abandoned" his father to his death. Thanks to a combination of resources that included ITS, we were able to tell Sol that his father did not die immediately after they got separated, but survived until the liberation and died a few days later. We also determined his grave location. Sol had to wait more than 70 years to know the truth. When we showed him a photo of his father that we managed to find, Sol looked at his father's face and apologized to him.[37]

There is a growing interest in the United States in tracing family roots. We have noticed a dramatic increase in requests for research after we made more names available online, especially after we automated requests for copies of documents. Typically people start with a simple Google search and end up at the USHMM Holocaust and Victims database. If they find metadata but cannot see the original document online because of European privacy laws, they can request a copy by clicking on a link that instantly emails it to them. Recently we have noticed an increase in research requests after people find basic name-related information on our website and then click on the link to the ITS research request form to conduct research on individuals at the USHMM. Often the ITS con-

---

[37] Ancestry on Youtube: "Yes, That's My Father". Available at: https://www.youtube.com/watch?v=D-ODdLRuJs. Last accessed: 31.7.2019.

tains much more information than what we can put online. The 2007 opening of the ITS has raised people's expectations but not always reasonably.

The fact that early on the ITS digital collection was too often presented as the "largest closed Holocaust related archives in the world" led many to expect the ultimate treasure trove. Too often this expectation is based on the assumption of the Nazis' legendary record keeping. However, most people who contact us have no knowledge of the ITS or other collections that could help. What they are looking for is answers, documentation, confirmation of what they already suspect, or new details, and, often, closure.

Changes in the Impact on 2G and 3G

Beyond changes in the research process, the impact ITS research has had changed significantly. ITS post-war materials are the most relevant and richest, especially for 2G, even if the latter are not homogenous. There are big differences in the needs of people born after the Holocaust in Europe generally, in the DP camps in particular, or in the United States. The ITS contains information about DPs that is often surprising to 2G requesters who often do not expect so many details, including some that bring back memories of childhood. The DP2 card file contains the registration files of children signed by at least one parent. Combined with Care and Maintenance files, these present a vivid picture of DP camp life. Medical information and brief psychological evaluations are sometimes available. Such documents are often sensitive and need to be contextualized as the products of harried social workers hardly trained to deal with thousands of traumatized DPs.

A few years ago, I attended a panel about DP camps at a conference held at the USHMM. During the discussion, a gentleman asked where he could find information about his parents, Ukrainians who ended the war in a DP camp. I soon found 105 images of pages of ITS documents about him, born in 1947 in the Cornberg DP camp,[38] 101 images of pages of documents about his younger sister, born in 1948, 47 images of pages of documents about his father, born in 1912, and an inquiry card about his mother. Those papers contained many details about their lives as DPs: the father's struggle to work as a tailor; the mother's hospitalization in DP hospital in Fulda for long periods, and a little boy (the requester) too young for Kindergarten playing outside when the weather was good; we found a photo of his baby sister. The father was in several DP camps between 1945

---

38 Card reference "Care and Maintenance" file, 0.1/27088722/ITS Digital Archive, USHMM.

and 1950 in Allendorf, Cornberg,[39] Leipheim Airport, and Bad Aibling in Upper Bavaria[40] Some of those camps including Cornberg hosted large numbers of Ukrainians.[41] The Child Search file contained memos and correspondence by the IRO Child Care Office about the little boy's health, suggesting that maybe some "food cod liver oil" might help.[42] We also learned that the father had "difficulties in working during his first months at Leipheim – as he had no sewing machine."[43] Later on the IRO requested that the father be transferred with his son to Bad Aibling where he could get a job. He is described as "active, honest, and a good worker."[44] As we sifted those files, the gentleman shared with me some of his childhood recollections, allowing me to learn firsthand about the life of a Ukrainian family hoping to rebuild their life in Canada. The requester mentioned that in the DP camp, he had had a sweater with three buttons on top of one of the shoulders. A photo of him wearing this exact sweater appears in his DP file.[45] The level of detail that the post-war collections can provide is quite phenomenal. Eventually the family was able to immigrate to the US, leaving Bremerhaven for New York on October 7, 1951 on the *USNS General Hersey*.[46] Their ITS documents not only contained information about four people, but also about the historical context of DP camps, the social workers who helped people return to as normal a life as possible, the medical and psychological help DPs received from overwhelmed staff, and much more.

But the impact of ITS research goes further. Following his research, my requester decided to help us reach out to the Ukrainian community in North America to let them know about the ITS and the research services that the USHMM provides. So far we have met with great success in cities such as Cleveland, where the community is quite significant. Starting that journey with a person

---

39 Application for IRO Assistance form, 3.2.1.1/79259728/ITS Digital Archive, USHMM. Ukrainian DPs in Cornberg DP camp are mentioned in *The Ukrainian Weekly*, 13, 1946. Available at: http://www.ukrweekly.com/archive/1946/The_Ukrainian_Weekly_1946-13.pdf. Last accessed: 6.8.2019.
40 A.E.F. Assembly Center Registration Card, 0.1/27087632/ITS Digital Archive, USHMM. On the topic of the IRO Children's Village Bad Aibling, see: Christian Höschler: *Home(less): The IRO Children's Village Bad Aibling*, Berlin: epubli, 2017.
41 Wsevolod W. Isajiw and Roman Senkus: *The Refugee Experience: Ukrainian Displaced Persons After World War II*, Canada: Canadian Inst of Ukranian Study Pr, 1992, 28.
42 Correspondence files of Children identified by name, 6.3.2.1/84298528/ITS Digital Archive, USHMM.
43 Social history – interview, 6.3.2.1/84298538/ITS Digital Archive, USHMM.
44 Correspondence files of Children identified by name, 6.3.2.1/84298530/ITS Digital Archive, USHMM.
45 Photography, 6.3.2.1/84298521/ITS Digital, USHMM.
46 Ship manifest, 3.1.3.2/81680604, 81680676, 81680677/ITS Digital Archive, USHMM.

born in a DP camp in 1947, we now have a partnership with the Ukrainian Museum and Archives (UMA) in Cleveland. This is just one example of how the ITS collection can impact lives and communities. It also illustrates the fact that the ITS collection significantly modified the way the USHMM conducts outreach to some non-Jewish communities such as the Polish, Ukrainian, and Baltic. Reaching out to such North American communities opens new perspectives. Sitting with Ukrainian-Americans who were born in DP camps and searching for ITS materials that they never imagined existed is quite an experience. The ITS collection allows us to conduct research for a wide range of groups that the museum recognizes as victims of Nazi persecution.[47]

Sometimes the ITS reveals family secrets – whether for better or sometimes worse depends on the nature of the information and whether the requester is a 2G or a 3G. The main difference between the latter is the distance in time that separates them from their relatives' experience. The 2Gs are more often strongly affected by such information when their parents did not mention it to them. They can feel that they have been left in the dark, and that their parents' experience will never be completely accessible to them. A few thus feel somehow "betrayed." Breaking the news that your father had been married to someone else before he met your mother after the war might be difficult to hear for some 2Gs but might be considered "cool" by 3Gs. The time distance between the 3Gs and the Holocaust is in a sense comparable to the distance between the 2G and the First World War. While the Holocaust remains part of the 2Gs' childhood and often directly shaped their lives, it is already history to the 3Gs.

The ITS collection also enhances our ability to reunite family members from these generations, though here space permits reference to only a few cases. Iris, who lives in Israel, decided to begin research into her father's family from Krakow.[48] Based on what she had been told, her father, Jakob (today, Yehoshua, and still alive), was the only survivor. Iris did not know where to start, and contacted the USHMM to inquire about her father's siblings. After a few weeks we sent her the ITS documents that recorded her father's imprisonment in the Krakow ghetto, his transportation in March 1943 to Plaszow when the Krakow ghetto was liquidated and, after liberation by the Red Army, his arrival in March 1944 in Lerida, Spain with other refugees.[49] Jakob sailed to Haifa on the *S/S Guine* on

---

[47] The Museum collects documentation from Jews and non-Jews who were displaced, persecuted, or discriminated against due to the racial, religious, ethnic, social, and political policies of the Nazis and their collaborators between 1933 and 1945.
[48] Iris Trzafrir on Youtube: "Discovering family after 70 years – produced by Alon Degani". Available at: https://www.youtube.com/watch?v=VoPdB3lecVA. Last accessed: 6.8.2019.
[49] Lists of refugees in Spain, 3.1.1.3/78788907, 78789170, 78788993/ITS Digital Archive, USHMM.

October 23, 1944[50] arriving via Portugal on November 5.[51] We also sent documentation about one of Iris's aunts, Jakob's sister Lea (or Sheindela). Scheindela was deported to Buchenwald on August 4, 1944, where she received the prisoner number 1095.[52] The ITS Buchenwald collection contains her prisoner registration card, an office card, an effects card, a prisoner questionnaire, and an employment card. What Iris' family had not known was that Scheindela too had survived the Holocaust and was registered as a DP under the Allied Expeditionary Forces.[53] She was sent to Hebertsfelden,[54] near Eggenfelden, Germany where she resided after the war[55] and was registered as a member of the Jewish community, who received German ration cards.[56] In March 1949, Scheindela eventually emmigrated to Palestine.[57] The documentation we sent to Iris left no doubt about Scheindela arriving in Palestine five years after her brother Jakob. Sadly, nobody in the family knew that she had survived and had been living only few kilometers away from her brother. Scheindela had since passed away, but had had two children. Therefore, while it was too late for Jakob to reconnect with his sister, he did meet his nephews. They now have a bigger family thanks to the ITS materials we sent.

The original missed opportunity is not as strange as it might seem at first. Individuals started to search for their loved ones during and immediately after the Second World War when they could request the help of the *International Tracing Service* in Arolsen. But back then the search meant going through millions of names indexed on cards and dispersed in various files and collections that each required a different way of searching due to their very nature. Searching prisoner files from a concentration camp demands a different association of information than looking for a name on a post-war ship manifest. The nature of requests about individuals for previously unknown information has not changed

---

50 S/S. "Guine" to Haifa, 3.1.1.3/78789104, 78789107/ITS Digital Archive, USHMM.
51 List of immigrants who arrived in Palestine from Portugal on Nov. 5, 1944, 3.1.1.3/78777147/ITS Digital Archive, USHMM.
52 Internment book (numbers) of Concentration Camp Buchenwald (women), 1.1.5.1/5271642/ITS Digital Archive, USHMM.
53 DP 2 Card File, A.E.F. DP Registration Record of Lola Ehrlich, 3.1.1.1/66999891/ITS Digital Archive, USHMM.
54 A.E.F. Assembly Center Registration Card of Lola Ehrlich, 0.1/64574223/ITS Digital Archive, USHMM.
55 DP Card File of Lola Ehrlich, 3.1.1.1/66999890/ITS Digital Archive, USHMM.
56 Liste der Mitglieder der jüdischen Gemeinde Eggenfelden die deutsche Lebensmittelkarten beziehen, 3.1.1.2/81976379/ITS Digital Archive, USHMM.
57 Jewish Displaced Persons who have been repatriated to Israel, 3.1.3.2/81646359/ITS Digital Archive, USHMM.

dramatically since then. But what did is the technology that allows researchers to cross reference millions of pieces of data. Thanks to the technology and to increasing access to more resources, we often succeed where our predecessors might not have.

Here is a research case that illustrates how ITS research can contribute to turn a missing opportunity to reunite two brothers during the chaotic post-war period into a late success. It also demonstrates that the issue of repatriation versus emigration of Polish DPs could make a remarkable research project. The ITS collection is not only about the Holocaust. It contains a vast amount of information about Polish-born DPs. Of course, this topic could require the study of thousands of personal files, and cross referencing them with other ITS sub-collections as well as with resources from other archives. Yet no one has undertaken such research so far. Repatriation was a priority for the post-war Polish authorities. Former forced laborers come to mind, but a more complex goal was returning Polish children. The ITS collection contains invaluable documentation on Polish children – both Jewish and non-Jewish – after the war. Children were treated separately by case workers in Arolsen, who created a separate Child Tracing Service. Depending on children's age and what they could remember and convey to social workers, cases could be extremely challenging. The work of the Red Cross is a research topic in itself, including its "mistakes" along the way and how they can be corrected today thanks to the ITS. A few years ago, the USHMM was contacted by American Red Cross staff working on the case of Polish twins separated at birth in 1947. One lived in California, the other in Poland. Some 200 pages of ITS materials eventually helped us reconnect the brothers separated in a chaotic post-war Europe. Everything started with a letter from the Polish Red Cross containing information on the twins' mother, Elżbieta, whose *Tracing* and *Documentation* File (*T/D*) contained 42 pages of documents.[58]

Elżbieta had been living near Kassel, Germany[59] from May 10, 1944 through March 31, 1945,[60] along with other Polish citizens, she had been working at Henschel and Sohn, a company that manufactured Panzer tanks employing forced

---

58 Elzbieta Jankowska, T/D file 170590, 6.3.3.2/87317372–87317394/ITS Digital Archive, USHMM.
59 Elzbieta Jankowska, A.E.F. D.P. Registration Records, DP 2 Card Files, 3.1.1.1/67445127, 67445130/ITS Digital Archive, USHMM. Elzbieta Jankowska United Nations Displaced Person/Refugee Identity Card, 3.1.1.1/67445128/ITS Digital Archive, USHMM.
60 Liste aller Personen fremder Nationalität, die für kürzere oder längere Zeit im Stadtkreis Kassel untergebracht waren, aber nicht mehr in Kreise wohnen, 2.1.1.1/70427204/ITS Digital Archive, USHMM. First page of that list, 70427199/ITS Digital Archive, USHMM.

laborers.[61] Medical records also appear in the ITS, so we were able to learn that on May 6, 1946, Elżbieta requested admission to the Sophienhaus Women's clinic in Kassel. [62] From the registrar's office in Kassel, we know that she bore twins on June 1, 1946.[63] In 1946 and again in 1948, she submitted applications for assistance.[64] What is interesting here is that the 1946 application includes her two sons, while the second application, submitted in 1948, contains only her name. In the latter she answered negatively to the repatriation question and wrote that she wanted to go to the United States. From various documents,[65] it seems that Elżbieta was again admitted to a DP hospital on February 10, 1948, this time in Merxhausen. January 1949, found her at the Graf Haeseler-Kaserne DP camp in Kassel. The *T/D file* contains complementary information about Elżbieta's ill health, the separation of the two brothers from their mother, and their repatriation to Poland. After leaving the hospital Elżbieta initiated a search for her children with the local Polish Red Cross but had neither money nor help. Sadly, she had a heart condition and passed away without learning what had happened to her sons. ITS material clarified many things. The boys had been repatriated to Poland, and because of their mother's illness they ended up in an orphanage. The ITS archives also contain copies of the brothers' birth certificates. But their names do not appear thereon, only the fact that they had been born to an unmarried "Elżbieta." The babies were actually named Georg and Lucjan, had been in a DP camp in Hofgeismar, Germany. A record from the Child Tracing Service Index indicates that they had been at the UNRRA children's center in Aglasterhausen, Germany, when their mother created their case, but had been repatriated to Poland, on June 13, 1947. Their case was closed on May 13, 1948, after they were adopted out to different families.

The correspondence contained in the *T/D file* records the reasons why the two brothers were separated. Georg never received any notice of death for his mother, and did not know about the existence of his twin brother. Georg grew up in Poland and in 1965, when he was 17, he learned for the first time that he

---

61 List of all persons of United Nations and other foreigners, German Jews and stateless persons who were temporarily or permanently stationed in the community, but are no longer in residence, 2.1.1.1/70427290/ITS Digital Archive, USHMM.
62 Liste aller ärztlichen und gesundheitsbehördlichen Aufzeichnungen Sophienhaus, 2.1.1.1/70429294/ITS Digital Archive, USHMM.
63 List of Births of all persons of United Nations and other foreigners, German Jews and stateless persons 2.1.1.3/85950301/ITS Digital Archive, USHMM.
64 Care and Maintenance file of Elzbieta Jankowska, 3.2.1.1/79219792/ITS Digital Archive, USHMM. Application for Assistance PCIRO, 3.2.1.1/79219794/ITS Digital Archive, USHMM.
65 Registrierbücher des DP-Hospitals Merxhausen, 3.1.1.2/82013266, 82013257, 82013288, 82013236, 82013237/ITS Digital Archive, USHMM.

had a twin brother and that he had been adopted. He soon moved to California, where he started an originally unsuccessful tracing case with the Red Cross to find his brother. Only in 2014, however, did Lucjan visit the orphanage where he had been a baby, discovering that he had had a twin brother. He opened his own tracing case with the Polish Red Cross in 2014. Finally, there was enough information to connect some dots. At that time, the Polish Red Cross contacted the American Red Cross, who in turn contacted us. Thanks to the digital ITS and other databases, we were able to put pieces together and succeeded in what had been impossible in the chaos that followed the Second World War. Soon the twin brothers were reunited and discovered when their mother had died, that she had looked for them, and that their father had been an American soldier who returned to the US prior their birth. After 68 years they saw each other for the first time since their separation.[66]

This case study illustrates that searching for a name can lead to a life-changing experience. But beyond the dramatic individual story, studying the materials shows how challenged the DP aid network had been in the immediate post-war period, the difficulty of keeping families connected when one member got separated, the even more complex work of UNRRA and IRO social workers helping children who were too young to remember much (in some instances, not even knowing their names), and the individual impact of the decisions made by administrators. Much has been written about the immediate post-war period, but the ITS brings an unmatched intimacy to individual stories. On the other hand, the ITS also allows researchers to draw upon a variety of sources to paint those stories back into a bigger picture of a changing post-war world. ITS is one place where macro- and micro-history intertwine.

Conclusion

The ITS collection has generated more interest from the youngest generations. It is unfortunately too late for the majority of survivors, but their descendants can now explore it along with other resources. According to a recent survey of 1,350 American adults – commissioned by the *Conference on Jewish Material Claims Against Germany* – 45 percent are unable to name any concentration camp or

---

66 Red Cross: "Red Cross Helps Twins Reunite after Nearly 70 Years". Available at: https://www.redcross.org/about-us/news-and-events/news/red-cross-helps-twins-reunite-after-nearly-70-years.html. Last accessed: 21.8.2019; American Red Cross on Youtube: "Twin Brothers Reunited after 68 years in Poland". Available at: https://www.youtube.com/watch?v=WWrCGpltGTA. Last accessed: 6.8.2019.

ghetto.⁶⁷ This is not an isolated phenomenon. Despite a larger Holocaust education elaborated plan deployed over the last decades in France, a recent poll revealed that 21 percent of young people aged 18 to 24 never heard of the genocide of the Jews, while the number only reached 2 percent for people over 65.⁶⁸ At a time of worldwide rising antisemitism this shows the need for ways to teach younger generations about what happened more than 70 years ago.

Whether survivors talked much about their experiences or not, the second generation tends to have read quite extensively about the Holocaust, while the 3G needs more historical context to accompany any ITS documents. It is not uncommon for 3Gs to be exposed to Holocaust history for the first time through ITS research requests. ITS thus becomes their portal to a broader knowledge, and sometimes leads to more in-depth research. During the USHMM's twentieth-anniversary events in 2013, we conducted basic ITS on-site research in Los Angeles, where we met a 3G who was so amazed by the ITS documents we found about her grandfather that she wanted to volunteer for the Museum. Another 3G was a fellow at the Museum working on technical options of computer recognition based on ITS materials.⁶⁹ Working with the Museum's ITS experts, he ended up requesting research about his grandmother, which opened a completely different world to him because he saw the actual application of his theoretical work and the impact ITS can have on people. While ITS research carries an intimate emotional charge for most 2Gs, it actually opens a new world for most 3Gs. The experience of thousands of individuals shows how the ITS can make history more accessible to a wide range of users.

---

67 "The study also revealed a generational difference in knowledge. For example, though 11% of all respondents either hadn't heard of the Holocaust or weren't sure if they had, that number was 22% among Millennials. And, while 41% of respondents overall did not know what Auschwitz was, that figure was 66% among Millennials". Lily Rothman: "Survey Reveals Gaps in Knowledge of Holocaust History", in *Time*, April 12, 2018. Available at: http://time.com/5235725/holocaust-history-survey/. Last accessed: 6.8.2019.
68 Fondation Jean Jaurès: "L'Europe et les génocides: le cas français". Available at: https://jean-jaures.org/nos-productions/l-europe-et-les-genocides-le-cas-francais. Last accessed: 6.8.2019.
69 Benjamin Charles Germain Lee: "Line Detection in Binary Document Scans: A Case Study with the International Tracing Service Archives", Submitted to *IEEE Big Data 2017*: 2ⁿᵈ CAS workshop, October 10, 2017; "Machine Learning, Template Matching, and International Tracing Service Digital Archives: Automating the Retrieval of Death Certificate Reference from 40 Million Document Scans", in: *Digital Scholarship in the Humanities*, fqy063, 9.11.2018. Available at: https://doi.org/10.1093/llc/fqy063. Last accessed: 6.8.2019.

Ramona Bräu, Kerstin Hofmann and Anna Meier-Osiński
The New Tasks and Challenges for Tracing

Abstract: The scope of the work carried out by the *Tracing Department* at the *Arolsen Archives* has changed in many ways since the re-opening of the archive in 2007. This change reflects the evolution from the *International Tracing Service*, an authority with a clear and finite mandate, to the *Arolsen Archives*, an open, networking, and modern knowledge repository. On the one hand, the service of providing information has been adapted to the needs of the applicants both in form and scope, and on the other hand, new areas of responsibility have been added, such as the support of visitors and proactive research within the framework of projects, PR activities and social media.

Introduction

When the *Arolsen Archives*, then known as the *International Tracing Service* (ITS), re-opened their archive in 2007, not only did this change both the way this unique organization was perceived and the image it projected, it also heralded the start of an intensive relationship between its staff and the general public. Relatives, researchers and other interested parties had been denied access to the documents for decades and relatives often had to wait years for replies to their inquiries. Now they were finally able to view the holdings of the archive on site in Bad Arolsen once more or could ask for copies of documents to be sent to them. This changed expectations of service as regards both quantity and quality.

Despite the manifold possibilities of today's interconnected online world, the original core task of the tracing service, which was to help survivors search for relatives and friends, was and still is an element of the service offering that is very much in demand. The article uses three examples to illustrate the development and change in *tracing* since the opening of the archive 1. the development of the information from the archive from a bureaucratic certificate to a service according to the changed needs of the inquirers, 2. the establishment of a visitor service for family members, and 3. the *#StolenMemory* campaign for returning effects.

A Journey through the Documents – From Information Provider to Research Assistant

The change is most evident in the way inquiries about individuals are processed, which for decades satisfied bureaucratic requirements above all. The so-called certificates sent out by the ITS with information from the archive were summarized copies of the pertinent personal data from the documents, which mainly listed details of persons and sojourns with references to times and places; alternatively, negative certification was given if no documents were available. The indexed collections that were evaluated were divided into the chronological-thematic categories 1. Concentration Camps and Detention Sites, 2. Wartime and 3. Postwar as well as 4. Child Search Branch and 5. General Documents, and these categories defined the organizational structure of the institution at the same time. Copies of documents were never provided, regardless of whether the inquiry had been submitted by a public authority, a legal representative, or the individuals concerned. Nevertheless, the content of these letters was of decisive importance in hundreds and thousands of claims for compensation or reparation.

This resulted in information on individuals who had been persecuted by the Nazi regime being collected over a period of several decades in the case files used for processing inquiries, known as *Tracing/Documentation* files (*T/D files*). This means that in over three million cases, not only are the inquiry and the response to the inquiry on file, but also all the information divulged to the ITS by external sources, as well as all the knowledge discovered about the fate of an individual during the course of the investigations, even if there is no information in the proper documentary holdings.[1] As a result, this collection of administrative documents – thanks to a period of closure of just 25 years – provides a valuable basis for case processing. Nowadays, relatives receive labeled color copies of all the documents relating to an individual that are not covered by the period of closure or by any other data protection measures.

In addition, inquiries about individuals are now processed on a more holistic basis with a unifying view over all the holdings as indexing and archival description constantly simplify the search process. Not least due to the improved technical possibilities – about 85 percent of the document holdings of the *Arolsen Archives* have now been digitized – the business of processing cases has developed into a comprehensive archival information service over the past ten years. This means that hundreds of thousands of copies of documents have

---

[1] Sub-collection 6.3.3.2: Repository of T/D cases, ITS Digital Archive, Arolsen Archives.

been sent to families in electronic form over the years. As the service offered by the organization has developed, so have the motivation and the expectations of the people who submit inquiries.

While in the majority of cases it was of utmost importance for the generation of the survivors to obtain proof of the injustice they had suffered or to obtain certainty about the whereabouts and often the death of relatives and friends, the generations that followed focused their interest on other questions. The generation of the children (2nd generation) and the generation of the grandchildren and great-grandchildren (3rd/4th generation) differ from one another in this respect. The inquiries received and preserved by the *Arolsen Archives* over more than seven decades reflect this in many ways, although it should be mentioned that the three million files relating to individuals are a unique collection of sources which has not yet been subjected to academic evaluation and which is growing all the time. In addition to an analysis of the origin, background, age, gender, motivation or knowledge of the people who submit inquiries, an examination of the style of language used might also be revealing with regard to the relationship between the ITS and the victims of Nazi persecution and their relatives, for example. There is clear documentary evidence of the changes in the relationship: at first, humble applicants faced an all-powerful authority, later came angry inquirers and now informative visits are arranged for family groups.

Numerous studies have now been made of the consequences the trauma experienced by the Holocaust and camp survivor generation had on their children, who often also suffer from traumatization themselves.[2] Talking or remaining silent about the time of persecution leads to very different dynamics between parents and children. Children often make the decision to write to the *Arolsen Archives* very late, either when they are already very old themselves, or shortly before, but more often after, the death of their parents. Some of them turn to the archive in a state of obvious desperation because the information passed on to them by their families is either nonexistent or very vague. Others tell of extensive research which they have already carried out. What these inquirers have

---

[2] On the transmission of trauma as a long-term consequence of experiences of dictatorship, see: Ira Brenner: "Stacheldraht in der Seele: Ein Blick auf die generationsübergreifende Weitergabe des Holocaust-Traumas", in Liliane Opher-Cohn, Johannes Pfäfflin, Bernd Sonntag, Bernd Klose, Peter Pogany-Wnendt (eds.): *Das Ende der Sprachlosigkeit? Auswirkungen traumatischer Holocaust-Erfahrungen über mehrere Generationen*, Gießen: Psychosozial-Verlag, 2001, 113–137; Felix Kolmer and Jost Rebentisch: "Folgegenerationen der Überlebenden nationalsozialistischer Verfolgung – Herausforderungen und Perspektiven", in Thorsten Fehlberg, Jost Rebentisch and Anke Wolf (eds.): *Nachkommen von Verfolgten des Nationalsozialismus*, Frankfurt/Main: Mabuse, 2016, 195–200.

in common, however, is the search for certainty. There has been a marked decrease in the number of cases involving requests for certification that can stand up in court during legal proceedings concerning questions of inheritance or compensation claims; these are of course closely connected with the political developments of reparation legislation.

For the children, attaining certainty about the fate of their parents and the fate of their families of origin is often part of a process of ascertaining their own identity. For this generation, knowledge about origin and descent functions as a kind of anchor for a sense of belonging and context in family-centered and social frames of reference, but this knowledge is often linked with uncertainties and traumas. Staff are faced with a very wide variety of different questions as a result. These range from requests for information of a general nature, as details of the dates and places pertinent to a family's history before, during and after the Second World War are unknown or only vague, through to concrete questions concerning tattooed prisoner numbers, living conditions in the camps, reasons for imprisonment, the whereabouts of fellow prisoners, detailed descriptions of events and the locations of graves, to mention but a few examples. The possibility of uncovering a family secret or even of coming across another branch of the family creates an element of uncertainty that seems to function as a driving force and as an impediment at the same time.

However, the 3rd and now the 4th generations are much less inhibited in their quest for information and often have less concrete previous knowledge about the Second World War and/or their family history – what they have instead are expectations of entering into a dialogue. The use of online offerings and social media is changing the way staff and users interact with each other. Staff members assist users in their search for information by helping them to carry out research in the holdings of the *Arolsen Archives*, by providing further references or contextual knowledge, or by preparing a visit to Bad Arolsen and providing advice and assistance on site. Thus the information from the archive is now seen as a starting point, or as another jigsaw piece in the puzzle presented by a specific search and also, increasingly, as an element in a process of self-publication. It is becoming more and more usual for users to post photos, documents and stories to supplement the material provided by the online collections of the *Arolsen Archives*. Users are becoming multipliers beyond the concrete context of their own families. What the effect of this development will be on the 20,000 inquiries submitted each year up until now[3] and how the target groups

---

3 See the annual reports of the *Arolsen Archives*, formerly the ITS. Available at: https://arolsen-archives.org/downloads/. Last accessed: 2.9.2019.

of the *Tracing Department* will change as a result will be seen in the coming years and will depend on how the transformation processes of family remembering and remembrance develop in the 3rd and 4th generation. However, interest in the *Arolsen Archives* does not seem to be waning.

Visits by relatives of victims of Nazi persecution to the *Arolsen Archives*

The *Arolsen Archives* have seen an increase in the numbers of relatives of victims of Nazi persecution visiting Bad Arolsen in recent years. These visitors make a conscious decision to travel to Bad Arolsen to view the original documents containing information about their relatives on site. Those who live overseas often combine their visit to the *Arolsen Archives* with a trip through Europe. They feel a real need to visit the various stations on the path of persecution experienced by their family members, most of whom are now dead. They want to see with their own eyes where their relatives were born, where they became victims of Nazi persecution, but also where they turned their backs on Europe forever.

For many from the generation of the grandchildren and great-grandchildren (3rd and 4th generation) in particular, it is no longer enough to receive "only" digital copies of the documents held in the *Arolsen Archives*. They want to see the original documents and hold them in their own hands in order to gain an impression of what happened to their grandparents, and sometimes even to their great-grandparents, under Nazi dictatorship and in the immediate post-war period. What the relatives need from the *Arolsen Archives* has also changed accordingly. For the generation of the grandchildren, unlike for the survivors and their children, the Holocaust and Nazi persecution are part of a story which they did not experience themselves and which their parents only experienced indirectly. From this follows that their need for knowledge is considerable, not only knowledge about the documents held in the *Arolsen Archives*, but also knowledge about the context in which they were created.

A visit to Bad Arolsen gives them the opportunity to ask questions and fill in the gaps in their family history. In September 2018, for example, Lucy Stoxen from Australia visited the *Arolsen Archives* with her husband and two small children as part of a round trip through Europe. She had heard about the possibility of visiting the archive in Bad Arolsen by chance through a member of her church. The past was never discussed in her family. It was not until after her grandmother Helena had died that she received a list of almost 60 names of members of her direct family who had been murdered in concentration camps and extermination camps. Almost all the members of this Jewish family in Amsterdam were deported directly to Auschwitz or Sobibor via the Westerbork transit camp and murdered. Only four members of Lucy's immediate family survived the Holocaust – including her mother and grandmother.

Fig. 1: Lucy Stoxen with her husband and children at the ITS, Bad Arolsen, 23.7.2018 (ITS Photo Collection, Arolsen Archives)

Unlike her relatives, Lucy's grandmother, who was pregnant at the time, was deported to Theresienstadt in August 1944, the only member of her family to be sent there. Shortly after her arrival, she gave birth to Lucy's mother Ellis. Together with her new husband and her daughter, Helena emigrated to a small town in Australia after the liberation. She drew a very definite line under the past: Nazi persecution and the loss of her family were never mentioned. She had no contact with other survivors. Not until she was an adult did Lucy's mother find out that she was not born in Amsterdam, as she had always assumed, but in the Theresienstadt ghetto. In the majority of cases, only three documents exist in the *Arolsen Archives* for each of her relatives: the index card from the *Judenrat (Jewish council)* file in Amsterdam, the transport list of Westerbork transit camp, and the list of murdered Dutch Jews.⁴ Lucy and her family find some comfort in the fact that their ancestors did not have to spend more than a few days in the extermination camps before they were murdered. "I am the right one to now finally collect all the information about the family", said Lucy on her visit to the *Arolsen Archives*. "I would like to be able to tell my children the story of their family."⁵

Visits from relatives are very important for the *Arolsen Archives*, as the documents preserved in the archive only tell part of the story. A broader picture of the deceased only emerges through the memories of the relatives, any photographs they may have and the knowledge handed down to them. It is not uncommon for the *Arolsen Archives* not to find out that victims of Nazi persecution survived and were able to start a new life after being liberated by the Allies until staff have the opportunity for personal conversations with relatives. This is one of the reasons why visits from relatives are nowadays recorded on video with their consent. Thanks to the new media database of the *Arolsen Archives*, these recordings can be shared with visitors if required. Family members who are unable to come to Bad Arolsen themselves can share in the visits in this way.

Visiting the archive is important for many relatives, even if their inquiries have met with a "negative" response, i.e. if there are no documents in the archive about the persecution of the persons concerned. In cases like these, a visit to Bad Arolsen is still worthwhile because it provides people with the opportunity to talk to a visitor support assistant from the *Tracing Department* and to use the reading room to search the holdings of the archive themselves. How can it be that no documents about the deceased relatives have been preserved? What search options are there? What does a certain abbreviation on a specific document mean? Answers to these questions and explanations of the historical context are just as important as the opportunity to talk about previous and future family research. Visits to the *Arolsen Archives* from relatives have changed considerably in recent years – and the support provided to visitors has been professionalized in parallel: no longer do visits simply provide the opportunity to view the documents, they now provide the opportunity to receive assistance in the search for information. Visiting relatives feel a real need to carry out their own research, to understand what happened and to record the results of their re-

---

4 Sub-collection 1.2.4.2: Index cards from the Judenrat (Jewish council) file in Amsterdam; sub-collection 1.1.46.1: List Material Westerbork, folder 1 to 10: transport lists of Westerbork transit camp; folder 14 to 39: lists of Jewish victims of the Nazi regime in the Netherlands 1941–1945, ITS Digital Archive, Arolsen Archives.
5 Video recordings of the visit of Lucy Stoxen in July 2018, Media Database of the Arolsen Archives.

search for posterity and this is becoming increasingly important; the service provided by the archive is evolving to meet these needs.

Research Project on Effects for Relatives and the #StolenMemory Campaign

The so-called effects kept in the archive in Bad Arolsen are a special collection. In the 1960s, the ITS received around 5,000 personal items, most of them belonging to political prisoners, most of whom had been deported to concentration camps. Most of these effects were seized by the British Army during the liberation of the Neuengamme concentration camp and were handed over to the ITS in the early 1960s via the *Administrative Office for Internal Restitution* in Stadthagen. In addition to personal items from the Neuengamme concentration camp, the *Arolsen Archives* also hold a much smaller number of personal effects from the Dachau concentration camp and the Hamburg Gestapo, from the Amersfoort police transit camp and the Compiègne deportation camp. In the years that followed, the ITS endeavored to return the effects to their owners, often with the assistance of the worldwide network of *Red Cross Societies* and memorial sites. In subsequent years, only a few returns of effects took place, and no search activities were carried out by the ITS. In 2009, the ITS carried out research on the collection of effects which were not identifiable by name, with the result that the owners of a large proportion of the effects could be named and the effects could be attributed correctly. In 2011, in a further attempt to support efforts to return the effects, the list of the names of the owners of the approximately 3,200 effects still held by the ITS at the time were published online.

Then, in the autumn of 2015, the collection of personal effects became one of first three sub-collections to be made visible and searchable in the online archive of the ITS (*Digital Collections Online*).[6] Since then, it has been possible to search all the photos of the effects for names and, if available, dates of birth, as well as to filter the names by nationality and by place of detention. This functionality is intended to enable volunteers all over the world to help the *Arolsen Archives* search for the rightful owners and to attract the attention of the public to this special temporary collection. Publishing the collection online led to the successful return of many effects. This was made possible by the support of volunteers,

---

6 See today's online archive of the *Arolsen Archives*. Available at: https://collections.arolsen-archives.org/en/search/. Last accessed: 2.9.2019.

most of whom were from the Netherlands at first. As a result of a Dutch TV news story about the online publication, two brothers were finally able to read a farewell letter from their father, which was "delivered" to them with a delay of more than 70 years.[7]

In the autumn of 2016, the ITS launched the *Returning Effects* project to help promote the search all over the world and return effects to families. As part of this project, the ITS began to carry out systematic research in its own holdings to document and evaluate the paths of persecution of the approximately 3,200 owners of the effects for the first time; information on places of residence and old addresses are particularly important here. Most of the victims of persecution were political prisoners: a large proportion of them (about 900 people) came from Poland, about 300 came from the former Soviet Union, about 680 from Germany and there were over 50 from the Netherlands, from France and from Spain, as well as from 30 other countries. Effects belonging to Jewish persecutees are an exception.

The information contained in the documents held at the *Arolsen Archives* (such as transport lists, prisoner registration cards etc.) provide important clues as to how to begin the real-life search for the survivors themselves or their relatives. Within the last two and a half years, nearly 400 effects have been returned to close relatives, including daughters, sons, and grandchildren. This was only possible through external investigations and through the support of various authorities such as register offices located all over the world, through cooperation with memorial sites, especially in Poland and including the Auschwitz and Stutthof memorials, through the assistance of the international prisoners' associations, and through the initiative of individuals in Poland, the Netherlands, Norway, France, Belgium and Spain.

Personal encounters with relatives frequently take place in Bad Arolsen when effects are returned in person, or in the relatives' home countries, and often involve their travelling long distances from the USA, France or Poland. These encounters emphasize how important it is to find the next of kin, because the objects kept in the *Arolsen Archives* are mainly pocket watches, wristwatches, jewelry, wedding rings, personal documents like birth certificates, school reports, identity papers, correspondence, everyday items and family photos, all of which are of inestimable value to the relatives. In many cases, these personal belongings function like a key that the relatives now hold in their hands, or like a trig-

---

[7] Arolsen Archives: "Sons Receive their Father's Farewell Letter after 72 Years". Available at: https://arolsen-archives.org/en/news/sons-receive-their-fathers-farewell-letter-after-72-years/. Last accessed: 2.9.2019.

ger that helps people start to find out about their own family history. The effects and documents provide important information that can fill in the gaps in the life stories of their relatives or they function like jigsaw pieces in the reconstruction of paths of persecution which were often unknown or only partly known beforehand. Over 70 years have since passed and this period of time should not be underestimated. The same can be said of how important it still is for families to find out about the history of their relatives and, as is frequently the case, even to find closure by clarifying their fates. In many cases, the objects concerned are familiar to the children from their childhood. Items like a pocket watch that was taken out of a father's waistcoat pocket on a Sunday and on its reappearance 70 years after its owner's murder immediately rekindles childhood memories of a beloved father. Only relatives have this kind of emotional knowledge and personal memories of the victims of persecution whose last personal belongings were taken away from them before their deportation to the concentration camps and now wait in the *Arolsen Archives* to be returned to their rightful owners.

Both the knowledge and the memories are a valuable supplement to the information and documents held by the *Arolsen Archives* on those who suffered persecution under the Nazi regime. Meetings with the relatives are, therefore, part of the process of remembering those who were persecuted and murdered, and they play a part in remembrance too. These objects are often the only things left and thus the very last things that can bear witness to the life of fathers, mothers or brothers before their persecution and murder. The successful searches that culminate in the return of personal belongings and the reactions of the families validate the special and intensive efforts made by the *Arolsen Archives* to return the objects to relatives. In 2016, for example, for the very first time at the age of 75 years, Joost de Snoo from the Netherlands, who has the same name as his father, was able to hold a photo in his own hands that showed himself as a toddler together with his parents. His father died during his imprisonment in a camp when Joost junior was just four years old. The photo belongs to Main Collection Group 1. *Incarceration Documents* and can be found in the subcollection *Personal Effects from the Neuengamme Concentration Camp*.[8]

In the wake of this very successful research and return project, the ITS launched the *#StolenMemory* campaign in 2018, which takes the form of a ready-to-print exhibition and tells the stories of the owners of the effects. The exhibition includes large-format posters displaying the names of the concentration camp prisoners and photos of the objects belonging to them. Focusing on successful searches that have culminated in the return of personal belongings,

---

8 1.2.9.3/108014563/ITS Digital Archive, Arolsen Archives.

Fig. 2: Joost de Snoo jun. with his parents, early 1940s (Effects from the Neuengamme concentration camp, 1.2.9.3/108014563/ITS Digital Archive, Arolsen Archives)

and highlighting what this means to the families, it also shows objects whose rightful owners the *Arolsen Archives* are still searching for and describes the fates of the people who originally owned them. The exhibition has so far been shown in various place, including Paris, Athens, Innsbruck, Luxembourg, Brussels and Venice. Furthermore, exhibitions at various locations in Poland took place in 2019 (80 years after the beginning of the Second World War), including two exhibitions in Oświęcim with a thematic and a geographical connection to the Auschwitz extermination camp and to people from the region who still have not been found. The collection of personal effects lends itself particularly well to using the regional connections of persecutees from specific places. Public searches for those concerned are then launched. These searches can be part of a school project, for example. Many effects, such as student ID cards, contain important information on the victims of persecution that supplements the information contained in the documents held by the *Arolsen Archives* and often provides numerous clues as to their paths of persecution. Of great importance for the relatives in this context are the documents kept in the archive, which include information on the date of death or the location of graves as well as old addresses and the places of residence of the missing persons.

The research and the successful returns of effects which have taken place over the past two and a half years have shown that searching and finding families in Eastern and Central Europe is not only about returning personal belongings to the families, but is also still inextricably linked to the clarification of fates. In many of the cases which the *Arolsen Archives* have researched in Poland, Russia and the Ukraine and which resulted in contact being made with the families, often with the children of victims of persecution, nothing was known about the whereabouts of the missing relative, let alone about their path of persecution, for over 70 years – until their belongings were returned to their families. Moreover, because most of the victims of persecution did not survive – the effects belonging to Polish persecutees from the Neuengamme concentration camp include items belonging to a large number of individuals who burned to death on the *Cap Arcona*[9] – most of the families do not even know where their loved ones are buried or where a memorial is located. Seventy years on, families are often now able to come to terms with the fates of their relatives, to visit their resting place and light a candle for them.

---

9 At the end of April 1945, the Neuengamme guards sent the remaining inmates on a northward march to keep them from falling into the hands of the advancing British. In Lübeck they were divided among several ships. On May 3, 1945, the British Royal Air Force mistook the Cap Arcona and the Thielbek for German troop carriers and sank them in the Bay of Lübeck.

In the case of Władysław Śliwiński, his granddaughter, Agnieszka Śliwińska from Warsaw, was not able to clarify his fate until after his personal effects had been returned. Her grandmother took the uncertainty about what had happened to her beloved husband with her to her grave a few years ago. Once the *Arolsen Archives* had located her grandfather's grave, Agnieszka was not only able to have a gravestone put up for Władysław at the cemetery in Gardelegen on behalf of her grandmother, but she was also able to have his prisoner number replaced by his name in the local memorial book. This was marked by an official ceremony on 14th of April 2019. The documents containing information on the site of the grave can be found in sub-collection *5.3.2, Attempted Identification*. These documents were created between 1950 and 1951. However, this collection also contains many documents which had already been created in the latter half of the 1940s.[10]

Another noteworthy case is that of the three Warsaw women, Janina Dobrowolska and her two underage daughters Halina and Barbara, who were deported to the Ravensbrück concentration camp with their mother during the Warsaw Uprising. At the beginning of 2019, jewelry and wristwatches belonging to the three women could be returned to the granddaughter/daughter/niece.

Up until then Halina Dobrowolska's daughter had not known where her aunt Basia (Barbara), her mother's sister who was just 17 years old at the time, had met her death in a bombing raid shortly before liberation by the Allies. *T/D file* 4698 on Barbara Dobrowolska provides information on her mother Janina's unsuccessful search for her daughter Basia, a search that remained fruitless until she died. Her daughter was still missing. Not until the discovery of documents held at the *Arolsen Archives* on various evaluations, including among other things evaluations of data on *unknown foreign fatalities and unknown fatalities from concentration camps and their grave sites* in sub-collection *5.3. Death Marches/Identification of unknown dead* did it become clear that Barbara was buried in

---

10 Cf. archival description 5.3.2. "The archive group 'Attempted Identification' is a collection of work and results of the ITS program of the same name. It contains, among others, correspondence, eye-witness reports, reports and protocols on the 'evacuation' of concentration camps and death marches passing through accommodation of prisoners on the death marches, certification of deaths, documents on burials, indexes of the deceased of the concentration camps and death marches lists of unknown dead as well as evaluations regarding unknown foreign fatalities, identification lists of deceased prisoners based on prisoner numbers, exhumation of deceased prisoners, lists of reburied bodies from mass graves, lists pertaining to the maritime disaster involving the Cap Arcona, Athen and Thielbeck, outcome of the search for graves of unknown foreigners and concentration camp prisoners, information on the results of the identification measures, results of the investigations of graves, results of the identification based on prisoner numbers, routes of the death marches."

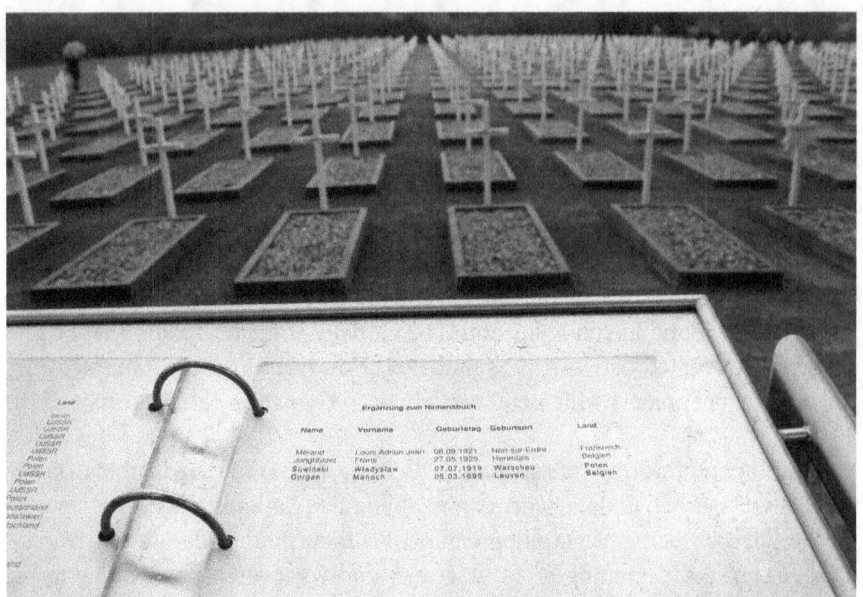

Fig. 3: Additional information in memorial book on Władysław Śliwiński, cemetery of the Memorial Barn Isenschnibbe Gardelegen, 14.4.2019 (ITS Photo Collection, Arolsen Archives)

International Tracing Service
Records Branch. Arolsen.

Attempt.identific.: made
G A R D E L E G E N - Sachsen-Anhalt. No. 59150

Attempted identification of unknown dead

Information given in File 34/1 Hq's 1st. Platoon 3046 QM.Gr.Registration Co.Ser.102 Inf.Div.US-Army from 25.4.45

C.C. Number 59150 died on 11.4.45 in Gardelegen buried in Gardelegen 21.-25.4.45

Evacuation march from CC. Mittelbau-Dora.

Inmates of camps in this march from CC.: 1.) Buchenwald, 2.) Mittelbau-Dora, 3.) Auschwitz, 4.) Gross-Rosen....

Number	Conc. Camp	Name and other information	yes/no	Reason
59150	Buchenwald	SCHACHROW, NICOLAJ Russ. born 26.11.19 SMOLENSK	no	[illegible] 13.11.44 15.11.44 [illegible] FURA
59150	Neuengamme	SLIWINSKI, Wladislaw born 7.7.19 - Polish	yes	[illegible]
	Auschwitz	not found	—	—
	Gross-Rosen	not found	—	—

Conclusion 59150 [illegible]

Attempted identification made [illegible]

Arolsen [illegible] Checked by

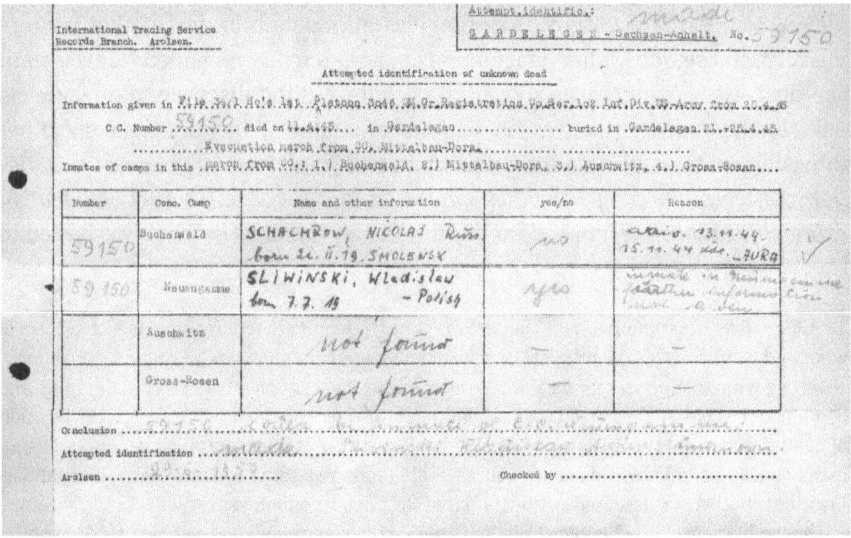

Fig. 4: Władysław Śliwiński. Attempted identification of unknown dead No. 59150 died in Gardelegen, 1950 (5.3.2/84614933/ITS Digital Archive, Arolsen Archives)

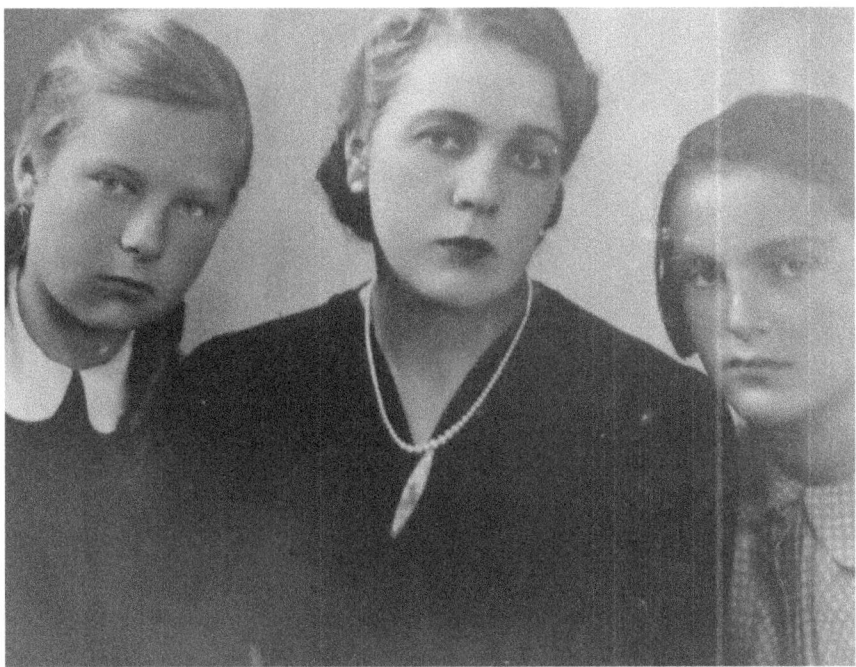

Fig. 5: Janina Dobrowolska (center) with her two daughters Halina (left) and Barbara (right), c. 1939/1940 (Private collection of Marzenna Wierzbowska-Sobczyk, Warsaw)

the cemetery in Celle. The *Attempted Identification of Unknown Dead* document held in the *Arolsen Archives* states that Barbara Dobrowolska died in Celle and was buried in Celle. The document can be found in the sub-collection *Attempted Identification*.[11]

A necklace with a Mother-of-God pendant, a bracelet and a delicate ring are the only remaining personal belongings of 17 year-old Barbara.[12]

---

[11] Attempted Identification of Unknown Dead – Cemeteries: results of the identification based on prisoner numbers: Evaluation and results forms of the ITS-Records Branch – for identified dead according to cemeteries along the stages of the death marches. 1.1.1950 – 31.12.1951
[12] Effects of Barbara Dobrowolska. Available at: https://digitalcollections.its-arolsen.org/01020903/name/thumbview/192227/211033. Last accessed: 2.9.2019.

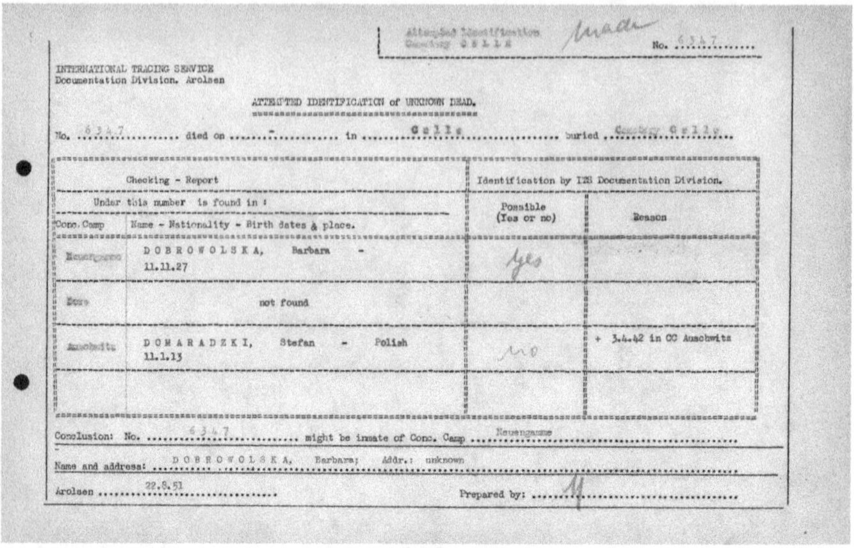

No. 6347

INTERNATIONAL TRACING SERVICE
Documentation Division. Arolsen

ATTEMPTED IDENTIFICATION of UNKNOWN DEAD.

No. 6347 died on - in Celle buried Cemetery Celle

Checking - Report		Identification by ITS Documentation Division.	
Under this number is found in :		Possible (Yes or no)	Reason
Conc. Camp	Name - Nationality - Birth dates & place.		
Neuengamme	DOBROWOLSKA, Barbara - 11.11.27	yes	
	not found		
Auschwitz	DOMARADZKI, Stefan - Polish 11.1.13	no	+ 3.4.42 in CC Auschwitz

Conclusion: No. 6347 might be inmate of Conc. Camp Neuengamme

Name and address: DOBROWOLSKA, Barbara; Addr.: unknown

Arolsen 22.8.51 Prepared by:

Fig. 6: Barbara Dobrowolska. Attempted identification of unknown dead No. 6347 died in Celle, 1951 (5.3.2/84613964/ITS Digital Archive, Arolsen Archives)

Conclusion

The tasks of the Tracing Service have constantly changed during the decades of its existence. However, with the challenges and opportunities offered by the opening of the archive and the technical possibilities of the twenty-first century, Tracing is at the beginning of a complete reorientation of its tasks. The expectations of the users and the possibilities of a constantly improving digital database point the way to more and more interactive search support, which makes the *Arolsen Archives* the knowledge and information center on Nazi persecution for members of the 3rd and 4th generation as well as for the interested public. Visitor support and campaign work already enrich the internal and external perception of the former formal bureaucratic department for the provision of information.

Fig. 7a/b/c: Jewellery of Barbara Dobrowolska (Effects from the Neuengamme concentration camp, 1.2.9.3/108004952/108004951/108004953/ITS Digital Archive, Arolsen Archives)

Collections and Activities of Archives Dealing with Nazi Victims

Henning Borggräfe, Isabel Panek

Collections Archives Dealing with Nazi Victims

The Example of the Arolsen Archives

Abstract: After the Second World War, millions of persons were missing, with relatives, friends and the governments of their home countries searching for them. Knowledge about the crimes committed by the Nazis was still fragmentary. Against this background, a new type of archive emerged that broke with established archival principles: *collections archives* were created for specific purposes in the period following 1945 – the search for victims and survivors of Nazi persecution, the criminal prosecution of perpetrators or remembrance of the crimes which were committed. This paper uses the history of the *Arolsen Archives* to examine two issues which, while being relevant to archives in general, were and are particularly important for *collections archives*. The first of these issues is the collection and organization of documents. The second issue concerns independent research and questions of access to the holdings of *collections archives*. The intention of this chapter is not only to help readers understand the history of the *Arolsen Archives* and the structure and usability of their collections, but also to begin to identify the peculiarities and challenges which are particular to this new type of *collections archives*.

Introduction

In response to Nazi persecution and the turmoil of the Second World War, a new type of archive emerged that broke with established archival principles: *collections archives* were created by different organizations for specific purposes in the period following 1945. The various activities which these organizations were involved in – the search for missing persons, the criminal prosecution of perpetrators or remembrance of the crimes which were committed – enriched these archives over decades. Later on, many of them were brought closer into line with conventional archives in terms of working practices and some were even integrated into conventional archives. However, certain special features of this new type of archive still endure.

One of the largest of these new *collections archives* came into being at the *International Tracing Service* (ITS), now known as the *Arolsen Archives*, in the town of Arolsen in north Hesse, Germany.¹ However, other tracing bureaus and related institutions also built up similar collections for the purpose of clarifying fates. In Germany, these included the collections of the *Tracing Service of the German Red Cross*, the *Church Tracing Service* or the *German Office for the Notification of Next of Kin of the Former German Wehrmacht* (German acronym: WASt), which was recently taken over by the Federal Archives. A different purpose, criminal prosecution, led to the creation of other collections which were similar in structure. Early examples include the collection built up by Simon Wiesenthal and others at the *Jewish Historical Documentation Center* in Linz and the collection created by the *Main Commission for the Prosecution of Crimes against the Polish Nation* in Warsaw; a later addition was the collection set up at the *Central Office of the Judicial Authorities of the Federal States for the Investigation of National Socialist Crimes* in Ludwigsburg, which was established in 1958. By contrast, most modern *collections archives* were created for the purposes of commemoration and remembrance. Examples include *Yad Vashem* in Jerusalem, founded in 1953 already, and the *United States Holocaust Memorial Museum* in Washington, DC, founded in 1993 – alongside the *Arolsen Archives*, these are probably the largest examples of this new type of archive – but there are also hundreds of other documentation centers and memorial site archives throughout Europe and beyond.²

Not only does the founding history of these institutions have a common historical point of reference, their development was intertwined and involved close cooperation which sometimes went as far as to include frequent sharing of collections of original documents or copies of collections. A comprehensive history of the new *collections archives* is nonetheless a desideratum of historical research. The first difficulty encountered when trying to describe this new type of archive is what to call them – we suggest using the term *collections archives*.³ The institutions of the archiving world are of little help in this respect. Archives of this type are not mentioned in archival manuals, at least not in those which

---

1 On the history of the *Arolsen Archives* see Henning Borggräfe, Christian Höschler and Isabel Panek (eds.): *A Paper Monument: The History of the Arolsen Archives, Exhibition Catalogue*, Bad Arolsen: Arolsen Archives, 2019.
2 For an extensive overview of many of the archives which hold Holocaust-related collections, see https://portal.ehri-project.eu/institutions. Last accessed: 12.7.2019.
3 Our thanks go to Christian Groh, Head of Archives at the *Arolsen Archives*, for his valuable contribution to discussions about this term.

are available in the German language.[4] The *International Council on Archives* (ICA) lists the *Arolsen Archives* under "archives of international organizations" and separates them from the other institutions mentioned above. The *Association of German Archivists* groups the *Arolsen Archives* together with the "archives of academic institutions", a categorization which is equally unhelpful.

This chapter uses the history of the *Arolsen Archives* to examine two issues which, while being relevant to archives in general, were and are particularly important for *collections archives*. The *first* of these issues is the collection and organization of documents, which is interesting for the very reason that the principles of archiving stipulate that the "natural" place for any of the documents in the archive to be would actually be in another archive. The second issue concerns independent research and questions of access, which were challenging because *collections archives* initially served one specific purpose only, and that purpose did not include historical research or call for external access as a matter of course.

The intention of the present chapter is not only to help readers understand the history of the *Arolsen Archives* and the structure and usability of their collections, but also to begin to identify the peculiarities and challenges which are particular to this new type of *collections archive*. In future, it would be desirable to conduct systematic research into the history of these institutions which have emerged since 1945 in connection with the critical analysis of Nazi crimes. This seems important, not least in an epistemological sense, in order to better understand how our modern methods of research, education and remembrance in relation to Nazi crimes and their victims were and are themselves shaped by the new *collections archives*.

Collecting and Organizing Beyond the Principle of Provenance

The ITS, now known as the *Arolsen Archives*, collected more than 30 million originals and copies of documents from concentration camps and prisons, on Nazi forced labor, and on Displaced Persons (DPs) for the purposes of tracing missing persons and clarifying fates, but also to furnish proof of individual persecution for compensation claims, for example. The most important finding aid is an

---

4 Cf., for example, Norbert Reimann: "Grundfragen und Organisation des Archivwesens", in Norbert Reimann (ed.): *Praktische Archivkunde. Ein Leitfaden für Fachangestellte für Medien- und Informationsdienste, Fachrichtung Archiv*, Münster: Ardey-Verlag, 2014, 25–54, here 36–46.

enormous *Central Name Index* which contains more than 50 million reference cards.

Searching for documents and organizing them in such a way that they can be evaluated efficiently in respect of individual persons were the main tasks of the ITS for decades. This approach is, however, extremely questionable from a conventional archival perspective. The reason for this is a basic principle which has been adhered to in the world of archiving for over 100 years, the "principle of provenance: the basic principle that records/archives of the same provenance must not be intermingled with those of any other provenance."[5] This principle ultimately defines both the area of responsibility of archives – they hold the records of specific bodies – as well as the internal organization of the collections. This principle is of such central importance that it is mentioned in the ICA's Code of Ethics: "Archivists should appraise, select and maintain archival material in its historical, legal and administrative context, thus retaining the principle of provenance, preserving and making evident the original relationships of documents."[6]

Adhering to this principle does not, of course, mean that archives simply take hold of history. Every archive and every collection was created in, is part of and marked by specific political and cultural contexts. This also holds true for *collections archives* like the *Arolsen Archives*. However, there is also an additional special dimension which applies to *collections archives*: "[F]or historians using the ITS, teasing out historical meaning is especially challenging. [The sources] are arranged in order to facilitate the tracing process and not historical research."[7] Their specific purpose gave rise to various peculiarities which apply to *collections archives* as opposed to conventional archives. These peculiarities will be described in the following four sections of this chapter using the history of the *Arolsen Archives* as an illustration.

---

5 Peter Walne (ed.): *Dictionary of Archival Terminologies/Dictionnaire de terminologie archivistique. English and French with Equivalents in Dutch, German, Italian, Russian and Spanish*, 2nd revised Edition, Munich, New York, London, Paris: KG Saur 1988, 121.
6 ICA Code of Ethics. Available at: https://www.ica.org/en/ica-code-ethics. Last Accessed: 25.7.2019.
7 Dan Stone: "The Memory of the Archive: The International Tracing Service and the Construction of the Past as History", in *Dapim: Studies on the Holocaust* 31, 2, 2017, 69–88, here 74.

Purpose-Related Document Acquisition and Autonomous Production of Source Material

The world of archiving, based as it is on the principle of provenance, does not allow for the existence of a *collections archive* like the *Arolsen Archives*. The *Arolsen Archives* do not have a mandate to preserve all the records of specific bodies, but instead collect all the documents which seem important for their specific purpose, without paying any attention to institutional, regional or national boundaries. In addition, however – and here they come closer to the principle of provenance in their own peculiar way – they create sources which have their very own historical value and they do so on a large scale in the normal course of the very activities they pursue.

A search for the beginnings of the *Arolsen Archives* soon brings holdings to light which were not collected but were produced autonomously. Because many Nazi crimes were either not well documented or were not documented at all, the ITS already began to search for evidence in the late 1940s. For example, in order to collect evidence of the death marches endured by many concentration camp prisoners towards the end of the war, the ITS questioned thousands of local authorities and former prisoners, as well as examining burial sites and mapping the routes of the marches.[8] The resulting collection and another similar one containing thousands of questionnaires with information provided by former prisoners about hundreds of places of detention were some of the first documentary holdings to be kept in Arolsen.

However, the large collections of documents which the Allies seized at the end of the war for tracing purposes or requisitioned from the Germans later on were not yet stored in Arolsen at the end of the 1940s. Instead, they were held by zonal tracing bureaus originally set up by the victors. Later, the ITS was to take over the bureaus in the American, British and French zones. But it was not until these bureaus stopped conducting active field searches for missing persons and documents in 1950,[9] and transferred their holdings to Arolsen that an archive that was referred to as such came into being there. The objective, which was to conduct research on individuals quickly, had a decisive impact on the way the archive was organized and one of the reasons for this was that the task of providing confirmation of the history of persecution of specific indi-

---

8 Sebastian Schönemann: "Die Untersuchungstätigkeit des International Tracing Service zu Todesmärschen. Das Programm 'Attempted Identification of Unknown Dead'", in: *Gedenkstättenrundbrief* 159, 2011, 28–33.
9 See the chapter by Christian Höschler and Isabel Panek in this volume.

viduals for compensation claims or immigration proceedings was gaining importance at the same time.

First of all, the *Concentration Camp Documents Section* came into being at the beginning of the 1950's. It held valuable documents that the Allies and survivors had managed to rescue from Buchenwald, Dachau, Mauthausen, and other camps. In addition, this department also held all the other documents on concentration camp prisoners from any number of different sources – ranging from documents produced by top Reich authorities to post-war lists of liberated prisoners drawn up by survivors' initiatives. Up until 1952, the ITS also received hundreds of thousands of lists of foreign forced laborers from the zonal tracing bureaus which had been closed. These lists had been compiled by German authorities on the orders of the Allies during a large-scale foreigner tracing campaign which was started in 1945/46. Along with registration documents for foreign forced laborers from hundreds of different provenances, these documents formed the nucleus of the new *Wartime Documents Section*. At the end of 1952, the ITS received 30 tons of DP registration documents which had been produced by the Allies. This new material led to the creation of a third collection, the *Postwar Documents Section*.[10]

However, the two largest collections held by the *Arolsen Archives* were not collected, they were produced by the ITS itself. This seems to be characteristic of *collections archive*s. The *Central Name Index* (CNI) deserves first mention here. This index contains references to the whereabouts of the victims of Nazi persecution derived from field searches, tracing inquiries, and the evaluation of the documents. Whenever material reached the ITS, person-related information was *carded*, and these reference cards were then sorted into the CNI in an alphabetic-phonetic order. The digitally available CNI, which was declared part of the world's documentary heritage by the UNESCO in 2013, includes more than 50 million references to approximately 17.5 million individuals. The CNI also provides researchers with a unique tool for conducting fast searches for individual persons across all the collections.[11]

The second collection of documents produced by the organization itself are the *Tracing/Documentation Files* (*T/D files*). There are almost three million of these files containing all the ITS correspondence on individual Nazi victims

---

[10] ITS Executive Board: Monthly Report for the Month of August, 1953, 11.4/4595/ITS Archive, Arolsen Archives.

[11] For a case study based on the CNI see Henning Borggräfe: "Die Rekonstruktion von Verfolgungswegen im NS-Terrorsystem: Eine Fallstudie zu Opfern der Aktion "Arbeitsscheu Reich", in Henning Borggräfe (ed.): *Freilegungen: Wege, Orte und Räume der NS-Verfolgung*, Göttingen: Wallstein, 2016, 56–82.

from the early post-war years on. Strictly speaking, this is nothing more than correspondence with users of the archive, which is not usually seen as a source of any great value. However, the situation is quite different here, as many inquiries contain descriptions of individual experiences which can be seen as ego documents. They also contain tens of thousands of pieces of information that are not to be found in any documents, either in Arolsen or elsewhere. Finally, the files are also a primary source which can inform personal and institutional debate on Nazi crimes and their consequences as well as providing a record of the changing social and political treatment of former victims of persecution.[12]

The Shaping and Reshaping of Archival Holdings Over Time

The ITS collected millions of documents on the subjects of detention, forced labor and displacement and organized them thematically in accordance with their purposes. The same organizational structure was established in all three sections of the archive: documents relating to individuals were stored in mixed card indexes which were sorted alphabetically. Documents containing lists of names were placed in thematic file series which were internally structured by subject matter, geography or chronology. Documents which did not contain any names were stored in separate file series, which were later brought together in the *Historical Section*. So the holdings were not organized according to the principle of provenance in Arolsen, but according to what is known as the principle of pertinence, which is given a bad press in specialist publications: "A principle, now rejected, for the arrangement of archives in terms of their subject content regardless of their provenance and original order."[13]

Structuring the holdings was a process which sometimes took decades and consisted of several different steps. The collection connected with the campaign to trace foreigners which dates back to 1945/46 is a good example. The main objective of the campaign was to gather documents containing information on the fate of foreign forced laborers. In the winter of 1945/46, the four occupying pow-

---

[12] This is also significant for the history of the experiences of marginalized groups subjected to persecution. See Henning Borggräfe and Hanne Leßau: "Die Wahrnehmung der NS-Verbrechen und der Umgang mit den NS-Verfolgten im International Tracing Service", in Henning Borggräfe, Hanne Leßau and Harald Schmid (eds.): *Fundstücke: Die Wahrnehmung der NS-Verbrechen und ihrer Opfer im Wandel*, Göttingen: Wallstein, 2015, 23–44.
[13] Walne (ed.): Dictionary of Archival Terminologies, 121.

ers issued orders to German municipalities, companies, the judiciary and the police, social insurance funds, hospitals, etc. to this end. These bodies produced hundreds of thousands of lists of foreigners as a result. Not only did the occupying powers define different specifications for the lists, they also pursued the campaign with varying degrees of intensity.[14]

All the material was supposed to be sent to the zonal tracing bureaus, which would then forward it to Arolsen. However, as a result of the incipient Cold War, hardly any lists were received from the Soviet zone. Similarly, the Soviet zonal tracing bureau was subsequently not integrated into the ITS. So while the campaign to collect documents was itself shaped politically, the holdings were shaped for a second time by the zonal tracing bureaus. The staff who worked there dissolved the provenances and resorted the material in accordance with the geographical origins of the lists and then in accordance with the nationality of the people.[15] When it became apparent that there were gaps in the material, further tracing campaigns were launched in the late 1940s, mostly in the British zone, in order to complete the data. The new material was simply inserted into the existing structure. Decades later, the same thing happened at the ITS once again, this time in connection with material from archives in the former GDR and in western Poland that could be copied after the end of the Cold War. In the 1950s, once all the documents from the zonal tracing bureaus had been transferred to their new central location, the *Wartime Documents Section* at the ITS, they were reshaped again. The material from all the zones of occupation, which had already been sorted by district and then within the districts by nationality, was now sorted internally again according to specific list types which had been defined in the US zone for the purposes of the foreigner tracing campaign and which had been stamped on the documents.[16] Finally, in the 1980s, the ITS moved parts of the collection to other parts of the archive because it held the view that they concerned other persecution complexes. This applied to lists of foreign inmates held in German police and judicial prisons, for example.[17]

Today, anyone looking for documents produced by a municipal authority for the foreigner tracing campaign will find individual parts of the lists and the as-

---

[14] On the Foreigner Tracing Operation, see Sub-collection 6.1.1: Predecessor Organizations, Folders 74–79.

[15] See for example Headquarters Search P.W. & D.P. Division [British Zone], Library Section, 15.9.1947, 6.1.1/82515429–82515431/ITS Digital Archive, Arolsen Archives.

[16] For example, there were specific list types for foreigners who had lived in the location during the war, who had died there during the war, or who still lived there when the lists were compiled.

[17] Today such lists can be found in Sub-Collection 1.2.2.1: List Material Group Prisons & Persecution.

sociated cover letters at various different locations in the collection on the foreigner tracing campaign, but that is not all. They will find other parts of the lists scattered over other collections. Thus the documentary holdings of the *Arolsen Archives* as they are today have not only been shaped by those who created them in the first place, but also by different phases of archival processing that must be disclosed by *collections archives* and taken into account by those researchers who work with their collections. The signature systems of the ITS archive, which were changed repeatedly, are also part of the problem. Resorting and relocating documents has torn old signatures apart.[18]

Political-Cultural Selection Processes in the Acquisition of Documents

Collections archives broke with another core principle of archiving too: archival records are traditionally defined as being characterized by their uniqueness; unlike books in libraries, they are kept in one place only.[19] However, the ITS and other *collections archives* did not only acquire original documents, they also copied millions of documents and sorted them into their collections. The acquisition of documents, whether by transferring originals, microfilming or later by creating digital copies, is probably the clearest expression of the political and cultural conditionality of the collections – because inevitably it was always a question of selecting what should and what should not be collected.

The ITS was involved in searching for and copying documents right from its inception. However, starting in the 1980s there was a sharp rise in new acquisitions which intensified still further after the end of the Cold War. At this time, it became apparent that the ITS archive contained no information on large numbers of persecutees from Central and Eastern Europe who were turning to Arolsen in their hundreds of thousands looking for proof of their persecution for compensation claims. As a result, ITS teams traveled through Germany and Europe to acquire, copy or microfilm documents. As early as in September 1989, ITS staff were able to film the death books of Auschwitz, for example. The Red Army had seized these documents in 1945. Soviet archives were inaccessible until 1989. By microfilming the documents in Moscow, the ITS gained access to evidence of

---

18 See Uwe Ossenberg: *The Document Holdings of the International Tracing Service. Using the Digital Archives in the Context of their Creation and Evolution, A Guideline*, Bad Arolsen: ITS, 2009, 47–63.
19 Reimann: "Grundfragen und Organisation des Archivwesens", 29.

the deaths of thousands of victims of Nazi persecution in the Auschwitz concentration camp for the first time.[20] But staff often had to work under pressure of time in difficult conditions when they microfilmed documents. They focused on recording the names. This is why the documents are often illegible and questions as to minimum archival standards for the quality of document copies in relation to the originals inevitably arise.

However, the selection processes which were applied in connection with document acquisition seem to be of even greater importance. The ITS did not usually acquire or copy complete archival holdings, but focused its interest instead on those people it saw as falling under its mandate – i.e. on foreign civilians and victims of Nazi persecution. Until well into the 2000s, the management of the ITS clung to an outdated definition of who was considered to be a victim of Nazi persecution which had been laid down by the West German authorities in the 1950s for use in connection with compensation claims. However, this definition came under massive criticism as a result of the social debates surrounding *forgotten victims* which arose in the early 1980s. Moreover, the staff, who often lacked historical knowledge, were only given a vague outline of the tasks they were to perform before they set off on these trips to acquire documents or began to inventory the new material.[21] The process of securing the files from the Bonn Prison in 1983 is a case in point. The ITS often acquired files, some of them originals, shortly before they were due to be destroyed, as was the case here. Germany had no laws requiring authorities to hand over their files to a state archive at the time. After acquiring the documents, ITS employees took the original prisoner books and redacted the names of all the prisoners who did not belong to the narrowly defined target group. An associated card index was sorted, documents on prisoners of war were handed over to the WASt (German acronym of the German Office for the Notification of Next of Kin of the Former German Wehrmacht), and all the cards that did not appear to be relevant were destroyed.[22]

Far from being an isolated case, this was typical for the acquisition of documents pertaining to police and judicial prisons which presented staff with a heterogeneous group of subjects. The "Prisons/Persecution Group" sub-collection, which comprises several thousand folders, is full of lists which have been blacked out or rendered partially illegible by masking, as well as index cards or prison files that were sorted in accordance with the obsolete definition of

---

20 Borggräfe/Höschler/Panek (eds.): *A Paper Monument*, 150–153.
21 Interview by the authors with ITS Staff Members J.P. and C.S., 21.11.2018, ITS Object Collection, Arolsen Archives.
22 Borggräfe/Höschler/Panek (eds.): *A Paper Monument*, 156–157.

the target group before the originals were acquired or before the documents were microfilmed.[23] So document acquisition at the ITS does not only reveal the extent to which the ITS remained oblivious to public debate and new research on the persecution of social outsiders and other *forgotten victims* between the 1980s and the 2000s. It also begs the general question as to which criteria and which methods *collections archives* used when acquiring documents as well as to what extent the decisions made when selecting documents can be understood by users today.

The Opportunities and Challenges of Digitization

A fourth special feature of the *Arolsen Archives*, as they are now known, and of some other large *collections archives* is that they have become pioneers in the digitization of archival material since the 1990s. The reason for this is probably that there is a great deal of public interest in the subject of Nazi crimes. They pushed and continue to push ahead into a brave new world full of opportunities but also full of risks – and these too are to receive at least brief mention in the present chapter.

Digitization started at the ITS in the late 1990s to speed up the process of providing information from the archive. A backlog of hundreds of thousands of inquiries had built up in Arolsen by then. In 1997, the IT service provider Ossenberg & Schneider presented an initial concept for a completely digital workflow for processing inquiries at the ITS. It covered digital research in the CNI and in all archival holdings. While space between the rows of shelves was limited, it was hoped that working at computer terminals would enable a much larger number of employees to carry out research in parallel. As had been recommended, the ITS and the service provider started by implementing partial solutions. The first major project was launched in 1998/99 and involved scanning the CNI. The major collections of the archive followed one by one. The process lasted up until the early 2010s. Since then, digitization has mainly focused on the large collection of the *T/D files*. About 85% of the archival holdings have already been digitized.[24]

The focus on tracing missing persons meant that cataloguing was not primarily carried out at the level of holdings or files at the ITS, although progress

---

23 For another example, see Prisoners' book from Butzbach prison, 1934–1943, 1.2.2.1/ 11559710–11559840/ITS Digital Archive, Arolsen Archives.
24 Borggräfe/Höschler/Panek (eds.): *A Paper Monument*, 158–163.

has recently been made on this. Instead, indexing was carried out at document level: names, dates and places, and sometimes also information on nationality, religion, etc. were entered into the archival database. Although some large gaps still exist, many holdings can be filtered very precisely according to a range of socio-biographical or geographical criteria. However, although this sounds like good news for users, it raises questions at the same time, because digitization is another form of shaping which involves only some content being made machine-searchable while other content is not.

An example of this is the collection of the 196,000 Care and Maintenance files of the *International Refugee Organization* (IRO). The DPs who still remained in occupied Germany used these files to apply for support between 1947 and 1951.[25] Researchers can not only search the collection by names, but also filter for people of a specific age, gender, place of origin, claimed nationality, or religion, or filters can be set for the camps where and dates when the applicants were registered. However, there is still a long way to go before the entire content of the files are machine-searchable. The following information is not yet accessible, for example: details of the whereabouts and workplaces of the DPs during the last 12 years, the reasons why they did not want to return to their home countries, their emigration destination or the decisions made by IRO officers on their applications. As was the case with the way the holdings were re-sorted at the physical level and with the selection processes involved in document acquisition, *collections archives* need to provide transparent information about the purpose of digitization and indexing, the method used and the criteria applied.

In principle, it would be possible to link documents of the same origin digitally and, in doing so, to reorganize *collections archives* virtually in accordance with the principle of provenance – in other words, to bring them into line with the prevailing norms of the archive world. The ITS took this path on a trial basis around 2010[26], but quickly abandoned it due to the resource requirements. Indexing the holdings more deeply within the existing system of pertinence seems to make more sense as Optical Character Recognition (OCR) and clustering, plus a system of keywords on top of that, enable users to restore original connections themselves if required, without a new and separate digital structure having to be maintained parallel to the analog structure of the archive.

---

25 Henning Borggräfe: "Exploring Pathways of (Forced) Migration, Resettlement Structures, and DPs' Agency: Document Holdings and Research Potentials of the Arolsen Archives", in *Historical Social Research*, forthcoming.

26 Karsten Kühnel: Usability of the Archives of the International Tracing Service (ITS), in *Archivar* 65, 2, 2012, 170–172.

However, digitization not only opens up brand new prospects in connection with indexing, it also provides new possibilities for users in particular. This applies to the way access is organized. Thanks to the internet, access is increasingly becoming possible at the global level – as well as to the way users conduct research in the holdings – and the millions of indexed data sets are contributing to the creation of a brand new source. In future it will be necessary to explore the potential of these aspects and discuss their consequences in detail.

Historical developments in the area of research which is extraneous to the intended purpose of the archive and the thorny issue of access to *collections archives* will be considered in the second part of this chapter, using the history of the *Arolsen Archives* as an illustrative example.

Research and Accessibility in Connection with Archival Collections

Over the past three decades many conferences, discussion panels and publications, both in the world of archiving and in the humanities in general, have touched on the questions of what archives are, what function they have and whether they should play an active role in historical and socio-political debates in order to keep memory alive.[27] There has been lively debate on the relationship between conventional archives and the public as well as exploration of the question of whether archives should be seen as part of the culture of remembering and the politics of history, or whether they are merely places where memory is managed:

> [W]hether their character – to use Aleida Assmann's terminology – is that of a passive storage memory which secures so-called authentic memory more or less objectively so that it can be activated by others for the dialogue between the generations and transferred to con-

---

27 Within the fields of philosophy and cultural sciences, the term "archive" and the process of archiving are increasingly being used metaphorically, are understood as a cultural technique, less institutional. See Knut Eberling and Stephan Günzel (eds.): *Archivologie: Theorien des Archivs in Philosophie, Medien und Künsten*, Berlin: Kadmos, 2009; Markus Friedrich: *Die Geburt des Archivs. Eine Wissensgeschichte*, Munich: Oldenburg, 2013; Michel Foucault: *Archäologie des Wissens*, Frankfurt/Main: Suhrkamp, 17. edition, 2015; Rainer Hering and Dietmar Schenk (eds.): *Wie mächtig sind Archive? Perspektiven der Archivwissenschaft*, Hamburg: University Press, 2013.

temporary functional memory if required, or whether they have to be seen at least to some degree as part of this functional memory which intervenes on a daily basis.[28]

These discussions about the interactive relationship between storage memory and functional memory touch on fundamental questions related to the accessibility and academic evaluation of archival holdings by external users as well as by archive staff. There is also the question of the extent to which archives can be "part of this functional memory which intervenes on a daily basis" by means of educational work, their own exhibitions, publications and events. The concept of opening up archives as a matter of principle to a historically interested public and the general access to cultural heritage which goes with this, which Jacques Derrida sees as being the "essential criterion" for "real democratization", emerged during the course of the French Revolution already.[29] In the decades that followed, different rules of access developed in different countries and, in the twentieth century in particular, they began to be enshrined in laws. In Germany, the process of opening up state archives to the public went hand in hand with the professionalization of historical scholarship and the emergence of the profession of the archivist at the end of the nineteenth century. But it was only subsequently to the debates on informational self-determination which had been raging since the 1970s that laws were introduced at federal and state level between 1987 and 1997 to regulate questions of data protection and personality rights in the context of archiving and usability.

However, the ITS, known today as the *Arolsen Archives*, were and still are an international institution and as such are not subject to these German archive laws. Initially set up and managed by the Allies, in 1955 responsibility for the institution was transferred to the *International Committee of the Red Cross* (ICRC) and an *International Commission* (IC) was established to guarantee protection of the collections. The Bonn Agreements – which provide the basic legal framework for the ITS – defined the main tasks of the institution as follows:

> [T]racing missing persons and collecting, classifying, preserving and rendering accessible to Governments and interested individuals the documents relating to Germans and non-

---

28 Hermann Rumschöttel: "Gedächtnisverwaltung oder Erinnerungskultur? Zur geschichtspolitischen Funktion der Archive", in: Verband deutscher Archivarinnen und Archivare e.V. (VdA) (eds.): *Lebendige Erinnerungskultur für die Zukunft. 77. Deutscher Archivtag 2007 in Mannheim*, Fulda: Selbstverlag des VdA, 2008, 35.

29 Jacques Derrida: *Dem Archiv verschrieben. Eine Freudsche Impression*, Berlin: Brinkmann und Bose, 1997, 14–15.

Germans who were interned in National-Socialist concentration or labor camps or to non-Germans who were displaced as a result of the Second World War.[30]

So it was that the core task of tracing and documenting came to be supplemented by the task of rendering the documents accessible to interested individuals. However, as was also the case with other early *collections archives*, this did not play a central role at first. Instead, tracing and documenting, the dominant activities at the time, took place primarily outside the public sphere and involved direct contact between the ITS and other tracing and documentation centers on the one hand and survivors and relatives of victims of Nazi persecution on the other. At the same time, during the early post-war period, neither contemporary historical writing nor public memory of the Nazi era paid much attention to the fates of individual victims of Nazi persecution. As a result there was no great interest in access to the ITS from either perspective.

The first factual evaluations of the documents were born of necessity. They were made by staff in connection with tracing activities, because knowledge about Nazi crimes was fragmentary at first and many pieces of information had to be collected and evaluated before they could be used. The collections were then opened up to survivors, academics and memorial initiatives who were able to search the holdings on site. This first phase of openness began at the end of the 1960s and lasted until the end of the 1970s. ITS staff also supported external projects during this period. At the beginning of the 1980s, the ITS archive gradually closed to the public and wound down most of its own historical projects. This launched a debate which was to last for over two decades centering on accessibility to the documents kept in Arolsen and involving controversial discussion of the main task and the intrinsic character of the institution. It seems that an interesting question to be explored in future might be on the one hand whether it is typical for *collections archives* to carry out their own intensive research in the context of their daily work (tracing activities, criminal prosecution etc.), and on the other hand, whether a difficult relationship to the issue of external access is also peculiar to *collections archives*, especially when remembering and remembrance are not their primary purposes.

---

30 Abkommen über die Errichtung eines Internationalen Ausschusses für den Internationalen Suchdienst, in: *Bundesanzeiger*, 7, 241, 14.12.1955, 3.

Knowledge Production at the ITS: Early Research Projects on Places of Detention and Nazi Crimes

Up until the beginning of the 1980s, under the leadership of the Allies and under the first directors appointed by the ICRC, the ITS conducted a number of large-scale evaluations which were based on the task of clarifying fates and which can be seen in retrospect as autonomous research projects. The search for missing persons and the process of providing information to state authorities in connection with the emigration of DPs or compensation, for example, went hand in hand with the acquisition and evaluation of documents. The ITS often lacked the specific knowledge needed in order to respond to the many inquiries it received. This included knowledge of particular places of detention and of complex crimes such as the death marches, the network of sub-camps belonging to the large concentration camp complexes or the medical experiments carried out on concentration camp prisoners. In order to gain knowledge in these areas, staff evaluated the documents on a thematic basis, conducted research at the sites of the crimes and produced contemporary sources by questioning survivors, for example. Questionnaires were the central research tool during this early period. The first questionnaire was circulated as early as in March 1946. In addition to questions on the construction and closure of places of detention, on the number of prisoners and the number of those who died, it also included questions on the whereabouts of the camp documents.[31]

At a meeting of national tracing bureaus held in Arolsen in the autumn of 1948, the participants agreed to draw up a comprehensive *master list* of all the places of detention in Europe to serve as a reference book for their daily work.[32] As the international center for tracing and documentation, the ITS was commissioned to compile this list. In 1949, the ITS published the *master list* under the title *Catalogue of Camps and Prisons in Germany and German-Occupied Territories*. It was created on the basis of the so-called camp lists that had been drawn up previously by national tracing bureaus to determine the location of places of detention, as well as on an initial evaluation of documents confiscated from the Nazis, and on interviews with survivors. In addition to concentration

---

[31] Amended Questionnaire on Camps, 6.1.1/82501260/ITS Digital Archive, Arolsen Archives.
[32] Minutes of the Conference of the National Tracing Bureaus Representatives, 30.9–2.10.1948, 6.1.1/82516578/ITS Digital Archive, Arolsen Archives.

camps and sub-camps, prisons and penitentiaries, this more than 480-page long catalogue also already listed places of civilian forced labor and ghettos.[33]

The knowledge gained from the evaluations was also recorded in special indexes, on maps, and later in a hanging file system in which originals or copies of documents on individual camps were kept.[34] This collection was created in parallel to the archival collection and was managed by the *Historical Section*. Work on the documentation continued in this department until the early 1980s. The catalogue was last published in 1979 under the changed title *Register Of Places Of Detention Under The Reichsführer-SS 1933–1945*.[35] However, many forced labor camps and ghettoes which had been listed in the earlier catalogue from 1949 were not included in this register. These omissions and the attending loss of knowledge should be seen in the context of Federal German compensation policy. From the 1950s on, the catalogue was no longer used exclusively by the ITS and other related tracing and documentation centers in order to determine the location of places of detention in connection with tracing inquiries. Instead, it had become a reference book which was used on a daily basis by Federal German compensation authorities. This also made the ITS the central point of contact for the authorities when it came to the evaluation and official recognition of individual camps in the context of compensation proceedings, despite the fact that the ITS was not an academic institution like the Munich *Institute for Contemporary History*, which was charged with rendering expert opinions connected with the Nazi period.[36] Its expanded remit brought the work of the ITS into the discourse of the politics of history and the politics of dealing with the past in Germany. And there were repeated tensions with the German govern-

---

[33] International Tracing Service: *Catalogue of camps and prisons in Germany and German-occupied territories Sept. 1st, 1939-May 8th, 1945*, Arolsen: ITS, 1949. Not until the middle of the 1990s did historical scholars begin to produce comprehensive "reference books" on places of detention during the Nazi era. The ITS was also involved in these projects. See the nine-volume work by Wolfgang Benz and Barbara Distel (eds.): *Der Ort des Terrors. Geschichte der nationalsozialistischen Konzentrationslager*, Munich: C.H. Beck, 2005–2009.

[34] The indexes and maps were used in the day to day work of identifying locations in connection with the clarification of fates. During the digitization of the main holdings groups, the original documents were taken out of the over 12,000 hanging files and sorted into the newly created archival collection 1.1.0.7: Compilation of Information Regarding Various Detention Sites and Camps.

[35] For a detailed description of the genesis of the catalogue of camps and prisons and the early testimonies which were used in order to produce it, see Susanne Urban: "Mein einziges Dokument ist die Nummer auf der Hand..." *Aussagen Überlebender der NS-Verfolgung im International Tracing Service*, Berlin: Metropol, 2018.

[36] See https://www.ifz-muenchen.de/das-institut/gutachten/. Last accessed: 25.7.2019.

ment, which wanted the catalog to be restricted to places of detention which the government had recognized in the context of compensation claims.

Access to the Archival Holdings: Between Openness and Isolation

Parallel to the work being done on the catalogue of camps and prisons and on the medical experiments conducted on concentration camp prisoners,[37] it was possible for survivors, academics and memorial initiatives to carry out research in Arolsen from the late 1960s onwards. At the same time, the ITS also supported important memorial and research projects undertaken by other institutions, including the *Memorial Book of the Federal Archives for the Victims of the Persecution of Jews in Germany*.[38] This phase of openness was closely linked to the management culture of Swiss national Albert de Cocatrix, who was the director at the time. He had come to Arolsen as the deputy director in 1955 and led the ITS from 1970 to 1977. He was a staunch upholder of the way the organization had seen itself in the early days, i.e. as being in the service of the survivors, and he entered into intensive dialogue with victims' associations. At the same time, he took part in academic conferences where he presented the holdings of the ITS and promoted their use. At the VI International Medical Conference of the FIR in Prague in 1976, Cocatrix commented that document acquisition had contributed to the very positive development of the ITS over the past decades and that it had become "t h e documentation center for the period of persecution."[39] In line with this self-confident attitude, the annual reports of the 1970s proudly record visits from academics, students and memorial initiatives, such as the visit of the young academic Falk Pingel in 1974, who predominantly studied the collection of the Buchenwald concentration camp, or the research visits of Rüdiger Lautmann and Richard Plant, who were engaged in pioneering research on the persecution

---

[37] In the 1960s, the ITS checked applications for compensation made by former concentration camp prisoners who had been victims of experiments. This was difficult at first because the documents held by the ITS were incomplete and hard to decipher. For this reason, collections of materials and evaluations on the subject of experiments on human beings in concentration camps were created, research was conducted in other archives and memorial sites, and contact was established with former prisoners. A total of 59 evaluations were produced.
[38] For contextualization of the genesis of the Memorial Book within the work of the Federal Archives, see the chapter by Tobias Hermann in this volume.
[39] Speech made by A. de Cocatrix at the International Medical Conference, Prague, 1976, 13 Soz 34/Library, Arolsen Archives.

of homosexuals. Lautmann's team was even allowed to borrow documents on a temporary basis and take them to Bremen.[40]

The ITS also cooperated with other institutions that were creating *collections archives* of their own and were involved in dealing with Nazi crimes, such as the *Central Office* in Ludwigsburg, with whom the ITS was in close contact from 1959 until the beginning of the 1980s. The two organizations exchanged documents and each allowed the other access to its own files.[41] During his period as director, de Cocatrix applied a flexible interpretation of the four mandates of the ITS which were defined in the Bonn Agreements as follows: collection, ordering, preservation and rendering access to the documents. However, the broad definition applied to accessibility led to conflicts with the ICRC, the governing body of the ITS, because of its intrinsic commitment to humanitarian ideals and neutrality. Seen from this perspective, the humanitarian mandate was only concerned with tracing missing victims of Nazi persecution, clarifying fates and documenting the persecution of individual victims.

Cocatrix's successor Philipp Züger implemented this narrow interpretation of the mandate consistently from 1978 onwards. Together with his deputy Charles-Claude Biedermann, who took over from him as director in 1985, they gradually closed the archive both to the interested public and to researchers, wound down most of the historical projects run by the ITS and discontinued support for the criminal prosecution of former Nazi perpetrators. During the course of these changes, the *Historical Section* was renamed the *General Documents Section*, a more neutral sounding name. On the one hand, Züger and Biedermann justified this about-face by invoking the ICRC's self-image as a neutral, humanitarian institution as well as a narrower interpretation of the four mandates of 1955. There was no longer any talk of "rendering access" to the documents. From then on, the documents were to be "reviewed" instead. On the other hand, they also employed arguments based on issues of data protection and personality rights, which had gained political and social significance in the Federal Republic of Germany in the context of debate surrounding informational self-determination. At the ITS, this new sensitivity with regard to handling personal data affected data acquisition in the 1980s most of all. Social security authorities and many companies became increasingly cautious and were only willing to release documents if the ITS would not pass them on to third parties – such as critical historians whose research was putting increasing pressure on companies as far

---

[40] 11/45582/ITS Archive, Arolsen Archives. See Rüdiger Lautmann: *Seminar: Gesellschaft und Homosexualität*, Frankfurt/Main: Suhrkamp, 1977; Richard Plant: *The Pink Triangle. The Nazi War Against Homosexuals*, New York: Holt, 1988.
[41] See the chapter by Kerstin Hofmann in this volume.

as questions of compensation were concerned from the mid 1980s on. The isolation of the ITS from the public and from the world of historical scholarship was supported by the *International Commission* (IC) of the ITS, the ICRC and the Federal Government. At its annual meeting in 1984, the IC decided that document acquisition and the humanitarian mission should be given priority and voiced its support for the ITS director's restrictive attitude to academia. The Belgian representative to the IC, Fernand Erauw, made the following statement: "Our objective is now [...] to obtain all the information we can about the past." For this reason, the principle that "researchers are not allowed to research in the ISD [ITS] archives from now on" had to be upheld.[42]

This policy of isolation weighed even more heavily because the 1980s were a time of intense debate about the Nazi past in West German society. Under the motto *dig where you stand*, memorial initiatives explored local aspects of Nazi history that had sunk into oblivion and expressed solidarity with *forgotten victims*. They accused the ITS of actively preventing a critical analysis of Nazi history and of "protecting the perpetrators" and they protested against the isolation of the ITS archive. The path which led to the archive reopening its doors to the public in 2007 was long and stony and involved many different parties. In the 1980s, protest came predominantly from within Germany. From the mid-1990s, protests became both more vigorous and more international: survivors' associations, the directors of various concentration camp memorials, researchers and committed individuals published numerous resolutions demanding access to the documents which were kept in Arolsen. At the same time, they harshly criticized the long waiting times for information needed in connection with pension and compensation claims. Most of these claims concerned victims of Nazi persecution from Central and Eastern Europe and they had been piling up since the late 1980s. Four resolutions will serve as examples illustrating the broad spectrum of the protests: in 1995, more than 50 academics signed a resolution at the international conference on *The National Socialist Concentration Camps 1933–1945. Development and Structure* in which they demanded access to the holdings and offered assistance from concentration camp memorials in fulfilling the humanitarian mission. At the same time, over 200 academics from the fields of the humanities and social sciences, trade unionists, politicians and publicists formulated the same demands in a resolution initiated by Frank-Uwe Betz. One year later, the *Amicale Internationale KZ Neuengamme*, the umbrella organization of the former prisoners of the Neuengamme concentration camp and their relatives, who had cooperated closely with Albert de Cocatrix three decades ear-

---

42 Minutes of the IC meeting, Bonn, 10.5.1984, 12.2.17.1/159/ITS Archives, Arolsen Archives.

lier, published a statement in which it emphasized that research into Nazi crimes was also an "act of intangible recognition." For this reason, they too considered access to the ITS archive to be indispensable. And the two other major Holocaust *collections archives*, the USHMM and *Yad Vashem*, which argued for opening the archive in their function as advisory members of the IC, also spoke out in 1996 when they presented a joint *Proposal for Opening the ITS Archive*.[43] In this proposal, they suggested that the holdings of the ITS be fully digitized and made available to the member states of the IC. Their intention was to avoid lengthy debates on data protection in the member states of the IC and make the digital copy available to the public in accordance with the data protection regulations of their countries.

In view of the massive public protest and accompanying scandal in the German media, the topic of "accessibility" was a constant point of discussion at the annual meetings of the IC in the years that followed. In consequence, there was an initial partial opening in 1996, which applied to the so-called non-personal general documents, and in 1998, the IC resolved to reopen the ITS archive, but emphasized the overriding priority of the humanitarian mission and with it the necessity of dealing with the backlog of inquiries.[44] Over the years that followed, the topic was discussed repeatedly by the IC, examined at greater depth by various working groups, and deferred on numerous occasions during the same period. There was disagreement and ignorance about data protection issues and possible rules of access because, as an international institution, neither the national archive laws of Germany nor the archive laws of any of the federal states could be applied to the ITS, and comparison with the legal position of national Red Cross societies also proved difficult. At the same time, there was also disagreement as to whether the collections of the ITS could even be described as archives and whether the holdings should be transferred to other institutions, such as the archives of the concentration camp memorials, the *Federal Archives* or the *Holocaust Memorial* in Berlin, which was under development at the time.

The renewed opening of the archive in 2007 was largely due to the work of historian Paul Shapiro from the USHMM, who continuously increased political and media pressure at international level from 2001 onwards. Not only did he

---

43 11.16/1296–1297/ITS Archive, Arolsen Archives; A selection of resolutions can also be viewed in the online exhibition "A Paper Monument: The History of the Arolsen Archives", see www.arolsen-archives.org/exhibition. For a chronological overview, see also: Frank-Uwe Betz: "Verdrängung ex ante. Über die Abwehr des Zugang zum ITS-Archiv", in *Mittelweg*, 36, 1998, 41–48.
44 Researchers tried to circumvent this isolation by going to *Yad Vashem* to view the ITS holdings that had been microfilmed in Arolsen in the 1950s and integrated into the *Yad Vashem* collection. See the chapter by Zvi Bernhardt in this volume.

show great persistence in putting the topic on the agenda of the annual IC meetings year after year, he also sought allies among politicians, researchers and survivors.[45] His efforts to sensitize the members of the *Task Force for International Cooperation on Holocaust Education, Remembrance and Research*, which was renamed the *International Holocaust Remembrance Alliance* (IHRA) in 2013, to the issue of access to the documents held in Arolsen are a good example of his approach. As members of the Task Force, nine member states of the IC which were opposed to opening up access to the ITS archive had actually committed themselves to campaigning for free access to archives that preserve Holocaust related documents by signing the *Stockholm Declaration* of 2000: "We share a commitment to throw light on the still obscured shadows of the Holocaust. We will take all necessary steps to facilitate the opening of archives in order to ensure that all documents bearing on the Holocaust are available to researchers."[46] At the same time, Shapiro arranged for the publication of a number of newspaper articles and invited the then German Minister of Justice, Brigitte Zypries, to a meeting and a press conference in Washington one month before the IC convened in April 2006. At the press conference, Zypries announced that the German government was now committed to providing access to the ITS archive and would take steps to accelerate the process. In May 2006, the IC voted unanimously to reopen the collections in Arolsen to the interested public and researchers.

As well as deciding to open the ITS archive, the IC also adopted the proposal that USHMM and *Yad Vashem* had put forward in the mid 1990's already to hand over digital copies of the ITS archive to all the member states of the IC. This means that today, the digital ITS archive is additionally held by seven partner institutions of the *Arolsen Archives* which are known as copyholders.[47] As a consequence of the opening, the ICRC withdrew from the management of the ITS in 2012. The *International Commission* took over responsibility for the ITS itself and pushed ahead with a new course of intensified modernization, openness and networking. Since 2015 this has resulted in more and more entire collections

---

[45] For a chronological overview of the efforts he undertook, see Paul A. Shapiro: *Opening the Archives of the International Tracing Service (ITS) How did it happen? What does it mean?* Available at: https://vwi.ac.at/images/Downloads/SWL_Reader/Shapiro/SWL-Reader-Shapiro.pdf. Last accessed: 12.7.2019.

[46] Available at: https://www.holocaustremembrance.com/index.php/stockholm-declaration. Last accessed: 12.7.2019.

[47] See https://arolsen-archives.org/suchen-erkunden/#faq. Last accessed: 1.8.2019.

gradually also being published in an online archive. All the documentary holdings from concentration camps and ghettoes can now be viewed online.[48]

The ITS thus left the extreme isolation it had been in since the beginning of the 1980s and is now open to users all over the world. This profound transformation can also be seen as a typical feature of *collections archives*. As well as making no distinction between originals and copies when they integrate documentary holdings into their collections, they also tend to share documentary holdings in their entirety with other institutions. At first this was done to promote the core task of tracing and documenting victims of persecution – today the aim is to make the holdings available to a wider public. Unlike conventional archives, *collections archives* evidently do not really see themselves in the role of the sole repository of authentic memory. In addition to the preservation of cultural heritage for current and future generations, they consider their core tasks to be the provision of easy and, ideally, global access and, in connection with this, the promotion of active learning and remembering from and with archive documents. Especially if they have not recently been integrated into state archives, the *collections archives* that were established for specific purposes after 1945 in response to Nazi crimes and the turmoil of the Second World War must be seen much more as "part of this functional memory which intervenes on a daily basis" than conventional archives. However, because many conventional archives are also currently working on providing easier access and showing greater social engagement, it remains to be seen to what extent this development will further reinforce the special role of *collections archives* or whether *collections archives* are perhaps playing a pioneering role in a general trend here, which will lead to a harmonization in the world of archiving in the medium term.

---

[48] Available at: https://collections.arolsen-archives.org/search/. Last accessed: 12.7.2019.

Rebecca Boehling
From Tracing and Fate Clarification to Research Center

The Role of International Players and Transnationalism in Shaping the Identity of the ITS

Abstract: The more international influence there was on and within the ITS, the more likely the ITS and its staff were to manifest and reflect a transnational culture of memory of and for an increasingly broadly defined group of victims. This was true early on due to its very international staff; however, with growing Cold War constraints and priorities and an increasing reliance on regional German staff under *International Committee of the Red Cross* (ICRC) management, the identity and volume of those served by the ITS narrowed. Only as a result of renewed international pressure following the end of the Cold War were ITS records opened to the public, with copies of the original documents made available to survivors and their families. The ITS changed its practices from using and considering ITS documents exclusively as a means to trace the fate and/or whereabouts of individuals persecuted and/or displaced by the crimes and aggression of the Nazi regime because of a growing understanding by the international community that these documents constituted an end in themselves. This change coincided with the *International Commission* for the ITS and its affiliated member state archives playing an increasingly pro-active supervisory role over the ITS. This, in turn, encouraged the ITS to conceive of and reconstitute itself as an archive, serving globally both victims and their descendants as well as scholars and journalists for historical research and documentation purposes.

Introduction

From my vantage point as the first director recruited and appointed by the *International Commission* for the *International Tracing Service* (ITS), I am struck by the apparent correlation between the number of international players involved in shaping the ITS, and the level of commitment to the mission of serving the breadth of victims of the Nazi regime, whether in terms of traditional tracing, fate clarification and documentation for restitution or memorialization. These international players include Allied agencies and their representatives, members of the *International Commission* for the ITS and the related archival partner institu-

OpenAccess. © 2020 Rebecca Boehling, published by De Gruyter. [CC BY-NC-ND] This work is licensed under the Creative Commons Attribution-NonCommercial-NoDerivatives 4.0 License.
https://doi.org/10.1515/9783110665376-014

tions, as well as international staff working at the ITS, whether Displaced Persons (DPs) or their spouses, especially those representing supranational, even transnational interests. The more international the influence was on and within the ITS the more likely the ITS and its staff were to manifest and reflect a transnational culture of memory, one transcending nationalism and national identity, and to advocate for an increasingly broadly defined group of victims. An increase in transnational influences made the ITS more inclined to conceive of itself as serving historical research and documentation purposes. In contrast, national interests and national legislation based upon racial and cultural biases against Roma and Sinti, homosexuals, those deemed physically or mentally "abnormal" or non-conformist in their behavior, and political biases against communists and other leftists in the West worked against a widening of the understanding of which innocent people had been incarcerated, tortured, even killed or worked to death by the Nazis.[1] An international declaration of human rights in 1948 may have purported to protect a panoply of rights for all, but not even all UN member states signed on and certainly the practices and legislation at home in many member states fell far short of the Universal Declaration of Human Rights.[2] For much of its history the understanding of who had been victimized by the Nazis and who thus deserved recognition and compensation was culturally and politically and socially biased at the ITS, just as it was among many of its Allied founders.

Early History of the ITS

When the ITS began its work as the *International Tracing Service* in early 1948 its main task was tracing those civilians missing because of Nazi persecution and the war in Europe. The ITS was the successor to SHAEF's Tracing and Locating Unit as well as the Central Tracing Bureau, which was created first under the *United Nations Relief and Rehabilitation Administration* (UNRRA) and then, as of 1947, under UNRRA's successor, the *International Refugee Organization* (IRO). In the midst of conquering Germany and the liberation of surviving victims of Nazism, the Allies, in particular the British and Americans, collected docu-

---

[1] In the Soviet bloc, the tendency was to focus on the victimization of communists while downplaying racial persecution, including the specific genocidal policies against Jews or Sinti and Roma, while playing down the persecution of Communists was the norm at the ITS under ICRC and western influence.

[2] For the text and voting information on the Universal Declaration of Human Rights, see: https://www.ohchr.org/EN/UDHR/Pages/UDHRIndex.aspx. Last accessed: 30.3.2019.

ments that survived the attempted destruction of records of concentration camps, prisons as well as of forced labor. These documents became part of the collection that moved to Arolsen, documents that could help trace the path of persecution both of victims who did and those who did not survive. The ITS, under the jurisdiction of the IRO, also documented the post-war whereabouts of survivors of Nazi persecution and those left displaced from their homelands, the so-called Displaced Persons (DPs), whose housing, care and maintenance as well as preparation for either repatriation or emigration the IRO managed. This in turn helped facilitate family reunification, a traditional goal of tracing organizations.

The Second World War Allies created the ITS to trace civilians from all the Allied countries, referred to at the time as the united nations, a term first coined by United States President Franklin D. Roosevelt in the Declaration by United Nations of January 1, 1942, when representatives of 26 nations pledged their governments to continue fighting together against the Axis Powers. This declaration predated the October 1945 founding of the United Nations organization, and included only those nations united in opposition to Germany and her allies.[3] The identity of the ITS continues to this day to be shaped by the Second World War (WWII) Allies, although neither exclusively nor consistently over this entire time by the same Allies conceived of in 1942, as the "united nations".

In the transition from UNRRA to the IRO, the Soviets withdrew their direct participation in the IRO's tracing efforts and never agreed to share responsibility for DPs. The Soviets never acknowledged DPs as a phenomenon in the way the western Allies, especially the US and Britain construed and then organized them. In contrast to its role in UNRRA, the Soviet Union did not join or back the IRO. So by the time the ITS was officially created, the Soviet Union had disengaged from Allied post-war tracing tasks. It did not participate in providing support for DPs, criticizing those resisting repatriation to the Soviet Union, its newly acquired territories, and eastern European countries that increasingly were becoming Sovietized and thus part of the new Eastern bloc. This meant that the new "International" Tracing Service in Arolsen, as initially conceived, was not truly international; in practice it did not involve all the "united nations" of all the WWII Allies that had fought and defeated Nazi Germany. This would also come to mean that under this limited western Allied control, the ITS would not provide easy access to information to or about Eastern Europeans, beyond those individuals already in Western Europe as DPs. Nor did the files left behind

---

[3] United Nations: "History of the United Nations". Available at: https://www.un.org/en/sections/history/history-united-nations/index.html. Last accessed: 29.3.2019.

in Nazi sites of persecution in Eastern Europe find their way into the ITS document collection. This also limited the ability of the ITS to provide information to Eastern Europeans or those whose persecution had taken place in sites of persecution in Nazi-occupied Eastern Europe, even when, or if, the ITS tried to do so.

Of course this is only part of the story. Britain and the US, the primary players in the IRO, also increasingly ignored Soviet requests for repatriation of their citizens. This was especially true for Soviet requests for repatriation of people from recently Soviet-annexed areas like the western Ukraine, because Britain and the US did not recognize the legitimacy of this Soviet acquisition. Under the cover of care and maintenance, the IRO, and thus indirectly as its record keeper, the ITS, sometimes even assisted in harboring Eastern Europeans as DPs who had displayed highly suspect collaborative behavior during the German occupation of the East and thus helped them emigrate to countries like the US or Britain, either because of their political, especially anti-Soviet or anti-communist, intelligence or military-related scientific expertise. This Cold War activity limited the potential of the ITS to develop a supra- or transnational identity, making it from the beginning a western institution, dedicated to serving the western Allied governments and select Allied victims of the Nazis.[4]

Who Fell under the ITS Mandate? The Role of National Identity and the Cold War

But how did the ITS define who counted as victims of the Nazis and thus fell under its mandate? As Henning Borggräfe and Hanne Leßau remind us, even in the early years of the ITS and its predecessor institutions, nationality took on more significance in the practice of responding to tracing and fate clarification inquiries rather than type of persecution or basis of victimhood. In fact the nationality of the sought-after person or the person doing the seeking could determine whether the inquiry fell under the ITS's tracing mandate or not.[5] This,

---

[4] For more on the ITS as a western pawn, specifically an extension of US foreign policy in the Cold War, see Jennifer L. Rodgers: "Archive of Horrors, Archive of Hope: The ITS in the Postwar Era", in Elizabeth Anthony, Rebecca Boehling, Suzanne Brown-Fleming and Susanne Urban (eds.): *Freilegungen: Spiegelungen der NS-Verfolgung und ihrer Konsequenzen*, Göttingen: Wallstein, 2015, 17–34, here 25–26.

[5] Henning Borggräfe and Hanne Leßau: "Die Wahrnehmung der NS-Verbrechen und der Umgang mit den NS-Verfolgten im International Tracing Service", in Henning Borggräfe, Hanne Leßau and Harald Schmid (eds.): *Fundstücke: Die Wahrnehmung der NS-Verbrechen und ihrer Opfer im Wandel*, Göttingen: Wallstein, 23–44, here 25. See also in the same volume Henning

however, was not simply due to one's geopolitical position within the Cold War division of Europe. Initially citizens of defeated Germany and of Nazi Germany's allied countries did not fall under the UNRRA or IRO tracing mandates and thus were not eligible to request information or assistance from the ITS. In fact, unless they were Jewish, Germans, regardless of their level of persecution, were rarely eligible to be regarded as DPs or to receive the care and maintenance that DP status carried with it.

As the need for both evidence for the prosecution of war crimes as well as the basis for restitution for victims or their heirs arose, these Nazi documents held at the ITS served a judicial purpose as well. They were requested for use by German and Allied courts and offices for prosecution purposes, while survivors and the families of victims, including those from Germany and those from Nazi-allied countries, also sought to provide proof of their persecution. As Jennifer Rodgers tells us, this proof was used for purposes of "certifying claims and issuing death certificates for social welfare and indemnification programs."[6] This broadened the functions of the ITS records beyond tracing missing persons to tracing one's path of persecution and tracing the identities and behavior of perpetrators. Such uses, however, did not lead to a reconceptualization of the ITS as a research center, or even an archive. The character of the IRO, as the ITS was known in the region for years, and by some of the older generation in the area even today, was affected by the fact that UNRRA and its successor the IRO, as relief agencies, both served and employed Displaced Persons at the ITS.[7] Those Displaced Persons, including some from eastern Europe who did not wish to be repatriated, also played a special role in providing first

---

Borggräfe: "Zum Geleit", 7–8, and Harald Schmid: "Zwischen Achtung und Ächtung: Opfer nationalsozialistischer Herrschaft im Bild der deutschen Öffentlichkeit", 10–22, here 17. They in fact show that it was not just nationality that determined whether one was deemed a victim worthy of ITS assistance. The ITS staff were affected by their surrounding culture's understanding of who had been victimized by the Nazis for Nazi-defined reasons, as opposed to for allegedly criminal and therefore not specifically Nazi, or even 'unwarranted' reasons, thus justifying the incarceration or even the resulting death. The authors argue that ironically even when West German society, at least its historians and intellectuals, came to realize that victims of the Nazis included those the Nazi records labeled "asocials", "criminal" elements, homosexuals, those involuntarily sterilized, so-called Gypsies, forced laborers and not just political and racial victims, the ITS staff under ICRC leadership continued to use the 1950s' restrictive definitions of who constituted legitimate victims of the Nazis, and who thus were worthy of compensation.
6 Jennifer L. Rodgers: "'Humanity's Ancestral Inheritance': The International Tracing Service, 1942–2008", Arolsen Archives website, see https://arolsen-archives.org/content/uploads/humanitys-ancestral-inheritance-rodgers.pdf. Last accessed: 2.9.2019.
7 Rodgers: "Archive of Horrors, Archive of Hope", 28.

hand-knowledge of forced labor and/or incarceration along their own paths of persecution and displacement. Such DPs were predisposed to a commitment to preserving the historical record of persecution alongside the information needed for tracing missing persons and reuniting families, which however does not mean they were immune to ethnic and nationalist biases, or antisemitism, for that matter. But like many DPs not wishing to return to their homelands, many former Nazi victims working at the early ITS were inclined to distance themselves from strong nationalism and national allegiances. But although more inclined toward what we would now call transnationalism, such DPs were of course also likely to share the anti-communism of their homelands as well as that of the Western Allies, which was becoming ever more overt.[8] This was especially true during the tensions of the Cold War in Europe from 1948 onward, and particularly as of 1951 as the (western) *Allied High Commission for Germany* (HICOG) took over responsibility from the IRO for administering the ITS, with the United States taking on the leadership role.[9]

It is significant that the international staff of the early ITS, well into the 1950s, identified with at least some of the people whose records they oversaw and for whom they did tracing and documentation work. They were contemporaries and in some cases they shared similar fates, or they identified with the Allied soldiers, seen as liberators, who had defeated those Germans they considered perpetrators. A number of Allied civilians also worked alongside the DPs at the early ITS. Most were less likely to identify with the local Germans, although they surely came into contact with them in their daily lives, but not so often in their ITS workplace. It was several years after the founding of the ITS before significant numbers of local Germans worked in regular staff positions

---

8 Anna Holian: *Between National Socialism and Soviet Communism: Displaced Persons in Postwar Germany*, Ann Arbor/Michigan: University of Michigan Press, 2011, 119; Diane Afoumado: "The 'Care and Maintenance in Germany' Collection – A Reflection of DP Self-Identification and Postwar Emigration", in René Bienert, Rebecca Boehling and Susanne Urban (eds.): *Freilegungen: Displaced Persons. Leben im Transit: Überlebende zwischen Repatriierung, Rehabilitation und Neuanfang*, Göttingen: Wallstein, 2014, 217–227, here 225. See also Laura J. Hilton: "The Experiences and Impact of the Stateless in the Postwar Period", 156–172, here especially 167. Also in the same volume, see Ruth Balint: "The Use and Abuse of History: Displaced Persons in the ITS Digital Archive", 173–186.

9 Charles Elbot, son of Hugh, G. Elbot, head of the Executive Board of the ITS during the HICOG period, described his father as "a Cold War warrior". In explaining his father's commitment to working at the ITS, Charles also stressed Hugh's concern for the survivors and victims of the Nazis. Telephone conversation with the author, 21.7.2019.

at the ITS.[10] This seems to correlate with both the age- and presumably health-related retirements of DPs as well as the 1951 to 1955 control of the ITS by the *Allied High Commission for Germany*, and then the 1955 takeover of the administration of the ITS, at the request of the western Allies, by the *International Committee of the Red Cross*.

The Hegemonic Role of the United States

The Americans, who led the ITS under its HICOG control phase from 1951 to 1955, oversaw a period of ever-decreasing transnational influence in and on the ITS. Jennifer Rodgers argues that the ITS, especially in the 1950s, gave inquiries from US agencies precedence over other requests.[11] This would not be surprising given the location of the ITS in the US zone of occupied Germany, the fact that the US provided the single highest contribution to the funding of the IRO and held the largest number of officers in the IRO Secretariat,[12] and that the ITS was led from 1951 to 1955 by an American. All of the DP camps directly run by the IRO were in the US zone of occupied Germany, while the IRO had a more limited oversight role over those in the British occupation zone. All of this points to the hegemonic role of the US within the IRO, even before the HICOG phase. During the HICOG phase itself, the US chaired the tripartite Executive Board of the ITS, which represented the three Western Allies, the British, French and Americans. It is not surprising during both the IRO and the HICOG phases that the ITS would have shown precedence to US agency requests.

It should be noted that soon after the American head of the HICOG tripartite Executive Board of the ITS, Hugh G. Elbot, took over his supervisory position at the ITS in 1951, he felt compelled to report to his superiors in Frankfurt that "about 45 top Nazis (including SS leaders, Gestapomen [sic] and Golden badge-party members) and about 5 Communists were recently removed, after having been employed under IRO supervision for several years." He noted the

---

10 This information derives from conversations I had while director of the ITS from 2013 to 2015 with older and recently retired ITS staff as well as with older Arolsen locals as well as from photographs and signatures on early documents from the ITS. A detailed analysis of personnel records would be necessary to confirm the exact nationalities of the staff at any given point, especially prior to 1955.
11 Rodgers: "Archive of Horrors, Archive of Hope", 25.
12 "International Refugee Organization", in *Yearbook of the United Nations*, 1951, 990–991. Available at: https://read.un-ilibrary.org/united-nations/yearbook-of-the-united-nations-1950_418b1872-en#page8-9. Last accessed: 20.3.2019.

strong opposition of the German manager and other Germans to the removal of "those elements."[13] Elbot, a German-speaking Jewish refugee from Czechoslovakia, who fled Central Europe in 1938 and joined the US military during the war, had misgivings about German influence at the ITS, but such misgivings were not typical, however, of his superiors in HICOG or the State Department.[14]

Following the 1954 repeal of the Occupation Statute in Germany, an *International Commission* (IC) of nine member states (Belgium, the Federal Republic of Germany, France, Israel, Italy, Luxembourg, the Netherlands, the United Kingdom, and the United States) was formed to charge the ITS with continuing its tracing services while protecting and utilizing the documents in Arolsen. During the HICOG phase the US government had hoped it would not be long before it could turn over the ITS to German control. But several of Germany's former WWII foes and, not unexpectedly, Israel, resisted this idea. Some Western Allies, including countries with sizable numbers of Nazi victims, were wary of Germans having control over the ITS, yet did want West Germany to pay for its staff and operations. Even the US representative on the Executive Board overseeing the ITS during the HICOG phase, Hugh G. Elbot, argued against his employer, the State Department, in advocating against turning over the ITS to the Germans "for the sake of posterity" and in order to safeguard the records and their accessibility.[15]

The government of the young Federal Republic was disappointed that an *International Commission* was formed to oversee the ITS. The Federal Republic did agree to shoulder the expense of funding the ITS, its operations and staff, partly to diffuse international tensions over the issue of potential German control over the ITS.[16] The ITS's reliance on German funding did of course spell greater German influence and a steady increase in the number of German staff working at the ITS. Germany was anxious to dispel distrust among its new-found Cold War

---

13 Hugh G. Elbot to G. J. Swope, Memo on "Future of the ITS", 6.2.1952, 2, 6.1.1/82507305/ITS Digital Archive, USHMM.
14 Charles Elbot (son of Hugh G. Elbot), telephone conversation with the author, 21.7.2019.
15 Charles Elbot, telephone conversation with the author, 21.7.2019. Although the US representative to HICOG's tripartite Executive Board overseeing the ITS, Hugh G. Elbot, wanted the ITS to remain under international control and not come under German control, the US State Department under John Foster Dulles advocated turning the ITS over to the Germans. According to Charles Elbot, Hugh G. Elbot's son, his father's persistent opposition to turning over the ITS to Germany, as expressed to his superior Dulles, helped prevent this from happening. See also Hugh G. Elbot to G. J. Swope, "Future of the ITS", 6.2.1952, in which Elbot argued that the "Germans, if left alone, would tend to reemploy unreliable elements." 6.1.1/82507305/ITS Digital Archive, USHMM.
16 Rodgers: "Archive of Horrors, Archive of Hope", 27.

allies in the midst of achieving stronger western integration and full sovereignty. The first major West German law to indemnify victims of the Nazi regime went into effect in 1953 (*Bundesentschädigungsgesetz* or BEG), providing compensation to both non-German and German victims, at least as defined at the time. But victims had to provide proof of internment, and it quickly became clear that the Nazi concentration camp and prison records held at the ITS were critical evidence.[17] Alongside its various *"Wiedergutmachung"* programs to show it was rehabilitating itself, the Federal Republic had come to realize it might save money by using ITS documents to certify claims of persecution and death rather than risk facing redundant claims.[18]

In the Bonn Accords of 1955, the *International Commission* had oversight authority over the ITS, yet did not want to manage it directly. The IC sought an institution that would be seen as neutral and apolitical, at least as defined within the constraints of the anti-communist, anti-Soviet West in the midst of the 1950s Cold War. Because the Red Cross, with its various national branches, in particular the British Red Cross, had been involved in the early tracing tasks taken on by the ITS and its predecessor organizations, the decision was made to ask the *International Committee of the Red Cross* (ICRC) to provide the administrative structure under which the ITS was to function: a Swiss delegate of the ICRC, accountable both to the ICRC and the *International Commission*, was to oversee the ITS's day-to-day operations while reporting to the Commission at its annual meetings.[19] Under ICRC management and with the approval of the IC, the ITS staff acted primarily as a tracing service for victims of Nazi crimes, providing documentation on victims' paths of persecution and fates, while, like other tracing services, helping to reunite families. Occasionally it would also provide documentation on perpetrators to judicial authorities. Civilian victims and their descendants had the right to request information from the ITS pertaining to their individual cases, but they were not granted direct access to the documents.[20]

---

17 Jean-Marc Dreyfus: "Opening the Nazi Archives at Bad Arolsen", Books&ideas.net, 11.4.2013, 3–4. Available at: https://booksandideas.net/IMG/pdf/20130411_dreyfus_arolsen_en.pdf. Last accessed 29.3.2019. Original French version first published by Laviedesidees.fr, 11.9.2008. Translated by Eric Rosencrantz.
18 Rodgers: "Archive of Horrors, Archive of Hope", 26–27.
19 As an ICRC delegate, the ITS director was paid directly by the ICRC and had diplomatic immunity in Germany.
20 Paul Belkin: "Opening of the International Tracing Service's Holocaust Era Archives in Bad Arolsen, Germany", Congressional Research Service Report for (US) Congress, 11.12.2007. Available at: https://www.everycrsreport.com/reports/RS22638.html. Last accessed: 18.2.2019.

The Role of Swiss Management: The *International Committee of the Red Cross* (ICRC)

Switzerland had been one of the 20 member states of the IRO, the headquarters of which were in Geneva, Switzerland, yet Switzerland had not fought against the Axis Powers, and thus was not an IC member. Instead the Swiss-run ICRC, also headquartered in Geneva, provided the director of the ITS, who formally reported both to the ICRC and to the *International Commission*. The Western Allied governments considered the ICRC, with its Swiss origins and headquarters, as both neutral and apolitical. By agreeing to administer the ITS, the ICRC had hopes of compensating for its less than stellar moral role on behalf of Nazi victims during the war. One might have thought that ICRC management would have made the ITS more transnational, or supranational during its administrative management of the ITS from 1955 until 2012, especially as compared to the HICOG phase. Instead the ICRC continued the HICOG policy of rejecting inquiries from the Eastern bloc, arguing that such requests were of a political nature, while claiming that the ITS under the ICRC was focused on "humanitarian" requests.[21]

In hiring more Germans from the area around Arolsen to replace the previously more international and more formally educated staff, the ITS under the ICRC took on a more provincial tone.[22] Its German staff had minimal direct experience with victims of Nazism and were less well-versed in the historical or geographical context of Nazi persecution and atrocities across Europe. The requests for information that the ITS staff provided were based on documents indexed solely by names, documents primarily authored by Nazi officials. Under ICRC management, fewer and fewer of the staff were equipped to interpret the information they were providing to victims and their descendants.[23] Had the ITS

---

21 Rodgers: "Archive of Horrors, Archive of Hope", 27.
22 There are no universities in the vicinity of Arolsen, with the closest a hundred kilometers away in Göttingen in what had been the Kingdom of Hanover, and later became Lower Saxony, but at the end of the war was in the British zone of occupation, unlike Arolsen in the state of Hesse in the US zone. Such boundaries made it very unlikely that those in the Arolsen area would have ever pursued studies at the University of Göttingen. The University of Kassel, some 50 km away from Arolsen, was not founded until the 1970s.
23 During my ITS directorship veteran staff confided in me how under ICRC management they had rarely been encouraged to do research themselves or to consult with each other about ways to piece together or interpret information. There was allegedly an unwritten policy under the long-time (1985–2006) ICRC director, Charles-Claude Biedermann, not to hire college graduates or anyone with a German *Abitur* (advanced pre-university high school degree). Biedermann pro-

under the ICRC decided to open the ITS for research, few on the staff would have been able to help facilitate it. On the other hand, the staff would have benefitted from the knowledge of researchers and made better use of the early historical information and analysis that had been prepared explicitly by an international historical division in the early years of the ITS, but which they were rarely encouraged to use. According to Susanne Urban, director of the ITS Research and Education Department from 2009 until 2015, these historical materials, including the approximately 1100 completed *Death March and Concentration Camp Questionnaires* that were sent out in 1950 to generate and revise a *Catalogue of Camps and Prisons* were used less and less by the ITS staff to answer inquiries or provide information to authorities after 1951. Instead they were stored in a basement in one of the ITS buildings until 2009, after the ITS had officially opened for research two years before.[24]

There is evidence that the ITS intermittently did provide replies to historical inquiries from the mid-1950s until the mid-1970s. In fact, while under the direction of Albert de Cocatrix from 1970 to 1977, the ITS became actively engaged in corresponding with and receiving visitors, including scholars. This policy changed with his departure, resulting in an overall decline in inquiries under his successor, Philipp Züger. Then in 1985, under the leadership of Charles-Claude Biedermann, who remained director for over 20 years, access to ITS files and many of its facilities became off-limits without the director's explicit authorization.[25] The decade prior to the reunification of Germany, while first Züger and then Biedermann were the ITS directors, coincided with a wave of popular and scholarly interest in National Socialism and the Third Reich in West Germany and WWII globally. The number of survivors of Nazi persecution was of course steadily declining, but a younger generation of historians and descendants of survivors began asking more questions. While Biedermann was director of the ITS, the number of inquiries skyrocketed, as did the backlog and wait time for those hoping for answers. With the collapse of the Soviet Union the ITS was able to acquire copies of new records held in the former Eastern bloc, which increased the volume of requests and raised expectations about speedy replies and

---

moted a very secretive and closed environment at the ITS, allegedly banning staff from talking about their work, not only outside work but also generally with each other while at work.
24 Susanne Urban: "'Mein einziger Dokument ist der Nummer auf der Hand'. Schriftliche Aussagen Überlebender im Archiv des ITS", in René Bienert, Rebecca Boehling and Susanne Urban (eds.): *Freilegungen: Überlebende – Erinnerungen – Transformationen*, Göttingen: Wallstein, 2013, 173–197, here 188–190.
25 Dreyfus: "Opening the Nazi Archives at Bad Arolsen", 5–6.

scholarly access. The compensation claims of former forced laborers from Eastern Europe also placed Arolsen's records in demand.[26]

The ITS as an Archive for Research?

Although the ITS records were increasingly utilized from the 1950s onward for judicial and restitution proceedings as well as to document victims' paths of persecution and occasionally still to reunite families, within the ITS and among its ICRC leadership, the ITS continued to be understood primarily under its initial mandate and name, as a tracing service. Except during this brief period in the 1970s under Albert de Cocatrix, its potential for research was stifled; its identity as an archive, a treasure trove of historical documents, suppressed. Even as survivors and family members of victims sent in documentation in the so-called correspondence or T/D files that supplemented the materials the ITS initially had from former concentration camps and prisons and that it became the repository for, there was little sense of the ITS constituting an archive. This was true even as the ITS actively sought and gathered documents and copies of documents from archives to supplement its collections.[27]

The decision in the 1990s to digitize the documents was less a reflection of this attitude changing, or of the recognition for the need for preservation, than of the need to speed up the process of searching within the documents, without staff having to move the original documents constantly from place to place, risking misfiling and loss. Yet in many ways this mass digitization process made it ever more clear, to outsiders, if not insiders, that the ITS had become an important repository of records for the history of the victims of the Nazi regime as well as for the criminal behavior and bureaucratic nature of the Nazi regime as it gathered and tortured and killed those it perceived as enemies.

During much of this more than a half century of ICRC management the documents of the ITS remained closed both to the public and to scholars – a policy that by the 1990s provoked increasingly strong criticism of the institution, from the international scholarly community as well as from the IC. In the IC more archivists and historians of the Holocaust and Nazi Germany came to take seats alongside the diplomats, without voting rights, of course, to represent the inter-

---

26 Ibid., 6–7.
27 Jan Erik Schulte: "Nationalsozialismus und europäische Migrationsgeschichte: Das Archiv des Internationalen Suchdienstes in Arolsen", in *Zeithistorische Forschungen/ Studies in Contemporary History*, 4, 2007, 223–232, here 225.

ests of the historical record as well as the legacy of those countrymen and countrywomen who had suffered at the hands of the Nazis and their allies.

The May 2006 decision of the *International Commission* to open up the ITS for historical research, concomitant with the recall of Biedermann, marked not only a remarkable change in accessibility but a new understanding of the ITS as an archive. Yet this did not come overnight. In 1995 the IC had voted to open up the ITS records to research, but the leadership of the ITS, citing concerns with the fact that ITS records referred to individuals and citing various data privacy laws in Germany and other parts of Europe that restricted access to personal data, had managed to fend off the opening, except to those general historical documents not pertaining to individuals.[28] More than a decade passed with increasing rumors of scandals related to Biedermann and practices within the ITS alongside pressure from scholars and the media before the IC was able to prevail.

Interestingly enough for me, as the first post-ICRC director of the ITS, few of the histories of the ITS focus much attention on the *International Commission*. The assumption is that the ICRC was able to act autonomously, at least within the constraints of German financial accountability and labor law, under which all the employees fell, except the ICRC staff, who were on temporary assignment in Arolsen. Until a detailed study of the ICRC and its relations with the *International Commission* is undertaken, we will not know in any detail how much autonomy the ICRC had and how and at which junctures the IC pulled in the reins. We do know that when revelations reached the public about the abuse of power of the ICRC Director Biedermann and the arbitrary practices of granting select people access to the archives, while resisting granting access even to members of the *International Commission*, that calculated pressure led to Biedermann's departure and the opening of the archives in late 2007. CBS's *60 Minutes* highlighted the significance of this opening, thanks especially to Paul Shapiro and the United States Holocaust Memorial Museum, with its unfortunately ill-named investigative report entitled *Hitler's Secret Archive*, which aired in December 2006.

I would suggest that it was really only at this point, with digitization underway already several years, that internally the ICRC and some of the staff had begun to think of the ITS as an archive. The opening of the archive of the ITS to the public may have transformed the external perception of the identity of the ITS as an archive that had long served the purposes of a tracing service to that of an archival repository for historical research, in particular for researchers and journalists anxious to delve into the records. Of course once researchers en-

---

[28] Ibid., 225.

countered the pitfalls of the OuS (Ossenberg und Schneider) software system used to classify the digitized documents primarily for name research their initial enthusiasm was somewhat dampened.

The core Inquiry (once called the Humanitarian Branch) and Tracing staff, with their lack of familiarity with other archives, typically thought of the documents in the ITS as a means to the end of answering survivor and family requests for information about victims or DPs. Yet once the ITS was open to the public, survivors and relatives of victims from across the world came personally to the ITS to see the relevant documents, and eventually once the ICRC no longer managed the ITS, to get copies of them and to meet with the staff to get (and to provide) more context to understand what the documents meant. This began to transform the significance of the documents for the Inquiry staff, at least those who met with or talked to or corresponded with inquirers. The documents and the archive as a whole started to constitute what child survivor and former International Criminal Court judge and ITS visitor Thomas Buergenthal called "sacred ground."[29] Once the Research and Education Department was created and the Archives Department was more fully developed a growing segment of the ITS staff came to think of the records in the archives as not just a means but an end in themselves. The Archives Department oriented itself to facilitating research by the public, whether scholars or journalists or pupils. Yet the ITS, and in particular its German government funders, still needed to be sure that the staff of what was once called the Humanitarian Branch and the ever-smaller Tracing Service Division with its ties to other Red Cross and Red Crescent and Magen David Adom tracing services across the world, would be able to find the documents they needed to focus on answering the 1,000 plus per month survivor and family inquiries about individuals (name searches).

Conclusion

So what are the implications of the changing practices of the ITS and its managers and staff, from using and considering ITS documents as a means to trace the fate and/or whereabouts of individuals persecuted and/or displaced by the crimes and aggression of the Nazi regime, on the one hand, to the growing understanding of these documents as an end in themselves by the *International Commission* for the ITS and its affiliated member state archives as well as by re-

---

29 Thomas Buergenthal used this terminology in his keynote address on the occasion of the ICRC departure ceremony on November 29, 2012 in Bad Arolsen.

cently hired academics on the ITS staff? I would argue that there is a danger of the ITS becoming seen as "just an archive," downplaying its relevance as both "sacred ground" for survivors, victims and their descendants, particularly as younger researchers and officials grow accustomed to conducting digital searches and never seeing or appreciating actual paper archives or valuing the documents in and of themselves, with their original signatures and handwritten details. Even the Federal Republic of Germany, the host country and *International Commission* member and the ITS's sole official funder, has not always understood the value of these "papers" in and of themselves, as evidenced by the manner in which they were long maintained and stored.

The misunderstanding that digitization of the documents could render unnecessary the preservation of the original documents has been countered by the growing role of archivists and historians both within the ITS and the *International Commission*, including of course the institutional partner, the *German Federal Archives*, and the ITS's affiliated member state archives. The reaction of *Betroffene*, such as Thomas Buergenthal, and their relatives when they come to Bad Arolsen to see the actual documents, not only pertaining to, but sometimes written or at least signed by, their loved ones has enhanced the value of the documents. This is of course evidenced by the entry of the ITS archive into UNESCO's Memory of the World and the official recognition by the IC and the German funding host, of the necessity of a climate-controlled archival facility for the records of the ITS. The *International Commission*, which in the last decade and a half has played such a key role in assuring that the ITS archives is appropriately preserved and maintained and made accessible to the public, will likely receive a much more prominent place in the history of the ITS, as should the ITS staff, who despite their administrative challenges and obstacles, have worked to fulfill the mission of the ITS, in all its changing dimensions.

Kerstin Hofmann
"It is our job to find out who did what."
The *Central Office* in Ludwigsburg and Cooperation with the ITS

Abstract: Nazi crimes have been subject to systematic investigation in the Federal Republic of Germany since 1958. The investigative authority responsible for this matter, the *Central Office of the Land Judicial Authorities for Investigation of National Socialist Crimes* (Zentrale Stelle der Landesjustizverwaltungen zur Aufklärung nationalsozialistischer Verbrechen), or *Central Office* for short, was dependent on cooperation with international archives and tracing services right from the very start. The *International Tracing Service* (ITS) was an important partner for the exchange of information and documentary evidence as well as for finding witnesses. After more than 20 years, the fruitful cooperation between the *Central Office* and the ITS ended at the beginning of the 1980s, when the ITS archive closed its doors to outsiders. Until it reopened in 2007, the Directorate of the ITS denied German law enforcement agencies access to the world's most comprehensive archive on Nazi persecution for reasons connected with data protection.

Establishment of a *Central Investigative Authority*

In the summer of 1958, the so-called *Ulm Einsatzgruppen* trial (*Ulmer Einsatzgruppenprozess*) drew the attention of both the public and the media to the fact that, in spite of the *Nuremberg trials*, a great many Nazi crimes still had not been investigated, nor had legal action been taken against the perpetrators – especially if the victims were of foreign nationality or if the crimes were committed on foreign soil.[1] The *Central Office of the Land Judicial Authorities for the Investigation of National Socialist Crime*s was established in order to put an end to this deplorable state of affairs. Systematic investigations have been carried out

---
[1] For an overview of how the Federal Republic of Germany first began to deal with Nazi crimes, see Jörg Osterloh and Clemens Vollnhals (eds.): *NS-Prozesse und deutsche Öffentlichkeit. Besatzungszeit, frühe Bundesrepublik und DDR*, Göttingen: Vandenhoeck & Ruprecht, 2011.

OpenAccess. © 2020 Kerstin Hofmann, published by De Gruyter. This work is licensed under the Creative Commons Attribution-NonCommercial-NoDerivatives 4.0 License.
https://doi.org/10.1515/9783110665376-015

into Nazi criminals in Ludwigsburg ever since December 1958.[2] Up until then, West German law enforcement agencies had only taken action, and even then only very reluctantly, if Nazi crimes had come to their knowledge by coincidence – in the 1950s, the media had already coined the phrase *Public Prosecutor Mr Coincidence* – or as a result of criminal charges being brought in isolated cases. Before the establishment of the *Central Office*, public prosecutors were not obliged to open a preliminary inquiry into a Nazi crime if it had been committed outside the territory of the Federal Republic of Germany and if its perpetrator was unknown or if his or her place of residence could not be determined.[3]

The Mission and the Work of the *Central Office*

In the administrative agreement of November 1958, the investigative mandate of the *Central Office* was clearly defined by the justice ministers and senators of the federal states: the mission of the authority was and still is to collect, inspect and evaluate all the material on Nazi crimes available both in Germany and abroad.[4] The main objective of the investigators is to identify complex offenses which can be defined in terms of a specific place, time and group of perpetrators as well as to determine which of the persons involved can still be prosecuted and to find out their whereabouts. When it first began carrying out investigations the jurisdiction of the *Central Office* was very limited. According to the administrative agreement, initially it was only responsible for all Nazi crimes committed against civilians outside the territory of the Federal Republic of Germany and extraneous to the act of war itself. This meant that crimes committed in concentration camps like Buchenwald or within the framework of the "euthanasia" campaign in Grafeneck were excluded from systematic investigation at first. In the 1950s, the prevailing opinion in West German society held that a *line should be drawn* under the Nazi past. A large part of the population blocked out their own complicity with or share in the responsibility and adhered to the mistaken belief that the

---

2 The paper is based on Kerstin Hofmann: *"Ein Versuch nur – immerhin ein Versuch": Die Zentrale Stelle in Ludwigsburg unter der Leitung von Erwin Schüle und Adalbert Rückerl (1958–1984)*, Berlin: Metropol, 2018.
3 Adalbert Rückerl: *NS-Verbrechen vor Gericht: Versuch einer Vergangenheitsbewältigung*, Heidelberg: C.W. Müller, 1982, 128.
4 Administrative agreement on the establishment of a *Central Office of the Land Judicial Authorities for the Investigation of National Socialist Crimes*, 6.11.1958. Available at: http://www.zentrale-stelle.de/pb/site/jum2/get/documents/jum1/JuM/Zentrale%20Stelle%20Ludwigsburg/Verwaltungsvereinbarung%20ZSt.pdf. Last accessed: 11.5.2019

crimes which had been committed in the name of National Socialism had been dealt with adequately once the *Nuremberg trials* had been held and the (main) culprits convicted.⁵ The strict limitations on its jurisdiction were not lifted until the imminent expiry of the statute of limitations for murder in the mid 1960s – which would also apply to Nazi crimes which had gone unpunished as yet.⁶ It was not until the end of 1964 that the investigative authority was also given jurisdiction over "crimes committed extraneously to the actual act of war on the territory of the Federal Republic during Nationalist Socialist rule by those in power during the Third Reich or by others acting on their behalf". Consequently, the *Central Office* was finally allowed to open pre-trial preliminary inquiries into crimes which had been carried out right on the doorstep of West German society in Dachau, Buchenwald or Ravensbrück. Nazi crimes which had been carried out by the supreme Reich authorities, such as the *Reich Security Main Office* (*Reichssicherheitshauptamt* [RSHA]), did not fall within the competence of the *Central Office* at the express request of the Federal German justice ministers and senators. These were subject to the jurisdiction of the Attorney General (*Generalstaatsanwalt*) at the *Berlin Court of Appeal* (*Kammergericht Berlin*), where pertinent preliminary inquiries were already pending.⁷ What was completely new was that the preliminary inquiries were not only opened on the basis of a complaint against a suspect, as was customary for public prosecution services. Pre-trial preliminary investigations could now be initiated as soon as information of any kind whatsoever was available to the investigators indicating that a crime may have taken place that had not yet been investigated or that a person who may have been involved in a crime had not yet been found. Starting points included, for example, the person of the accused, even if no clearly

---

5 Shortly after the subsequent *Nuremberg trials* had ended, calls for the criminal prosecution of Nazi perpetrators to come to an end could already be heard with increasing frequency in the Federal Republic of Germany. Influenced by the onset of the Cold War and plans to rearm West Germany as a "bulwark against Bolshevism", the Allies began to grant early release to large numbers of Nazi criminals they had previously convicted to prison sentences. By 1958, the Nazi criminals convicted in the *Nuremberg Einsatzgruppen trials* (Case IX), for example, had all been gradually released early "on parole" and the crimes they had committed were forgotten. Cf. Andreas Eichmüller: *Keine Generalamnestie. Die Strafverfolgung von NS-Verbrechen in der frühen Bundesrepublik*, Munich: Oldenbourg, 2012.
6 Not until 1979 did the German Parliament decide to lift the statute of limitations for murder, thus putting an end to the 20-year-long debate surrounding the issue of the time for prosecuting Nazi crimes. Since then, Germany subscribes to the principle that there is no statute of limitations for murder. Cf. Marc von Miquel: *Ahnden oder amnestieren? Westdeutsche Justiz und Vergangenheitspolitik in den sechziger Jahren*, Göttingen: Wallstein, 2004.
7 Administrative agreement of 6.11.1958.

defined suspicion existed as yet, a deed, an administrative district or a (concentration) camp, as well as evidence of crimes committed by an SS unit or duty station. The most important question to be answered in respect of all these criteria was whether or not proceedings dealing with the same subject matter were already pending before a West German court. If not, those cases which gave rise to the suspicion that a punishable offence which was still prosecutable had been committed were assigned the file reference "AR-Z". All other cases, such as petitions filed by private individuals, were assigned the file reference for the general register, "AR".

In the early years, the work of the investigators was based on the so-called snowball system, as newly initiated preliminary investigations often gave rise to evidence of further crimes. Despite the unique and heterogeneous nature of the investigations, a plan of work soon emerged.[8] The first step in any pre-trial preliminary investigation was always to consult the in-house archive: the *Central Index*, the collection of documents and other materials, and any parallel files which may have existed.[9] Once the subject matter of the proceedings had been clarified on the basis of the knowledge gleaned so far, it was important to begin to find out the whereabouts of the accused as quickly as possible and, if diplomatic relations with the Federal Republic of Germany existed, to submit requests for legal assistance to the various countries in which the Nazi perpetrators resided. By submitting inquiries to the *Federal Archives*, or more precisely to the *Military Archives* in Freiburg, the investigators found out which Wehrmacht units or duty stations had been stationed at the place where and at the time when the crime was committed. The next step was to check this information with the assistance of the *German Office for the Notification of Next of Kin of the Former German Wehrmacht* (*Deutsche Dienststelle für die Benachrichtigung der nächsten Angehörigen von Gefallenen der ehemaligen deutschen Wehrmacht* [WASt]).[10]

---

8 Einführung in die Arbeit der Zentralen Stelle [ca. 1969], B 162/20054, Federal Archives (German acronym: BArch).
9 In 2010 the *Federal Archives* assumed the task of taking on those documents of the *Central Office* that are no longer used for criminal prosecution as archival materials and of making them accessible to the interested public: Collection BArch B 162.
10 As of January 2019: Department of the *Federal Archives* for information on personal data related to world wars I and II (PA).

The Search for Nazi Perpetrators

In addition to administrative staff, the staff of the *Central Office* consisted of public prosecutors, judges and police officers seconded to Ludwigsburg, who, especially in the early years, had to obtain a thorough grounding in the subject of Nazi crimes, which was new to them at first.[11] In practice, as opposed to in theory, the search for potential Nazi criminals was beset by unusual obstacles at the pre-trial preliminary investigation stage. A considerable measure of creativity was required of the investigators who worked in Ludwigsburg, as they often had to deviate from their usual working methods when investigating the whereabouts of perpetrators and witnesses. One of the investigators, for example, sought a particularly brutal Nazi criminal who came from East Prussia. However, neither the *Central Index*, nor the dog tag directories contained any information about the accused under the name which was known to the investigator concerned. Not until he turned to a colleague who was born in East Prussia for advice and showed him the name of the man which had been transcribed phonetically from witness statements did he find out that the name of the person he was looking for was actually spelt completely differently in written German. Using the Germanized name, it was possible to identify the Nazi perpetrator. However, the pre-trial preliminary investigations had to be brought to a close without any result as the man had died six months previously.[12]

The public prosecutors and police detectives working in Ludwigsburg proceeded according to geographical and, in individual cases, factual aspects. Each of them was responsible for a department which was structured in accordance with the territorial borders in existence during the war, and had to acquire extensive specialist knowledge about the administrative and police personnel deployed in this area as well as about their lines of command. In order to keep track of all the proceedings and of all the documentary evidence which had been evaluated, the investigators developed the *Central Index*, which remains to this day their most important investigative tool. It is an index of names which is filed in three separate ways: it is kept as an alphabetical index, as an index of places and as an index of units or duty stations. All

---

11 Staff turnover was very high at the *Central Office* in the first decade of its existence, as many public prosecutors who had voluntarily agreed to their secondment had underestimated the extent and the cruelty of the Nazi crimes being investigated in Ludwigsburg and filed an application for transfer back to their home authority shortly after their arrival.
12 Interview conducted by the author with E. Frick, a former employee of the *Central Office*, 12.2.2013.

known information is noted on the index cards. In addition to the personal data – of suspects and witnesses alike – this information includes the rank, the unit concerned and the location. In order to facilitate the coordination of ongoing proceedings, the same procedure is used for file references, for references to information found in documents, and to information on interrogations and on the outcome of proceedings. Several cards were sometimes created for one and the same person. This occurred if, for example, different spellings were used, if only phonetic information was available, or even only cover names.

A special *index of proceedings* was set up in parallel to the *Central Index*. It served as the basis for overviews of proceedings which were compiled regularly and sent to public prosecution services and courts throughout Germany to provide an overview of the Nazi proceedings which were pending there. Another important investigative tool was the *collection of documents*. This collection contains reproductions of documents whose originals are stored in archives located in Germany and abroad. Special finding aids were created and made available to all staff in order to render the constantly growing collection of documents manageable. Charge sheets and judgements were also collected to enable staff to make quick comparisons without having to consult the relevant files. The *collection of expert opinions* served a similar purpose, especially those dealing with issues of contemporary history, issues of superior orders and problems connected with foreign law. The corpus, which was built up and maintained by the investigators themselves, was supplemented by evaluations of press releases, a collection of photographs of uniforms, and a collection of testimony and documents recording the extent and the horror of Nazi crimes.

As well as finding the accused themselves, the Ludwigsburg investigators also had to find potential witnesses. Thanks to *indexes of hometowns* and *information offices*, this was a relatively *simple* procedure for persons who lived in the Federal Republic of Germany. However, when it came to foreign witnesses, public prosecution services were dependent on support from the *World Jewish Congress*, (WJC) or – as described below – the *International Tracing Service* (ITS), for example.[13]

Although the *Central Office* investigated using the same methods as a public prosecution service, it did not have the same investigative powers and therefore had no authority to issue directives. In practice, this meant that the Ludwigsburg investigators were allowed to collect documentary evidence in foreign archives, but they were not allowed to conduct interrogations, question witnesses, make arrests or even to bring charges against anyone independently. Instead, they

---

13 Rückerl: *NS-Verbrechen*, 262–263.

had to rely on the cooperation of the competent public prosecution services and local criminal police departments. The final step was to forward the pre-trial preliminary investigation file to the local public prosecution service with jurisdiction over the place of residence or place of stay of the (main) perpetrator. The *Central Office* was not and is not competent to open proper preliminary inquiries or even to bring charges.[14]

The Laborious Search for Documentary Evidence

During the early years of the *Central Office* in particular, it was especially important to build up the in-house archive systematically. Gathering the evidence required for the investigations was associated with numerous difficulties, as it was usually in the possession of foreign archives. A large proportion of the relevant German files had been confiscated by the victorious Allied powers at the end of the war and taken out of the country. It was not until the end of the 1950s that the Western Allies began to return documentary evidence to the Federal Republic of Germany, with the exception of smaller holdings.[15] The first step was to strengthen the links with domestic institutions and archives that had existed since the *Ulm trial* and to establish contact with archives in other countries. The first head of the *Central Office*, Senior Public Prosecutor Erwin Schüle, was instrumental in this process. Before being appointed head of the *Central Office*, he had led the investigations of the Ulm public prosecution service into the *Einsatzkommando Tilsit* and had then represented the prosecution in the *Ulm Einsatzgruppen trial*. Not only did this make him very familiar with the subject matter, it also provided him with important contacts to archives and historians.[16]

Fact-finding trips to evaluate the holdings of international archives played a particularly important role. Not only did these trips enable the investigators to find important evidence, they also helped increase recognition of the *Central Office* and provided opportunities for networking. It was not without reason that Erwin Schüle ironically described himself as a "commis voyageur of justice", i.e. as a traveling salesman of justice.[17]

---

14 Ibid., 144–145.
15 Cf. Andreas Eichmüller: *Keine Generalamnestie. Die strafrechtliche Verfolgung von NS-Verbrechen in der frühen Bundesrepublik*, Munich: De Gruyter Oldenbourg, 2012, 369.
16 Schüle's Nazi past and the problematic way he dealt with it are described in detail in: Hofmann: *Zentrale Stelle*.
17 "Ohne Schelle im Wald", in *Der Spiegel*, 12.8.1959.

A visit to Washington in the summer of 1960 made a lasting impression on him. Together with two colleagues, he carried out research in the archival holdings of the *Federal Records Center*, the *National Archives* and the *Library of Congress*, all of which were largely unindexed. The investigators were so surprised by the amount of evidence they found there that in their interim report they described their "initial shock at the sheer abundance of material". During the very first days of their visit to the *National Archives*, they came across the files of the personal staff of *Reichsführer-SS* Heinrich Himmler, which were, however, in a terrible condition:

> It would be a massive understatement to use the term higgeldy-piggeldy to describe the state of these files. For example, the first sheet of paper might contain a request for information on the number of people with a "Grecian nose", while a second sheet has an instruction to some commander of the security police and the SD about security police measures which have been taken, and the third sheet contains a recipe, dated the end of 1944, mark you, for making Old Germanic mead for the 1944 Yuletide celebration![18]

As far as the public prosecutors were concerned, these chaotic documents brought the important personal and professional realization that the power of the SS had been far greater and more comprehensive than they had previously assumed:

> There was no sphere in which they had no influence, quite simply as a result of the fact that Himmler had managed to place his cronies in the individual ministries and authorities or had given prominent deputies an equivalent SS rank with the result that all these people provided "their Reichsführer" with reports on all the most confidential proceedings in the Foreign Office, etc.[19]

Among the documents they sifted through were the official reports sent to Berlin from Auschwitz, Bergen-Belsen, Krakow, and several hundred other places. The Ludwigsburg investigators came across the same names again and again in these documents, which made it clear to them that "hundreds of Hitler's worst murderers were still running free".[20] Given the abundance and the informational value of the material they found in the USA, they came to the conclusion that the archives located in the countries of the Eastern Bloc also needed urgent evaluation. Although Erwin Schüle, Head of the *Central Office*, suggested contact be made

---

18 Schüle to Haußmann 1.8.1960, EA 4/106 Bü 1, Central State Archives of Stuttgart.
19 Ibid.
20 Schüle as cited in: Frederic Sondern: "Das Gewissen Westdeutschlands", in *Das Beste aus Readers Digest* 10, 1962, 37–42, here 40.

with Poland in particular as soon as he returned, the judicial authorities of the federal states did not pass any such resolution.[21]

During the course of their almost two-month stay in Washington, the investigators had over 10,000 documents microfilmed for later detailed evaluation in Ludwigsburg. The documents they found in the American archives happened to include the official report of an SS man in which he reported that his submachine gun was unusable after he had had to fire over 800 single shots in an execution. It was only after subsequent investigations had been carried out in Ludwigsburg and after the man had been interrogated that it became apparent that this execution was, in fact, a previously unknown mass crime in Poland, which involved the murder of 18,000 people in just one day. After his arrest, the former SS man stated that he had supervised the shootings from a propeller-driven aircraft, as the execution field had been too large to be surveyed from the ground.[22]

The Head of the *Central Office* gave an extremely positive verdict on the fact-finding trip. Initial distrust of their plans and the criticism that the Federal Republic had left it too long before making efforts to investigate Nazi crimes and atone for them had soon been replaced by an easy working relationship.[23] However, the archival research did not always go quite so smoothly. Schüle's successor as Head of the *Central Office*, Senior Public Prosecutor Adalbert Rückerl, emphasized that bureaucracy was an important aspect of the trips made abroad by staff from the Ludwigsburg authority that should not be underestimated. "The difficulties in obtaining documents were supposedly of a technical nature, but in actual fact the difficulties were more of a bureaucratic kind".[24]

The bureaucratic hurdles often concealed political interests. At the end of their fact-finding trip in early September 1960, the investigators handed the German Embassy in Washington a package of six reels of microfilm containing images of selected and certified documents, the descriptions of the individual images, and correspondence with various West German public prosecution services. They asked the Embassy to send these materials to the *Central Office*

---

[21] Rückerl: *NS-Verbrechen*, 157. Only when the statute of limitations on the prosecution of murder, which was scheduled to take effect in 1965, entered the realm of public debate did the *Central Office* obtain authorization to undertake its first official fact-finding trip to Warsaw.
[22] "Auf der Suche nach den Hauptschuldigen", in *Frankfurter Allgemeine Zeitung*, 4.4.1961.
[23] Ibid.
[24] Adalbert Rückerl: "Die Zentrale Stelle der Landesjustizverwaltungen zur Aufklärung von NS-Verbrechen", in Evangelische Akademie Bad Boll (ed.): *Die Justiz und der Nationalsozialismus (II). Die Bundesrepublik Deutschland und die NS-Verbrechen. Tagung vom 20. bis 22. März 1981*, Bad Boll 1981, 35–50, here 39.

in Ludwigsburg by courier mail.[25] The packages that the investigators had sent from the USA by normal post arrived in Ludwigsburg at the beginning of October. However, there was still no sign of the documents which had been sent by courier mail and which were urgently needed for ongoing preliminary inquiries. In response to his repeated inquiries, Erwin Schüle was informed by the Federal Ministry of Justice on October 4, that the parcel had accidentally been left in Washington and was now being sent to Germany by normal mail, packed in a sea bag. Four weeks later, on November 2, when the parcel had still not arrived at the *Central Office*, Schüle asked the Stuttgart Ministry of Justice to inquire in Bonn about its whereabouts. He was then told that as of November 4, the Foreign Office in Bonn still had not received the microfilmed documents. Meanwhile, the Ludwigsburg investigators were receiving more and more inquiries from German public prosecution services and courts, who urgently needed the microfilmed and evaluated evidence for pending investigations.[26] On November 19, 1960, more than two months after Schüle had handed the parcel over to the German Embassy in Washington, the documents finally arrived in Ludwigsburg. The consignment, which was undamaged and still in its original packaging, was not accompanied by a letter from the Foreign Office, nor was there any indication of when it had been posted in Bonn. The only sign that it had been sent via Bonn was a strip of paper identifying the sender as the Forwarding Office of the Foreign Office in Bonn.[27]

Senior Public Prosecutor Heinz Artzt, who was responsible at the *Central Office* for investigating Nazi crimes committed in France, had similar experiences. In 1961 concrete information which had come to his knowledge led him to try to gain access to the private *Centre de Documentation Juive Contemporaine* (CDJC) in Paris and to the files of French military courts, as he suspected that important documentary evidence was held there. Politically, his efforts turned out to be highly explosive, despite the fact that he was only following the investigative mandate of the *Central Office*. This was because the Federal government under Konrad Adenauer was putting France under a great deal of pressure at the time to stop the trials which were pending against German Nazi criminals there and to release those Germans who had already been convicted. The Foreign Office went by way of the Ministry of Justice of Baden-Württemberg to inform the Ludwigsburg investigators that the German Embassy in Paris would for "under-

---

25 Telegram from the German Embassy (Washington D.C.), 3.10.1960, B 83/58, Political Archive of the Foreign Office, Berlin.
26 Schüle to the Ministry of Justice of Baden-Württemberg (JuM BW), 4.11.1960, B 83/58, Political Archive of the Foreign Office, Berlin.
27 Schüle to the JuM BW, 19.11.1960, B 83/58, Political Archive of the Foreign Office, Berlin.

standable reasons", appreciate it if they abandoned their plans to inspect the records held in France. The *Central Office* insisted on the need to evaluate the archival materials. In 1964 and 1965, two investigators were finally granted access to the documentary evidence held by the *Center of Contemporary Jewish Documentation* and were allowed to evaluate a large number of court files for the purposes of their investigations.[28]

Notwithstanding these "bureaucratic" obstacles encountered in connection with the evaluation of Western Archives, the greatest problems lay in procuring documents from the countries of the Eastern Bloc, especially the GDR. As Nazi crimes were classified as political crimes in the GDR, Interpol also refused to cooperate with the *Central Office* and invoked its statutes when it declared that it had no mandate to deal with them.[29]

Cooperation between Ludwigsburg and Arolsen

As well as establishing contact with archives all over the world, it was also important to develop links with institutions and archives within the Federal Republic of Germany. In the first six months which followed the establishment of the *Central Office*, Erwin Schüle traveled extensively within Germany. The *Institute for Contemporary History* in Munich, the *State Archive Depot* (*Staatliches Archivlager*) in Göttingen, the *Wehrmacht Information Office for War Losses and POW's*, and the US-American administrated *Berlin Document Center* (BDC) were among the organizations visited by the investigators. Schüle presented the activities of the *Central Office* in an effort to promote future cooperation. The *Document Center* in particular was very important in the early 1960s as it held the personnel files of SS officers, the personnel files kept by the *SS Race and Settlement Main Office* (*Rasse- und Siedlungshauptamt der SS* [RuSHA]), the full central index of members of the NSDAP, and documents containing personal data which came from a large number of other authorities. Despite the reservations which the USA still had in respect of the German population, the Ludwigsburg public prosecutors were given unrestricted access to the documentary evidence held by the BDC. However, much to the investigators' regret, the majority of the

---

28 Cf. Bernhard Brunner: *Der Frankreich-Komplex: Die nationalsozialistischen Verbrechen in Frankreich und die Justiz der Bundesrepublik Deutschland*, Göttingen: Wallstein, 2004.
29 Willi Dreßen: "Im Dienst der Gerechtigkeit. 30 Jahre Zentrale Stelle der Landesjustizverwaltungen zur Aufklärung von NS-Verbrechen in Ludwigsburg", in *Freiheit und Recht*, 34, 1988, 7–10, here 9.

files there were unsorted and had not been described in accordance with archival standards.[30]

The *Central Office* and the ITS first came into direct contact in the spring of 1959. On April 13, 1959, Senior Public Prosecutor Schüle approached the ITS in order to introduce himself and his authority and discuss the potential for cooperation. The Director of the ITS, Nicolas Burckhardt, replied immediately, thus laying the foundation for the fruitful cooperation between the two institutions – even though the content of the first letter from Arolsen was extremely sobering:

> The International Tracing Service has records of prisoners from the concentration camps. It does not have any documents on SS camp personnel. [...] The International Tracing Service does not deal with the prosecution of crimes committed by former concentration camp personnel and has no records relating to this matter.[31]

Although the *Central Office* and the ITS had a completely different perspective on the mass crimes of the National Socialists, what they had in common was the search for documentary evidence and documentation of the crimes which had been committed. Contact between Ludwigsburg and Arolsen soon intensified as both parties profited from working together. The *Central Office*, which was still in the process of being set up, received important information for their investigations from the ITS – especially in connection with concentration camps. For its part, the Tracing Service benefited from the many trips made by the Ludwigsburg investigators to archives in foreign countries. The *Central Office* sent finding aids to Arolsen on a regular basis and informed Arolsen when new documents came to light. The first personal contact between the two institutions took place at the end of June 1959, when a Ludwigsburg investigator traveled to Arolsen specially to talk to Albert de Cocatrix, the Deputy Director of the ITS, about the interfaces of their joint work.[32]

Exchange of Documents and Information

The first copies of documents from Ludwigsburg to reach the ITS arrived at the end of July 1961. Prior to this the Ludwigsburg investigators had discovered the death book of the Natzweiler II registry office for 1943 while evaluating the docu-

---

30 Interview conducted by the author with E. Frick on 12.2.2013.
31 Cf. ITS to *Central Office*, 20.4.1959, GA III-14/1, Central Office, Ludwigsburg.
32 Memorandum on the official visit to Arolsen and Göttingen on 29.6.1959, 8.7.1959, GA III-14/3, Central Office, Ludwigsburg.

ments that had been microfilmed in the summer of 1960 during a visit to the *World War II Records Division* in Alexandria, USA.[33] Schüle's subsequent offer to send prints of the microfilm in question to Arolsen was gratefully accepted by Nicolas Burckhardt as a "valuable addition" to the archive's existing holdings.[34] In addition to the documents from the Natzweiler concentration camp, the film rolls also contained other microfilmed material which was of great interest to the ITS, such as reports on various ghettos, deportations of the Jewish population and medical experiments performed on human subjects. However, unlike the death book, these documents were classified. In order to circumvent the promise given to the US government that the documents would only be used for purposes connected with the German justice system, the Head of the *Central Office* made the following suggestion to the ITS:

> The original number of each document is included in the document description which is available to you. So, if you compile a list of the documents you would like and send this list to the Department of State – Historical Division – in Washington, stating the reasons why you require them, I am convinced that they will also make microfilm copies of these documents available to you.[35]

It was no accident that the *Central Office* was so helpful. Close cooperation with the ITS was important for the investigative authority as the ITS had access to archives and institutions which were closed to the *Central Office* in its function as a judicial body of the Federal Republic of Germany. Polish archives belonged to this category, to mention but one example. So it was that in the mid-1970s, the then Deputy Director of the Ludwigsburg investigative authority, Senior Public Prosecutor Heinz Artzt, traveled specially to Arolsen to clarify "how the documents sent to the ITS by the (Polish Main Commission[36]) could be used without embarrassing the ITS in front of Poland".[37] Albert de Cocatrix had no qualms about sharing the documents received from Warsaw with law enforcement agencies and consequently with the *Central Office* too. He did this despite the fact

---

33 Death register of the registry office Natzweiler II, 1943, 1.1.29.1/3139791/ITS Digital Archive, Arolsen Archives.
34 *Central Office* to ITS, 15.6.1961, and ITS to *Central Office*, 16.6.1961, GA III-14/4, Central Office, Ludwigsburg.
35 *Central Office* to ITS, 26.6.1961, GA III-14/6, *Central Office*, Ludwigsburg. Cf. also *Central Office* to ITS, 27.07.1961, ibid.
36 *Główna Komisja Ścigania Zbrodni przeciwko Narodowi Polskiemu*, today: *Instytut Pamięci Narodowej* (IPN). For a description of the conflict-ridden working relationship of the *Central Office* and the *Polish Main Commission*, see Hofmann: *Zentrale Stelle*, 186–222.
37 Memorandum of 24.7.1975, GA III-14/72, Central Office, Ludwigsburg.

that the Polish Main Commission had previously asked him not to share the material with the *Federal Archives* in Koblenz under any circumstances. All Cocatrix asked was that the documents provided by the ITS not be listed in the finding aids which were sent out from Ludwigsburg to West German public prosecution services on a regular basis.[38]

Senior Public Prosecutor Artzt used his visit to Arolsen to address another topic that was of great concern to his authority: finding witnesses and survivors of the crimes committed by the Nazis. Many of the witnesses needed for investigations into concentration camp crimes also lived behind the *Iron Curtain*. During the early years in particular, the *Central Office* was dependent on the cooperation of victims' associations for help in this respect. Not only did they provide the investigative authority with the addresses of the witnesses it needed in Germany and abroad, they also established contact with witnesses living in the countries of the Eastern Bloc.[39] As the central point of contact and main information office for survivors of the Nazi dictatorship and their relatives, the ITS also had important contacts to potential witnesses.[40] In addition to the documents related to specific persons, which could be accessed through the *Central Name Index* (CNI), the Tracing Service also had countless volumes of place and address books that could be used to identify even the tiniest of Polish, Russian and Czech hamlets. Albert de Cocatrix was happy to share this information with the *Central Office*. He also promised to help the Ludwigsburg investigators find out the correct spellings of Polish, Russian and Czech names and implement a phonetic search modeled on the CNI.[41]

Despite the fruitful exchange of documents between Ludwigsburg and Arolsen, the cooperation between the *Central Office* and the *International Tracing Service* was also marked by numerous conflicts. For example, in the 1960s, ITS employees were strictly prohibited from appearing as witnesses in court. The Directorate in Arolsen adopted the position of the *International Committee of the Red Cross* (ICRC), which held that it was not the job of the Tracing Service to assist in the investigation of Nazi crimes. If ITS staff were still invited sum-

---

[38] Memorandum of 13.8.1975 on the visit to the ITS in Arolsen on 4./5.8.1975, GA III-14/80, Central Office, Ludwigsburg.
[39] Report on the activities of the Central Office in the period between 1.12.1958 and 1.6.1959 (as of 1.5.1959), 14.5.1959, EA 4/106 Bü 4, Central State Archives of Stuttgart.
[40] See for example sub-collection 11.15 Strafverfolgung, file 1978–2007 569: Staatsanwaltschaften, ITS Archives, Arolsen Archives.
[41] Memorandum of 13.8.1975 on the visit to the ITS in Arolsen on 4./5.8.1975, GA III-14/80, Central Office, Ludwigsburg. Cf. also ITS to *Central Office*, 18.9.1969, GA III-14/46, Central Office, Ludwigsburg.

moned to appear in court as witnesses, they had to refuse to testify. There was just one exception to the rule: if the interrogation was conducted by a delegated or requested judge in Arolsen and was thus not dealt with in a public hearing. Furthermore, the Directorate ordered that original documents kept in Arolsen could only be used as documentary evidence in Nazi trials if a police officer traveled to Arolsen with the copies which were relevant to the proceedings in question in order to verify the authenticity of the said copies on the premises before giving evidence as a witness in court.[42]

The End of the Fruitful Cooperation

At the beginning of the 1980s, the close relationship between the ITS and the *Central Office* finally came to an end. Despite the existence of certain points of friction, the cooperation had been very valuable to both institutions for many years. It was easy for public prosecutors and investigators from Ludwigsburg, or from anywhere else in the Federal Republic of Germany for that matter, to view or evaluate documents at the ITS or even have copies of documents sent to their own offices. ITS employees, on the other hand, spent periods of several weeks at the *Central Office* on a number of occasions in order to evaluate files which were important for the compilation of the list of imprisonment sites.[43]

The breakdown in the relationship coincided with a momentous change at the helm of the ITS: Philipp Züger took over as the new Director and Charles Biedermann was appointed his Deputy.[44] In November 1981, Adalbert Rückerl, who succeeded Erwin Schüle as Head of the *Central Office* in 1966, described the new situation as follows in a report to the supervising authority of the *Central Office*, the Baden-Württemberg Ministry of Justice:

> I have been approached by a number of people recently who have drawn my attention to the fact that the evaluation of documents held by the ITS has become increasingly problem-

---

[42] Report of the Justice Ministry of North Rhine-Westphalia, 11.09.1963, GA III-14/13, Central Office, Ludwigsburg.
[43] Register Of Places Of Detention Under The Reichsführer-SS 1933–1945, Arolsen, 1979. Cf. ITS letter books; also *Central Office* to JuM BW, 26.11.1981, GA III-14/101, Central Office, Ludwigsburg.
[44] Cf. Henning Borggräfe, Hanne Leßau: "Die Wahrnehmung der NS-Verbrechen und der Umgang mit den NS-Verfolgten im International Tracing Service", in Henning Borggräfe, Hanne Leßau, Harald Schmid (eds.): *Fundstücke: Die Wahrnehmung der NS-Verbrechen und ihrer Opfer im Wandel*, Göttingen: Wallstein, 2015, 23–44.

atic since the retirement of the long-standing and very cooperative Director of the ITS, Dr. Cocatrix, who has been replaced by Dr. Züger.[45]

The background to this report to the Stuttgart Ministry was a memorandum from the Frankenthal Public Prosecution Service (Rhineland-Palatinate) to the *Central Office*, which stated that a request for assistance addressed to the ITS by the Public Prosecution Service had been refused – the Prosecution Service had asked for permission to evaluate transport lists from the Auschwitz concentration camp for criminal prosecution purposes. The Directorate of the ITS had gone on to explain that the ITS would only process requests submitted to the Tracing Service via the Federal Ministry of the Interior. Public prosecutors and investigators involved in pertinent Nazi investigations were no longer permitted to evaluate documentary evidence from the ITS archive or even to make copies of documents. Rückerl, who was concerned about access to important evidence for ongoing and future investigations – a serious obstacle to investigative work – asked the Ministry of Justice to examine ways in which an agreement could be reached with the management of the ITS to ensure effective and, if necessary, rapid use of the documents held there for the purposes of criminal prosecution work.[46] However, this request was unsuccessful. What is more, Züger, the then Director of the ITS, confirmed his hostile stance in a communication to the Ministry of Justice of North Rhine-Westphalia:

> The International Tracing Service has received a mandate from the Allied governments, including the Federal Republic of Germany, to provide former victims of Nazi persecution and their legal successors with information from their documents for humanitarian purposes. As a Red Cross organization, the International Tracing Service does not have a mandate to provide evidence to be used against war criminals.[47]

---

[45] *Central Office* to JuM BW, 26.11.1981, GA III-14/101, Central Office, Ludwigsburg.

[46] *Central Office* to JuM BW, 26.11.1981, GA III-14/101, Central Office, Ludwigsburg. Director Züger had previously allowed the Frankenthal public prosecution service to view a transport list from the Dachau concentration camp. However, he had only granted this exemption because the legal provisions had not been completely clear at the time and "the whole thing was in a state of upheaval".

[47] Justice Ministry of North Rhine-Westphalia to Federal Ministry of the Interior, 25.7.1980, GA III-14/14–18, Central Office, Ludwigsburg. The *Central Office* only conducts investigations into Nazi crimes, war crimes are explicitly excluded from its remit. For information on differentiating between war crimes and Nazi crimes, see: Heinz Artzt: "Zur Abgrenzung von Kriegsverbrechen und NS-Verbrechen", in Adalbert Rückerl (ed.): *NS-Prozesse. Nach 25 Jahren Strafverfolgung: Möglichkeiten, Grenzen, Ergebnisse*, Karlsruhe: C. W. Müller, 1971, 163–194.

An increase in the workload due to inquiries from Federal German judicial authorities cannot have been the reason for the hostile stance of the ITS. The so-called *Multi-Year Plan* drawn up by the ITS for 1981 contains the following information on this subject:

> The inquiries received from investigative authorities, primarily public prosecution services or state offices of criminal investigation, pertaining to inmates of concentration camps or their "Kommandos" have also contributed to a reduction in the workload. It was usually sufficient to check with the Central Name Index department in order to identify the place of detention or find out the current address of the persons concerned. [...] The number of inquiries from investigative authorities began to drop in 1976.[48]

Züger placed more emphasis on the strict data protection regulations which the ITS had to comply with in connection with the acquisition of new documents. He explained that health insurance companies, local authorities, public archives and, above all, businesses would refuse to provide the ITS with information unless the latter could produce express authorization from the person concerned. For reasons connected with data protection, the evaluation of documents from concentration camps would, therefore, no longer be allowed. As far as the Directorate was concerned, data protection and the commitment to neutrality were more important than the prosecution of Nazi crimes.[49] This stance is completely at odds with the preface to the ITS Annual report for 1981. Philipp Züger used the following words:

> The International Tracing Service possesses a part of this [National Socialist; note from the author] documentary material. Closely packed, sheet for sheet, this inventory of slavery measures 6 kilometers in length and bears testimony to the boundless depravity of those who ordered such things. Most of the authors of these documents have sunk, nameless, into eternal oblivion. [...] In memory of [the] victims of persecution, coming generations will return again and again to these documents which will forever remain a shameful stain on our culture – but which have been purified by the names of the victims which appear on them.[50]

In its 1981 strategy plan, the *International Tracing Service* makes the following boastful claim: "The tiniest of clues found by the International Tracing Service

---

48 The tasks of the International Tracing Service: targets for the individual working areas 1.7. 1981–31.12.1985, Multi-Year Plan, 6. In 1960, 33,973 inquiries had been received from judicial authorities, in 1980 this number had dropped to 1,970.
49 Cf. Sub-collection 11.5 data protection, file 1978–2007, 465: Auskunft, Amtshilfe, Prinzip, ITS Archives, Arolsen Archives.
50 Preface to the 1981 Activity Report of the ITS.

in its documents can provide help today to the people persecuted by the Nazi regime."[51]

Data protection – or rather the protection of Nazi perpetrators from West German law enforcement agencies – put a stop to the cooperation between the *Central Office of the Land Judicial Authorities for the Investigation of National Socialist Crimes* and the *International Tracing Service* after over 20 years, at the end of 1981. In 1993 – after years of complete silence – the investigators in Ludwigsburg were surprised by post from Bad Arolsen: the *International Tracing Service* sent them a letter thanking them for the good working relationship which had been non-existent for over ten years. Cooperation between Ludwigsburg and Arolsen did not resume until 2007, when it was rekindled as a result of the radical transformation and the reopening of the ITS. It continues to this day.

---

[51] The tasks of the International Tracing Service: targets for the individual working areas 1.7.1981–31.12.1985, Multi-Year Plan, 3.

Tobias Herrmann
The *Federal Archives* and its Role in German Politics of Remembrance

Abstract: Historical remembrance in Germany after the Second World War has had its own traditions and developments. The focus has mainly been on the time of the Nazi terror regime, and – to a lesser extent – the SED dictatorship of the GDR. Archives, particularly the *Federal Archives* as an institution at the national level, continue to play an important role in the context of this remembrance. In this chapter, following a short contextualization with regard to the political framework of remembrance, the different "activities" of the *Federal Archives* in terms of dealing with the Nazi past are presented, as are the experiences gained throughout this process. In doing so, it is important to differ between activities resulting from the legal obligations of the *Federal Archives* on the one hand, and those that, strictly speaking, would not have necessarily had to be taken up by the *Federal Archives* on the other hand. Finally, the self-image of the *Federal Archives* as an active part of current politics of remembrance will be discussed.

Introduction

In Germany today, historical remembrance primarily focuses on the critical examination of the two dictatorships which took place during the twentieth century, especially in relation to the unprecedented scale of the crimes perpetrated by the Nazi dictatorship from 1933 to 1945, and the SED dictatorship from 1949 to 1989. The *Federal Archives* also plays an important role in processing the history of the GDR; however, this essay follows the theme of *Tracing and Documenting Nazi Victims* and aims to focus on the commemoration of the period of National Socialist tyranny, and considers the *Federal Archive's* contribution to this undeniably political task. The focus will be principally, though not exclusively, directed towards the "victims."

Politics of Remembrance in the Federal Republic of Germany: The Historical Context

The early years of remembrance and analysis in the Federal Republic of Germany are distinguished by the almost complete absence of archival sources. The majority of the documents held in the Reich ministries and archives that had not already been destroyed were confiscated by the Allied Powers and taken to each of these countries. During its first years of existence from 1952, the *Federal Archives* was effectively an archive without records. It was only from the mid-1950s that the records, which were primarily held in the USA and the United Kingdom, were handed back to the *Federal Archives*. Academic work on these records was expected to be explicitly encouraged, which is why official records and *documentation* dating back to before May 23, 1945 – as long as they were not of a personal nature – were specifically excluded from the 30-year rule that was otherwise applicable.

Documents that were taken to Moscow – apart from the large volumes of archival material from a wide range of sources to which Russia now believes it has unalienable rights, defines as *trophies* and does not intend to hand back – were returned to the GDR and ended up in three different archives (the *Central State Archives*, the archives at the *Institute for Marxism-Leninism* and the archives at the *Ministry for State Security*). These archives were not readily accessible, if accessible at all.[1]

It is only possible and necessary to provide a brief summary here of how research into the Third Reich evolved in the West. In the early years, which were marked by a society-wide *Konsens des Verschweigens* (concealment by consensus), the prime focus was on the structures of the Nazi state and those of the SS concentration camp system. The research did not focus on people (except for the main perpetrators Hitler, Himmler, Göring, Goebbels, etc.) or on everyday life. After the television series *Holocaust* was aired at the end of the 1970s, interest in critically examining the mass murder of European Jews started to extend beyond specialist historical research.

A huge surge in research into National Socialism coincided with German reunification which brought the German archives and any archive holdings related to the National Socialist era all under one roof at the *Federal Archives*. Notably,

---

[1] See, for example, Heinz Boberach: "Die schriftliche Überlieferung der Behörden des Deutschen Reiches 1871–1945. Sicherung, Rückführung, Ersatzdokumentation", in Heinz Boberach and Hans Booms (eds.): *Aus der Arbeit des Bundesarchivs*, Boppard: Harald Boldt, 1977, 50–61.

the transfer of documents from the former *Berlin Document Center* into the *Federal Archives* helped to focus the spotlight on the personal aspects – with respect to the "perpetrators" in this case – which was now no longer the sole province of academic research. Documents relating to the period between 1933 and 1945 are the most commonly requested items in the *Federal Archives* to date. In the last few decades, the numerous memorials surrounding the Nazi era which have emerged, the many notable television documentaries, and recently the historical commissions that have investigated Nazi continuities and the presence of officials in post-war government departments who were tainted by their association with the Nazi regime, have all depended on the efficient work carried out by the Archives' employees.

Activities Related to the Politics of Remembrance Carried Out by the *Federal Archives* (1) on the Basis of Statutory Responsibility

The *Federal Archives* plays a very important role in commemorating the Third Reich purely on account of its awareness of its statutory responsibilities:

> The remit of the Federal Archives is to safeguard the Federal Government's archival materials in perpetuity, to make good use of them and utilize them in a scholarly way. It guarantees access to the Federal Government's archival materials whilst respecting the need to protect private or public interests.

This is how the *Federal Archives*' core function is described in § 3, para. 1 of the *Federal Archive Act* (*Bundesarchivgesetz*) dated March 10, 2017. Documents relating to the legal predecessors of the Federal Government are also naturally part of the "Federal Government's archival materials", which include, for example, documents relating to central civilian and military agencies which operated during the Third Reich until May 1945, and the NSDAP, its subdivisions and affiliated associations. The term *documentation* encompasses much more than just files and index cards.

The staff who have worked at the *Federal Archives* over the past decades have very efficiently performed the task of making good use of the documentation by opening up access to the archival materials and providing advice to users. The question of whether a regular preliminary appraisal should take place before cataloguing does not usually arise for records from the period between 1933 and 1945. In view of the fact that there are a large number of gaps in the archival legacy and due to the specific nature of this period of German history, the archivists follow an unwritten rule that a cassation will only happen in very rare cases which must be thoroughly justified.

Even just listing the most important archival holdings from the National Socialist period, which are often used thousands of times, would firstly make very dry reading and secondly take up too much space at this point.[2] I would therefore like to briefly highlight the final clause of § 3 of the aforementioned *Federal Archive Act:* "This [guaranteeing access to the archival material] can also be provided through digitization and making the information accessible to the public via the internet."

Due to the fact there are now around 415 kilometers of documents – of which around 100 kilometers are from the period up to 1945 – the *Federal Archives* is under pressure to set priorities for digitization over the foreseeable future. The digitization of the NSDAP membership registry was considered to be a particularly high priority: the project has now been completed. This registry by definition focuses on people. It is not yet possible to provide open access to it via the internet and it does provide more information on the "perpetrators" than on the "victims" of the regime if users decide to use any of these terms. However, digitizing this register plays a key role in safeguarding the archival holdings over the long term as it is now no longer necessary to use the fragile index cards in their original format. In addition, processing personal enquiries using the digital research methods that are now possible significantly expedites processing times, which is expected to free up resources for other fields of work. It will also mean that the protection period for personal data, which has so far prevented the entire register from being available online, will essentially have expired in around ten years.

Among the documents selected for digitization, which will be available for anyone to access and use via the internet, are the record groups *NS 8 Rosenberg Chancellery (Kanzlei Rosenberg)*[3] and *NS 30 Reichsleiter Rosenberg Taskforce (Einsatzstab Reichsleiter Rosenberg)*[4] which are of central importance for provenance research, and specifically for the reconstruction of property and the expropriation of art and cultural assets. Particularly illuminating records are also expected

---

[2] For further details, see the summary of the EHRI online course entitled "Modern Diplomatics of the Holocaust": https://training.ehri-project.eu/holocaustrelevante-best%C3%A4nde-des-bundesarchivs. Last accessed: 28.6.2019.

[3] See Invenio: https://invenio.bundesarchiv.de/basys2-invenio/direktlink/47f30320-f947-4edd-8049-f3fb8b010675/. Last accessed: 28.6.2019.

[4] See Invenio: https://invenio.bundesarchiv.de/basys2-invenio/direktlink/7ac6d63f-7cf5-40b2-a375-dd93c010a349/. Last accessed: 28.6.2019.

to be accessible soon online in their entirety from the *post-war record group* (*Nachkriegsbestand*) B 323 *Trusteeship of Cultural Assets at the Munich Regional Finance Office* (*Treuhandverwaltung von Kulturgut bei der Oberfinanzdirektion München*).

Activities Related to the Politics of Remembrance Carried Out by the *Federal Archives* (2) which Transcend Statutory Responsibility

In addition to these obvious activities, a range of other services have become available over the decades for a variety of reasons and have each been conceived in different ways. The *Federal Archives* did not necessarily have to make them available, however, they have undeniably strengthened the role this organisation has played in German politics of remembrance. In many cases, current outcomes have been underpinned by very close partnerships with other institutions. The *Federal Archives* has to some extent been appointed to deal with the administration of the end product. At the beginning of a project, the amount of work that would actually be involved in maintaining or developing the results was not always properly assessed and staffing levels do not always appear to be sufficient. I believe that the key point to consider is that many of these services have proven to be effective, are well-recognized and strongly support many other key players in the field of remembrance.

These services, operations or activities have been divided into three areas in this essay and can only be outlined in the broadest terms. A key component of the politics of remembrance in the Federal Republic of Germany is without doubt the *German Memorial Book for the Victims of the Holocaust who originated from Germany*.[5] The original impetus for this project stemmed from *Yad Vashem* during the 1960s. The first edition of the printed version was produced in close partnership with the *International Tracing Service* (ITS). When it was published in 1986, it included the names of approximately 128,000 Jewish victims who once lived within the territory which was then designated as the former Federal Republic of Germany and West Berlin. Reunification then presented the project with a completely different basis for this work: The second edition of the *Memo-*

---

5 See Hans-Dieter Kreikamp: "Erinnerungen an den Holocaust – Der Beitrag des Bundesarchivs zur historischen und politischen Aufarbeitung", in Angelika Menne-Haritz and Rainer Hofmann (eds.): *Archive im Kontext. Festschrift für Hartmut Weber zum 65. Geburtstag*, Düsseldorf: Droste, 2010, 67–76.

rial Book published in 2006 subsequently listed the names of 150,000 victims from the territory of the German Reich following the national borders which were drawn up in 1937. There were then no further plans to produce another printed edition and an online version was created instead which has significantly widened the circle of users and has facilitated dialogue about entries which may be potentially incorrect.[6] The online *Memorial Book* currently holds over 170,000 names – unfortunately, this number sometimes causes confusion and is misused by revisionists. The *Federal Archives* clearly lays out its position in the introduction to the online *Memorial Book*.

On a technical level, the *Memorial Book* is also closely linked to the list of Jewish people living in the German Reich from 1933 to 1945, which is known as the *List of Residents*. Due to the ad hoc nature of the collection of data records which were created up to 2003 as part of the process of identifying potential beneficiaries of insurance claims which have not yet been paid out, the project group at the *Federal Archives* worked in partnership with the *Foundation "Remembrance, Responsibility and Future"* (German acronym EVZ) from 2005 to 2007 to compile an academically well-substantiated list which, in addition to those who died, includes emigrants, survivors and people whose fates are uncertain.[7] The databases containing the *List of Residents* and the *Memorial Book* were consolidated in 2006 and this database is now being managed at the *Federal Archives* on an ongoing basis. This involves consolidating the data records and removing duplicates, incorporating feedback, evaluating literature and researching new sources. Unlike the *Memorial Book*, the *List of Residents* cannot be published on the internet for data protection reasons, however, it is issued to selected institutions in Germany and abroad on a regular basis after it is updated. We assume that between 1933 and 1945 there were approximately 650,000 Jewish inhabitants in the German Reich according to the borders that were drawn up in 1937.[8] A complex project is currently being carried out to bring the databases in line with the latest technical standards. Some political leaders are under the misapprehension that databases are somehow "complete" and "cost neutral" after the content has been pulled together. However, the opposite turns out to be

---

6 *The Memorial Book of the Federal Archives for the Victims of the Persecution of Jews in Germany (1933–1945)*, see: http://www.bundesarchiv.de/gedenkbuch/. Last accessed: 28.6.2019.

7 See Nicolai M. Zimmermann: "The List of Jewish Residents in the German Reich 1933–1945". Available at: http://www.bundesarchiv.de/EN/Content/Publikationen/essay-zimmermann-list-of-jewish-residents.html. Last accessed: 28.6.2019.

8 Nicolai M. Zimmermann: "Was geschah mit den Juden in Deutschland zwischen 1933 und 1945? Eine Dokumentation des Bundesarchivs", in *Zeitschrift für Geschichtswissenschaft*, 64, 2016, 1045–1058.

true – human and financial resources need to be regularly invested to ensure that the databases can be used easily and conveniently over the long term. In addition to their core responsibilities, the permanent archive staff have to continually maintain the databases and ensure the information is readily available because the original project staff – often historians without any specialist training in archive management – are usually only employed on a temporary basis.

The online information portal *Forced Labor in the National Socialist State*[9], which is available in German, English and Russian, is based on a list that was compiled to determine compensation payments in the late 1990s. The *Federal Archives* has been responsible for developing the portal since 2007 which is also funded by the *Foundation "Remembrance, Responsibility and Future"* (EVZ). It contains a great deal more information than just names and is interactive to a certain extent because other institutions can contribute additional data once they have registered via an online maintenance module. A key element of the portal is the *Directory of Detention Facilities* which offers a range of options for specialist research. Information concerning relevant archive holdings, compensation and reparation efforts, interviews with former forced laborers and workers, an online bibliography, basic historical information on the subject and virtual document generation are also available.

The *Inventory of Sources on the History of Euthanasia Crimes between 1939– 1945 (Inventar der Quellen zur Geschichte der Euthanasie-Verbrechen 1939–1945)* was *frozen* at the point it was last updated in 2003[10]; the latest published list of names of the victims of Nazi *Euthanasia*, whose medical records are available at the *Federal Archives*, are discussed briefly at the end of this essay. At this point, it is important to at least mention the educational archival materials that are on offer at the branch office of the *Federal Archives* in Ludwigsburg. This is where since 2000 the *Federal Archives* has provided access to information curated by the still active *Central Office of the Land Judicial Authorities for Investigation of National Socialist Crimes (Zentrale Stelle zur Aufklärung nationalsozialistischer Verbrechen)*.

Thanks to a long and successful partnership with the Baden-Württemberg Ministry of Education and Cultural Affairs, it has been possible to put on weekly events for local school students which extend well beyond conventional archive work in terms of content and timeframes. Various modules are used to help the students learn to work with archival sources, to appreciate the standpoints of both "perpetrators" and "victims" more fully and ideally to understand how

---

9 Available at: http://www.bundesarchiv.de/zwangsarbeit/. Last accessed: 28.6.2019.
10 Available at: http://www.bundesarchiv.de/geschichte_euthanasie/. Last accessed: 28.6.2019.

mass crimes perpetrated by the National Socialists happened and how similar attempts might be resisted. The documents held at the *Central Office* enable two key questions to be considered at the same time: How did the terror regime operate? And, how have National Socialist crimes been legally processed in the Federal Republic of Germany, especially under a legal framework that was scarcely capable of taking punitive action against crimes of this magnitude? This demonstrates how the *Federal Archives* and its partners are playing an important role in the politics of remembrance in a different kind of way beyond merely providing archive materials and online services, yet this type of education on historical themes appears to a lesser extent to have become more obsolete and redundant than ever before.

In addition to the *Federal Archives*' core responsibilities as defined by the *Federal Archive Act* that have been previously mentioned, academic research is also an important activity, which – some may say regrettably – only a few colleagues are actually able to perform. There are a few editorial groups at the *Federal Archives* who are responsible for editing Federal Government cabinet meeting transcripts and documents relating to German domestic policy; however, the *Federal Archives* also plays a role in editing sources concerning the history of the Third Reich. In the case of the publication entitled *The Reich Chancellery's Files* (*Akten der Reichskanzlei*) – a project undertaken in partnership with the *Historical Commission at the Bavarian Academy of Sciences and Humanities* – additional staff were employed in order to finish the outstanding volumes dedicated to Hitler's government as quickly as possible. During work on the project entitled *Persecution and Murder of the European Jews by Nazi Germany 1933–1945* (*Die Verfolgung und Ermordung der europäischen Juden durch das nationalsozialistische Deutschland 1933–1945* [VEJ]), representatives from the *Federal Archives* were on the editorial board and helped the editorial staff at each organization to research and evaluate sources.

I would like to highlight at this point collaborative work that was carried out during projects such as the *European Holocaust Research Infrastructure* (EHRI),[11] which includes the involvement of both the *Federal Archives* and the *Arolsen Archives* during the second phase of the project. In my opinion the various contributions made by the *Federal Archives*[12] to this project – which has been commended by the European Commission on several occasions – are impressive,

---

[11] EHRI website: https://ehri-project.eu/. Last accessed: 28.6.2019.

[12] For example, information from the seminar "Aktenkunde des Holocaust" (Understanding Documentation on the Holocaust), has been incorporated into the online course "Modern Diplomatics of the Holocaust". Available at: https://training.ehri-project.eu/unit/6-modern-diplomatics-holocaust. Last accessed: 28.6.2019.

however, they largely happen incidentally which ultimately leads me on to discuss the extent to which boundaries are set in terms of the perception of non-statutory duties when it comes to the politics of remembrance.

Assessment of the Current Situation

In comparison to the majority of state, municipal and other archives in Germany, the *Federal Archives* might be well advised to exercise a certain degree of restraint when it comes to complaining about inadequate staffing, insufficient funding and a lack of attention from supervisory authorities. Admittedly, the *Federal Archives* has not just acquired considerably higher volumes of archive material in recent years, but has also taken on a much larger number of new responsibilities without seeing any adjustments to staffing levels to keep pace with these changes. Since it can be expected that there will not be a significant increase in the number of permanent positions in the short term, the *Federal Archives* has no other option but to carefully review all of the tasks, re-prioritize them and identify which areas it will no longer be possible to continue dealing with in the usual way. Both the *Federal Archives* and the *Arolsen Archives* are right in the middle of this process at the moment. Drawing on the results of a personnel requirements report (PBE) carried out by an established consultancy firm, I would like to focus on one point that highlights the magnitude of the challenges.

As part of this process, a calculation was made of the number of man-years, broken down by department, that would be required to work at the current level on records that have not yet been analyzed. Even for *Department R* (German Reich), which was in existence until the autumn of 2018 and was responsible for the archival legacy of the civil authorities from the period to 1945, this would amount to 540.2 years. In other words, it would be necessary to employ an additional 540 people to reduce the backlog of records that have not been analyzed within one year.

These types of figures sound dramatic, however, this effect is not really the prime concern. It is possible to draw various conclusions from this and other results produced in the PBE report and to pose a number of different questions: Would cataloguing records which have not really been analyzed before help to further research in a significant way even when there has been hardly any demand for them so far? Is it really necessary to analyze all of the records to the same depth and according to the same standards as they would initially have been subject to completely different conditions over 50 years ago? Is it possible to transfer personnel from different areas with smaller backlogs into departments with particularly high levels of backlogs? These questions cannot and should not be answered definitively here; they provide the basis for reflection and strategic realignment which is already under way at the *Federal Archives* and elsewhere.[13] When analyzing the figures, it is certainly no longer possible to be surprised by these findings: The *Federal Archives* does not wish to lose its relevance as a participant in a German politics of remembrance. If new responsibilities are entrusted to the *Federal Archives* in the future, these can only be offset by creating new jobs – or specific tasks will no longer be performed in the same way as they used to be. These kinds of questions will become increasingly relevant following the integration of the *German Office for the Notification of Next of Kin of the Former German Wehrmacht* (*Deutsche Dienststelle für die Benachrichtigung der nächsten Angehörigen von Gefallenen der ehemaligen deutschen Wehrmacht* [WASt]) into the *Federal Archives* from January 2019. For example, this department is now also responsible for managing the database containing information on Soviet prisoners of war.

As we reach the end of this essay, a topical issue within remembrance politics should have come to the fore concerning a decision the *Federal Archives* had to reach following in-depth discussions together with other relevant participants which has received the approval of many parties: The question concerning the publication of the names of victims of the Nazi *Euthanasia Program* has been the subject of intense debate across society for a long time. Due to the fact that physical and mental disabilities continued to be stigmatized in the Federal Republic of Germany, until recent times individual family members and the working group called the *Association of Victims of Euthanasia* (*Bund der 'Euthanasie'-Geschädigten*) objected to the publication of the names.[14] As far as the *Federal Archives* and many other agencies are concerned, this is outweighed by the consideration that in a time of inclusion victims of the Nazi *Euthanasia Program* should no longer be kept secret. It is also believed that the relevant archival sources should be handled in a more liberal way in the interests of academic and genealogical research. The *Federal Archives* has stated its position on its website in order to avoid any further misunderstandings[15]: Only the names, dates of birth and the names of the institutions associated with approx-

---

13 See: *Das Bundesarchiv im digitalen Wandel*, Forum. Das Fachmagazin des Bundesarchivs, 2018. Available at: http://www.bundesarchiv.de/DE/Content/Publikationen/Forum/forum-2018.html. Last accessed: 28.6.2019.

14 See https://www.euthanasiegeschaedigte-zwangssterilisierte.de/themen/erinnerungspolitik/. Last accessed: 28.6.2019.

15 See http://www.bundesarchiv.de/DE/Content/Artikel/Ueber-uns/Aus-unserer-Arbeit/euthanasie-im-dritten-reich.html. Last accessed: 28.6.2019.

imately 30,000 people, and not the records themselves, have been published. These patient records are held at the *Federal Archives* in *record group R 179, Chancellery of the Führer, Central Office IIb (Kanzlei des Führers, Hauptamt IIb)*.

Archives are places where reliable and authentic sources are stored and made accessible for everyone, and where views and interpretations of history can be developed or potentially revised. Without the contribution of archives and not least the *Federal Archives* – whether resulting from a statutory mandate or factors beyond this – public remembrance would be incomplete. The *Federal Archives* is aware of the tasks associated with this and will always endeavor to tackle them with the right degree of integrity and professionalism.

Carola Lau
Institutes of National Remembrance and their Role in Dealing with National Socialism

An Examination of the Issues, Debates and Public Perceptions

Abstract: In the context of debates on recent episodes of national history, specialized archival and research facilities were founded in several countries in East-Central and Eastern Europe. Often referred to as "Institutes of National Remembrance", they were supposed to dedicate their work to both the communist and National Socialist (occupation) periods. The following chapter explores the debates surrounding the creation of these institutions in Poland, Slovakia and the Czech Republic, as well as their realization and their subsequent activities in dealing with the Nazi period. In terms of the scope of their research activities, their public profile and the degree of meaning that was attached on a political level, work on the archival legacy of the communist state security services significantly overshadowed the way the National Socialist period was dealt with. However, in terms of the way the period 1938/39 to 1945 was remembered, the institutes could also achieve political meaning and public awareness, and thus contribute to a significant commemorative culture, especially in terms of raising questions relating to how the whole of society associates perpetrators and victims within a context of foreign domination and complicity.

Introduction

Following the collapse of the communist system in Central and Eastern Europe at the end of the 1980s and the beginning of the 1990s, debates were held in the former Eastern bloc countries surrounding the way the histories of these nations should be critically examined and processed. Against this backdrop, proponents in favor of critically examining the previous political systems set up specialized state-run archives and research institutions which focused on the recent past. In many cases, this work centered on the socialist systems which had immediately preceded this period and the archives compiled by the former state security services.[1] The purpose of some of these institutions – often entitled *Institutes of Na-*

---

1 See also Carola Lau: *Erinnerungsverwaltung, Vergangenheitspolitik und Erinnerungskultur nach*

OpenAccess. © 2020 Carola Lau, published by De Gruyter. This work is licensed under the Creative Commons Attribution-NonCommercial-NoDerivatives 4.0 License.
https://doi.org/10.1515/9783110665376-017

tional Remembrance – was primarily to critically examine the decades between 1938/39 and 1989/90 which therefore included the National Socialist era and period of occupation. Consequently, the political will to focus on the recent past, and particularly the communist past, opened up the potential for the National Socialist era and the Second World War to be re-examined on an institutional basis.

The following essay examines three *Institutes of National Remembrance*[2] – the *Institute of National Remembrance* (*Instytut Pamięci Narodowej*, IPN) in Poland, the *Nation's Memory Institute* (*Ústav pamäti národa*, ÚPN) in Slovakia and the *Institute for the Study of Totalitarian Regimes* (*Ústav pro studium totalitních režimů*, ÚSTR) in the Czech Republic. From a comparative perspective, the objective of this essay is to outline the starting position which led to the establishment of the institutes and the debates surrounding their organization. The essay also aims to describe the structure and subsequent activities of the institutes and the role they played in stewarding national historical consciousness, in promoting a culture of remembrance and in shaping policies for dealing with the political past. The analysis will focus on the way the National Socialist era (period of occupation) is dealt with which will be evaluated within the wider debate about the recent past which has taken place in the countries under consideration. It also aims to examine the degree of importance that can be attached to this period when the institutions were being established and later on in terms of their self-perception, and when this might be relevant on a political and public level.

1989 – Institute für nationales Gedenken im östlichen Europa im Vergleich, Göttingen, V&R unipress, 2017.
2 In the following essay, the title "Institute of National Remembrance" will be used as a generic term for the three institutes that are being examined, even though the Czech institute has a different name. In the Czech Republic, right up until the end of the legislative debate, the institute which finally came to be called the ÚSTR was originally going to be called the 'Institute of National Remembrance' (*Ústav paměti národa*) to conform with the name given to the institutions that had been previously set up in Poland and Slovakia. The term *pamięć* (Polish), *pamäť* (Slovak) and *paměť* (Czech) which is used in the Slavic institutes' nomenclature is usually referred to as *Gedächtnis* (memory) in German. The titles of the above institutions are therefore translated in the literature as the "Institutes of National Memory." However, due to their activities as preservers of a specific memory and through their role of actively promoting a specific type of remembrance, the term "Institute of National Remembrance" is considered to be more accurate for the purpose of this essay.

The Starting Position

The *Institutes of National Remembrance* that are being considered in this essay were established only years after the regime changes in Poland, Slovakia and the Czech Republic. Thus, during the time they were established and developed – in Poland in 1998, in Slovakia in 2002 and in the Czech Republic in 2007 – they were inevitably placed within the context of previous debates on how each nation should deal with their recent pasts. During this period especially, the process of decommunization, otherwise known as lustration, defined the political and public debate on this subject in the Czech Republic and Poland. This refers to the process of purging certain public offices of individuals who were regarded as being tainted by their official or unofficial involvement with the communist intelligence services or, as was the case in the Czech Republic, who were high-ranking members of the Communist Party. Corresponding laws were enacted to address this issue in both countries during the 1990s.[3] Highly controversial questions were raised relating to the value and credibility of the records which had been collected under the legacy systems. These questions formed the basis of decisions concerning whether an individual was deemed to be tainted or not by the past. The publication of lists[4] of individuals who were alleged to be tainted by their past activities was already adding heat to the debate in the Czech Republic back in 1992. It is clear that this was a burning issue in the Czechoslovak Federation and in the following years in the Czech Republic due to the fact that the *Office of the Documentation and the Investigation of the Crimes of Communism* (*Úřad dokumentace a vyšetřování zločinů komunismu*, ÚDV) was established in 1995 thanks to the existence of two former institutes that had been

---

3 In the Czechoslovak Federation, a law had already been passed in 1991 described as the law "On enforcing further conditions relating to the execution of some of the functions in the public bodies and organizations in the Czech and Slovak Federal Republic, the Czech Republic and the Slovak Republic". This was followed in Poland in 1997 by the law "On disclosure of work or service for state security bodies or unofficial cooperation with them in the period between 1944–1990 by individuals performing public functions."

4 The former dissident and staunch anti-communist Petr Cibulka published the "Cibulka Lists" in 1992 in the magazines *Rudé krávo* and *Necenzurované noviny* which specified the names of 160,000 alleged collaborators of the Czechoslovak state security services. The lists had not been officially corroborated and were strongly contested by the accused and many other individuals.

set up in the Ministry of Interior. The ÚDV specifically focused on carrying out investigations into crimes committed by state agencies between 1953 and 1989.[5]

After Slovakia had separated from the Czech Republic, it was only at the end of the 1990s, that there was again a greater focus on critically examining the nation's recent past.[6] This resulted in the parliament enacting laws in 1999 and 2002 which were intended to help arrange compensation for victims who were deported to Nazi concentration camps and prison camps from 1939 to 1945 or settlements for members of the Slovak resistance movement and former political prisoners.[7] Yet, during 1999, the former Slovak Justice Minister Ján Čarnogurský was unable to push through a law to establish a Slovak institution along the same lines as the Czech ÚDV. He was only able to set up the *Office of the Documentation of the Crimes of Communism* at the Justice Ministry of the Slovak Republic (*Oddelenie pre dokumentáciu zločinov komunizmu Ministerstva spravodlivosti Slovenskej republiky*, ODZK).

During the 1990s in Poland on the other hand, an institution, which had been in existence for quite some time, was widening the scope of its activities to include the critical examination of Stalinist crimes prior to December 31, 1956. This work was carried out from April 1991 by the *Central Commission for the Prosecution of Crimes against the Polish Nation – Institute of National Remembrance* (*Główna Komisja Badania Zbrodni przeciwko Narodowi Polskiemu – Instytut Pamięci Narodowej*) whose objective was to gain new insights into the past and start criminal proceedings by using new witness statements and accessing archives that had not been available until that point.[8] The institution arose from the *Central Commission for the Investigation of German Crimes in Poland* (*Główna Komisja Badania Zbrodni Niemieckich w Polsce*) which was founded in

---

[5] The ÚDV continues to exist today as part of the Police of the Czech Republic under the jurisdiction of the Ministry of the Interior. See https://www.policie.cz/clanek/urad-dokumentace-a-vysetrovani-zlocinu-komunismu-679905.aspx. Last accessed: 6.3.2019.

[6] Very little relevant legislation was passed until Prime Minister Vladimír Mečiar was voted out in 1998. The collections of records belonging to the former Slovak state security services had also not been made available at this point. The "Law on the Immorality and Injustice of the Communist Regime", which was approved by the Slovak parliament in 1996, was only really symbolic in nature.

[7] A list of all of the laws relating to this theme is available on the ÚPN website: https://www.upn.gov.sk/sk/dokumenty/. Last accessed: 6.2.2019.

[8] Witold Kulesza: "Verbrechen im Parteiauftrag als Gegenstand des Strafverfahrens in Polen", in Dagmar Unverhau and Roland Lucht (eds.): *Lustration, Aktenöffnung, demokratischer Umbruch in Polen, Tschechien, der Slowakei und Ungarn*, Münster: LIT, 2005, 43–46.

November 1945.[9] This was then renamed the *Central Commission for the Investigation of Hitlerite Crimes* (*Główna Komisja Badania Zbrodni Hitlerowskich w Polsce*) in 1949.[10]

The main focus of its work at that time was to document and research events that occurred during the war and when Poland was occupied, using witness statements, inspections of crime scenes and disinterments, whereas crimes committed during 1939 to 1941 during the Soviet occupation and German crimes committed in what became the former Polish eastern territories after 1945 were not dealt with.[11] The Commission acted as an instrument of the Polish government to help determine policies for dealing with the past. It regularly criticized what was alleged to be West German revisionism and referred in positive terms to the efforts that were being undertaken in the GDR to critically examine the past. However, it did work in partnership with Western European and American authorities and with the West German *Central Office of the Land Judicial Authorities for Investigation of National Socialist Crimes* (*Zentrale Stelle zur Aufklärung von NS-Verbrechen*) in Ludwigsburg.[12] During the 1960s, the Commission was part of anti-Zionist campaigns, however, it denied antisemitism in Polish society and the participation of some Polish citizens in the Nazi persecution of the Jews.[13]

In 1984 political decision makers added *Institute of National Remembrance* to the Commission's title and explicitly mandated the Commission to focus on three key areas: prosecution, archive management and research.[14] The role of the research department was to develop proposals for educational initiatives[15] and to shape the idea of Polish national remembrance in a more active way in

---

[9] Council of Ministers of the Republic of Poland, 1945. Decree of November 10, 1945 on the *Central Commission and the District Commissions for the Investigation of German Crimes in Poland* (Dziennik Ustaw 1945 no. 51 item. 293).

[10] Andreas Mix: "Juristische Ermittlungen und historische Forschung in Polen. Von der 'Hauptkommission' zum Institut des Nationalen Gedenkens", in Wolfgang Benz (ed.): *Wann ziehen wir endlich den Schlussstrich? Von der Notwendigkeit öffentlicher Erinnerung in Deutschland, Polen und Tschechien*", Berlin: Metropol, 2004, 75–94, here 80.

[11] Ibid., 76 and following.; Council of Ministers, 1945, art. 3 b).

[12] Mix, 2004, 77 and 81 and following; Kulesza, 2005, 43.

[13] Mix, 2004, 85.

[14] Council of State of the Republic of Poland: Law of April 6, 1984 on the *Central Commission for the Investigation of Hitlerite Crimes – Institute of National Remembrance* (Dziennik Ustaw 1984 no. 21 item. 98), art. 2 and art. 9.1.

[15] Ibid., art. 5.

keeping with the Commission's new title.¹⁶ The epithet *Institute for National Remembrance* ultimately outlasted the regime change in 1989/1990.

The debates surrounding the establishment of the *Institutes of National Remembrance* took place in the Czech Republic and Poland within the context of previous controversies that had been fought out in the political and public arenas. After the debates on decommunization or lustration, the situation was now characterized by a desire to regulate the storage and access to the records produced by the state security services. After years of modest activity and influenced by developments in its neighboring countries, political decision makers in Slovakia also became more interested in grappling with their country's recent past. The question of how to deal with the collections of documents from the communist era that could now be accessed had become an extremely delicate matter because only a short amount of time had elapsed since the events under scrutiny had passed. The whole issue was also very sensitive because it had the potential to result in specific consequences for both private individuals and public figures. This could not apply (anymore) to archive collections from previous periods, including those from the National Socialist era (period of German occupation). A critical analysis of communism was now being seen as a higher priority in all three countries, as demonstrated by the drive during the 1990s to institutionalize efforts to re-examine the past by focusing attention on Stalinist and communist crimes through the work of institutions that had recently been set up or former institutions that were realigning their focus. The parliamentary and public de-

---

16 The first Polish Institute of National Remembrance was initiated in 1944 by the *Polish Committee of National Liberation* (*Polski Komitet Wyzwolenia Narodowego*) in Lublin. According to the co-founder of the institute, the author Helena Boguszewska, it was intended that the Institute would focus on, "the martyrdom under the occupation, the struggle against Hitlerism and the reorganization of the political system." See also Helena Boguszewska: *Nigdy nie zapomnę [I will never forget]*, Warsaw: Wiedza, 1946, 38. The Institute tried, among other things, to preserve documents and other testimonies from Majdanek concentration camp and, until it was renamed in 1948 and closed in 1950, it devoted much of its efforts to documenting and publishing materials. See Iwona Pachcińska: *Władysław Bartoszewski. Doktor Honoris Causa Katolickiego Uniwersytetu Lubelskiego Jana Pawła II* [Władysław Bartoszewski. Degree honoris causa from the John Paul II Catholic University of Lublin.]. Lublin, 2008. Available at: http://www.kul.pl/files/254/bartoszewski_DHC_KUL.pdf. Last accessed: 4.6.2019, 21 and 32. In terms of content, the Institute critically examined German war crimes in Poland, Polish collaboration with the German occupying forces and Polish history from the suppression of the 1863 January Uprising until the end of the Second World War, and therefore specifically the role of the labor movement. It also documented information about concentration camps, places where mass executions had taken place and estimated the extent of Poland's losses due to the war. See Krzysztof Pilawski: "Prawo do pamięci [A Right to Memory]", in: *Przegląd*, n.d. Available at: https://www.tygodnikprzeglad.pl/prawo-do-pamieci/. Last accessed: 4.6.2019.

bates surrounding the *Institutes of National Remembrance* were a natural continuation of this development.

The Process of Establishing the Institutes

The establishment of a Polish *Institute of National Remembrance* constituted one of the most important aspects of the work that was being undertaken to process the recent past by the conservative-liberal government during the legislative period from 1997 to 2001. Even though the coalition government had a clear majority in the Sejm (the lower house of the Polish parliament), the decision to establish the institute was accompanied by long and heated parliamentary debates, a declaration by the Senate (the upper house of the Sejm) and a veto by President Aleksander Kwaśniewski[17] which was finally overruled by the Sejm. The project received a great deal of media attention. It was repeatedly stressed throughout the parliamentary debate that redefining the way the records were managed and accessed should mean that the files formerly created by the intelligence services should no longer be used as a "political tool or a way to blackmail the nation".[18] Changing the way the files were controlled was intended to sever the "hellish umbilical cord" that existed between the current constitutional intelligence services and the former communist secret police.[19] The People's Republic of Poland was described by conservative members of the Sejm as an "unlawful state" (*państwo bezprawia*) and a "totalitarian state" (*państwo totalitarne*).[20] Through its work, the new institution was expected to expose crimes perpetrated by the state and reveal "the true face of the communist state."[21] However, members of the SLD party criticized the legally designated terms "communist state" and "communist crimes", and deemed them to be ideological, a

---

[17] Kwaśniewski was a member of the *Democratic Left Alliance* (*Sojusz Lewicy Demokratycznej*, SLD) which was one of the successors of the defunct Polish *United Workers Party* (*Poska Zjednoczona Partia Robotnicza*, PZPR).

[18] "[...] instrument[...] walki politycznej i mechanism [...] zbiorowego szantażu [...]", from a speech by Marek Siwiec, for a similar argument see the speeches by Jan Lityński and Bogdan Pęk, at the parliamentary debate on 2.4.1998, (first reading), stenographic report, third period of government, session 15, agenda item 14.

[19] "[...] piekielną pępowinę [...]", speech by Janusz Pałubicki, ibid.

[20] Speeches by Jan Lityński, Piotr Żak and Janusz Pałubicki, ibid.

[21] "[...] prawdziw[e] oblicz[e] komunistycznego państwa", speeches by Janusz Pałubicki, Stanisław Iwanicki and Piotr Żak, ibid.

form of propaganda and part of a non-legal language.[22] The SLD party also proposed that the period that the new institution covered should be extended to incorporate 1918 onwards because this included crimes which had been committed during the Second Polish Republic that needed to be critically examined. The proposal was not successful.[23] The debate surrounding the way the records should be managed and accessed therefore clearly exemplified the different ways the past activities of both the Polish People's Republic and the Second Polish Republic were being assessed by political parties who were involved in this process.

On the other hand, discussions concerning the way the period of Nazi occupation was evaluated, or at least more detailed references to this era, were not included in the debate. This is despite the fact that the draft legislation stipulated that the *Central Commission for the Prosecution of Crimes against the Polish Nation – Institute of National Remembrance* should be integrated into the new institute which would mean that the work of the former institute – and especially its work on this period – would be incorporated into the work of the new institute. Ironically, the participants in the parliamentary and public debates which focused on processing Poland's recent past completely obscured the way the Central Commission and the *Institute of National Remembrance* had evolved before 1989.

The political context from which the preceding institutes arose with its clearly defined political objectives and processes was also not part of the discussions. As the coalition government thought that integrating criminal prosecution, educational activities and archive management into one institution would be appealing and beneficial, they were clearly not interested in critically examining the former institute and its background history when setting up the new institute. The SLD as the successor of the Polish *United Workers' Party* was also not very interested in critically examining this aspect of the government's project as this would have meant adopting a critical stance towards the institutions that were run during the period of the Polish People's Republic. In December 1998, the Polish Sejm passed the law *On the Institute of National Remembrance*

---

22 Speech by Marian Marczewski, ibid.; speeches by Janusz Zemke and Bogdan Lewandowski, debate in the Sejm on 9.9.1998 (2nd reading), stenographic report, third period of government, session 27, agenda item 2.
23 Speech by Katarzyna Maria Piekarska, debate in the Sejm on 9.9.1998 (second reading), stenographic report, third period of government, session 27, agenda item 2.

and the Commission for the Prosecution of Crimes against the Polish Nation[24] without having addressed the period between 1939 and 1945 in a more comprehensive way.

Meanwhile in Slovakia in 2001, a group of parliamentarians led by Ján Langoš (who would later become the director of the institute), pressed ahead with passing the law *On access to documents compiled by the state security services during the time of oppression from 1939 to 1989 and on the Nation's Memory Institute*, an Institute of National Remembrance which was intended to be based on the Polish model (*Ústav pamäti národa*, ÚPN). Although President Rudolf Schuster vetoed a "package of anti-communist laws"[25] and therefore also the ÚPN law, he was overruled as far as the latter was concerned. Even though media coverage during this period included issues such as the past activities of Slovak judges, or the fact that important state officials used to be members of the Communist Party, it was not focused on uncovering such stories. Moreover, the drafting of the new law did not capture the attention of the media in Slovakia and as a consequence neither the attention of the broader public.[26] The legislative debate ran relatively smoothly despite the presidential veto and did not feature much in the way of dissent.

However, a large proportion of parliamentarians clearly expressed their opinions about the need for a critical analysis of the past, made a clear assessment of the recent decades of Slovak history and focused the spotlight on crimes that had been committed under the previous systems and on the victims. Langoš provided exhaustive figures relating to the victims of German National Socialism in Slovakia and of Soviet communism in Czechoslovakia from 1939 to 1989 to support his argument that this was an era marked by continuous oppression and a lack of freedom. He clearly defined the period between 1939 and 1989 as a "totalitarian past" (*totalitná minulost*) which was characterized by "repressive institutions" (*represivnych inštitúcií*).[27] It was never really in doubt in parlia-

---

24 Ustawa z dnia 18 grudnia 1998 r. o Instytucie Pamięci Narodowej – Komisji Ścigania Zbrodni przeciwko Narodowi Polskiemu (Dziennik Ustaw 1998 nr 155 poz. 1016) Tekst ogłoszony [adopted text], hereinafter the IPN Law.
25 Patricia Ďurišková: "Medzi sudcami nad'alej zostanú bývalí tajní [Former secret service agents still working as judges]", in *Pravda*, 21.8.2002, 1–2, 1.
26 The magazine *Kritika & Kontext* described a culture of "silence" that had been ongoing for a number of years in politics, the media, the academic world and among the general public. Miroslav Kusý et al.: "Dedičstvo ŠtB na Slovensku [The legacy of the ŠtB in Slovakia]", in *Kritika & Kontext*, 2–3, 29–39.
27 Speech by Ján Langoš, National Council of the Slovak Republic, parliamentary date on 9.7.2002, stenographic report, period of government 1988 to 2002, session 61.

ment that the periods of National Socialism and the People's Republic should both be viewed as a "time of oppression".

Langoš stressed several times that the National Socialist and Bolshevik-communist ideologies were both foreign sets of beliefs that had not originated in Slovakia and that they had been brought into the country by Germany and Russia.[28] In doing so, he also avoided attributing any responsibility or even guilt to the Slovak people as a whole. Although during the debate Langoš touched upon the Slovak state between 1939 and 1945, and the persecution of the Jewish population in this region, he did not mention Slovak policy makers, their party and affiliated organizations such as the Hlinka's Slovak People's Party and its paramilitary wing, the Hlinka Guard, or the Hlinka Youth.[29] This was interesting given that leading Slovak players had worked quite separately from Germany towards finding "a solution to the Jewish question".[30] Even the politician and Roman Catholic priest Jozef Tiso – described a few years later as "our most controversial historical figure"[31] by a journalist in the magazine *Týždeň* – was not mentioned by any of the participants in the debate, despite the fact that as a leading politician in the Slovak state[32] he should have been the focal point of the debates surrounding the way the state was evaluated.

An externalization of responsibility was not only evident in the use of the expression "era of oppression", which already implied that it was impossible for the Slovaks to make any decisions regarding their own degree of responsibility, but could also be seen in the way that the initiator of the law would only refer to the terms "National Socialist" and "communist" and failed to recognize that the Slovak state could be characterized in its own right as having developed from an authoritarian to a totalitarian regime which had some fascist elements.[33] The parliamentary debate did not prompt an analysis of the Slovak state between

---

28 Speech by Ján Langoš, National Council of the Slovak Republic, parliamentary debate on 19.8.2002, stenographic report, period of government 1998 to 2002, session 63.
29 Speech by Ján Langoš, National Council of the Slovak Republic, parliamentary date on 9.7.2002, stenographic report, period of government 1988 to 2002, session 61.
30 Ivan Kamenec: "The Slovak state, 1939–1945", in Mikuláš Teich et al. (eds.): *Slovakia in History*, Cambridge: Cambridge Univ. Press, 2011, 175–192, here 184; Tatjana Tönsmeyer: *Das Dritte Reich und die Slowakei 1939–1945. Politischer Alltag zwischen Kooperation und Eigensinn*, Paderborn: Schöningh, 2003, 336.
31 Martin Hanus: "Čas na rozsudok [Judgement Time]", in *Týždeň*, 29.8.2005, 16–23, 17.
32 Tiso was Prime Minister and President of the Slovak State from 1939 to 1945 and "leader and president" between 1942 and 1945.
33 Ivan Kamenec describes the development of domestic policy in the Slovak state as a development "from an authoritarian regime to totalitarianism with significant fascist elements, but also with several specifically Slovak features." Kamenec, 2011, 182–183.

1939 and 1945. This aspect was pushed into the background instead, which was in contrast to the speeches that were made concerning the opening of the archives on the former communist intelligence services. The Slovak *Law on National Remembrance* was passed in August 2002.[34]

In the Czech Republic, parliamentary debates were repeatedly held for many years regarding the establishment of a new institute that would manage the archives and help to process the nation's recent past. It was envisaged that this institute would bring together documentation, academic research and file collections, foster relationships with other institutions, and enhance public awareness. Draft legislation from 1999 that was connected to this relating to the Memorial to the Era of Oppression 1939 to 1989 (Památník doby nesvobody 1939 to 1989)[35] and draft legislation relating to the *Institute for the Documentation of Totalitarian Regimes* (*Institut pro dokumentaci totality*)[36] from 2001 basically differed in that it was envisaged that the second bill would limit the institute's activities to the period between 1949 and 1990.

It was not until 2006 that a group of liberal-conservative members of parliament were able to launch an initiative to establish an *Institute of National Remembrance* (*Ústav paměti národa*, ÚPN). The most significant change was that the project was intended to reach well beyond previous initiatives in terms of the way the collections of documents relating to the former intelligence services would be managed, making it possible to access the documents in a new and efficient way.[37] It is also probable that this was influenced by the increasing numbers of revelations in the Czech Republic concerning public figures who were accused of collaborating with the former Czech state security service.[38] It was also repeatedly discussed in an extremely heated debate whether the entire

---

[34] Act no. 553/2002 of August 19, 2002 entitled "On disclosure of documents on the activities of the state security services from 1939 to 1989, on the establishment of the Slovak Nation's Memory Institute and on the amendment of certain laws", 553/2002 Z. z.

[35] Senate of the Czech Republic, Návrh zákona o Památníku doby nesvobody [draft bill on the Memorial to the Era of Oppression], parliamentary paper 450/0, 1999.

[36] Chamber of Deputies of the Parliament of the Czech Republic, Application by the parliamentary members Václav Krása, Marek Benda, Josef Janeček and others relating to the adoption of the law on the Institute for the Documentation of Totalitarian Regimes and the amendment of certain other laws, parliamentary paper 1118 – 1st reading, session 43, 11.12.2001.

[37] Senate of the Czech Republic, Application by the Senate relating to the adoption of the law on the Institute of National Remembrance and the amendment of certain other laws. 21.8.2006, parliamentary paper 15/0.

[38] Signatories of Charter 77, and Czech singers and actors, reported unofficial collaboration with the state security service.

period between 1949 and 1990 that was being examined by the institute could be described as totalitarian.

Criticism was also voiced about the fact that initially the draft bill stipulated that the new institute would only focus on the period between 1948 and 1990.[39] It was also argued that if the institute also incorporated the period from 1939, it would be in a position to continue the work of the Czech *Government Commission for the Prosecution of Nazi War Crimes* which had been abolished in 1990.[40] However, a broader debate was not held on the inclusion of this period of history, or on the activities of the former Commission, despite the fact that this timeframe had been ultimately agreed by consensus by all of the parties involved. The fact that it was being implied that communism and National Socialism were both similar totalitarian systems was also not critically examined by the members of parliament. In June 2007 the law *On the Institute for the Study of Totalitarian Regimes, and the Security Services Archive and amendments to certain other laws* was enacted.[41]

The debates surrounding the establishment of the *Institutes of National Remembrance* showed that there was already a clear imbalance with regard to political and public input and the way that this period, which was characterized by communism and National Socialism/fascism, would be dealt with in terms of content. This was undoubtedly because issues that were raised concerning the immediate past and the fiercely debated interpretations of state socialism during these periods were utterly overwhelming. Moreover, this provided a hint of the types of agendas that would be carried out by the new institutions. In addition, aspects which were not being examined at this time, such as the tendency to externalize in the legislative text and the way previous institutions had politicized history, certainly played a key role in the future activities of the institutes. In terms of the suppression of specific historical aspects, it was significant that the origin and historical context relating to the name *Institute of National Remembrance*, which originated in Poland and was adopted in draft legislation in Slovakia and the Czech Republic, was not the subject of discussion or examined critically in any of the debates at all.

---

39 Not only the Greens but also the Social Democrats and the Communists supported the idea of extending the timeframe to include 1938 to 1945.
40 Speech by Karel Černý, parliamentary debate on 7.11.2006, Chair of Deputies of the Czech Parliament, Application by the Senate relating to the adoption of the law on the Institute of National Remembrance and the amendment of certain other laws, parliamentary paper 15–1st reading.
41 Zákon ze dne 8. června 2007 o Ústavu pro studium totalitních režimů a o Archivu bezpečnostních složek a o změně některých, Sbírka zákonů Nr. 181/2007.

Activities Undertaken by the *Institutes of National Remembrance*

According to the preamble to the law on the Polish *Institute of National Remembrance*, the objective of this institute is to preserve the memory of the immense sacrifices, losses and harm suffered by the Polish people during and after the Second World War, to represent the patriotic legacy of the Polish people in their struggle against the occupiers, National Socialism and communism, and to convey the actions of Polish citizens in their attempt to secure an independent Polish state and to defend the ideals of freedom and human dignity. The law also emphasized the commitment that had been made to prosecute crimes against humanity and war crimes, as well as the Polish state's commitment to pay compensation to all victims. The text specifically identified the occupying forces, National Socialism, communism and the machinery of the People's Republic as the "perpetrators" whose crimes should be prosecuted, disclosed and remembered. The law vehemently condemned both the period of German occupation and the People's Republic of Poland along with their ideologies.

The Slovak legislators adopted this wording almost to the letter in the preamble of the Slovak *Law on National Remembrance*. Only the term "National Socialism" was replaced with the term "fascism". The specific circumstances relating to the years 1939 to 1945 when Slovakia was a "protectorate" of the German Reich were not mentioned, even though this is clearly different to the period of German occupation in Poland which happened at the same time. The expression "era of oppression" that was used to describe the timeframe that would be the focus of the ÚPN's work reflected once more the tendency to externalize responsibility that had already been part of the parliamentary debates. It set the starting point as April 18, 1939 when the government of the Slovak state passed the first legislation known as the "Jewish Laws" which marginalized Jewish citizens. However, the law does not name any leading figures who passed laws such as the Decree of April 18, 1939 and the parties and organizations of this state whilst it examines the departments of the state security services from the 1940s in greater detail.[42]

---

[42] The way § 8 of the law is worded, which emphasizes that the ÚPN should judge the "participation of native and foreign individuals" in the fascist and communist system, does very little to attenuate this impression. As has already been stated, this is especially relevant given that specific National Socialist and fascist organizations are not mentioned throughout the entire legislative text.

The preamble of the Czech law on the *Institute for the Study of Totalitarian Regimes* also describes the twentieth century as an era that is marked by two totalitarian regimes and their communist and National Socialist ideologies. It identifies two key periods in which human rights were suppressed and democratic principles were violated: The "era of oppression" between 1938 and 1945 and the "period of totalitarian communist rule" from 1948 to 1989. In using the words "totalitarian and authoritarian regimes of the 20th century" the law is referring to the criminal organizations that followed communist and National Socialist ideologies in equal terms and it therefore treats National Socialism and communism as part of the same continuum of totalitarian rule.

In its preamble, the law clearly refers to preceding projects that have already been described in which accounts of the consequences of the regimes especially, from the violation of human rights to the destruction of nature, can also be found in an almost identical form. The legislators referred here to the Czech *Law on the Illegitimacy of the Communist Regime* that was enacted in 1993. It is therefore not surprising that the statements in the law relating to the ÚSTR appear to be more relevant for the Czechoslovak Socialist Republic than for the period between 1938 and 1945. Despite explicitly mentioning both regimes and ideologies, the law clearly aligns with statutory regulations that had been put in place since the first half of the 1990s in the Czech Republic to tackle the subject of the country's communist past. References to the period of German occupation between 1938 and 1945 look like they were added later, which corresponds with the way in which the parliamentary debates actually progressed.

The three institutes therefore had a broadly defined remit which encompassed archiving and providing access to documents, carrying out research and public relations, and assisting with the prosecution of criminal offenses. The Polish IPN stood apart from the others in that it had its own department, the *Central Commission for the Prosecution of Crimes against the Polish Nation* (*Główna Komisja Ścigania Zbrodni przeciwko Narodowi Polskiemu*), which had the legal powers to initiate criminal proceedings and to prosecute. In 2007 the IPN was also mandated to carry out a fourth function which involved dealing with lustration procedures in what was called the *Lustration Bureau* (*Biuro Lustracyjne*).[43] Meanwhile, a Witness Office was set up at the ÚPN in Slovakia and a Working Group for Oral History was established at the ÚSTR in the Czech Republic. The *Security Services Archive* (*Archiv bezpečnostních složek*, ABS) was unique to the Czech Republic and reported directly into the ÚSTR. It still had its own

---

[43] For further information on the structure of the IPN, refer to the institute's website at https://ipn.gov.pl/pl/o-ipn/struktura/36493,Struktura.html. Last accessed: 4.6.2019.

remit with regard to providing access to and publishing documents whereas a department responsible for digitizing archive material was again directly attached to the ÚSTR.[44]

In line with the goals that had already been set out during the legislative debates in all three countries, the institutes were first and foremost expected to take ownership of the documents compiled by the former state security services and make them accessible to the public. The fact that control over the archives was held by civil institutions and not institutions that were connected to the current state security services was particularly important for legislators in Poland and in Slovakia. In 2005 the IPN in Poland finally took over the "[...] biggest archive operation in the history of Poland and perhaps in the whole of Europe".[45] This is how a former employee described this project which involved the transfer of over 80 kilometers of files into the archives. The ÚPN in Slovakia had to enforce its legal rights over the Slovak security services and the Czech Republic when taking over the relevant archive materials,[46] finally acquiring over 1.8 kilometers of records in paper form and on microfiche. By contrast, it was much quicker and easier for the ÚSTR in the Czech Republic to acquire the 18 kilometers or so of records during 2007 and 2008.[47]

In all three countries the majority of the archive collections came from the former communist intelligence services, which were compiled from the current Department of the Interior, the Defense Department and the Department of Justice. These documents were what made the institutes unique now they were accessible for the first time in this format for research and for use by the general public. Even though discussions surrounding the credibility, comprehensiveness and fundamental significance of the former state security service files have never

---

44 For further information on the structure of the ÚSTR, refer to the institute's website at https://www.ustrcr.cz/o-nas/organizacni-struktura/. Last accessed: 4.6.2019.

45 "To była największa operacja archiwalna w dziejach Polski, a kto wie, czy nie całej Europy." Antoni Dudek: *Instytut. Osobista historia IPN* [*The Institute. A Personal History of the IPN*], Warsaw: Wydawnictwo czerwone i czarne, 2001, hereinafter: Dudek, 2011, 94.

46 Ústav pamäti národa (eds): *Výročná správa o činnosti 2003* [*Annual Activity Report 2003*], Bratislava. Available at: http://www.upn.gov.sk/data/upn-vyrocna-sprava-2003.pdf. Last accessed: 4.6.2019, 12. ÚPN: "Institut des nationalen Gedenkens – Slowakei", in BStU (ed.): Das "Europäische Netzwerk der für die Geheimpolizeiakten zuständigen Behörden." *Ein Reader zu ihren gesetzlichen Grundlagen, Strukturen und Aufgaben*, Berlin, 74–83, 78.

47 Ústav pro studium totalitních režimů (ed.): *Výroční zpráva Ústavu pro studium totalitních režimů za rok 2007* [*2007 Annual Report of the Institute for the Study of Totalitarian Regimes*], Prague. Available at: http://www.ustrcr.cz/data/pdf/uredni-deska/zprava2007.pdf. Last accessed: 4.6.2019, 6.

abated,[48] and the newly established institutes were criticized for their lack of transparency when opening up the collections of records,[49] the archives undoubtedly provided the first ever opportunity to carry out systematic academic research on the structures, mechanisms and employees of the former state security services.[50] Although both periods under assessment were mentioned in the legal preambles, the fact that the work carried out by the institutes focused on the activities of the state security services was to all intents and purposes a logical outcome.

By contrast, considerably less attention was given to document collections that related to the period before 1945, which is certainly due to the fact that these collections were smaller in size[51] and were not perceived to be as current. However, they also had far less potential to be used in a way that would unleash a scandal. Whereas exhibitions to raise public awareness were conceived that focused on the people who were presumed to have worked full-time and on an informal basis for the communist intelligence services,[52] potentially scandalous lists were circulated and public figures were held accountable for their words and actions,[53] there were no discussions in the political and public arenas

---

[48] "Dôverníci o spolupráci vediet' nemuseli [Employees responsible for confidential information would not have known they were collaborating]", in Sme, 21.10.2002, 3.
[49] The IPN in Poland was criticized because it is said that a clear succession of people consulted the files and external academics were the last to be granted access. See Dudek, 2011, 79–80. It was only in 2012 that the IPN also published an inventory on its website that included more detailed information on individual documents.
[50] Antoni Dudek and Andrzej Paczkowski: "Polen" in Łukasz Kamiński (ed.): *Handbuch der kommunistischen Geheimdienste in Osteuropa 1944–1991*, Göttingen: Vandenhoeck und Ruprecht, 2009, 265–339, here 330.
[51] See also the detailed information on the structure and scope of the archive collections on the websites of IPN: https://ipn.gov.pl/pl/archiw/zasob/31615,Zasob-archiwalny-Instytutu-Pamieci-Narodowej.html; UPN: https://www.upn.gov.sk/archivne-fondy/klasifikacna-schema.php; and ÚSTR or ABS: https://www.abscr.cz/fondy-a-pomucky/pruvodce-po-fondech-sbirkach/#schema. Last accessed: 4.6.2019.
[52] In 2006 the IPN in Poland arranged a series of exhibitions entitled "Twarze bezpieki" (Faces of the Stasi) which examined the people behind the regional structures of the former state secret services. The exhibitions run by the Institute included photos and information relating to individuals who worked as full-time staff. They were shown in many Polish towns and cities. The ÚSTR in the Czech Republic also organized an exhibition along the same lines called "Tváře moci" (Faces of Power).
[53] For example, reference was made to the debates surrounding Lech Wałęsa's collaboration with the communist secret police in Poland, the allegations against Milan Kundera in the Czech Republic and the Wildstein List in Poland which was published by the journalist Bronisław Wildstein in 2005. The List contained approximately 240,000 names linked to former agents, unofficial employees and "operational contacts" of the state security services, and peo-

about the archive collections that related to the role individuals played in the National Socialist and fascist regimes. Within the institutes there was only a minor scandal at the IPN in Poland when it became clear that its predecessor had sent and consequently lost a large number of original documents to predominantly foreign agencies, including the *Central Office of the Land Judicial Authorities for Investigation of National Socialist Crimes* in Ludwigsburg. An investigatory commission at the IPN ascertained that over 6,900 documents had been lost, of which there were no copies in Poland,[54] and finally referred the case to the public prosecution authorities. However, the department of prosecution, after three years in 2009, dropped the case.[55]

Despite the lack of public attention, the institutions' work relating to the period before 1944/45 became more visible in terms of investigative work, publishing information, and running research and educational programs. Even though there was considerably more focus on the period after 1945 in the institutes' own journals, monographs, anthologies, memoirs, films and exhibitions, the period between 1938/39 and 1945 was also covered. A research department was set up at the ÚSTR in the Czech Republic to focus on the period between 1938 and 1945 which, among other things, researched and published materials relating to issues such as political repression and resistance during the period of occupation in the protectorate of Bohemia and Moravia, the prison system between 1938 and 1989 and resistance and persecution of Christians under National Socialism and communism from 1939 to 1989.[56] In terms of the disclosure of victims and "heroes" of the Czech Republic's recent past, as well as documenting the names of people who were executed due to political reasons, who died in prison

---

ple who were also alleged to have been recruited as informants although they had never given their consent.

54 Instytut Pamięci Narodowej (ed.): *Informacja o działalności Instytutu Pamięci Narodowej – Komisji Ścigania Zbrodni przeciwko Narodowi Polskiemu w okresie 1 stycznia 2008 r.–31 grudnia 2008 r.* [*Information relating to the activities of the Institute of National Remembrance – Commission for the Prosecution of Crimes against the Polish Nation from January 1, 2008 to December 31, 2008*], Warsaw. Available at: https://ipn.gov.pl/pl/o-ipn/informacje-o-dzialalnos/24314,w-okresie-1-stycznia-2008-r-31-grudnia-2008-r.html. Last accessed: 4.6.2019.

55 Instytut Pamięci Narodowej (ed.): *Informacja o działalności Instytutu Pamięci Narodowej – Komisji Ścigania Zbrodni przeciwko Narodowi Polskiemu w okresie 1 stycznia 2009 r.–31 grudnia 2009 r.* [*Information on the activities of the Institute of National Remembrance – Commission for the Prosecution of Crimes against the Polish Nation from January 1, 2009 to December 31, 2009*], Warsaw, 33. Available at: https://ipn.gov.pl/pl/o-ipn/informacje-o-dzialalnos/24313,w-okresie-1-stycznia-2009-r-31-grudnia-2009-r.html. Last accessed: 4.6.2019.

56 See also the ÚSTR website at https://www.ustrcr.cz/uvod/doba-nesvobody-1938-1945/. Last accessed: 4.6.2019.

and who died trying to cross national borders between 1948 and 1989, the ÚSTR also chronicled the names of Czechoslovakians who were executed at Plötzensee Prison in Berlin and at Pankrác Prison in Prague by the Gestapo during the Second World War.[57]

Of the three countries being examined, only the *Central Commission for the Prosecution of Crimes against the Polish Nation* in Poland has been able to carry out investigative work and has been directly involved in criminal proceedings. From 2006 it focused on crimes perpetrated after 1956 when the public prosecutors based there had first given priority to the Stalinist crimes.[58] In keeping with the IPN law's focus on "National Socialist crimes" (*zbrodnie nazistowskie*), starting with the invasion of Poland by the German Wehrmacht on September 1, 1939, the Central Commission also turned its attention to the murder of Jewish citizens, the abuse of detainees, the execution of resistance fighters by the Gestapo, deportations into the General Governorate (the German zone of occupation established after the invasion of Poland), torture and abuse in forced labor camps, the execution of members of the Polish Home Army, the liquidation of ghettos on Polish territory and mass murder that was carried out there, mass executions of Polish citizens, the murder of patients in psychiatric institutions and forced labor within the territory conquered by the Third Reich.[59] In 2004 the IPN initiated the international search for twelve perpetrators of "National Socialist crimes" through Interpol.[60] It investigated crimes committed by the Wehrmacht

---

[57] Ústav pro studium totalitních režimů (ed.): *Výroční zpráva Ústavu pro studium totalitních režimů za rok 2008 [2008 Annual Report of the Institute for the Study of Totalitarian Regimes]*, Prague. Available at: http://www.ustrcr.cz/data/pdf/uredni-deska/zprava2008.pdf. Last accessed: 4.6.2019, 28 and following. See also the ÚSTR website at https://www.ustrcr.cz/uvod/popraveni-plotzensee/ and https://www.ustrcr.cz/uvod/pankracka-sekyrarna/. Last accessed: 4.6.2019.

[58] Instytut Pamięci Narodowej (eds.): *Informacja o działalności Instytutu Pamięci Narodowej – Komisji Ścigania Zbrodni przeciwko Narodowi Polskiemu w okresie 1 stycznia 2007 r.–31 grudnia 2007 r. [Information on the activities of the Institute of National Remembrance – Commission for the Prosecution of Crimes against the Polish Nation from January 1, 2007 to December 31, 2009]*, Warsaw, 15. Available at: https://ipn.gov.pl/pl/o-ipn/informacje-o-dzialalnos/24313,w-okresie-1-stycznia-2009-r-31-grudnia-2009-r.html. Last accessed: 4.6.2019.

[59] Instytut Pamięci Narodowej (ed.): *Informacja o działalności Instytutu Pamięci Narodowej – Komisji Ścigania Zbrodni przeciwko Narodowi Polskiemu w okresie 1 lipca 2000 r.–30 czerwca 2001 r. [Information on the activities of the Institute of National Remembrance – Commission for the Prosecution of Crimes against the Polish Nation from July 1, 2000 to June 30, 2001]*, Warsaw, 33 and following. Available at: https://ipn.gov.pl/pl/o-ipn/informacje-o-dzialalnos/24321,w-okresie-1-lipca-2000-r-30-czerwca-2001-r.html. Last accessed: 4.6.2019.

[60] Instytut Pamięci Narodowej (ed.): *Informacja o działalności Instytutu Pamięci Narodowej – Komisji Ścigania Zbrodni przeciwko Narodowi Polskiemu w okresie 1 lipca 2003 r.–30 czerwca*

in Poland which were not classed as war crimes by German investigative authorities but as crimes carried out as part of the resistance struggle which led to the proceedings being halted in Germany.[61] And it achieved some success in repealing judgments that had been reached by German special courts against Polish citizens during the period of German occupation by the German public prosecution authorities.[62] From the start of its investigatory work, the Central Commission cultivated a working relationship with the German *Central Office of the Land Judicial Authorities for Investigation of National Socialist Crimes* and other foreign investigative and prosecuting bodies.[63]

The investigative work carried out by the IPN also meant that historical materials could be processed and previously unknown testimonies obtained and used as the basis of academic research and publishing activities relating to the cases in question.[64] IPN public prosecutors interviewed 600 witnesses about the forced displacement of approximately 20,000 Poles from the area around the town of Żywiec by German occupiers at the end of 1940 during what was called *Action Saybusch*, and handed over the collection of documents relating to the investigations to the Public Education Office at the IPN where it was used to form the basis of a publication.[65] The institute's references to the

---

2004 r. [*Information on the activities of the Institute of National Remembrance – Commission for the Prosecution of Crimes against the Polish Nation from July 1, 2003 to June 30, 2004*], Warsaw, 9. Available at: https://ipn.gov.pl/pl/o-ipn/informacje-o-dzialalnos/24318,w-okresie-1-lipca-2003-r-30-czerwca-2004-r.html. Last accessed: 4.6.2019.

[61] Instytut Pamięci Narodowej (ed.): *Informacja o działalności Instytutu Pamięci Narodowej – Komisji Ścigania Zbrodni przeciwko Narodowi Polskiemu w okresie 1 lipca 2002 r.–30 czerwca 2003 r.* [*Information on the activities of the Institute of National Remembrance – Commission for the Prosecution of Crimes against the Polish Nation from July 1, 2002 to June 30, 2003*], Warsaw, 36. Available at: https://ipn.gov.pl/pl/o-ipn/informacje-o-dzialalnos/24319,w-okresie-1-lipca-2002-r-30-czerwca-2003-r.html. Last accessed: 4.6.2019.

[62] IPN, 2004, 9.

[63] Instytut Pamięci Narodowej (ed.): *Informacja o działalności Instytutu Pamięci Narodowej – Komisji Ścigania Zbrodni przeciwko Narodowi Polskiemu w okresie 1 lipca 2001 r.–30 czerwca 2002 r.* [*Information on the activities of the Institute of National Remembrance – Commission for the Prosecution of Crimes against the Polish Nation from July 1, 2001 to June 30, 2002*], Warsaw, 8. Available at: https://ipn.gov.pl/pl/o-ipn/informacje-o-dzialalnos/24320,w-okresie-1-lipca-2001-r-30-czerwca-2002-r.html. Last accessed: 4.6.2019.

[64] IPN, 2004, 10.

[65] Instytut Pamięci Narodowej (ed.): *Informacja o działalności Instytutu Pamięci Narodowej – Komisji Ścigania Zbrodni przeciwko Narodowi Polskiemu w okresie 1 lipca 2004 r.–31 grudnia 2005 r.* [*Information on the activities of the Institute of National Remembrance – Commission for the Prosecution of Crimes against the Polish Nation from July 1, 2004 to December 31, 2005*], Warsaw, 50. Available at: https://ipn.gov.pl/pl/o-ipn/informacje-o-dzialalnos/24317,w-okresie-1-lipca-2004-r-31-grudnia-2005-r.html. Last accessed: 4.6.2019. Popular academic literature written

positive outcomes of its investigative work regardless of any actual convictions, make it even more obvious that both the institute and the Central Commission were always acutely aware of their limited success in the area of criminal prosecutions. This unquestionably related to the advancing years of the victims and perpetrators from the period of German occupation and the Stalinist era. The *Ostatni Świadek* (*The Last Witness*) campaign initiated by the IPN in 2012 appealed for elderly citizens to provide the IPN with information about possible crimes committed against the Polish population. In many instances it was presumed this would be the last opportunity to at least document these types of cases and perhaps make them public, even if it was not possible to carry out criminal proceedings.

One of the most important cases processed by the IPN, which was to profoundly shape the perception of the institute in Poland and abroad when it first started its work, were the investigations carried out by the Central Commission into the Jedwabne pogrom. The case concerned the massacre of Jewish residents in the town of Jedwabne in 1941 by fellow Polish citizens. Staff at the IPN analyzed the case files from 1949 and 1953, questioned witnesses in Poland and Israel and arranged disinterments in Jedwabne.[66] The institute established that at least 340 Jewish citizens were murdered or burned alive by their Polish fellow countrymen whilst German troops were present in the area. It also underscored the fact that these events were not unique. The subsequent public debates in Poland resulted in a comprehensive study by the IPN[67] and an emotionally charged debate across society and in the political arena surrounding the emphasis that is given to historical events in terms of the way the Polish see themselves and define their past, ranging from a "monumental history" to a "critical history" and from a "history of national glory" to "a history of national shame".[68] Alongside its publishing activities, the institute also undertook measures to increase public awareness. Seminars were organized for school students and teachers from the

---

by Mirosław Sikora and Monika Bortlik-Dźwierzyńska was published in 2010: *Aktion Saybusch. Wysiedlenie mieszkańców Żywiecczyzny przez okupanta niemieckiego 1940–1941* [*Action Saybusch. The Displacement of the Citizens from the Żywiec Region Through the German Occupation 1940–1941*], the author explicitly refers to the testimonies of hundreds of victims and witnesses that were collected and used as sources by the IPN District Commission in Katowice.

66 IPN, 2001, 10–11.
67 Paweł Machcewicz and Krzysztof Persak (eds.): *Wokół Jedwabnego* [*About Jedwabne*], Warsaw: IPN, 2002.
68 Andrzej Nowak: "Westerplatte oder Jedwabne", in Ruth Henning (ed.): *Die "Jedwabne-Debatte" in polnischen Zeitungen und Zeitschriften. Dokumentation*, Potsdam: Deutsch-polnische Gesellschaft Brandenburg, 2002, 354–357, here 355; Paweł Machcewicz: "Westerplatte und Jedwabne", in ibid., 358–361.

Jedwabne region[69] and the institute worked with the *Auschwitz-Birkenau Memorial and Museum* and the *Yad Vashem Holocaust Memorial* to compile information on thousands of Polish citizens who were murdered or had to suffer repression during the Second World War because they helped their fellow Jewish countrymen.[70] The institute wanted to use its internet portal entitled "A Life for a Life" to work against what was perceived as a one-sided view of Polish-Jewish relations which presented the Poles as perpetrators and Jews as victims.[71] The question of guilt surrounding the Holocaust is even to this day seen as a serious and delicate matter. This is demonstrated by the campaign initiated by the IPN already some years ago to challenge the international media's use of the expression "Polish concentration camps" which inferred that the camps had been set up by Poles. In the same context, in 2018, an amendment to the act on the IPN was signed into law in order to protect Poland's reputation.[72]

The way the IPN tackles this difficult chapter in Polish history and Polish-Jewish relations therefore demonstrates that even in a period of the recent past that was not overshadowed by the communist regime there were issues that awaited scrutiny, and questions raised about responsibility which could be seen to be of enormous current relevance. It also underscores the balancing act that the *Institutes of National Remembrance* must perform between academic research and often prescriptive educational work, especially when considering questions concerning the roles of victims and perpetrators. The fact that the IPN branch office in Białystok abandoned investigations concerning the events in Jedwabne in 2004 because it was not possible to identify any perpetrators who had not already been convicted in previous trials,[73] underlines how much importance can also be attributed to these kinds of questions beyond matters relating to criminal prosecutions. The general impact of the research findings was ultimately more modest by comparison which is reflected in the results of the surveys that were conducted when the major public debate was held in 2001: The majority of people surveyed said that they had heard of the events in Jed-

---

69 IPN, 2001, 71–72.
70 IPN, 2008, 10.
71 Dudek, 2011, 283–284. The portal can be accessed at http://zyciezazycie.pl/. Last accessed: 4.6.2019.
72 The amendment to the law initially criminalized undermining the reputation of Poland, threatening a possible prison sentence of up to three years, however, this was toned down following international protest.
73 Instytut Pamięci Narodowej – Oddziałowa *Komisja Ścigania Zbrodni przeciwko Narodowi Polskiemu* w Białymstoku: *Postanowienie o umorzeniu śledztwa [Decision on the Cessation of Investigations]*, S1/00/Zn, Białystok: IPN, 2003.

wabne and were aware that Jewish citizens had been the victims.[74] However, only part of those surveyed were aware of the key observation from the debate on Jedwabne, namely the fact that Polish citizens acted as perpetrators in this and similar cases.[75]

The ÚPN in Slovakia was not able to carry out its own independent investigations or lustration processes. It could only initiate criminal proceedings by collecting relevant material and handing it over to the public prosecutors. It focused especially on deaths in custody and border deaths before 1989, but this did not lead to criminal convictions.[76] This, the disclosure of information relating to groups of perpetrators and victims via registers and lists played an even more important part in how the ÚPN saw its role. In addition to registration protocols, which included information on official and unofficial employees of the Czechoslovak state security service or on officials from the Communist Party, the institute published information on the closure and "aryanization" of Jewish businesses, on the commanders of the Hlinka Guard, on the Jewish population in Slovakia in 1942 and on people who were deported to gulags.[77] Culpable organizations, such as the Hlinka Guard, and Jewish citizens who were persecuted between 1939 and 1945 were now also specifically named. The complexities of Slovakia's recent past are demonstrated in the way Slovak citizens who died fighting in conflicts with the Soviet Union when the Slovak state was an ally of the German Reich are presented by the ÚPN. They are regarded as a group of victims, similar to Jewish citizens who were persecuted by the same state.

In Slovakia, however, lists which focused on the period after 1945 and unofficial employees of the former state security services garnered considerable public interest as well. The involvement of Slovak priests in the former system particularly generated a great deal of interest in the media. The work of the ÚPN was therefore the focus of attention in two respects; first, because it dealt with the period when the cleric Tiso governed the Slovak Republic and therefore with the degree of influence and accountability prominent church officials had in issues such as the deportation of Jewish citizens. Second, on the publication of the

---

74 CBOS (ed.): *Polacy wobec zbrodni w Jedwabnem – Prezmiany społecznej świadomości* [*The Poles Response to the Crimes in Jedwabne – Shifts in Social Attitudes*], BS/120/2001, 2.

75 In September 2001, 30 percent of those surveyed could not specify who the perpetrators in Jedwabne were. Ibid.

76 Ústav pamäti národa (ed): *Výročná správa o činnosti 2007* [*2007 Annual Activity Report*], Bratislava, 28. Available at: http://www.upn.gov.sk/data/upn-vyrocna-sprava-2007.pdf. Last accessed: 4.6.2019, 28; see also written statements by the ÚPN to the author dated 22.7.2014.

77 All registers and lists can be accessed via the ÚPN website at https://www.upn.gov.sk/. Last accessed: 4.6.2019.

state security service records, reference was also made to the priests in various categories and in some cases they were also identified as being collaborators. The public debate surrounding the extent to which these and other individuals acted as unofficial collaborators, which also resulted in libel lawsuits against the ÚPN,[78] significantly overshadowed the disclosure of other groups of victims and perpetrators, and other activities that were being undertaken by the ÚPN. However, this was a deliberate strategic approach on the part of the institute. The ÚPN hoped to use these kinds of disclosures to initiate a kind of voluntary lustration process within the affected Slovak authorities and institutions without there being an explicit lustration law in place.[79]

Conclusion

Activities undertaken by the *Institutes of National Remembrance* in Poland, Slovakia and the Czech Republic formally focused on framing both the National Socialist/fascist and the period of state socialism as repressive systems to the same degree. However, as far as political and public perception was concerned, the prime focus was on the communist period. Most notably, in terms of the scope of their research activities, their public profile and the degree of meaning that was attached on a political level, their work on the archival legacy of the communist state security services significantly overshadowed the way the National Socialist period (period of occupation) was dealt with after 1989. This was due to the fact that, undeniably, concerning the communist period there was a lack of research and because it was now easier to access the source materials on this period.

However, this should be understood in light of the type of approach the institutes took to clarifying specific issues, especially in relation to the communist state security services. Activities related to the political past undertaken by the institutes – often in the form of lists – which focused on inclusion and exclusion through defining groups of heroes, victims and perpetrators, left very little gray areas when it came to individual guilt and involvement. Although relevant lists

---

[78] Ústav pamäti národa (ed): *Výročná správa o činnosti 2012* [*2012 Annual Activity Report*], Bratislava, 11. Available at: http://www.upn.gov.sk/data/upn-vyrocna-sprava-2003.pdf. Last accessed: 4.6.2019.
[79] See also the comments made by the first Chair of the ÚPN Ján Langoš in Nadya Nedelsky: "Czechoslovakia and the Czech and Slovak Republics", in Lavinia Stan (ed.): *Transitional Justice in Eastern Europe and the Former Soviet Union. Reckoning with the Communist Past*, London and New York: Routledge, 2009, 37–75, 55–56.

on the period between 1938/39 and 1945 also existed, they received far less public attention, supposedly because they were not seen to be as relevant and topical. The work of the *Institutes of National Remembrance* on the period of German occupation and the Second World War therefore appears to have been dealt with in an almost dispassionate way, even though this period of history in these countries was continuously processed in the form of infinite lists, and research and educational work.

Nevertheless, the institutes' work on the National Socialist/fascist period achieved political importance and was able to raise public awareness, especially in terms of raising questions relating to how the whole of society associates perpetrators and victims within a context of foreign domination and complicity. The debate in Poland surrounding Jedwabne clearly shows how the institute could certainly fracture views equally across the whole of society concerning the status of victims, perpetrators and heroes, but could then also contribute towards a renewed sense of self-assurance. In terms of the way the period 1938/39 to 1945 is remembered, the institutes could and can therefore try to shape significantly the commemorative cultures of their countries. Apparently, a broader level of public awareness requires to fathom controversies in areas of apparent consensus. However, it is questionable whether this would be helpful when considering the legitimate academic research and long-term educational activities carried out by the institutes. The self-perception of the *Institutes of National Remembrance* with their investigative and political drive relates primarily to the communist period – as could already be seen during the parliamentary debates. In the end, exactly this factor could have a positive impact on the way these institutions deal with the National Socialist/fascist period in their work.

Puck Huitsing and Edwin Klijn
Linking and Enriching Archival Collections in the Digital Age

The *Dutch War Collections* Network

Abstract: Digitizing collections offers new opportunities to link and connect historical data. In digital format, collections are no longer bound to the physical walls of the heritage institutions or the limitations of their original carriers. In machine-readable format, the information in collections can become part of the linked data-cloud, adding context and meaning to the individual resources. Based on their experience in the *Dutch War Collections* project, the authors claim that semantic web technologies can help heritage institutions to reinvent themselves as trusted digital expertise centers. More generally, connecting and enriching data will bring collections closer to a worldwide audience interested in the history of the Second World War (WWII).

Introduction

In the twenty-first century the digital revolution is reaching maturity at full speed. This will have huge consequences for heritage institutions, like for instance archives and documentation centers that hold document collections on the victims of Nazi persecution. Access to collections in the digital era requires new strategies, expertise and skills. Heritage institutions are challenged to re-evaluate their role and function. What is their added value? How to anticipate different forms of presentation and user groups? Basically, how do you claim your niche in the digital age?

This chapter attempts to provide some insights into relevant developments and explores ways for heritage institutions to adapt to the rapidly changing circumstances. The example of the *Dutch War Collections* (*Netwerk Oorlogsbronnen*) network serves as use-case. *Netwerk Oorlogsbronnen* is a cooperation of approximately 80 heritage institutions that hold collections on WWII. Its aim is to improve digital access to the joint collections through linking and connecting. In part 1, the conceptual framework is explained, part 2 expands on its implementation in practice, and part 3 reflects on new opportunities for both heritage and academic institutions to become part of the digital revolution themselves.

OpenAccess. © 2020 Puck Huitsing and Edwin Klijn, published by De Gruyter. This work is licensed under the Creative Commons Attribution-NonCommercial-NoDerivatives 4.0 License.
https://doi.org/10.1515/9783110665376-018

It is argued that in order to comply with today's and tomorrow's user demands collections should be perceived as building blocks for narratives that transcend the walls of the individual institutions. *Thematic intellectual management* is a conceptual framework in which the theme, not the collection holding organization, is leading. Digitization, automated text recognition and enrichment with semantic web technologies are helpful in turning documents into data, and data into information. There is a clear benefit for heritage institutions to cooperate with scholars and vice versa. The biggest beneficiary of such a joint effort would be the general audience looking online for information on their relatives, hometown or any related events that happened during WWII.

Part 1: The Concept of *Thematic Intellectual Management*
Multiple Narratives, Multiple Collections, One Theme

Today, 75 years after the end of WWII, there is still a continuous interest in what has become a historical beacon for reflections on human rights, suppression and freedom of speech. According to a survey performed by *Netwerk Oorlogsbronnen* in 2015, 70 percent of the Dutch population are convinced that knowledge on WWII contributes to a better understanding of today's world.[1] Currently, with the provision of information to all those interested in WWII, some important shifts in perspective are unfolding.

First of all there is a change in relation to usage of primary sources of information. In a few years' time there will be no survivors left to provide first-hand accounts from their own experience. Eye-witness narratives are a very powerful means. They translate the abstract concept of WWII into human narratives which people can relate to. When there are no more people to tell us about what happened during WWII, collections are our second-best option to experience what Dutch historian Johan Huizinga called "the historical sensation".[2] The heritage of the war in the care of professional institutions consists of a wide variety of documents, photos, films, objects, newspaper clippings, books, etc. They are dis-

---

[1] Netwerk Oorlogsbronnen: "Kenniscentrum Oorlogsbronnen. De Nederlandse belangstelling voor de Tweede Wereldoorlog. Hedendaagse interesse en informatiebronnen". Available at: https://www.oorlogsbronnen.nl/sites/default/files/Rapport%20De%20Nederlandse%20belangstelling%20voor%20de%20Tweede%20Wereldoorlog.pdf. Last accessed: 6.6.2019.

[2] Frank R. Ankersmit: *De Historische Ervaring*, Groningen: Historische Uitgeverij, 1993, 12.

persed across a multitude of museums, archives, libraries, research institutes, universities, etc. In the Netherlands alone there are over 400 professional organizations that hold collections on WWII. There is also a large network of private collectors, amateur historians and others in possession of original materials from WWII.

Second, the ways people consume information are gradually altering. Apart from history books, TV documentaries, exhibitions and – to a lesser degree – research in archives, the internet is gaining ground as a channel of information.[3] Especially for younger generations, if something cannot be found online, it does not exist at all. New generations are often unfamiliar with heritage institutions but simply looking for information. Most of them do not have the same frame of reference as their parents or grandparents. Also, primarily they are not interested in a specific object or collection, but in information on events, persons, places or specific topics.[4] At the moment, the answers to their questions lie hidden in a multitude of mainly analogue, undiscovered collections.

The digital revolution has only recently reached the heritage field. According to a survey held amongst European archives, libraries and museums in 2017 approximately 40 percent of all collections have not been catalogued in a collection database. Although most archives are involved in digitization activities, only ten percent of all their holdings had been digitized.[5] Digitization is costly, labor intensive and requires a kind of expertise that many heritage institutions do not possess. An increasing number of those institutions publish metadata on their holdings online. They do this with different standards in various systems. Data on what they have are usually presented on their own websites only. When collections have been digitized, it often means that the scans can be consulted online. Only in a few cases are the data searchable or linked to external sources of information.

In short, a gap exists between the data supply from heritage collections and the predominantly thematic questions end users have. In 2015 the *Dutch War Collections* network defined a concept called *thematic intellectual management*. To narrow the difference between demand and supply it is crucial to create digital cross-collection access to the virtual *Dutch collection WWII* on four axes: who,

---

3 Netwerk Oorlogsbronnen: Kenniscentrum Oorlogsbronnen.
4 Ibid.
5 G.K. Nauta, W. van den Heuvel and S. Teunisse: *Europeana DSI 2- Access to Digital Resources of European Heritage*. Available at: https://www.den.nl/uploads/5c6a8684b3862327a358fccaf100 d59668eedf1f7f449.pdf. Last accessed: 6.6.2019.

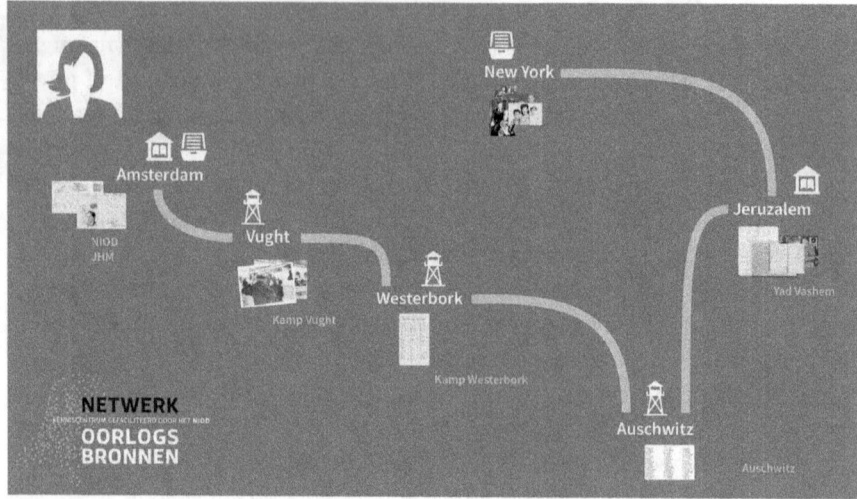

Fig. 1: One story, multiple collections (Netwerk Oorlogsbronnen)

what, where and when.[6] Preconditions for such an approach are a certain tolerance to the fact of life that institutions use different standards and systems. It also presupposes a willingness of institutions to openly share their data. *Thematic intellectual management* distinguishes between organizations that provide data and hubs that use their domain expertise to enrich the data. From a thematic and conceptual point of view, all information in the collections are building blocks that help users to construct their own narratives. The big challenge is to find ways to logically link these pieces of information and empower users to perform their own research.

Challenges for Heritage Institutions

Becoming a data-driven organization has a huge impact on the core business of heritage institutions. First of all it requires a shift in thinking. Users of collections are not only those who physically visit the reading room, but also people consulting the data online. Many heritage institutions have broad experience in trans-

---

6 Netwerk Oorlogsbronnen: "Program Plan Network War Collections". Available at: http://www.oorlogsbronnen.nl/sites/default/files/Programme%20plan%20Network%20War%20Collections_1.pdf. Last accessed: 6.6.2019.

forming analogue collections into data. These digital assets fuel web services but also serve as raw materials for researchers. Ideally, when creating indexes institutions share similar terminologies for concepts, places, persons, etc., provided and maintained by thematic organizations. As data suppliers organizations are trusted authorities that guarantee permanent access to digital objects. The prime responsibility of a data driven heritage institution is to provide high quality data. Access is not limited to metadata but ideally also to full-text documents.

Second, becoming part of a data network means a shift of perspective. Heritage institutions are used to attracting an audience that is specifically interested in their unique collections. In the digital domain most people are searching for information, not so much the collection of a single organization. Cooperation with other institutions in order to create an added value by linking data is of crucial importance for the online visibility of collections. Adding a thematic layer to the data is a joint effort of both the heritage institutions and thematic experts in the field. Also, other stake holders play an important part, for instance software suppliers and Digital Humanities researchers.

A third shift relates to the expertise at hand within organizations. What is needed is a thorough understanding of the basics of information technology, in particular collection management systems and software to create machine-readable texts and enrichments. Many institutions work with external software suppliers. For a successful cooperation, experts within the institutions need to be capable of translating user requirements into technical solutions. As technologies are rapidly changing, IT staff need to continuously keep track of what is happening around them.

A last shift is that heritage institutions become accustomed to a demand-driven market. On the web, audiences will not automatically come to your organization. Anticipating their questions and becoming part of the answer are keys in claiming one's stake online. As data supplier, your attractiveness increases if the data are presented where your target audience already is. Sharing data with platforms like *Wikimedia* is a viable strategy to reach out to new, sometimes unexpected users.

In short, moving from analogue to digital does not just require a one-time investment or a three-day training course for all staff members. It encompasses a complete reboot of the entire organization that may take years. Yet by initiating this process in time, heritage institutions can regain their reputation as trustworthy, knowledgeable, independent expertise centers.[7]

---

[7] Inge Angevaare: "Are Heritage Institutions 'Living the Digital Shift'?" Available at: http://www.ncdd.nl/are-heritage-institutions-living-the-digital-shift-dish2011-1/. Last accessed: 6.6.2019.

Research Infrastructures

In a digital environment, institutions can have different, often overlapping roles: data supplier, user of data or data improver. Knowledge on the contents of a collection is not necessarily limited to the organization that is responsible for preserving the originals. In a digital network, thematic parties and heritage institutions join forces to improve access to the collections, profiting from the best of both worlds. They can do so by sharing tools and data, but also by feeding knowledge systems with their expertise.

In the last few years, an increasing number of thematic cooperations have been launched. So-called *research infrastructures* bring together scholars and computer scientists to develop tooling for academic research. Thematic aggregators are collaborations of heritage institutions that automatically gather (harvest) metadata from collections and build one search entry that deeply links to the objects presented in the context of the institutional websites. One of the most successful research infrastructures in the field of war and genocide studies is EHRI (*European Holocaust Research Infrastructure*).[8] Examples of thematic aggregators are the fashion portal *ModeMuze*[9] and the regional portal *Brabants Erfgoed*.[10]

Thematic aggregators are driven by the urge felt by some heritage institutions to make their collections more visible to the world outside. The driving force behind this development has been the EU-funded heritage platform *Europeana*, which today unites over 57 million items from more than 3,500 heritage institutions.[11] *Europeana* encouraged institutions to open up their collection management systems for computers to harvest and share on other platforms besides their own websites. The target audience for most thematic aggregators is the general public. Research infrastructures were invented by scholars and computer scientists, most of which focus on the re-use of data, developing tools for scientific research. *Research infrastructures* generally serve an audience of experts.[12]

Despite the obvious differences, *research infrastructures* and thematic aggregators have a lot in common. First of all, they both depend on the availability of collection data. Greater digitization and standardization are beneficial to both.

---

[8] European Holocaust Research Infrastructure. Available at: https://www.ehri-project.eu. Last accessed: 6.6.2019.
[9] Modemuze. Available at: https://www.modemuze.nl/collecties. Last accessed: 6.6.2019.
[10] Brabants Erfgoed. Available at: https://www.brabantserfgoed.nl. Last accessed: 6.6.2019.
[11] Europeana. Available at: https://www.europeana.eu. Last accessed: 6.6.2019.
[12] European Research Infrastructures. Available at: https://ec.europa.eu/info/research-and-innovation/strategy/european-research-infrastructures_en. Last accessed: 6.6.2019.

Second, they are agorae for domain experts and other people interested in the topic concerned. Finally, they have a shared interest in enriching the metadata to increase their usability. Currently, research infrastructures and thematic aggregators are worlds apart, even though they are both working towards providing better access to collections. Tools developed in the field of Digital Humanities would sometimes also be beneficial for improving search-and-retrieval of collection data. The expertise of collection specialists would in some cases be very useful to build clever tooling. Approaching collections from a thematic perspective in the digital era means working in multidisciplinary cooperations in a networked environment to serve a worldwide audience.

A Use Case: *Dutch War Collections* (*Netwerk Oorlogsbronnen*)

Dutch War Collections originates from a large-scale preservation and digitization programme called *Heritage of the War*. Between 2006 and 2010, in more than 200 projects, large amounts of original documents, films, oral history, newspapers, pamphlets and other source materials were digitized and made available online. The assumption behind *Heritage of the War* was that once the eye witnesses passed away, collections would be the only remaining sources of information to keep the memory of WWII alive. Giving them a new life digitally would ensure their availability in the future.

Originally, *Dutch War Collections* started as a *Europeana*-style thematic aggregator. It periodically harvested the metadata from the local systems of the institutions and made them searchable through one singular online access point. From the start, the focus was not just on constructing a digital network. On a regular basis, conferences and expert meetings for collection experts were organized to encourage the involvement of the institutions in the joint effort. In 2015 its scope was broadened due to the shared ambition of some stakeholders who recognized the potential of further cooperation in the digital domain. Together with over 60 institutions in the war heritage field, a plan was compiled that translated the visions into a number of projects and activities.[13]

Essentially, *Dutch War Collections* moved from being a thematic aggregator to something that could best be described as a thematic platform. One of the biggest issues with aggregating huge amounts of collection data was that people

---

[13] Netwerk Oorlogsbronnen: "Program Plan Network War Collections". Available at: http://www.oorlogsbronnen.nl/sites/default/files/Programme%20plan%20Network%20War%20Collections_1.pdf. Last accessed: 6.6.2019.

searching on the portal site www.oorlogsbronnen.nl drowned in the overflow of information. What was needed was more context and better links between the data. The expertise was in the heads of the experts. Semantic web technology offered the tooling to datify their knowledge and use it to contextualize data from collections. *Dutch War Collections* became a platform that explored ways to put into practice the concept of *thematic intellectual management*. Conceptually, it has developed into a raw data factory that collects and enriches collection data on the basis of standardized reference data. The enrichment focuses on four elementary access points: who, what, where and when.[14]

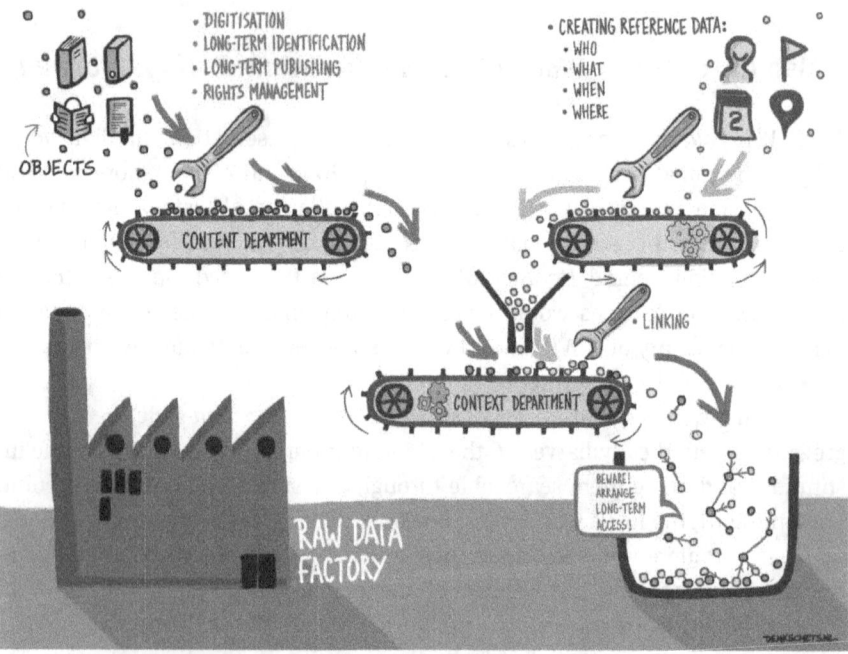

Fig. 2: Dutch War Collections as 'raw data factory' (Netwerk Oorlogsbronnen)

In 2015, *Dutch War Collections* changed its organizational structure. Heritage institutions with WWII collections were invited to officially become a partner. A steering group, consisting of some eminent stake holders, was put in charge of the governance of the network and its activities. *Dutch War Collections* gradually

---

[14] W3C, Semantic Web. Available at: https://www.w3.org/standards/semanticweb. Last accessed: 6.6.2019.

developed into a platform where heritage institutions cooperate to improve the visibility of their collections in the context of others. In *Dutch War Collections* digital services are developed that (semi-)automatically enrich the collection data of participants. Currently, *Dutch War Collections* has 81 consortium members, mainly museums, remembrance organizations and archives.[15] A small project team of six members, housed at *NIOD Institute of War, Holocaust and Genocide Studies* in Amsterdam, coordinates all projects and organizes fundraising. *Dutch War Collections* is supported by the Ministry of Health, Welfare and Sport, Fonds and several other funds.

Dutch War Collections embraces the philosophy that visibility of the collections is not only boosted by attracting users to one place, but in particular by ensuring that the data are presented where users already are. Experiments are done to link to *Wikidata* and other *Wikimedia*-platforms. Regional cooperation is also set up to create a network of satellite sites, focusing on the WWII history of a specific province or theme. For example, in the Dutch province of Gelderland in 2018 a site was launched that linked the items from a wide variety of collections to approximately 1,300 locations in the region.[16] In 2019, together with the *Indisch Herinneringscentrum*, a portal site was developed that specifically presents collection items that relate to the Dutch Indies during WWII.[17] Both the Gelderland and the Dutch Indies sites recycle collection data from the data repository of *Dutch War Collections*.

One of the main conclusions after three years of constructing the *raw data factory* is that semantic web technologies are very well suited to linking and connecting data. Events modelling, data visualizations, macro-analyses, query expansion; these are just some of the promising perspectives when data are connected in a linked data environment. Not only are the empirical foundations of historical research strengthened by interconnectivity, but clustering data around groups or events can lead to new insights in cause-and-effect relationships. By virtually tearing down institutional walls, phenomena like the Second World War can be studied from multiple perspectives: as a local, regional, but also as an international occurrence. New research questions may be formulated that were previously complicated or simply impossible to perform, like for instance, "What happened to Cornelis Gootjes during the war?", "What was the deadliest day during the Second World War?" and "What were the chances of survival in Camp Vught compared to Camp Westerbork?". In part 2 we will

---

15 As of June 6, 2019.
16 WO2 Gelderland. Available at: https://www.wo2gld.nl. Last accessed: 6.6.2019.
17 Dutch Indies in wartime. Available at: https://www.indieinoorlog.nl. Last accessed: 6.6.2019.

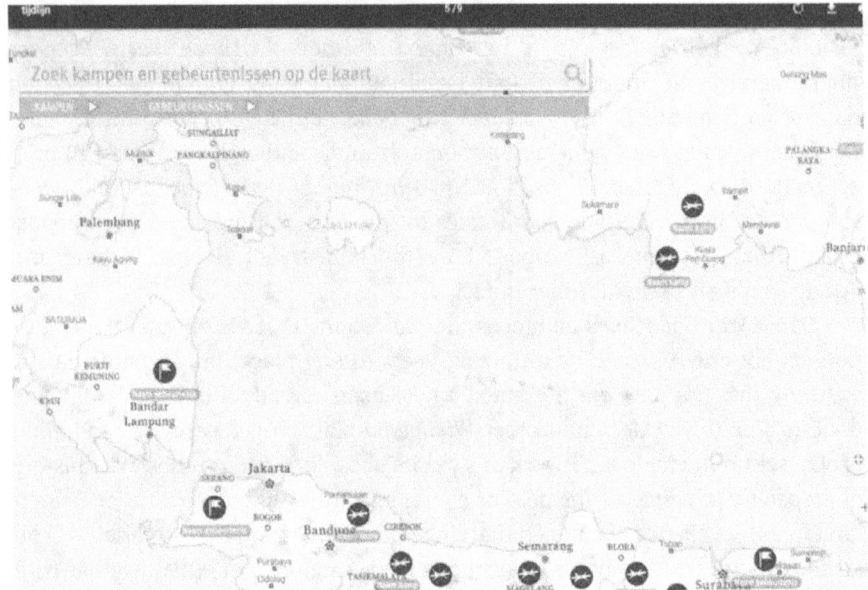

Fig. 3: Screenshot of portal 'Indie in Oorlog', powered by Dutch War Collections (www.indieinoorlog.nl. Last accessed: 22.8.2019)

take a closer look at how linking and connecting can be applied to contextualize historical resources.

Part 2: Practice

In the infancy of the web, *Hyper Text Markup Language* (HTML) was used to encode information. Although this was originally not the intention of its inventor Tim Berners-Lee, HTML soon developed into a language used to provide instructions to a computer on how to visually present information on a computer terminal. HTML did not actually tell the computer about the meaning of the information, it simply provided orders how it should be displayed. In 2002 Tim Berners-Lee, together with James Hendler and Ora Lassila, laid the foundations for the idea of the so-called *semantic web:*

> The Semantic Web is not a separate Web but an extension of the current one, in which information is given well-defined meaning, better enabling computers and people to work in cooperation. The first steps in weaving the Semantic Web into the structure of the existing Web are already under way. In the near future, these developments will usher in significant

new functionality as machines become much better able to process and *understand* the data that they merely display at present.[18]

The concept of the semantic web strongly evolves around the principle of structuring data at the root in such a way that it can be linked to other sources of information, thus turning *a web of documents* into a *web of data*.[19]

Archival collections are all about information. Documents, photographs, videos, books, newspapers, audio recordings are all information carriers that hold data that can be interlinked and applied to construct narratives. Currently, little is known about the exact contents of archival collections. Often, the metadata provided on specific archives or inventories are very generic, for example *Correspondence of the Jewish Council of Amsterdam with the municipal government*. Even when collections have been scanned at document-level, actually searching through them is not possible. Collections are also seldom presented in the context of other related archives.

The Foundations: Machine-Readable Text

When digitizing archival materials, scanning is just a first step. For a computer, a scan of a text page is no different than a holiday snapshot. To allow users to digitally search through all text within the documents, software is required that converts the characters in a scan into machine-readable text. The raw materials produced by this transformation also serve as a starting point for automatically linking the data to external sources of information. The error rate of the software transforming analogue text-based materials into machine-readable text depends on the quality of the original, as some of the cases below will illustrate.

For example, consider the diary entry of Westerbork camp prisoner Etty Hillesum on June 7, 1943. She provided assistance when the first train of children deported from Kamp Vught arrived at 4 AM in the morning:
If you apply *Optical Character Recognition* (OCR) software to interpret this image, it produces this machine-readable text:

---

18 Tim Berners-Lee, James Hendler and Ora Lassila: "The Semantic Web. A New Form of Web Content that is Meaningful to Computers Will Unleash a Revolution of New Possibilities", in *Scientific American*, May 2001. Available at: http://www-sop.inria.fr/acacia/cours/essi2006/Scientific%20American_%20Feature%20Article_%20The%20Semantic%20Web_%20May%202001.pdf. Last accessed: 6.6.2019.
19 W3C Semantic Web Frequently Asked Questions. Available at: http://www.w3.org/RDF/FAQ. Last accessed: 6.6.2019.

> Vught altijd veel luizen meekomen. Van 4 tot 9 heb ik met kleine
> huilende kinderen gesjouwd en bagage gedragen voor uitgeputte
> vrouwen. Het was hard- en hartverscheurend. Vrouwen met kleine
> kinderen, 1600 (vannacht komen er weer 1600), de mannen zijn op-
> zettelijk achtergehouden in Vught. De transporttrein voor morgen-

Fig. 4: Excerpt from: Etty Hillesum: *Etty. De nagelaten geschriften van Etty Hillesum 1941–1943*, Amsterdam: Balans, 1986, 639

> Vught altijd veel luizen meekomen. Van 4 tot 9 heb ik met kleine
> huilende kinderen gesjouwd en bagage gedragen voor uitgeputte
> vrouwen. Het was hard- en hartverscheurend. Vrouwen met kleine
> kinderen, 1600 (vannacht komen er weer 1600), de mannen zijn op-
> zettelijk achtergehouden in Vught. De transporttrein voor morgen-[20]

The manuscript of Etty Hillesums war diary was published in 1986. The neatly printed pages lead to a perfect digital transcription.

In the case of historical archives, the error rates of automated text recognition-software, commonly expressed in *Word Error Rate* (WER = percentage of words that has been incorrectly interpreted), very much depend on the condition of the original.[21] In 2017 the *Koninklijke Bibliotheek* (National Library of the Netherlands) measured a WER of approximately 11 with a small sample from 12 million digitized and OCR'd newspaper pages.[22] For instance, in 1945 the first eye witness accounts of what happened in Vught circulated in the Dutch underground newspapers. In *Moed en Vertrouwen* on May 5, 1945 war correspondent John O'Conner interviewed some Dutch children in camp Buchenwald.[23] Two of them were deported during the children's deportations in Vught:

Due to the clear type font, the excellent quality of the ink and the ample spaces between the lines, the OCR-result is near perfect.

> Ik sprak de negenjarige Josef Berger, die eerst in Vught, later in Sachsenhausen en tenslotte
> hier terecht was gekomen. Alleen omdat hij een Joods kind is. Hij is afkomstig uit Den

---

20 Etty Hillesum: *Etty: De nagelaten geschriften van Etty Hillesum 1941–1943*, Amsterdam: Balans, 1986, 639–640.

21 Final report on TRIADO enrichment phase. Available at: https://www.oorlogsbronnen.nl/final-report-triado-enrichment-phase. Last accessed: 6.6.2019.

22 L. Wilms: "Newspaper OCR quality – What do we have and how can we improve it?" Available at: http://lab.kb.nl/about-us/blog/%E2%80%8Bnewspaper-ocr-quality-%E2%80%93-what-do-we-have-and-how-can-we-improve-it. Last accessed: 6.6.2019.

23 *Moed en Vertrouwen: Weekblad voor de opbouw van Nederland*, 3/40, 1945. Available at: https://resolver.kb.nl/resolve?urn=MMNIOD05:000117247. Last accessed: 6.6.2019.

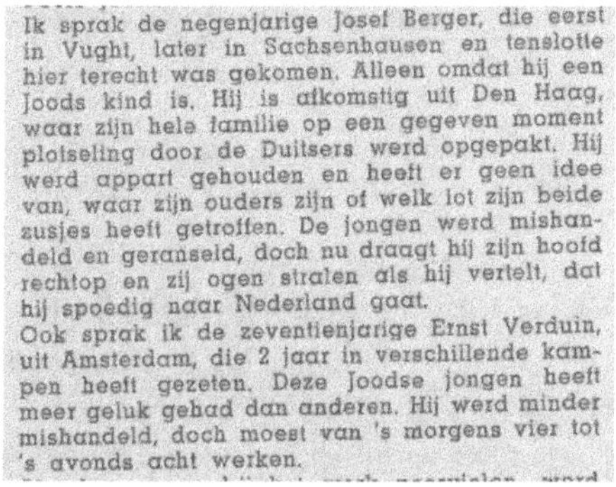

> Ik sprak de negenjarige Josef Berger, die eerst in Vught, later in Sachsenhausen en tenslotte hier terecht was gekomen. Alleen omdat hij een Joods kind is. Hij is afkomstig uit Den Haag, waar zijn hele familie op een gegeven moment plotseling door de Duitsers werd opgepakt. Hij werd appart gehouden en heeft er geen idee van, waar zijn ouders zijn of welk lot zijn beide zusjes heeft getroffen. De jongen werd mishandeld en geranseld, doch nu draagt hij zijn hoofd rechtop en zij ogen stralen als hij vertelt, dat hij spoedig naar Nederland gaat.
> Ook sprak ik de zeventienjarige Ernst Verduin, uit Amsterdam, die 2 jaar in verschillende kampen heeft gezeten. Deze Joodse jongen heeft meer geluk gehad dan anderen. Hij werd minder mishandeld, doch moest van 's morgens vier tot 's avonds acht werken.

Fig. 5: Excerpt from: Moed en Vertrouwen. Weekblad voor de opbouw van Nederland, 3, 40/1945

Haag, waar zijn hele familie op een gegeven moment plotseling door de Duitsers werd opgepakt. Hij werd appart gehouden en heeft er geen idee van, waar zijn ouders zijn of welk lot zijn beide zusjes heeft getroffen. De jongen werd mishandeld en geranseld, doch nu draagt hij zijn hootd rechtop en zij ogen stralen als hij vertelt, dat hij spoedig naar Nederland gaat. Ook sprak ik de zeventienjarige Ernst Verduin, uit Amsterdam, die 2 jaar in verschillende kampen heeft gezeten. Deze Joodse jongen heeft meer geluk gehad dan anderen. Hij werd minder mishandeld, doch moest van 's morgens vier tot 's avonds acht werken.

In the case of typewritten archival documents, the WER is usually worse, due to faded ink, the poor quality of the paper, stains or other forms of deterioration. For example, take this announcement by the camp staff in Kamp Vught (June 5, 1943) to inform prisoners of the deportation of the children.[24]

Here, due to the irregular font and the 'filling' of s, e and a, the quality of the OCR is rather poor.

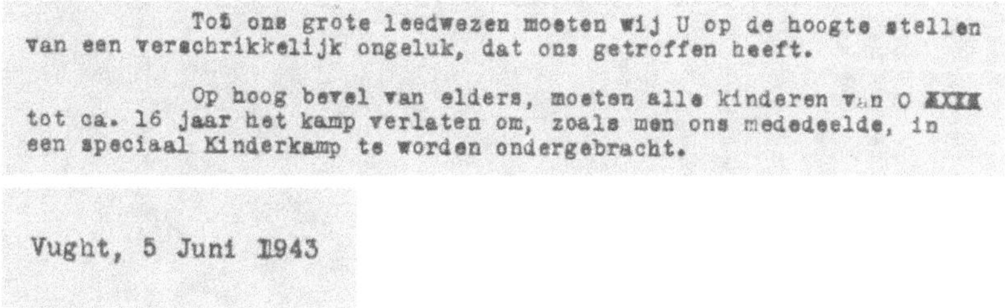

> Tot ons grote leedwezen moeten wij U op de hoogte stellen van een verschrikkelijk ongeluk, dat ons getroffen heeft.
>
> Op hoog bevel van elders, moeten alle kinderen van 0 XIII tot ca. 16 jaar het kamp verlaten om, zoals men ons mededeelde, in een speciaal Kinderkamp te worden ondergebracht.
>
> Vught, 5 Juni 1943

Fig. 6: Excerpt from document number: D000177, Collection Jewish Historical Museum, Amsterdam

---

24 D000177, Collection Jewish Historical Museum, Amsterdam.

> Tot ons grote leedwezen moeten wij ü op de hoogte "tellen
> tan een- vernchrikjcelijk ongeluk, dat ona getroffen heeft.
> Op hoog bevel van eldere, moeten alle kinderen van 0 XXXX
> tot da" 16 jaar het kamp verlaten om, zoals men one mededeelde, in
> een speciaal Kinderkamp te worden ondergebracht.
> Vught, 5 juni 1943

In the project TRIADO (*Tribunal Archives as Research Facility*), coordinated by *Dutch War Collections*, for a sample of 150 typewritten archival documents OCR'd with Abbyy Finereader 11, an overall weighted WER of 15 was measured.[25] Despite the fact that approximately one out of five words were incorrect, the user interface to perform a full-text search through the sample set of 160,000 pages still meant a spectacular improvement in the level of access.

By applying machine learning and artificial intelligence technology, automatic transcription of handwritten original texts is rapidly advancing. In the project READ, the software tool *Transkribus* is used to train software to recognize handwritten texts on the basis of a limited amount of training data.[26] Depending on the regularity of the original handwriting and the amount of training data in some projects WERs are measured that surpass the results measured with typewritten materials.

Increasingly, crowdsourcing or citizen science projects emerge to manually key in information from original documents. In 2017 *Nationaal Monument Kamp Vught*, in cooperation with *Dutch War Collections*, mobilized approximately 170 volunteers. In less than three months they entered data from 25,000 camp cards into an online database.[27] Recently a Dutch digitization company called *Picturae* launched a new version of their crowdsourcing platform (*Crowd Teaches Computer How to Read*) that uses the manual input of volunteers to train the computer in recognizing specific handwritings.[28]

---

[25] TRIADO Research Report. Available at: https://www.oorlogsbronnen.nl/final-report-triado-enrichment-phase. Last accessed: 6.6.2019.

[26] Transkribus. Available at: https://transkribus.eu/Transkribus. Last accessed: 6.6.2019.

[27] About the project, see www.oorlogsbronnen.nl/crowdsourcingsplatform-kamp-vught. Last accessed: 6.6.2019.

[28] About the project, see https://velehanden.nl/projecten/bekijk/details/project/amsterdam_correct_notarieel_transkribus. Last accessed: 6.6.2019.

Data Enrichment and Linking

Machine-readable text is required in order to make scans with text searchable, findable and attractive for re-use. Even if the text is not perfect, it can still be good enough to build search applications or make connections to other data. The sheer mass of data in itself provides computers with useful input for making an estimated guess on whether *Amste&dam* should really be *Amsterdam*. After creating machine-readable text reference data are added. In *Dutch War Collections* the focus is on four axes that coincide with the most frequently asked questions of web users: who ("What happened to grandfather during the war?"), what ("What was the Jewish Council of Amsterdam?"), where ("What happened to my hometown during the war?") and when ("When did the first transports from Amsterdam to Westerbork start?").

Machine-readable text can automatically be enriched with references to places, organizations, persons, events, dates, etc. For instance, when enriching the example from *Moed en Vertrouwen* used above, the results ideally are like this:

> Ik sprak de negenjarige **Josef Berger (https://data.niod.nl/WO2_biografieen/Josef-Berger)**, die eerst in **Vught (Wikidata_ID= Q12013510)**, later in **Sachsenhausen (Wikidata_ID= Q684765)** en tenslotte hier terecht was gekomen. Alleen omdat hij een Joods kind is. Hij is afkomstig uit **Den Haag (Wikidata_ID= Q36600)**, waar zijn hele familie op een gegeven moment plotseling door de Duitsers werd opgepakt. Hij werd appart gehouden en heeft er geen idee van, waar zijn ouders zijn of welk lot zijn beide zusjes heeft getroffen. De jongen werd mishandeld en geranseld, doch nu draagt hij zijn hootd rechtop en zij ogen stralen als hij vertelt, dat hij spoedig naar **Nederland (Wikidata_ID= Q55)** gaat. Ook sprak ik de zeventienjarige **Ernst Verduin (https://data.niod.nl/WO2_biografieen/Ernst-Verduin)**, uit **Amsterdam (Wikidata_ID= Q9899)**, die 2 jaar in verschillende kampen heeft gezeten. Deze Joodse jongen heeft meer geluk gehad dan anderen. Hij werd minder mishandeld, doch moest van 's morgens vier tot 's avonds acht werken.

Named Entity Recognition (NER) software is used to identify names in running text.[29] In TRIADO, experiments with NER were disappointing due to the fact that the software was not trained to deal with old Dutch and German. Automatically matching existing lists of names (persons, places) with the data proved to be a more effective method to identify names.[30] Apart from identifying names, one of the biggest challenges of automated data enrichment – especially in

---

[29] M. Gupta: "A Review of Named Entity Recognition (NER) Using Automatic Summarization of Resumes". Available at: https://towardsdatascience.com/a-review-of-named-entity-recognition-ner-using-automatic-summarization-of-resumes-5248a75de175. Last accessed: 6.6.2019.
[30] Research Report TRIADO. Available at: https://www.oorlogsbronnen.nl/final-report-triado-enrichment-phase. Last accessed: 6.6.2019.

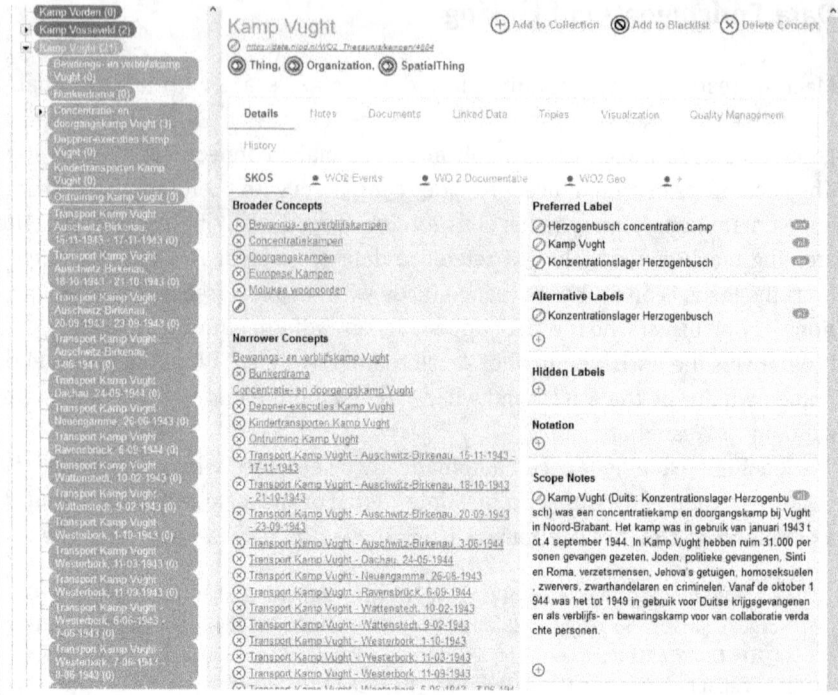

Fig. 7: WW2 Thesaurus at https://data.niod.nl/WO2_Thesaurus.html. Last accessed: 22.8.2019

case of full-text – is to find ways to cope with ambiguity. How do we know that in the excerpt above Vught and Sachsenhausen are referring to the concentration camps, not the municipalities? How do we know which Ernst Verduin is meant in this text? Archives with full-text data cannot be expected to go through these references manually to check for any mismatches. Further fine-tuning of the software with more context information may lead to higher probability rates, but there will always be a certain error margin.

Why is it so important to make links from the text to unambiguous reference data? First of all it allows us to digitally connect all examples above to the children's deportations that took place in Vught in 1943. Second, it provides the building blocks to any other related context. For linking data to organizations, concepts, events, corporations, camps and persons *Dutch War Collections* uses a linked open data WWII-thesaurus maintained by *NIOD Institute for War, Holo-*

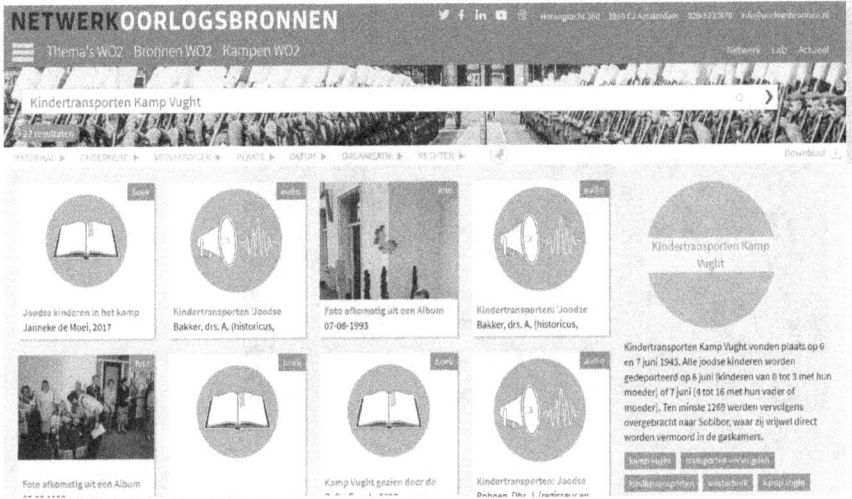

Fig. 8: Screendump from www.oorlogsbronnen.nl when searching for 'Kindertransporten'

caust and Genocide Studies.³¹ Its hierarchical structure – with broader, related and narrow terms – is extremely well fitted to record logical relationships and contextualize information. For example, the lemma 'Kamp Vught' has a scope note with a short summary of its history and references to alternative labels like its German name *Konzentrationslager Herzogenbusch*, geo-coordinates of the location and descriptions of related events, like for instance the two children's deportations in June 1943.

The information stored in the WWII thesaurus can be used on websites to provide extra information and create sophisticated search functions. In *Dutch War Collections* the data are also used to automatically interlink themes, persons, locations and events to descriptions of collection items, like oral history accounts, literature, photographs and archives.

Searching for *Kindertransporten Kamp Vught* returns 27 results from the collections of four different heritage institutions. There are references to videos, photos, literature and monuments. One of the most striking hits is an oral history video from Ernst Verduin. As a young boy, Verduin managed to be excluded from transportation, but was deported a few months later.

---

31 WOII Thesaurus. Available at: https://data.niod.nl/WO2_Thesaurus.html. Last accessed: 6.6.2019.

Fig. 9: Screenshot of oral history account of Ernst Verduin (http://getuigenverhalen.nl/inter view/interview-02-ernst-verduin. Last accessed: 6.6.2019)

Event Modelling

For the contextualization of metadata *Dutch War Collections* experiments with a method known as event modelling.[32] Events are defined as acts that relate to a moment in time and place, involving one or more actors in specific roles. In the case of our example, the event *Children deportation Vught* has this logical structure:

By recording encyclopedic information about persons, places, organizations, topics and acts in a thesaurus structure, it can be applied to provide contextual information to individual resources. For instance, if we take Etty Hillesum's report of the arrival of the children from Vught in Westerbork in the early morning of the June 7, 1943, the life events of Hillesum coincide with events relating to Kamp Vught. Schematically, this is visualized below:

---

[32] This model is loosely based on the Simple Events Modelling (SEM) concept. See W.R. van Hage, V. Malais, R. Segers, L. Hollink and G. Schreiber: "Design and Use of the Simple Event Model (SEM)", in *Web Semantics: Science, Services and Agents on the World Wide Web* 9, 2011, 128–136. Available at: https://homepages.cwi.nl/~hollink/pubs/vanHage2011SEM.pdf. Last accessed: 6.6.2019.

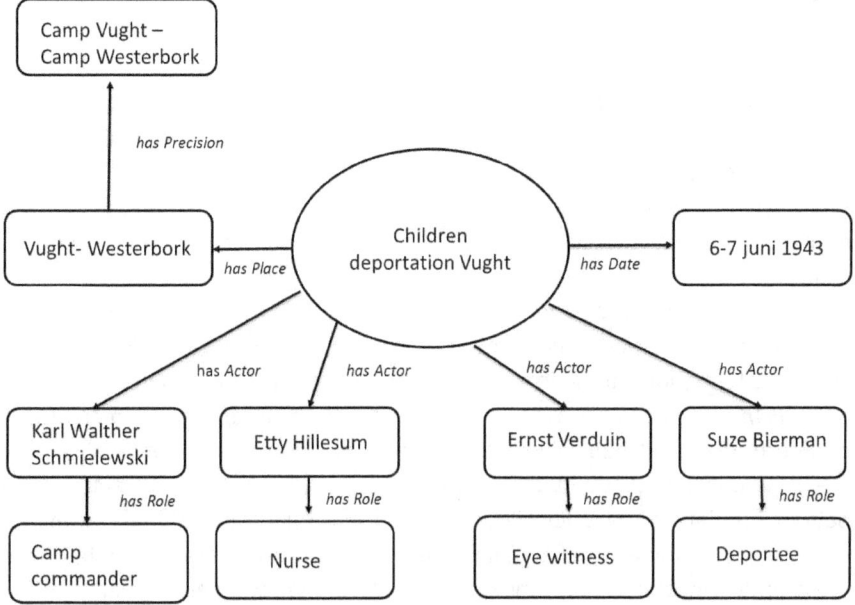

Fig. 10: Relational representation of children deportation that took place in Camp Vught (6/7 June 1943; Netwerk Oorlogsbronnen)

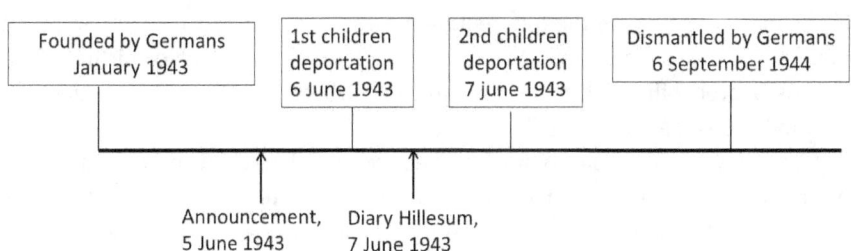

Fig. 11: Timeline about Camp Vught with related events (Netwerk Oorlogsbronnen)

When structuring information around events a web of interrelated occurrences is the result. Semantic web technology can help computers to make intelligent guesses when linking the data. Automatically connecting the data from original documents to events is still complicated.

War Lives

The main aim of *Dutch War Collections* is to improve the online visibility of all collection data. By linking the (meta)data of the collections to reference data, a thematic layer is created on top of all data available. The final goal is to supply users with sufficient information to conduct their own research. So in case of the Vught children deportations, facts about the event, the start and end data, related events, the geographical location(s) and any persons involved, can be presented.

Persons' names are probably the most popular entry point for web users. Currently in the Netherlands there are several organizations that offer online access to information on victims of persecution, such as for instance the *Jewish Monument* and the *War Graves Foundation*.[33] Some museums and remembrance organizations have their own data files with names. At the moment many of them can only be consulted under strict conditions, for instance by family members or scholars. Privacy legislation has caused organizations to be extremely careful with publishing this data online. Casual users are unfamiliar with these professional organizations and often do not know where to start.

In 2016, 13 partners of *Dutch War Collections* initiated a project called *War Lives* (*Oorlogslevens*). Its objective was to build an online web portal that would serve as a first entry point for anyone researching the whereabouts of specific persons during WWII. This concerns resistance fighters, victims of persecution, the military, collaborators and others with a specific relation to WWII. *War Lives* focused on developing a website that would allow searches through all names. Computer algorithms were also used to identify unique individuals within the mass of names in the different data files. By automatically comparing the first characters of a surname, together with the date and place of birth, it then returns a probability estimate that indicates whether two names are actually one and the same individual.

The War Lives-website (www.warlives.org) was launched in February 2020. Approximately 1 million names from 35 datasets were matched, tracing these names back to about 300,000 individuals. All names can be searched through one Google-like interface. The important life events (birth, arrest, imprisonment, etc.) are displayed on a timeline, together with references to the sources of information.

---

[33] Joods Monument. Available at: http://www.joodsmonument.nl; Oorlogsgravenstichting. Available at: http://www.oorlogsgravenstichting/zoeken. Last accessed: 6.6.2019.

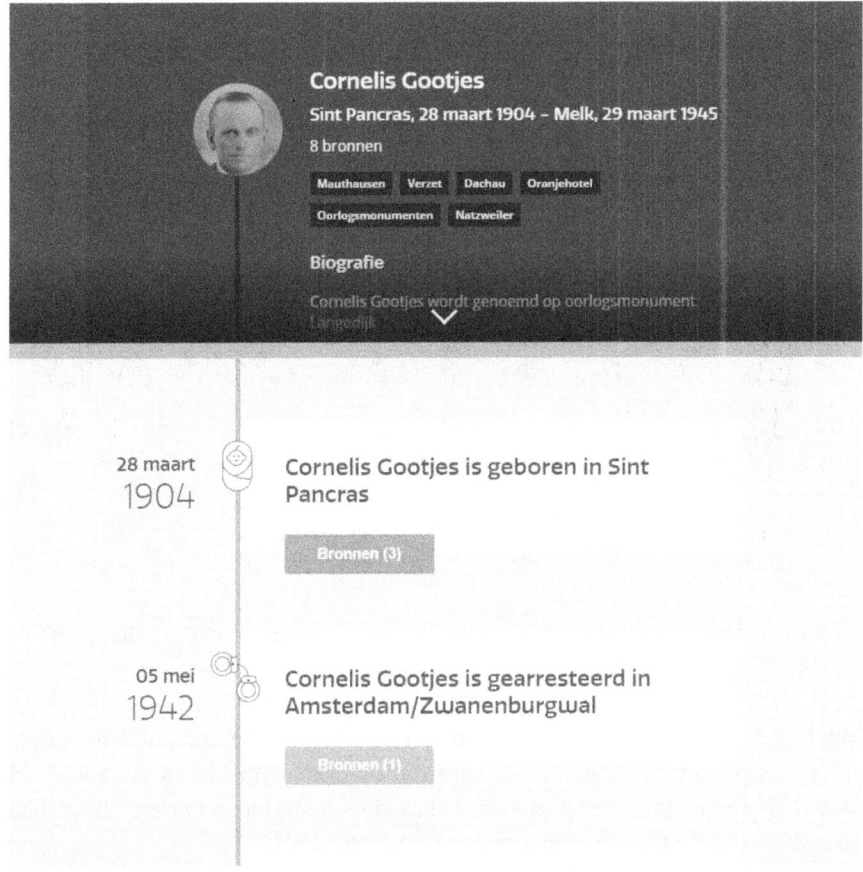

Fig. 12: Screendump of War Lives website: example of Cornelis Gootjes (www.warlives.org)

In May 2019, data from *Arolsen Archives* were integrated.[34] A wealth of additional information was added to the data from Dutch institutions. For instance, in case of Ernst Verduin, *Arolsen Archives* holds registration cards from the *Dutch Red Cross*, Buchenwald and the *Jewish Council* in Amsterdam.

The ambition of *Dutch War Collections* is to feed *War Lives* with more data in the next few years, also including international collection data. *War Lives* is meant to be a freely available online service for anyone looking for information on persons (victims of persecution, resistance fighters, military, collaborators, etc) in

---

34 Arolsen Archives. Available at: https://collections.arolsen-archives.org. Last accessed: 6.6.2019.

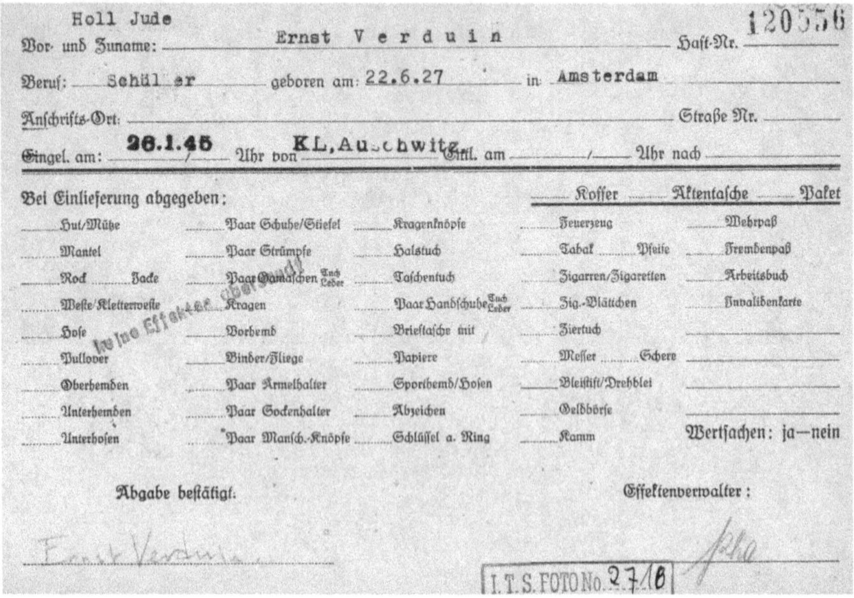

Holl Jude

Vor- und Zuname: Ernst V e r d u i n Haft-Nr. 120556

Beruf: Schüler geboren am: 22.6.27 in: Amsterdam

Anschrifts-Ort: Straße Nr.

Eingel. am: 26.1.45 Uhr von KL. Auschwitz Entl. am / Uhr nach

Bei Einlieferung abgegeben: Koffer Aktentasche Paket

Hut/Mütze — Paar Schuhe/Stiefel — Kragenknöpfe — Feuerzeug — Wehrpaß

Mantel — Paar Strümpfe — Halstuch — Tabak Pfeife — Fremdenpaß

Rock Jacke — Paar Gamaschen Tuch Leder — Taschentuch — Zigarren/Zigaretten — Arbeitsbuch

Weste/Kletterweste — Kragen — Paar Handschuhe Tuch Leder — Zig.-Blättchen — Invalidenkarte

Hose — Vorhemd — Brieftasche mit — Ziertuch

Pullover — Binder/Fliege — Papiere — Messer Schere

Oberhemden — Paar Ärmelhalter — Sporthemd/Hosen — Bleistift/Drehbleistift

Unterhemden — Paar Sockenhalter — Abzeichen — Geldbörse

Unterhosen — Paar Mansch.-Knöpfe — Schlüssel a. Ring — Kamm — Wertsachen: ja—nein

keine Effekten übergeben

Abgabe bestätigt: Ernst Verduin

Effektenverwalter:

I.T.S. FOTO No. 27(16)

Fig. 13: Buchenwald personal effects card from Ernst Verduin (1.1.5/7339907/ITS Digital Archive, Arolsen Archives)

WWII. Privacy legislation places restrictions on processing and publishing data of persons who are still alive. Another function of the *War Lives* service is to act as a digital national register that can be used by institutions to check their data in order to verify whether persons are deceased or not.

In 2019 to 2021 *Dutch War Collections* will be focusing on collecting more relevant data and improving the WWII thesaurus. In the next few years, *War Lives* will be merged with oorlogsbronnen.nl to reach a full integration of all available collection data on persons, organizations, events, geographical locations and specific WWII related themes. Apart from metadata about the collections, experiments are planned in 2020 that will also include full text collections, such as for instance all WWII newspapers now published on the Delpher-platform.[35] One of the main objectives now is to familiarize the audience interested in the WWII with the *Oorlogsbronnen*-service and the underlying collections. Some applications will also be developed to showcase its educational value and its potential for reaching out to a variety of different user groups.

35 Delpher. Available at: https://www.delpher.nl. Last accessed: 6.6.2019.

Conclusion

The aim of *Dutch War Collections* is to improve the online visibility and re-use of collection data. By collecting the data from the systems of the individual institutions and enrich them in line with the more thematically oriented questions of the end users ("who", "what", "where" and "when"), the *Oorlogsbronnen* services try to facilitate new perspectives on the shared collections. The semantic web technology used in *Oorlogsbronnen* is extremely well suited to practically implementing the key values of *Dutch War Collections:* open, (re)usable and available to a worldwide audience. There are other advantages as well, including the fact that sharing all information as open data on the semantic web is the best guarantee for its preservation over time.

The concept of *thematic intellectual management* is still under development. The first impression after three years of experimentation is that it seems to offer a valid theoretical framework to meet the user demands in the field of war heritage. Online people search for information, not so much individual items or documents. The shift to a digital mindset that perceives collections as reservoirs for all kinds of narratives is a complex and comprehensive one. Heritage institutions are all of a sudden called *content providers*. On the internet, institutional walls are torn down. It is all about gaining your ground as an expert and being where your target audience is. A shift to digital not only implies leaving old familiar paths, but also means discovering new paths that could strengthen the traditional role of heritage institutions as trusted custodians of cultural heritage.

Key preconditions for claiming one's stake online are openness and a willingness to cooperate. *Thematic intellectual management* requires the efforts of both heritage specialists and scholars. Humanities research is in need of collections in a re-usable, digital format. Academic expertise, datified in thesauri and other knowledge systems, contributes to deriving information from the data and putting it on the internet for all to use. Scholars can help heritage organizations prioritize collections for digitization. Tools from the digital humanity community sometimes have the potential to improve access to collection data considerably.

By virtually releasing the data from institutions and enriching them thematically, it is possible to perceive the same collection data from different angles: regional, national, local, personal, thematic, international. New digital technology allows us to automatically distill the information out of archives. As such, the web has enabled us to connect this information in unprecedented ways. Regarding which new research questions and insights this may lead is still unclear. For now, in the infancy of this development, science and heritage need to cross bridges and learn from each other, for their own benefit but most of all for the sake of all those interested in the history of the Second World War.

Contributors

DIANE F. AFOUMADO received her PhD in History from the University of Paris 10-Nanterre, France in 1997. She is currently Chief of the *Research and Reference Branch* at the *Holocaust Survivors and Victims Resource Center* at the *United States Holocaust Memorial Museum* in Washington, D.C. Formerly Assistant Professor of Contemporary History at the University of Paris 10-Nanterre and the *Institut National des Langues et Civilisations Orientales* (INALCO) in Paris, she worked for the two French Commissions related to compensation to Jewish victims (Prime Minister's Office). She also worked as a historian for the Archival Division of the *Centre de Documentation Juive Contemporaine – Mémorial de la Shoah*.

ZVI BERNHARDT has worked in *Yad Vashem* since 1994 and is currently Deputy Director of two related departments in *Yad Vashem's* Archive division: *The Hall of Names* and the *Reference and Information Department*.

RENÉ BIENERT holds a Master's degree in Ethnology, Cultural History and Sociology. Since 2017 he has worked for the *Vienna Wiesenthal Institute for Holocaust Studies* (VWI) where he is responsible for indexing, describing and raising awareness of the Simon-Wiesenthal collections and the Holocaust-related sub-collections from the archives of the *Jewish community* in Vienna. Bienert has been a research associate at the *Research and Education Department* of the *International Tracing Service* (ITS) with a focus on displaced persons and at Friedrich Schiller University in Jena where he worked on the project of redesigning the permanent exhibition titled *Ostracism and Violence 1937 to 1945* at the *Buchenwald Memorial*. Most recently he has been EHRI fellow at the *United States Holocaust Memorial Museum*. Apart from archival issues, his current working field covers the topics of forced migration, displaced persons and the prosecution of Nazi crimes since 1945.

REBECCA BOEHLING is Professor of History and Director of the Global Studies program at the University of Maryland, Baltimore County (UMBC). She has published on the US occupation of Germany, gender and immediate post-WWII West German politics as well as on German-Jewish families during and following the Holocaust. Her books include: *Life and Loss in the Shadow of the Holocaust: A Jewish Family's Untold Story* (Cambridge University Press, 2011) and *A Question of Priorities: Democratic Reforms and Economic Recovery in Postwar Germany. Frankfurt am Main, Munich and Stuttgart under U.S. Occupation, 1945–49*. (Berghahn Books, 1996). She is currently working on a study of denazification as transitional justice. She was the first director of the ITS following the departure of the ICRC from its management at the end of 2012 until the end of 2015. She currently serves as the Acting Director of the *National Institute for Holocaust Documentation* at the *U.S. Holocaust Memorial Museum*.

HENNING BORGGRÄFE is a historian and, since 2017, head of the *Research and Education Department* at the *Arolsen Archives*. He earned his Ph.D. in History in 2012 from Ruhr-University Bochum. Before he came to the ITS in 2014, he worked as a research assistant at the *Institute for Advanced Studies in the Humanities* (KWI) in Essen. He has published on nationalism, Nazi Germany, the history of sociology, and Germany's dealing with the Nazi past, including the books *Zwangsarbeiterentschädigung. Vom Streit um "vergessene Opfer" zur Selbstaus-*

söhnung der Deutschen (Göttingen: Wallstein 2014) and *Freilegungen: Wege, Orte und Räume der NS-Verfolgung* (ITS Yearbook 2016, editor).

RAMONA BRÄU joined the *Tracing Department* at the *Arolsen Archives* as deputy head in 2017. The historian whose work has chiefly focused on the European history of the first half of the twentieth century, put her scientific focus on the National Socialist Germany and occupied Poland during the Second World War. After working as a scientific trainee at the *Memorials Foundation Buchenwald and Mittelbau-Dora*, Ramona Bräu contributed her services as associate within the scope of the federal research project about the history of the *Reich Ministry of Finance*. In the course of her more than ten years working in various international projects, she gained experience and knowledge in and outside Europe. To improve the performance of the *Tracing Department*, Ramona Bräu, in her new position as Manager Digital Business Development, develops tools to improve the processing of incoming inquiries.

MAREN HACHMEISTER received her PhD in History from the Ludwig Maximilian University of Munich in 2018 with a dissertation entitled *Self-organization in State Socialism: The Red Cross in Poland and Czechoslovakia (1945–1989)*. She is currently a research associate at the *Hannah Arendt Institute for Totalitarianism Studies* at the *TU Dresden*. She previously held fellowships from institutions including the *German Historical Institute* in Warsaw, the *German-Poland Institution of Darmstadt* and the *Adalbert Stifter Association*. Hachmeister has published and presented on topics including the *Red Cross* in Central and Eastern Europe, blood donation and socialist humanitarianism.

TOBIAS HERRMANN, born in Aachen in 1975, studied History, Politics, Economics and German Philology at the Universities of Aachen, Nottingham and Bonn from 1994 to 2006. He received his doctorate at the University of Bonn in 2006 with a thesis on the beginnings of written local administration in the late middle ages. He completed a two-year-internship at the *German Federal Archives* in Koblenz, Berlin and Freiburg and the Archives School in Marburg in 2008 and was head of the *Ludwigsburg branch office* of the *German Federal Archives* from 2008 to 2012, responsible for the documents of the *German Central Office for the Investigation of National Socialist Crimes*. Since 2012, he has worked in the *department for General Archival Matters* of the *German Federal Archives* in Koblenz, responsible for public relations, international relations, web presence, strategic planning and more, since 2015 as head of department.

CHRISTIAN HÖSCHLER is a historian and Deputy Head of *Research and Education* at the *Arolsen Archives*. He studied History, English, and Educational Sciences and subsequently received his PhD from the University of Munich in 2017. His dissertation explored how displaced children were cared for in the American Zone of Germany in the late 1940s and early 1950s. At the *Arolsen Archives*, he works on the history of Nazi persecution, displacement, tracing and documentation, as well as educational approaches to teaching about the Holocaust, imprisonment and forced labor during WW2.

KERSTIN HOFMANN is a historian and research associate in the *Research and Education Department* of the *Arolsen Archives*. Prior to that she was responsible for the care of relatives visiting the *Arolsen Archives* and the knowledge management in the *Tracing Department*. She received her PhD in History from the University of Mannheim in 2017 with a dissertation titled

'*Ein Versuch nur – immerhin ein Versuch*' *Die Zentrale Stelle in Ludwigsburg unter der Leitung von Erwin Schüle und Adalbert Rückerl (1958–1984)*. Her research included the criminal investigation of Nazi crimes in the Federal Republic of Germany and the sociopolitical change in the Holocaust remembrance in Germany.

PUCK HUITSING studied History in Amsterdam and Change Management at SIOO in Utrecht. She was director of *Eenheid Oorlogsgetroffenen en Herinnering Tweede Wereldoorlog* (Unit War Victims and Remembrance WWII) at the Ministry for Health, Welfare and Sports from 2003 to 2010. Since June 2016 she is Program Director of *Dutch War Collections*.

CAROLA LAU holds a PhD in Eastern European History and a degree in International Business and Cultural Studies from the University of Passau. In her thesis she examined the *institutes of national remembrance* in Poland, Czech Republic, Slovakia, Romania, Hungary and Ukraine and their activities as "players" between historical research, memory cultivation and national politics of remembrance. She has published and presented on topics including *culture of remembrance*, civil society, corruption and human rights in Eastern Europe. She is currently desk officer for Poland at the Ministry of Justice and for European Affairs and Consumer Protection of the Federal State of Brandenburg.

LINDA G. LEVI is the Director of *JDC Global Archives* at the *American Jewish Joint Distribution Committee*. The JDC Archives, one of the most significant repositories in the world for the study of modern Jewish history with centers in New York and Jerusalem, includes 3 miles of text documents, 100,000 photographs, over 6,000 books, and over 1,000 audio-visual recordings including oral histories. A graduate of New York University, she received her MA from Brandeis University in Contemporary Jewish Studies. Ms. Levi has worked for the organization for over three decades and is an expert on Jewish communities around the world. She served as editor of: *The JDC at 100: A Century of Humanitarianism* published in 2019; *I Live. Send Help: 100 Years of Jewish History in Images from the JDC Archives* published in 2014, and *In Every Generation: The JDC Haggadah* which was published in 2010. She has published a number of professional articles and has lectured extensively about the *JDC Archives* and the history of the organization at academic, professional, and Jewish genealogy conferences.

EDWIN KLIJN has a Masters degree in Modern History and a postdoctoral degree in Historical Information Science. Previously, from 2009 to 2011, he was Project Manager for the project *Databank Digital Daily Newspapers* at the *Koninklijke Bibliotheek* (National Library of the Netherlands). Since 2011 he has been Program Manager of *Dutch War Collections*.

ANNA MEIER-OSIŃSKI was Head of the *Tracing Department* at the *Arolsen Archives* from 2015 until 2020. She currently holds the position of Outreach Manager for Central and Eastern Europe. She has a Master of Arts in Cultural History of Eastern and East Central Europe, Polish Studies and Political Sciences and graduated at the research center Eastern Europe at the University of Bremen and at the University of Gdańsk. Her Master's thesis *The Extermination of the Polish Elites in Gau West Prussia* is based on biographical interviews she had with former polish political prisoners from Concentration Camp Stutthof in 2005. Before coming to the *Arolsen Archives* she had been the Deputy Head of the Pedagogical Department at the *International Youth Meeting Center Oświęcim/Auschwitz* where she was responsible for the collaboration with the former prisoners and survivors of Auschwitz-Birkenau Concentration and

Extermination camp, the international educational programs and management of the department.

ISABEL PANEK is a historian and works in the *Eduction Department* at the *City Museum Leipzig*. From 2016–2019 she was a research associate at the *Research and Eduction Department* of the *Arolsen Archives*. She has co-curated the first permanent exhibition on the history of the *Arolsen Archives* titled: *A Paper Monument. The History of the Arolsen Archives*. Isabel Panek studied Medieval and Modern History as well as Educational Sciences in Frankfurt/Main and Leipzig. Her working field is the interface between research and education, her thematic focus being Nazi forced labor, the history of the concentration camps as well as the culture of memory and teaching of history after 1945.

CHRISTINE SCHMIDT is Deputy Director and Head of Research at *The Wiener Library*, where she oversees research and engagement, ensuring that the Library's outreach programme builds on the latest scholarship. Dr. Schmidt earned her Ph.D. in History from Clark University in 2003. She has held two post-doctoral fellowships from the *Hungarian Ministry of Education* and the *Fulbright Scholar Program*. From 2003–2005, she worked as an applied researcher at the *U.S. Holocaust Memorial Museum's Center for Advanced Holocaust Studies*, where she contributed to the first volume of *The Encyclopedia of Camps and Ghettos, 1933–1945* (2009). She published "Drops in the Ocean: Rescue Operations of Jews in Southern France and Hungary during the Holocaust" in *The Holocaust: Essays and Documents*, edited by Randolph Braham (2010). Another study derived from her post-doctoral research, co-authored with Gábor Kádár and Zoltan Vági, "Defying Genocide: Jewish Resistance and Self-rescue in Hungary," was published in *Jewish Resistance to the Nazis*, edited by Patrick Henry (2014). Her most recent studies on Hungarian Jewish women in Markkleeberg and the *Wiener Library*'s role in increasing access to the ITS archive have been published in the ITS Yearbooks (2015, 2016). She is currently conducting research on early tracing efforts, the *Child Search Branch*, and early Holocaust research at the *Wiener Library*.

DAN STONE is Professor of Modern History and Director of the Holocaust Research Institute at Royal Holloway, University of London. He is the author of some 80 scholarly articles and 16 books, including *Histories of the Holocaust* (OUP, 2010), *Goodbye to All That? The Story of Europe since 1945* (OUP, 2014), *The Liberation of the Camps: the End of the Holocaust and its Aftermath* (Yale, 2015) and *Concentration Camps: A Very Short Introduction* (OUP, 2019). He is currently completing a book on ITS, entitled *Fate Unknown*, to be published by Oxford in 2021, and writing a book on the Holocaust for Penguin's revived Pelican series.

SILKE VON DER EMDE is Associate Professor of German Studies at Vassar College, NY, where she teaches German language and literature, Women Studies, and Film. She is the author of *Entering History: Feminist Dialogues in Irmtraud Morgner's Prose* (Peter Lang, 2004), as well as several articles on memory, archive, GDR literature, feminist theory, and German film. She has also co-published articles on foreign language pedagogy. She is currently working on a book project tentatively entitled *Gendered Pasts: Women, Memory and Coming to Terms with the German Past(s)*.

www.ingramcontent.com/pod-product-compliance
Lightning Source LLC
Chambersburg PA
CBHW061931220426
43662CB00012B/1867